Pro Nagios 2.0

James Turnbull

Apress®

Pro Nagios 2.0

Copyright © 2006 by James Turnbull

ISBN-13: 978-1-59059-609-8

ISBN-10: 1-59059-609-9

Printed and bound in the United States of America 9 8 7 6 5 4 3 2 1

Lead Editor: Jim Sumser
Technical Reviewer: Justin Kulikowski
Editorial Board: Steve Anglin, Dan Appleman, Ewan Buckingham, Gary Cornell, Jason Gilmore,
    Jonathan Hassell, James Huddleston, Chris Mills, Matthew Moodie, Dominic Shakeshaft,
    Jim Sumser, Matt Wade
Project Manager: Elizabeth Seymour
Copy Edit Manager: Nicole LeClerc
Copy Editor: Liz Welch
Assistant Production Director: Kari Brooks-Copony
Production Editor: Kelly Winquist
Compositor: Linda Weidemann, Wolf Creek Press
Proofreader: Nancy Sixsmith
Indexer: John Collin
Artist: Kinetic Publishing Services, LLC
Cover Designer: Kurt Krames
Manufacturing Director: Tom Debolski

Distributed to the book trade worldwide by Springer-Verlag New York, Inc., 233 Spring Street, 6th Floor, New York, NY 10013. Phone 1-800-SPRINGER, fax 201-348-4505, e-mail orders-ny@springer-sbm.com, or visit http://www.springeronline.com.

For information on translations, please contact Apress directly at 2560 Ninth Street, Suite 219, Berkeley, CA 94710. Phone 510-549-5930, fax 510-549-5939, e-mail info@apress.com, or visit http://www.apress.com.

The source code for this book is available to readers at http://www.apress.com in the Source Code section.

To my parents, whose love of books and writing inspired me to write

Contents at a Glance

About the Author xiii

About the Technical Reviewer xv

Acknowledgments xvii

Introduction xix

CHAPTER 1   Installation 1

CHAPTER 2   Basic Object Configuration 29

CHAPTER 3   Security and Administration 87

CHAPTER 4   Using the Web Console 113

CHAPTER 5   Monitoring Hosts and Services 143

CHAPTER 6   Advanced Commands 207

CHAPTER 7   Advanced Object Configuration 249

CHAPTER 8   Distributed Monitoring, Redundancy, and Failover 269

CHAPTER 9   Integrating Nagios 299

CHAPTER 10 Developing Plug-ins 343

INDEX 367

Contents

About the Author xiii

About the Technical Reviewer xv

Acknowledgments xvii

Introduction xix

■CHAPTER 1   **Installation** 1

Positioning the Server. 1

Choosing Software and Hardware 3

Capacity Planning 4

Redundancy and Backup 5

Installing the Nagios Software. 5

    Prerequisites for Software Installation 6

    Installing the Nagios Server 9

    Installing the Nagios Plug-ins 17

Configuring Your Web Server for Nagios. 21

    Basic Configuration 22

    Virtual Server Configuration 24

    Configuring Your Web Server with an RPM Installation. 25

    Restarting Apache 26

    Testing. 26

Checkpoint 27

Resources. 28

    Mailing Lists 28

    Sites 28

■CHAPTER 2   **Basic Object Configuration**. 29

How Does Nagios Work? 29

How Is Nagios Configured? 30

    Getting Started with Your Configuration 32

    Specifying Your Configuration Files 32

Defining Nagios Configuration Objects 35

Defining Your First Host 36

Defining the Hostname and Address 37

Parents, Host Groups, and Contact Groups 38

Checking the Host 39

Notifications 45

Flapping 47

Event Handling 49

Retention of Status 50

State Stalking, Obsession, and Performance Data 52

Defining Services 54

Basic Service Directives 55

Service Checking 56

Service Status and Notifications 63

Service Flapping and Event Handling 65

Service Stalking and Obsession 66

Other Directives 66

Using Templates for Objects Definition 67

Contact Objects 72

Grouping Objects 75

Host Group Objects 76

Service Group Objects 77

Contact Group Objects 77

Defining Time Periods 78

Defining Commands 79

Check Commands 79

Event Handler Commands 83

Notification Commands 84

Checkpoint 84

Resources 85

■CHAPTER 3   **Security and Administration** 87

General Security Guidelines 87

Do Not Run Nagios As the root User 88

Securing and Administering for External Commands 88

Securing the Web Console 90

Web Console Authentication with Apache 91

Nagios Authentication and Authorization 97

Nagios Administration. 100

    Starting and Stopping the Nagios Server. 101

    Nagios init Script 106

    Logging 107

Checkpoints 110

Resources. 111

■CHAPTER 4   **Using the Web Console** 113

General 115

Monitoring. 115

    Tactical Monitoring Overview 115

    Service Detail 118

    Host Detail. 125

    Host and Service Group Views. 127

    Process Information. 130

    Scheduling Queue 132

    Other Items in the Monitoring Menu. 133

Reporting 134

    The Availability Report 134

    The Event Log Report 140

Configuration 140

Checkpoints 142

■CHAPTER 5   **Monitoring Hosts and Services** 143

Introduction to Monitoring 144

    Monitoring Hosts 144

    Monitoring Services. 145

Local Unix Monitoring 147

Monitoring Network-Based Services 154

Remote Monitoring 161

    Monitoring via NRPE 162

    Monitoring via SSH 175

    Monitoring via SMNP. 181

Monitoring Windows 187

    NSClient++ 188

Checkpoint 205

Resources. 205

    Books. 205

    Sites 205

∎**CHAPTER 6**   **Advanced Commands**. 207

Macros. 207
     On-Demand Macros 208
     Macros As Environmental Variables 209
Event Handlers. 210
Notifications 213
     Sending Notifications via Instant Messenger 217
     Notification Aggregation and Suppression 220
External Commands 221
     Processing Checks Results with External Commands. 224
     External Commands for Adaptive Monitoring 225
Performance Data 227
     Processing Performance Data 228
     Using Performance Data. 231
Checkpoints 246
Resources. 247

∎**CHAPTER 7**   **Advanced Object Configuration** 249

Host and Service Dependencies 250
     Service Dependencies. 250
     Service Dependency Shortcuts 253
     Inheritance 254
     Host Dependencies 256
Notification Escalations 258
     Service Notification Escalations 259
     Service Escalation Shortcuts 262
     Host Escalations. 264
Extended Host and Service Information Definitions. 265
Checkpoint 267

∎**CHAPTER 8**   **Distributed Monitoring, Redundancy,**
and Failover 269

Distributed Monitoring 269
     Distributed Server Configuration. 271
     Central Server Configuration 280
Redundancy and Failover. 289
     Configuring the Master Server. 290
     Configuring the Slave Server 294
     Failover Process. 297

Checkpoint 298
Resources. 298
  Sites. 298

■CHAPTER 9   **Integrating Nagios** 299

syslog-NG and Nagios 299
  Installing the Remote Host. 300
  Configuring the Nagios Server. 309
  Wrapping Up. 313
Snort 313
  Configuring Snort for Integration. 314
  Configuring syslog-NG 315
  Configuring Nagios 316
  Wrapping Up. 317
Integrating with MRTG, Cacti, and Related Tools. 317
  Querying MRTG Log Files 318
  Querying RRD Databases 322
SNMP Traps and Nagios. 323
  Receiving SNMP Traps 325
  Sending SNMP Traps 336
Checkpoint 340
Resources. 341
  Books. 341
  Sites. 341
  MIB Files 341

■CHAPTER 10   **Developing Plug-ins** 343

Writing Your First Plug-in. 343
Writing Perl Plug-ins. 350
Other Guidelines 355
  Specifying Threshold Ranges 355
  Specifying Performance Data 356
  Commands and Files. 357
  Plug-in Timeouts 358
  Command-Line Options 358
  Other Guidelines. 359

Nagios Event Broker 359

    Helloworld 360

    NDO Utilities 362

    Other Sources of Information. 365

Checkpoints 366

Resources. 366

■INDEX 367

About the Author

JAMES TURNBULL is a senior consultant with pure-play security consultancy B-Sec in Melbourne, Australia. He was previously an IT&T security manager at the Commonwealth Bank of Australia. James is an experienced infrastructure architect with a background in Linux/Unix, AS/400, Windows, and Storage systems. He has been involved in security consulting, infrastructure security design, SLA and support services design, and business application support. He has a strong interest in security metrics and measurement.

About the Technical Reviewer

JUSTIN KULIKOWSKI is a student at Pennsylvania State University achieving his BS in information sciences and technology. He takes a particular interest in backend administration, database-driven applications, security, and automation. Justin is active in the open source community, and fulfills various freelance requests varying from long-term server administration to short-term installation, configuration, and troubleshooting.

When not computing, Justin can be found performing in the Penn State Blues Band, where he plays mellophone. In his free time, Justin remains active on campus by developing applications that benefit students. Examples of this include a website built to notify students of class openings, and an e-commerce website built to provide a means for students to order products from local grocery food chains. To learn more, visit his website at `www.jpk236.com`.

Acknowledgments

Lucinda Mora—for her understanding and patience

Ruth Brown—for her friendship and support

Jim Sumser—for letting me do it all again

Dennis Matotek, Feodor Frukhtman, and Mark Chandler—for their comments and support

Mark Ferlatte—for his notification throttling script

Seva Gluschenko—for his check_rrd plug-in

Introduction

You are an IT manager in charge of numerous systems spread across multiple countries. It's 4:00 a.m. and you are in bed asleep. Your cell phone rings. It's the Help Desk calling to tell you that users in Indonesia can't access their email. You get up, dial into work, and start to diagnose the problem. After an hour of work you identify that the issue is disk space on the mail server in the Indonesian office. You clear some free space, confirm the users can access their mail, and go back to sleep.

This is a common scenario in the IT industry. IT staff are geographically and temporally separated from the systems and applications they manage. All troubleshooting, monitoring, and management of systems and applications occurs remotely. The systems and applications being managed are complex and hugely configurable. They are also made up of multiple components—hardware, software, networking devices, networks, and supporting infrastructure like environmental and electrical systems. In the event of a problem, many of these components need to be checked in order to eliminate them as a cause.

All this has resulted in monitoring, management, and troubleshooting becoming increasingly complicated and time consuming. No longer do IT professionals have time to individually review every log, every setting, and every variable on all the systems and applications they are responsible for. They need tools to automatically monitor the characteristics of the assets they are responsible for managing . . . tools that will detect anomalies, failures, or performance issues and alert IT staff via email, a pager, or an SMS message . . . tools that can automatically perform actions, such as restarting a service, in response to events they have detected. These types of tools perform functions generally known as enterprise management.

So what advantages does an enterprise management solution offer? Well, let's say that as an IT manager you have deployed an enterprise management solution. With this solution in place, let's revisit our troubleshooting scenario again. Instead of a call from the Help Desk, this time your cell phone beeps to indicate it has received an SMS message. You read the message:

```
4/21/05 04:54AM C:\ drive on server INDOEXCH01 has 1% of free space remaining.
```

You get up, dial into work, connect to the INDOEXCH01 server, clear some free space, confirm the server is functional, and then go back to sleep. Total elapsed time? Ten minutes. Now instead of your having to diagnose the problem, eliminate all the possible variables, review log files, and test multiple components, the actual root cause of the issue is presented directly to you.

In this book I am going to introduce the popular open source enterprise management tool Nagios. At the time of this writing, version 2.0 has just been released as the stable production version. This book takes advantage of this release to provide an introduction to Nagios and how you can use it streamline, manage, and monitor your IT assets.

What Is Nagios?

So what is Nagios?[1] It is an open source, Unix-based enterprise monitoring package with a web-based front-end or console. Nagios can monitor assets like servers, network devices, and applications, essentially any device or service that has an address and can be contacted via TCP/IP. It can monitor hosts running Microsoft Windows, Unix/Linux, Novell NetWare, and other operating systems. It can be configured to work through firewalls, VPN tunnels, across SSH tunnels, and via the Internet.

Nagios can monitor a variety of attributes on your assets. These can range from operating system attributes such as CPU, disk, and memory usage to the status of applications, files, and databases. You can use a variety of network protocols, including HTTP, SNMP, and SSH, to conduct this monitoring. Nagios can also receive SNMP traps, and you can build and easily integrate your own custom monitoring checks using a variety of languages, including C, Perl, and shell scripts.

The Nagios tool is capable of being deployed in a distributed model with multiple servers, collecting data about your assets and reporting them to a central server (which is ideal for organizations with disparate geographical locations that are controlled from a central site or network operations center). Nagios can also be configured as a robust redundant monitoring infrastructure that is capable of disaster recovery and failover modes of operation.

Nagios is developed by a single developer, Ethan Galstad, as an open source software project. This means that time between releases can be extensive but the overall product tends be to carefully and extensively tested. Additionally, many of the newer features tend to be released and stay in CVS versions of the package for long periods of time. These releases, while usually fairly stable, are generally not recommended for production use.

Who Should Read This Book?

This book is an introductory guide to Nagios 2.0. It presumes no prior knowledge of Nagios and indeed focuses entirely (with minor digressions) on the current version of Nagios. It is designed for system administrators, operations managers, IT managers, and support staff who need to deploy a tool to monitor and report on IT assets and applications.

The book starts from scratch and introduces how to install Nagios, build your basic monitoring configuration, and use the Nagios web console. It then covers some advanced topics such as escalations, dependencies, distributed monitoring, how to integrate Nagios with other tools, and how to develop your own monitoring checks. At the end of this book, you should have the ability to deploy and monitor using Nagios, to implement redundancy or failover capabilities with Nagios, to integrate Nagios into other tools such as MRTG and syslog-NG—and you should have an idea of where to look for additional knowledge and resources that might answer more advanced questions and issues.

The book presumes some experience with Unix and Windows platforms, as you will need to install and configure Nagios on a Unix-based host, and you will need to configure monitoring for your remote hosts and devices. This assumed prior knowledge includes the following:

---

1. Nagios is a recursive acronym for "Nagios Ain't Gonna Insist On Sainthood." It was previously known as "NetSaint."

- Knowledge of TCP/IP networking

- Some knowledge of firewalls, including `iptables`

- Some exposure to the Apache web server

- Ability to install and run software on Unix and Windows hosts

- The ability to use editors and command-line tools on Unix and Windows hosts

---

■**Note** If you wish to develop your own monitoring checks, you will need some knowledge of programming. Some commonly used languages for this purpose are C, Perl, Python, and shell script. See Chapter 10 for further details.

What's in This Book?

- Chapter 1, "Installation," deals with installing the Nagios server and its associated prerequisites, including a web server for the console.

- Chapter 2, "Basic Object Configuration," covers basic configuration of your monitoring environment and explains how the Nagios object model and object template system functions.

- Chapter 3, "Security and Administration," focuses on how to administer and secure Nagios servers and includes information on securing the web console, understanding general Nagios security, starting and stopping the Nagios daemon, and handling logs.

- Chapter 4, "Using the Web Console," deals with the Nagios web console.

- Chapter 5, "Monitoring Hosts and Services," addresses how to use Nagios to monitor your hosts and services. This includes monitoring by SSH, using SNMP and a variety of other methods. It includes details on how to monitor Unix and Windows hosts.

- Chapter 6, "Advanced Commands," covers advanced use of Nagios command objects, including macros, event handlers, advanced notifications, external commands, and performance data.

- Chapter 7, "Advanced Object Configuration," focuses on some of the objects that weren't covered in Chapter 2. These include notification escalations, host and service dependencies, and extended host and service information.

- Chapter 8, "Distributed Monitoring, Redundancy, and Failover," demonstrates how to configure a distributed monitoring model to allow you to distribute your monitoring load and to monitor hosts you may not be able to directly connect to because of network structure or segmentation. It also shows how to use Nagios in redundant and failover modes to enhance the resiliency and availability of your Nagios solution.

- Chapter 9, "Integrating Nagios," looks at how you can integrate Nagios with a number of other tools, including syslog-NG, SNMP, and MRTG.

- Chapter 10, "Developing Plug-ins," examines plug-in development and includes details on developing plug-ins in shell script and Perl. The chapter also covers the Nagios Event Broker, an integration engine and interface that allows integration with tools such as databases.

## CHAPTER 1

Installation

The first stage in deploying Nagios is installing the software and any required infrastructure. The Nagios installation process can be complicated, and you must follow a number of steps to ensure all the correct components are installed. This chapter takes you through those steps and explains several of the possible installation options and models from which you can choose.

By the end of this chapter you should have a good understanding of where to position your Nagios server or servers in your environment to best monitor all the required assets. You will also have some guidelines for selecting and sizing your Nagios hardware and choosing your operating system software. I will also cover the steps you need to take to install the Nagios server and the plug-ins. Finally, I'll demonstrate how to set up and configure a web server to run the Nagios web console.

Positioning the Server

Before you actually install the software itself, let's briefly look at where to locate your Nagios servers. Where you deploy your Nagios server(s) is an important part of your Nagios implementation. I'll briefly cover the broad issues involved in server deployment here to make you aware of them. I'll also go into these issues in more detail in later chapters when I look at monitoring hosts through firewalls and when I examine how to deploy Nagios in distributed and failover configurations.[1]

First, Nagios uses Transmission Control Protocol/Internet Protocol (TCP/IP) to monitor hosts and devices. Thus, you need to deploy your Nagios server or servers where they have network visibility of the hosts and devices that you require to be monitored. If you have firewalls, network links, network segregation, or filtering devices between your Nagios server(s) and the hosts to be monitored, then you may not have the visibility of the hosts required to monitor them. For example, if you rely on Internet Control Message Protocol (ICMP) pings to monitor the presence of a host, the intervening network devices must allow ICMP traffic to traverse them.

If this network visibility is not available, you may need to deploy an additional server or multiple additional servers to monitor those hosts. The best deployment model is to place the additional server(s) in a distributed configuration where remote Nagios servers send the results of checks back to a central server. This means you only need to monitor one web console and have only one set of notification infrastructure to maintain. This configuration does require the ability to manipulate the firewall or other network device between the central server and

---

1. See Chapters 5 and 8.

the distributed Nagios servers to allow the check and results traffic to traverse the network. You can see this configuration in Figure 1-1.[2]

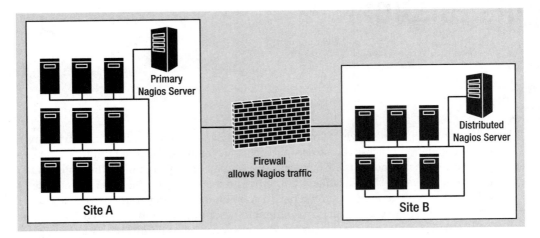

Figure 1-1. *Nagios servers in a distributed configuration*

If you cannot manipulate the intervening firewall or network device to allow this traffic through, then these servers may need to be configured as independent Nagios servers monitoring any hosts that are not visible and collecting and notifying any events detected on them. This does complicate your management regime, as each independently configured Nagios server would have its own web console that would need to be monitored and potentially its own notification infrastructure. I have demonstrated this configuration in Figure 1-2.

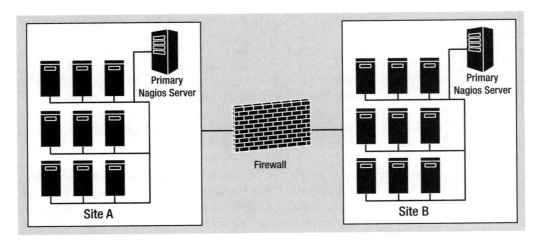

Figure 1-2. *Independent Nagios servers*

---

2. I discuss distributed configurations in Chapter 8.

Second, where you deploy your Nagios server(s) can have performance, availability, and security implications. These implications are most obvious when the hosts you are monitoring are geographically separated and connected via a network link or connection to the Nagios server.

From a performance perspective, if you are monitoring hosts in remote geographical locations from a centrally located server, then the checks and the results of these checks will be sent and received at the speed of the intervening connection. If this connection is very slow—for example, a dial-up connection—the delay between checks and results could be considerable. This is especially true if the Nagios server is sharing the intervening link with other applications and services. The delayed checks and results could mean that notification of an incident, outage, or event could be delayed. You should consider whether you need to deploy a local Nagios server to monitor any hosts to which you have a limited speed connection rather than attempting to monitor them from a remote site.

Additionally, from an availability perspective, if the intervening link between the Nagios server and the hosts fails, you will obviously lose visibility of the hosts being monitored. Here also you should consider whether a local Nagios server or potentially a Nagios design involving a failover configuration is an option that you could explore. In a failover configuration, if one of your Nagios servers fails then another server is configured to take over.

Lastly, from a security perspective, if you are monitoring hosts in a remote location via an intervening link, the traffic being carried on that link could be exposed to monitoring or subversion. This is particularly true if the intervening link between the server and the remote hosts is provided via the Internet.

Choosing Software and Hardware

Nagios is designed to primarily run on the Linux operating system. There is no particular Linux distribution recommended as an operating system platform for Nagios, and it should have no issues running on your preferred flavor of Linux.[3] Indeed, I have successfully run Nagios on Red Hat, Debian, Mandrake, SuSE, and Gentoo distributions. Nagios can also be run on other flavours of Unix, including Sun Solaris, IBM AIX, Mac OS X, and HP-UX.

You should choose the operating system platform that suits your environment. However, as the recommended platform is Linux, most documentation and support resources such as the forums and mailing lists usually offer advice and support information that assumes you are using Linux. Thus, for the purposes of getting the best possible support I recommend running on a Linux-based platform.

With regard to selecting hardware for your Nagios installation, I recommend running on Intel-based hardware. This is not to say you cannot run Nagios on other hardware. Indeed, Nagios also supports most other proprietary Unix hardware, including Scalable Processor Architecture (SPARC), Intel Itanium, Alpha, and PowerPC. From my experience, Intel-based hardware is the most commonly selected platform and thus the majority of support information available in mailing lists and forums refers to this platform. Additionally, because of Intel-based hardware's low cost, it is almost certainly the most cost-effective platform for a Nagios installation.

---

3. Statistics (www.nagios.org/userprofiles/quickstats.php) indicate that Red Hat is the most commonly used operating system for Nagios.

■**Note** For this book I have selected Red Hat Enterprise Linux ES Version 4 running on Intel-based hardware as the operating system and hardware platform for our Nagios installation.

Capacity Planning

Sizing a Nagios server is greatly dependent on the environment you intend to monitor. This is because the number of hosts and services you intend to monitor and check has a material impact on the size of the host you should select as a Nagios server. There are few ground rules available to determine exactly how many services and hosts you can monitor with a particular hardware configuration. The recommendations for sizing installations I have made are based on research and personal experience with a variety of Nagios installations.

As with most applications, the three factors impacting the performance of Nagios are CPU, memory, and disk space. Additionally, as with most applications the more of each factor available to your Nagios server, the better performance you will achieve. Table 1-1 provides some rough indications of the number of hosts you can monitor with particular configurations.

Table 1-1. *Nagios Hardware Sizing Figures*

# of Hosts Monitored	# of CPUs	CPU Speed	Memory	Disk Space
< 100	1	800MHz+	512MB+	5GB+
100–500	1	1GHz+	1GB+	10GB+
500–1000	1+	3GHz+	1GB+	20GB+
> 1000	1+	3GHz+	2GB+	40GB+

■**Note** Nagios will take advantage of symmetric multiprocessing (SMP) for some purposes. The primary Nagios process will only run on one CPU, but the checks on your hosts and services are spawned as separate processes and will generally be distributed automatically by your operating system's SMP code onto any additional available CPUs.

These are very arbitrary figures and can vary greatly depending on exactly what your environment looks like and how your Nagios server is configured. This is because for every host monitored you can monitor a varying number of services on that host; for example, you may only monitor disk space on one host but monitor disk space, Apache, Oracle, and FTP on another. You can also perform varying types, volumes, and frequencies of checks on those hosts and services that can influence the performance of your Nagios server. I'll discuss this in more detail in Chapter 2 when I look at configuring Nagios.

The disk space required by your Nagios server is also dependent on what data you collect and how long you keep that data. For example, if you send your data to a database you may require more storage than simply storing in the default Nagios files.

Due to the potential uncertainty in Nagios performance, I recommend that you err on the side of caution when sizing your hardware. Even then you may not be able to fully determine the size of the hardware you require until you have started adding hosts and services to be checked and monitoring the resulting performance of your Nagios server.

Tip To reduce the overhead of a particular server, you can also configure your Nagios installation as a "distributed" environment and deploy multiple Nagios servers. In this configuration you would deploy multiple servers that would conduct the checks of your hosts and services. These servers would then send the results of the checks back to a central server, which would collate and display these results. I discuss this configuration model in Chapter 8.

Redundancy and Backup

You should consider the importance of your monitoring environment to your organization and look at the redundancy and the backup of your Nagios servers. Generally, if you rely on your monitoring infrastructure to provide an integral part of your management infrastructure, you should purchase resilient hardware to run Nagios on. This hardware should include features like redundant power supplies, Redundant Array of Inexpensive Disks (RAID), and failover network connections.

You should also look at installing an additional server or servers to provide redundant monitoring capabilities in the event the primary or production Nagios server fails. These servers should be installed in a disaster recovery planning (DRP) site or an alternate location to prevent an outage in your primary site also taking out your redundant server(s).

Tip Obviously if the hosts and devices you are monitoring are located in one site and the nature of the outage is connectivity to that site, then the presence of redundant servers will not help you in monitoring the hosts at that site.

Also a consideration for your Nagios servers is backup and recovery. You should include your Nagios server(s) in your normal backup regime and disaster recovery planning.

Installing the Nagios Software

Now that we've briefly looked at positioning and selecting the right hardware and software for your Nagios installation, we can look at actually installing the Nagios software. Nagios installations consist of two major components: the Nagios server and the Nagios plug-ins. The Nagios server is the core of the Nagios solution and performs functions such as interpreting the configuration, running the web console, and initiating notifications and checks. The Nagios plug-ins provide the interfaces to hosts, devices, and applications to allow you to monitor them; for example, the plug-ins package includes a plug-in called `check_mysql` that allows you to monitor the status of a MySQL database. It also contains plug-ins that can check common network services via TCP, User Datagram Protocol (UDP), or ICMP and others that allow local resources such as CPU, memory, and disk space to be checked. The plug-ins are called by the Nagios server and the results of the checks fed back into the Nagios server and actioned. I'll discuss this process further in Chapter 2 when I cover configuring Nagios.

Prerequisites for Software Installation

There are also prerequisites for both the Nagios server and plug-ins. First, if you are compiling from source, you will need a C compiler to create both the Nagios server and the plug-ins. If you are installing the server and plug-ins from a package such as an RPM, you will not require the compiler. Second, if you choose to use the Nagios web console, your Nagios server installation requires two other prerequisites: a web server (the recommended server is Apache) and the `gd` library, which is used to display graphs and trending images.[4]

I'm not going to cover installing a C compiler. This is a basic component of most Linux distributions and indeed other Unix platforms. I will assume you are able to install a C compiler. I will briefly cover installing the Apache web server from source in the "Installing the Apache Web Server" section. Additionally, on most Red Hat systems you have the option to install the Apache web server as part of your server build or using an RPM after installation. I will also cover performing an installation via RPM. In the "Configuring Your Web Server for Nagios" section later in this chapter, I will discuss configuring the Apache web server to support the Nagios web console.

■**Tip** If you intend to integrate Nagios with any other packages—for example, the Multirouter Traffic Grapher (MTRG)—you need to have these packages installed. I talk about integration in Chapter 9.

Installing the Apache Web Server

There are three methods of installing the Apache web server: source, binaries, or via a package such as an RPM. I'll cover installing from source and via RPM in this section.

Installing Apache from Source

The fastest way to install Apache is probably via source. You can download the Apache source from the Apache Foundation website. At the time of this writing, the latest version of the Apache `httpd` daemon was 2.0.55.[5] The following lines show how to download and unpack the source package for the daemon:

```
puppy# wget http://www.apache.org/dist/httpd/httpd-2.0.55.tar.gz
puppy# tar -zxf httpd-2.0.55.tar.gz
```

---

4. `www.boutell.com/gd`

5. Also available is the 1.3.x branch of the `httpd` daemon if your environment still uses it.

You then need to change into the resulting directory and compile the `httpd` daemon. The `httpd` daemon has a `configure` script that needs to be executed, and then you can run `make` and compile the daemon. The `configure` script has a number of options that you may wish to change on your system; you can view these by executing `configure` with the `--help` flag. But generally you will not need to use any of these options for an installation to support the Nagios server. On the next lines, I run the `configure` script and then compile the daemon using the `make` command:

```
puppy# ./configure
puppy# make
```

Lastly I need to install the `httpd` daemon. This can be done using the `make install` command as you can see here:

```
puppy# make install
```

By default, this installs the `httpd` daemon underneath the directory `/usr/local/apache2/`. The `httpd` configuration is stored in the directory `/usr/local/apache2/conf/` and the `httpd` binary in the directory `/usr/local/apache2/bin/`. You can then start the `httpd` daemon using the following command:

```
puppy# /usr/local/apache2/bin/apachectl start
```

and stop it using this command:

```
puppy# /usr/local/apache2/bin/apachectl stop
```

Installing Apache from RPM

If you are running an RPM-based distribution, such as Red Hat, and you don't wish to install from source, you can also install from an RPM package. First, you may already have Apache installed on your host as it is a fairly standard installation option. You can check for the presence of the RPM by using the following command:

```
puppy# rpm -qa | grep httpd
httpd-2.0.52-19.ent
httpd-2.0.52-12.2.ent
```

In the previous lines you can see that version 2.0.52 of the `httpd` daemon is installed on our host and we don't need to install it. If the RPM is not installed, then the command will not return any results.

On Red Hat if the `httpd` package is not installed, you can install it via the `up2date` application like so:

```
puppy# up2date httpd
```

or, if you have taken the RPM from your installation media, by using the `rpm` command like so:

```
puppy# rpm -Uvh httpd-2.0.52-19.ent.rpm
```

Either option will install the `httpd` daemon and indicate any required prerequisite RPMs. The configuration files will be installed into the `/etc/httpd/` directory in the `conf` and `conf.d` subdirectories. The package installation will also create an `init` script for the `httpd` daemon. You can use this to start and stop the daemon.

■Tip If you do use an RPM-based distribution you could also install Apache using your distribution's package management application, such as APT, yum, or emerge.

Installing the gd Library and Includes

First, let's check to see if you have the gd library already installed. The easiest method for checking is to use the ldconfig command to see if the library is present:

```
puppy# ldconfig -p | grep 'libgd.so'
libgd.so.2 (libc6) => /usr/lib/libgd.so.2
libgd.so (libc6) => /usr/lib/libgd.so
```

If the command returns these messages, this indicates that the libraries are installed. You should confirm that the gd includes are also installed by using the find command to locate the file gd.h:

```
puppy# find / -iname gd.h
/usr/include/gd.h
```

The gd.h file might also be located in the directory /usr/local/include. Only if both the libraries and include file are installed is the gd library correctly installed.

■Tip On Red Hat systems you can check if the RPMs are installed by using the command rpm -q gd gd-devel. You can do the same on other package-based systems by querying for the relevant package names using your package management tool. The relevant package names for most common distributions are listed later in this section.

If the gd library and includes are installed, you can skip this section and continue to the section "Installing the Nagios Server." If the gd library is not installed, continue reading.

I will cover installing the gd library both from source and via a package. You will need to be logged on as the root user in order to install the gd library for both types of installation. First, let's look at installing the gd library from a source package and then via the packages available from your distribution.

If you want to install gd from source, you need to retrieve the gd package and unpack it as you can see on the next two lines:

```
puppy# wget http://www.boutell.com/gd/http/gd-2.0.33.tar.gz
puppy# tar -zxf gd-2.0.33.tar.gz
```

Once you have uncompressed the package, you will need to change into the resulting directory and configure, compile, and install the gd library. Example 1-1 shows the configuration and compilation process.

Example 1-1. *Configuring and Compiling the gd Library*

```
puppy# cd gd-2.0.33
puppy# ./configure
puppy# make
puppy# make install
```

By default, the `configure` process will install gd underneath the `/usr/local/lib` directory. You can override this location with the `--prefix` `configure` option, as you can see on this line:

```
puppy# ./configure --prefix=/usr/lib
```

There are also a variety of other `configure` options that you can display with the command on the following line:

```
puppy# ./configure --help
```

You can also install the gd library from a package. gd packages are available for most Linux distributions. On Red Hat you need to install two RPM packages: gd and gd-devel. You can see them being installed on the following line:

```
puppy# rpm -Uvh gd gd-devel
```

On Mandrake and Debian, you need to install the `libgd2` and `libgd2-devel` packages. Lastly, on Gentoo you need to `emerge` the gd package like so:

```
duckling# emerge gd
```

Installing the Nagios Server

After you have installed the required prerequisites, you can then install the Nagios server. The Nagios server is available as a source package and as a Red Hat RPM.[6] I will demonstrate how to install using both approaches. As a general preference I strongly recommend installing the Nagios server from source. This is principally because of the greater flexibility in configuring the Nagios server that installing from source allows. In the next section I show you how to install from source. If you wish to install from RPM, I recommend you still read the "Installing from Source" section, which contains other useful information about Nagios, before you go on to the "Installing via RPM" section.

■**Note** You will need to be logged on as `root` to install Nagios.

Installing from Source

You can obtain the Nagios server source package from the Nagios website at www.nagios.org/download/. At the time of this writing, the latest release of Nagios was version 2.0 and this book

---

6. At the time of this writing, older versions (generally version 1.2) of Nagios are available as Debian, Gentoo, and SuSE packages.

focuses on this release only.[7] From the Nagios website you will be directed to Sourceforge,[8] where you can select the mirror of your choice to download the Nagios server source code. Also on the Nagios download site is the MD5 checksum of the source package. Make a note of it as you should use it together with the md5sum command to confirm that the package you have downloaded has not been tampered with. In Example 1-2, I demonstrate downloading the Nagios server source package and confirming the checksum matches.

Example 1-2. *Downloading and Verifying Nagios*

```
puppy# wget➥
http://easynews.dl.sourceforge.net/sourceforge/nagios/nagios-2.0rc1.tar.gz
puppy# md5sum nagios-2.0rc1.tar.gz
051760458d961b6ee015b5932a8437c4  nagios-2.0rc1.tar.gz
```

Once you have downloaded and verified the checksum of the source package, you need to unpack it before compilation and change into the resulting directory:

```
puppy# tar –zxvf nagios-2.0rc1.tar.gz
puppy# cd nagios-2.0rc1
```

Before you install the Nagios server, you need to create a user and group to run Nagios as. In Example 1-3, I show how to create them.

Example 1-3. *Creating the Nagios User and Group*

```
puppy# groupadd nagios
puppy# useradd -g nagios -M nagios
```

The first command creates a group called nagios, and the second command creates a user also called nagios. The -g option adds the newly created user to the nagios group, and the -M option stops the creation of a home directory for the nagios user.

Creating an External Command Group

You may also need a group to allow you to run external commands. External commands enable you to interact with the Nagios server from external sources—for example, submitting commands from the Nagios web console to acknowledge an event or change a configuration setting. External commands are optional and many people do not enable them for security reasons as there is a risk that someone could submit an unauthorized external command. You can control whether external commands are accepted from within your Nagios configuration. I am going to set up the required group here. If you decide that you don't need external commands, you can leave them turned off in your configuration.

■Note I'll discuss securing external commands in Chapter 3.

---

7. At the time of this writing, Nagios 2.0 was issued as a release candidate. This book uses release candidate 1 of Nagios. By the time of publication, a production release of Nagios should be available.

8. www.sourceforge.net

To function correctly, external commands require authorization to interact with the web server and the Nagios server. This is provided by the group, which Nagios calls the command group, that I am about to create. The members of the command group need to be the user that your web server process runs as and the user that the Nagios server runs as.

First, determine the user that is running your web server. In the case of the Apache web server, this is usually apache or nobody. With Apache you can verify this by running the ps command to determine which user the httpd process is running:

```
puppy# ps -ef | grep 'httpd'
apache   32344 32341  0 14:24 ?        00:00:00 /usr/sbin/httpd
apache   32345 32341  0 14:24 ?        00:00:00 /usr/sbin/httpd
```

The first column indicates the user running the process, in this case, the user apache.

For the Nagios server process, the default user should be the nagios user that I have just created. In Example 1-4, I have created a command group and added the Nagios and web server process users to the group.

Example 1-4. *Creating a Command Group*

```
puppy# groupadd ncmd
puppy# usermod -G ncmd nagios
puppy# usermod -G ncmd apache
```

Compiling Nagios

Now that you have created the Nagios user and the required groups, you are ready to configure and compile Nagios. Example 1-5 shows the configure command I am going to use.

Example 1-5. *Nagios Server configure Statement*

```
puppy# ./configure --prefix=/usr/local/nagios --with-htmlurl=/nagios/➥
--with-cgiurl=/nagios/cgi-bin --with-nagios-user=nagios --with-nagios-group=nagios➥
--with-command-group=ncmd
```

As you can see from Example 1-5, the configuration process requires you to specify a number of options. Indeed, the six configure options used in Example 1-5 are critical to your Nagios configuration. Table 1-2 lists these options and their descriptions and defaults.

Table 1-2. *Nagios Critical configure Options*

Option	Description	Default
--prefix=*directory*	Base directory to install Nagios into	/usr/local/ nagios
--with-htmluser=*url*	The URL of the Nagios HTML files	/nagios/
--with-cgiurl=*url*	The URL of the Nagios CGIs	/nagios/cgi-bin
--with-nagios-user=*user*	The user the Nagios process will run as	nagios
--with-nagios-group=*group*	The group the Nagios process will run as	nagios
--with-command-group=*group*	Sets the group name for external commands	None

Let's look at how we can use each of these options. The first, `--prefix`, specifies the base installation directory for the Nagios server. The default setting is `/usr/local/nagios`. You can change this to whatever directory suits your setup. In the examples in this book, I have assumed the base installation directory has been used.

The second and third options specify settings for the Nagios web console. The `--with-htmlurl` option specifies the URL of the Nagios web console. This option defaults to the URL `/nagios/`. This means that when you connect your web browser to the Nagios web console you would use the URL `http://`*hostname*`/nagios/`. You would replace *hostname* with the hostname of your web server, for example `http://puppy.yourdomain.com/nagios/`. You can specify whatever URL location you wish here. You will need to make a note of what you do specify as the URL since you will need that information when you configure your web server in the "Configuring Your Web Server for Nagios" section.

The second web console option, `--with-cgiurl`, specifies the URL for the Nagios CGIs. The CGI represents the code for the Nagios web console. This option defaults to `/nagios/cgi-bin`. You can specify a different URL, but you will have to make a note of it when you configure your web server.

■**Caution** For the `--with-cgiurl` option you should ensure you do not specify a trailing `/` at the end of the URL. The trailing `/` at the end of the option will cause Nagios to fail to correctly compile.

The next options, `--with-nagios-user` and `--with-nagios-group`, allow you to specify the user and group that will run the Nagios server process. Both options default to `nagios`. I demonstrated creating a `nagios` user and group in Example 1-3 earlier in this section. You can specify any user or group, but the user and group both need to exist.

■**Caution** Don't run your Nagios daemon as the `root` user. Nagios does not require this level of privilege and is designed to drop privileges when it is started.

The last `configure` option in Table 1-2 allows you to specify the name of the command group. There is no default for this option. In Example 1-5, I have used the group `ncmd` I created earlier in this section. You can specify any group name as long as that group exists. The membership of the group should be the users running both the Nagios process and your web server process—in our case, the users `nagios` and `apache`.

There are also a number of other `configure` options that you can use with Nagios, and I've listed those in Table 1-3.

Table 1-3. *Additional Nagios configure Options*

Option	Description
`--with-command-user=`*`user`*	Sets the username for external commands
`--with-gd-lib=`*`/path/to/gd/lib`*	Specifies the location of the gd library
`--with-gd-inc=`*`/path/to/gd/includes`*	Specifies the location of the gd includes
`--enable-event-broker`	Turns on the Nagios Event Broker
`--enable-embedded-perl`	Turns on embedded Perl Nagios (ePN)
`--with-perlcache`	Adds caching of Perl scripts (requires ePN)
`--with-mail=`*`/path/to/mail`*	Specifies the location of the `mail` binary
`--with-init-dir=`*`/path/to/init`*	Specifies where to install the `init` script
`--with-lockfile=`*`/path/to/lockfile`*	Specifies where to locate the lockfile

The first option in Table 1-3, `--with-command-user`, is linked to the external command group I defined earlier. The command group usually contains the user the Nagios server runs as, together with the user your web server process runs as. You can change this behavior to define a separate command user rather than the user the Nagios server runs as. The user you specify here must also be added to the command group. This allows you to set different permissions for the user running the Nagios server process and the external command user. I recommend you leave this directive blank for most configurations.

The next two options are provided in the event that Nagios can't find your gd library and includes. With these options, you can specify the location of the library and includes. These options are required when the `configure` script cannot find the libraries or includes.

The `--enable-event-broker` option enables new functionality introduced with Nagios version 2.0 called the Nagios Event Broker (NEB). The Event Broker allows you to develop modules that take and broker events from Nagios—for example, adding an event broker module to log Nagios events to a database. As yet very little development has been done utilizing the broker and the documentation is somewhat sparse. I will discuss it further in Chapter 10.

The `--enable-embedded-perl` and `--with-perlcache` options enable the Embedded Perl Nagios (ePN) and caching of internal Perl scripts, respectively. The ePN is designed to enhance the use of Nagios with plug-ins written in Perl. I'll discuss ePN briefly in Chapter 10 when I talk about developing your own plug-ins. The `--with-perlcache` option has no effect unless the ePN has been enabled.

The `--with-mail`, `--with-init-dir`, and `--with-lockfile` options allow you to specify the location of the `mail` binary, the location of your `init` directory, and where to place the Nagios lockfile, respectively.

Once you have configured Nagios, you need to compile it using the `make` command and then install it. There a number of steps in the `make` process you will have to perform to install all of the components. I start with compiling the Nagios server source with the `make all` command like so:

```
puppy# make all
```

When this process completes, the message in Example 1-6 will be displayed.

Example 1-6. *Nagios Compilation Completion Message*

```
*** Compile finished ***

If the main program and CGIs compiled without any errors, you
can continue with installing Nagios as follows (type 'make'
without any arguments for a list of all possible options):

    make install
        - This installs the main program, CGIs, and HTML files

    make install-init
        - This installs the init script in /etc/rc.d/init.d

    make install-commandmode
        - This installs and configures permissions on the
          directory for holding the external command file

    make install-config
        - This installs *SAMPLE* config files in /usr/local/nagios/etc
          You'll have to modify these sample files before you can
          use Nagios.  Read the HTML documentation for more info
          on doing this.  Pay particular attention to the docs on
          object configuration files, as they determine what/how
          things get monitored!
    ...
```

The message in Example 1-6 describes the next steps in the make process that you need to take. First, the make install command installs the binaries, CGIs, and HTML files. Then, the init script is installed with the make install-init command. By default, the init script will be installed into the directory /etc/rc.d/init.d. You can override this with the directory of your choice by using the --with-init-dir=*directory* option when you run the configure script. Replace *directory* with the location of your init scripts.

So let's install the server components and the init script like so:

```
puppy# make install && make install-init
```

Next I will further configure Nagios to run external commands. I've already configured one of the other components, the command group, earlier in this section. This component, command mode, requires that we modify the ownership and permissions of a directory in your Nagios installation. These changes are required so that the directory can hold the external command file. The external command file is a named pipe that is created when Nagios is started and removed when Nagios is stopped. External commands are fed into this file, read by the Nagios server process, and actioned.

The external command file requires specific permissions to allow external command to be written to the file. First, the directory holding the file needs to be owned by the Nagios user and the command group I defined earlier. For example, using the examples in this chapter it would be the user nagios and the group ncmd. Second, you need to set the sticky bit on this directory to ensure that the command file inherits the permissions of the directory. In most

Nagios installations, the directory that is modified is /usr/local/nagios/var/rw. To perform this installation step I use the following command:[9]

```
puppy# make install-commandmode
```

The command mode directory will now have ownership and permissions like those displayed in Example 1-7.

Example 1-7. *Command Mode Directory*

```
puppy# ls -al /usr/local/nagios/var/rw
drwxrwsr-x  2 nagios ncmd   4096 Apr 30 01:46 .
```

■**Caution** You will note that the ncmd group has write access to the directory holding the external command file (and as a result of the sticky bit, also to the external command file itself). The user that runs your web server process or daemon also needs to be a member of the ncmd group. This membership allows external commands to be submitted from the web console. External commands, however, can be a security risk and it may be possible for an attacker to submit malicious or unwanted external commands. I will discuss some security measures to mitigate this risk in Chapter 3.

Finally, Nagios comes with a set of sample configuration files that provide an excellent starting point for configuring Nagios. These files are all suffixed with the term -Sample and will need to be renamed before you can use them to configure Nagios. You can install them with this command:

```
puppy# make install-config
```

Now that you have fully installed Nagios from the source package, let's quickly look at the directory structure of Nagios and learn where the various components are installed. Table 1-4 lists the directory structure I have just created beneath the base installation directory of /usr/local/nagios.

Table 1-4. *Nagios Source Directory Structure Beneath /usr/local/nagios*

Directory	Description
bin	Location of the binaries
etc	Location of the configuration files
sbin	Location of the CGI files
share	Location of the HTML files
var	Location of the log files
var/archives	Location of any archived log files
var/rw	Location of the external command file

---

9. If you don't use this install step, you can see instructions about how to do this at http://nagios. sourceforge.net/docs/2_0/commandfile.html.

Now you can skip to the "Installing the Nagios Plug-ins" section or keep reading if you are interested in seeing how you can install Nagios from an RPM package.

Installing via RPM

In addition to installing from source, you can install from an RPM package. These packages are designed for the Red Hat operating system but will also generally work on Mandrake and other RPM-based distributions. First, let's download a suitable RPM for Nagios. The Nagios RPMs are created by Dag Wieers and available from his site at http://dag.wieers.com/packages/nagios/. Dag's site contains RPMs for Red Hat 7.3, 8, and 9; Enterprise Linux versions 2.1 and 3; and Fedora Core.

■Tip Be aware that the RPM packages available at Dag's site can occasionally be slightly out of date and may represent earlier versions of Nagios. If you require the latest version I recommend you install from source as per the instructions in the "Installing from Source" section earlier in this chapter.

In Example 1-8, you can see the commands for downloading a Nagios RPM, this one for Red Hat Enterprise Linux version 4.

Example 1-8. *Downloading and Installing a Nagios RPM*

```
puppy# wget➥
http://dag.wieers.com/packages/nagios/nagios-2.0-0.b4.1.2.el4.test.i386.rpm
```

Once you have the Nagios RPM, you can install it using the rpm command. I show this process in Example 1-9.

Example 1-9. *Installing the Nagios RPM*

```
puppy# rpm –Uvh nagios-2.0.el4.i386.rpm
Preparing...                ########################################### [100%]
   1:nagios                 ########################################### [100%]
```

The RPM installation performs most of the same steps performed by installing Nagios from source. There are several subtle differences. First, the external command directory has its group set to the group used by the web server process; for example, for Apache it is set to the apache group. Thus the external command directory should look like this:

```
puppy# ls -al /var/log/nagios/rw
total 16
drwxr-sr-x  2 nagios apache 4096 Mar  5 17:57 .
drwxr-xr-x  4 nagios nagios 4096 May  9 21:12 ..
```

Second, the sample configuration files are installed but they are not suffixed with the term -sample.

Lastly, the RPM installation process does not use the default directory structure that the Nagios source package uses. Rather, it creates its own directory structure. Table 1-5 shows this structure.

Table 1-5. *Nagios RPM Directory Structure*

Directory	Description
/etc/nagios	Configuration files
/usr/bin/nagios	Nagios binary
/var/log/nagios	Log files
/var/log/nagios/rw	External command directory
/usr/share/nagios	HTML files
/usr/lib/nagios/cgi	CGI files
/usr/lib/nagios/plugins	Plug-ins

■**Tip** In this book I have assumed you have installed the Nagios server using the source package and with the default directory structure. If you have used RPMs or a different directory structure, you will have to change some of the examples and configuration settings to reflect your particular configuration.

Installing the Nagios Plug-ins

After you have installed the Nagios server, you need to install the Nagios plug-ins. The plug-ins are not contained in one single program but within a large collection of small programs. Each program is an individual plug-in that is designed to monitor a particular system, device, or application.

As with the Nagios server, you can install the plug-ins via source or from an RPM. Again, I recommend you install the plug-ins from source. I demonstrate how to install the plug-ins from source in the next section and via RPM in the section that follows. I recommend you read both sections to gain a full understanding of the entire process.

Installing the Plug-ins from Source

As with the Nagios server, you can obtain the plug-in source package from the Nagios website at www.nagios.org/download/. The download site redirects you to the Sourceforge website at http://sourceforge.net/projects/nagiosplug/, where you can select a suitable mirror to download the file. At the time of this writing, the latest version of the Nagios plug-ins is 1.4 and I have used this release for the purposes of this book.

In Example 1-10, I have retrieved the package from one of the Sourceforge mirrors and unpacked the plug-in source.

Example 1-10. *Downloading and Unpacking the Plug-in Package*

```
puppy# wget➥
http://easynews.dl.sourceforge.net/sourceforge/nagiosplug/nagios-plugins-1.4.tar.gz
puppy# tar -zxf nagios-plugins-1.4.tar.gz
```

Now change into the directory created when you unpacked the package. From here you can configure and compile the plug-ins. Before you configure and compile, you need to be aware that some of the plug-ins require prerequisites in order to compile and function. I have listed these plug-ins and their required prerequisites, including where you can find them and, if applicable, the name of the relevant RPM package,[10] in Table 1-6.

Table 1-6. *Plug-in Prerequisites*

Plug-in	Prerequisite	Source	Package Name
check_fping	fping utility	www.fping.com	fping
check_game	qstat utility	www.qstat.org	N/A
check_hpjd	NET-SNMP package	http://net-snmp.sourceforge.net	perl-Net-SNMP
check_ldap	LDAP libraries	www.openldap.org	openldap
check_mysql	MySQL libraries	www.mysql.org	mysql
check_pqsql	PostgreSQL libraries	www.postgresql.org	N/A
check_radius	radiusclient library	ftp://ftp.cityline.net/pub/ radiusclient/	radiousclient and radiusclient-devel
check_snmp	NET-SNMP package	http://net-snmp.sourceforge.net	perl-Net-SNMP
check_ifstatus	NET-SNMP package	http://net-snmp.sourceforge.net	perl-Net-SNMP
check_ifoperstatus	NET-SNMP package	http://net-snmp.sourceforge.net	perl-Net-SNMP
check_ups	Network UPS Tools	www.networkupstools.org/	N/A

■**Tip** More detailed information on the prerequisites for plug-ins is contained in the file REQUIREMENTS located in the Nagios plug-ins source package.

Each of these prerequisites can be downloaded from the source indicated, or you can install them via an RPM package or a package from your distribution's package management system. You don't have to download and install these prerequisites unless you require the plug-in that they support. If you do not install the prerequisite, the configure process will print an error message, and skip that plug-in and not compile or install it. Some of the prerequisites may already be installed, and this will also be indicated when you run the configure script.

The configure process also has a number of potential variables you can set. In Example 1-11, I show a typical configure statement.

---

10. Package names for other distributions should be similar to the RPM packages.

Example 1-11. *Nagios Plug-ins configure Statement*

```
puppy# ./configure --prefix=/usr/local/nagios --with-nagios-user=nagios➥
--with-nagios-group=nagios --with-cgiurl=/nagios/cgi-bin
```

The configure script in Example 1-11 uses the defaults we used earlier to configure the Nagios server. Whatever options you use here must match what was used previously. In Example 1-11, we have specified the default installation prefix of /usr/local/nagios and a user and group of nagios. Lastly, it specifies the URL of the CGIs, /nagios/cgi-bin. Table 1-7 shows a list of the other major configure options for the plug-in package and, if applicable, their defaults.

Table 1-7. *Nagios Plug-in configure Options*

Option	Description	Default
--prefix=*prefix*	Base directory for Nagios plug-ins	/usr/local/nagios
--with-cgiurl=*dir*	URL location of the CGI programs	/nagios/cgi-bin
--with-nagios-user=*user*	The user the Nagios process runs as	nagios
--with-nagios-group=*group*	The group the Nagios process runs as	nagios
--with-trusted-path=*path*	Sets the trusted path for executables	/bin:/sbin:/usr/bin:/usr/sbin
--with-pgsql=*dir*	Sets the path to PostgreSQL installation	N/A
--with-mysql=*dir*	Sets the path to the MySQL installation	N/A
--with-openssl=*dir*	Sets the path to OpenSSL	N/A
--without-openssl	Disables OpenSSL	N/A
--with-ping-command=*syntax*	Sets the syntax for the ping command	/bin/ping -n -U -w %d -c %d %s
--with-ping6-command=*syntax*	Sets the syntax for the IPv6 ping command	/bin/ping6 -n -U -c %d %s

Some of the options in Table 1-7 are self-explanatory but others need further description. The --trusted-path option sets the path used by executables called by plug-ins. The default should be sufficient for most purposes. The --with-pgsql and --with-mysql options both allow you to specify the location of your PostgreSQL and MySQL installations, respectively. The --with-openssl option allows you to specify the location of your OpenSSL installation. The --without-openssl option lets you disable the use of OpenSSL. The last two options, --with-ping-command and --with-ping6-command, control the variables used by the ping and ping6 commands when they are utilized by the plug-ins. These variables consist of normal options for these commands and Nagios macros.

■**Note** Nagios macros are variables, for example an IP address or a hostname, that are passed from the Nagios server to plug-ins. I'll discuss them in Chapter 2.

For example, for the ping command the default options are -n -U -w %d -c %d %s. This tells the ping command to output numerically only (-n) and print user-to-user latency (-U). It also specifies the ping count and deadline (the -c and –w options, respectively) with a value of the macro %d. It also uses the macro %s as the destination of the ping. On the next line, I show what the ping command would look like with the macros replaced with real values:

```
puppy# ping –n –U –w 2 –c 2 192.168.0.100
```

Changing these variables controls the information that Nagios receives from the ping command. You should only change these if you understand what the implications are of the change.

Now you have configured the plug-ins you need to make and install the plug-ins. You can see the required commands to do this on the following lines:

```
puppy# make
puppy# make install
```

The plug-ins will be installed into the directory /usr/local/nagios/libexec/ unless you override this with the --prefix configure option.

Installing the Plug-ins via RPM

In addition to installing from source, you can install the plug-ins from an RPM package. These packages are designed for the Red Hat operating system but will also generally work on Mandrake and other RPM-based distributions.

There are two prerequisites for the Nagios plug-in RPM: the fping package and the perl-Net-SNMP package. perl-Net-SNMP also has a number of prerequisites itself. Both of these packages are available from Dag Wieer's sites at http://dag.wieers.com/packages/fping/ and http://dag.wieers.com/packages/perl-Net-SNMP/, respectively. The prerequisites for perl-Net-SNMP are also available from Dag's site, and you can see the full list of them in Table 1-8.

Table 1-8. *Prerequisites for perl-Net-SNMP*

Prerequisite	URL
perl-Digest-HMAC	http://dag.wieers.com/packages/perl-Digest-HMAC/
perl-Digest-SHA1	http://dag.wieers.com/packages/perl-Digest-SHA1/
perl-Socket6	http://dag.wieers.com/packages/perl-Socket6/
perl-IO-Socket-INET6	http://dag.wieers.com/packages/perl-IO-Socket-INET6/
perl-Crypt-DES	http://dag.wieers.com/packages/perl-Crypt-DES/

First, download and install the RPMs that are perl-Net-SNMP's prerequisites. Next install the fping and perl-Net-SNMP packages as you can see in the following lines:

```
puppy# rpm -Uvh fping-2.4-1.b2.2.el4.rf.i386.rpm \
perl-Net-SNMP-5.0.1-1.2.el4.rf.noarch.rpm
warning: fping-2.4-1.b2.2.el4.rf.i386.rpm: V3 DSA signature: NOKEY, key ID 6b8d79e6
Preparing...              ######################################### [100%]
   1:perl-Net-SNMP  ######################################### [ 50%]
   2:fping          ######################################### [ 100%]
```

Now that you have installed the prerequisites, you can download a suitable RPM for the Nagios plug-ins. The Nagios plug-in RPMs, like those for the server, are created by Dag Wieers and available from his site at `http://dag.wieers.com/packages/nagios-plugins/`. Dag's site contains RPMs for Red Hat 7.3, 8, and 9; Enterprise Linux versions 2.1, 3, and 4; and Fedora Core.

In Example 1-12, I have downloaded and then installed the Nagios plug-ins using one of these RPM packages.

Example 1-12. *Downloading the Plug-in RPM*

```
puppy# wget➥
http://dag.wieers.com/packages/nagios-plugins/nagios-plugins-1.4-2.2.el4.rf.i386.rpm
puppy# rpm –Uvh nagios-plugins-1.4-2.2.el4.rf.i386.rpm
Preparing...                    ########################################### [100%]
   1:nagios-plugins             ########################################### [100%]
```

Your Nagios plug-ins are now installed. By default, they are installed into the directory `/usr/lib/nagios/plugins`.

Configuring Your Web Server for Nagios

The final step in your Nagios installation is to configure your web server to support the Nagios web console. I've assumed that you have used the recommended web server, Apache. But it should be relatively easy to adapt the instructions to suit most web servers. I have also assumed you have installed Nagios with the default base installation location of `/usr/local/nagios`. We will also cover securing the web console and the CGIs in Chapter 3.

■**Tip** You could also configure Nagios to use SSL (HTTPS) rather than HTTP. In the case of Apache, this is done by configuring your web server to support the `mod_ssl` module. You can read about how to do this at `http://httpd.apache.org/docs-2.0/ssl/`.

There are two ways you can configure Apache to present the web console. Each method results in the display of a different URL for the Nagios web console. The first is the recommended configuration, which locates the web console off the root of your host's web server. For example, navigating to the URL like `http://puppy.yourdomain.com/nagios/` will display the web console. This method is explained in the section "Basic Configuration."

The second method uses Apache's `VirtualServer` mode, and in this method navigating to a URL like `http://nagios.yourdomain.com` will display the web console. This method is explained in the section "Virtual Server Configuration."

I'll demonstrate how to configure using both methods. I don't recommend one method over the other. You should choose the method that best suits your environment.

■**Note** If you installed the Nagios server from an RPM package, you should also read the section "Configuring Your Web Server with an RPM Installation."

Basic Configuration

The basic configuration for the web console first involves defining some aliases to allow the Nagios HTML and CGI files to be externally addressable—for example, aliasing the directory containing the HTML files, /usr/local/nagios/share, to the URL /nagios/. The aliases you define will be based on the configure script choices, using the --with-cgiurl and --with-htmlurl options, you made when you configured the Nagios server. Then, you need to define the two directories holding the HTML and CGI files and their attributes to the Apache server using the Directory directive so that it can serve out the required pages.

All of this information needs to be placed into the Apache configuration file, usually called httpd.conf. On Red Hat systems, this file is usually located in the directory /etc/httpd/conf. If you have installed Apache from source, the httpd.conf file is located in the directory /usr/local/apache2/conf.

Let's start with the directive defining the location and attributes of the CGIs. Example 1-13 shows the sample configuration recommended for the CGI alias and Directory directive. I'll explain what each component of the example does next.

■**Caution** You need to place the alias and Directory directive for the CGI files above the alias and Directory directive for the HTML files in the httpd.conf file. This will prevent Apache from incorrectly parsing the aliases.

Example 1-13. *The CGI Alias and Directive*

```
ScriptAlias /nagios/cgi-bin /usr/local/nagios/sbin
<Directory "/usr/local/nagios/sbin">
    AllowOverride None
    Options ExecCGI
    Order allow,deny
    Allow from all
</Directory>
```

The first line is the CGI alias, which uses the ScriptAlias directive.[11] The ScriptAlias directive aliases the location of CGI-based scripts. It indicates that the files in the target directory are CGI scripts and hence should be processed by the mod_cgi script handler. The first variable of the ScriptAlias directive, /nagios/cgi-bin, should be the location you chose as the URL for your CGI scripts using the --with-cgiurl option when you configured the Nagios server. The second variable is the directory where the CGI scripts are located on your host, by default /usr/local/nagios/sbin. If you used different defaults, you must replace these variables with the correct URL and directory. If you do not specify the correct URL and directory here, the Nagios web console will not function.

---

11. You can read about the ScriptAlias directive at http://httpd.apache.org/docs-2.0/mod/mod_alias.html#scriptalias.

Directly after the `ScriptAlias` directive is the `Directory` directive, which defines the directory on your host holding the CGIs to Apache and sets a number of attributes, using additional directives, about that directory. These attributes are contained within the starting `<Directory "/path/to/CGIs/">` and ending `</Directory>` directive statements. You should ensure that the directory specified in the opening statement matches the directory on your host that holds your CGI files.

There are four additional directives defined in the `Directory` directive in Example 1-13. The first directive is the `AllowOverride` directive, which has been set to `None`. This disables the use of `.htaccess` files. I'll discuss why I am doing this when I look at authentication in Chapter 3. The second directive, `Options`, controls what server features are available in that directory. The `ExecCGI` variable tells Apache to allow CGIs to be executed in this directory.

The third directive, `Order`, controls the default access state. The variable `allow,deny` tells Apache that access is denied by default.

The last directive, `Allow`, is related to the `Order` directive and tells Apache which clients are allowed to connect to the web console. In Example 1-13, this is specified as `from all`, indicating that all clients can connect. I recommend you change this to a more restrictive setting that limits the clients that can connect to your web console. The `Allow` directive will take a number of options, including hostnames, IP addresses, and netmasks. For example, on the following line I have restricted access to the web console to two IP addresses:

```
Allow from 192.168.1.10 192.168.1.15
```

Or, as you can see on the next line, I could also allow access from an entire subnet:

```
Allow from 192.168.0.0/24
```

You can configure this to suit your own environment.[12]

Now that you have added the directives for the CGI files, you need to define the directives for the HTML files that make up the display portion of the web console. These directives should be placed below the CGI directives to ensure that Apache parses the aliases correctly. I have shown these directives in Example 1-14.

Example 1-14. *The HTML Alias and Directive*

```
Alias /nagios /usr/local/nagios/share
<Directory "/usr/local/nagios/share">
    AllowOverride None
    Options None
    Order allow,deny
    Allow from all
</Directory>
```

Like Example 1-13, the first line is an alias directive, this one the base `Alias` directive used for normal HTML files rather than CGI scripts. You need to ensure that the URL and directory indicated are both correct. The URL should be the same as the URL specified using the `--with-htmlurl` option. The directory should be the directory on your host that contains the Nagios HTML files.

---

12. You can read more about Apache access controls at `http://httpd.apache.org/docs-2.0/mod/ mod_access.html`.

Also present is the starting <Directory "/path/to/HTML/"> and ending </Directory> directive statements containing the defining attributes about the specified directory. These are only slightly different from the directives you defined as part of the CGI Directory directive.

The AllowOverride and Options directives are still present and are both set to None to specify that an .htaccess file and no additional server features are allowed. The Order and Allow directives are also identical to Example 1-13, and again I recommend you change the Allow directive to a more restrictive access list.

The final configuration should look like Example 1-15.

Example 1-15. *The CGI and HTML Aliases and Directives*

```
ScriptAlias /nagios/cgi-bin /usr/local/nagios/sbin
<Directory "/usr/local/nagios/sbin">
    AllowOverride None
    Options ExecCGI
    Order allow,deny
    Allow from all
</Directory>

Alias /nagios /usr/local/nagios/share
<Directory "/usr/local/nagios/share">
    AllowOverride None
    Options None
    Order allow,deny
    Allow from all
</Directory>
```

■**Note**   You will need to restart Apache before the configuration you have defined will take effect.

Virtual Server Configuration

The configuration of your Nagios web console as a virtual host is a simple process that builds on the configuration discussed in the "Basic Configuration" section. First, you enable name-based virtual hosting. Then the CGI and HTML directives from Example 1-15 are combined (with the CGI directives still first, followed by the HTML directives) and wrapped in a VirtualHost directive. You can see this in Example 1-16.

Example 1-16. *Virtual Host Configuration for Nagios*

```
NameVirtualHost *:80

<VirtualHost nagios.yourdomain.com>
    ServerAdmin admin@puppy.yourdomain.com
    DocumentRoot /usr/local/nagios/share
    ServerName nagios.yourdomain.com
```

```
    ScriptAlias /nagios/cgi-bin/ /usr/local/nagios/sbin/
    <Directory "/usr/local/nagios/sbin/">
         AllowOverride None
         Options ExecCGI
         Order allow,deny
         Allow from all
    </Directory>

    Alias /nagios/ /usr/local/nagios/share/
    <Directory "/usr/local/nagios/share">
     AllowOverride None
     Options None
     Order allow,deny
     Allow from all
    </Directory>
</VirtualHost>
```

The first line in Example 1-16, `NameVirtualHost *:80`, enables name-based virtual hosting, which allows you to host multiple sites on one Apache server. For example, `www.site1.com` and `www.site2.com` could be both hosted on the host `host1`.

■**Tip** You can read about virtual hosting at `http://httpd.apache.org/docs-2.0/vhosts/`.

Next is the `VirtualHost` directive. The directive has a variable of the name of the site you wish to use for the Nagios web console—in this case, `nagios.yourdomain.com`.

Some additional directives are required. We have specified these directly below the opening `VirtualHost` directive. The `ServerAdmin` directive specifies the site administrator's email address. The `DocumentRoot` directive specifies the base directory for your site. This should be set to the location of your Nagios HTML files; in Example 1-16 this is `/usr/local/nagios/share`, as we defined earlier. Lastly, we define the `ServerName` directive, which allows us to specify the name for your Nagios web console site. If you need to specify additional directives, you can specify any directive supported by Apache in a `VirtualHost` directive.

You then place the contents of Example 1-15, which we defined earlier with the CGI script `Directory` directive before that of the HTML `Directory` directive. You then close the `VirtualHost` directive.

■**Note** You will need to restart Apache before the configuration you have defined will take effect.

Configuring Your Web Server with an RPM Installation

If you've installed from a Nagios RPM. your configuration will already be partially done for you. The RPM will create a file called `nagios.conf` in the `/etc/httpd/conf.d/` directory. This file contains a configuration similar to the configuration described in the "Basic Configuration" section. You may need to modify this to meet your needs—for example, by changing the access control settings, based on the information in the previous sections.

The `conf.d` directory is designed to hold files that are included in your Apache configuration by using the `Include` directive in your `httpd.conf` file. You can see the `Include` directive that the Nagios RPM adds to the `httpd.conf` file on the next line:

```
Include /etc/httpd/conf.d/nagios.conf
```

You will need to ensure that this is not commented out in the configuration, and Apache will have to be restarted to ensure that the configuration has been updated.

Restarting Apache

Once you have configured Apache for the Nagios web console, you need to restart the Apache daemon to apply the configuration. On most systems, you can run the `init` script to do this. For example, on a Red Hat system you would use this:

```
puppy# /etc/rc.d/init.d/httpd restart
```

On other systems you can use the `apachectl` command like so:

```
puppy# apachectl restart
```

Every time you change your web server configuration, you must remember to restart Apache. Failing to restart the web server is a common trap that is hard to identify and can prolong troubleshooting.

Testing

Once you have restarted Apache, you can test the Nagios web console. Obviously, we haven't configured any monitoring yet, but you can still display the empty console screen to determine if your Nagios web console is configured correctly. You should see something like the screen displayed in Figure 1-3.

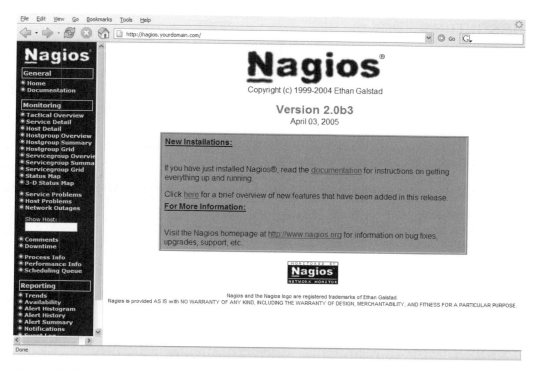

Figure 1-3. *The Nagios web console*

Checkpoint

- Ensure that you locate your Nagios server where you have network connectivity to the hosts and applications you want to monitor. If you can't get suitable network visibility of your hosts, you should look at deploying distributed Nagios servers. I examine distributed Nagios configuration in Chapter 8.

- If your hosts are located in one or more remote sites, you should also look at the option of using a distributed Nagios configuration.

- I have provided rough guidelines for sizing your Nagios server, but the requirements for monitoring can vary, depending on the environment you intend to monitor.

- If your Nagios solution is critical to your organization, make sure you purchase resilient and redundant hardware. Also remember to include your Nagios server(s) in your backup regime. You could also consider looking at a Nagios server in a failover configuration, where one server can take over from another in the event of a server failure.

- You can install the Nagios server and plug-ins from source or via RPMs. I recommend that you install from source to take advantage of the greater potential configurability.

- You can configure the Nagios web console in two different ways, in a directory underneath your host or in a virtual host configuration. You should choose the method that suits you best.

Resources

Here are some resources that you may find helpful.

Mailing Lists

- Nagios User Mailing List: `http://lists.sourceforge.net/mailman/listinfo/nagios-users`

- Nagios Announcements List: `http://lists.sourceforge.net/mailman/listinfo/nagios-announce`

- Nagios Developers List: `http://lists.sourceforge.net/mailman/listinfo/nagios-devel`

- Nagios Plug-in Help List: `http://lists.sourceforge.net/mailman/listinfo/nagiosplug-help`

Sites

- Nagios: `www.nagios.org/`

- Nagios RPM packages: `http://dag.wieers.com/packages/nagios/`

- Nagios Plug-in downloads: `http://sourceforge.net/projects/nagiosplug/`

- Apache Virtual Hosts: `http://httpd.apache.org/docs-2.0/vhosts/`

Nagios Prerequisites

- gd: `www.boutell.com/gd/`

Nagios Plug-in Prerequisites

- fping: `www.fping.com`

- qstat utility: `www.qstat.org`

- NET-SNMP package: `http://net-snmp.sourceforge.net`

- LDAP libraries: `www.openldap.org`

- MySQL libraries: `www.mysql.org`

- PostgreSQL libraries: `www.postgresql.org`

- radiusclient library: `ftp://ftp.cityline.net/pub/radiusclient/`

- Network UPS Tools: `www.networkupstools.org`

■ ■ ■

## CHAPTER 2

Basic Object Configuration

This chapter will get you started with the basic configuration of your Nagios server to provide monitoring for hosts and services. I'll begin by describing how Nagios works, move on to how it is configured, and then demonstrate how to create the basic configuration objects needed for monitoring your environment. I'll cover a number of topics in this chapter that form the basis for the principles and methods that Nagios uses to monitor your hosts and services. Some of these topics I'll cover in detail, but others I'll just introduce you to and then address them in greater detail in later chapters.

As a result of this process of gradual introduction, especially to the more advanced Nagios topics, I recommend you also read and use the Nagios documentation. The Nagios documentation is both expansive and highly detailed. It is a useful resource during the configuration process. The Nagios documentation is provided in HTML form with your Nagios installation and is viewable from the web console. The documentation is also available online at `http://nagios.sourceforge.net/docs/2_0/`.

How Does Nagios Work?

Let's quickly look at how the basics of Nagios work, starting with how to define your monitored environment. You do this by defining a series of objects that represent the characteristics of the environment being monitored. You begin by defining your assets to the Nagios server. Nagios calls them *hosts*. Then you define the attributes and functions of these assets. Nagios calls these *services*. Services can include attributes and functions such as an FTP daemon, an email server, an application, or a database. Services can also include the attributes of a host or application—for example, the amount of disk space free on a host or the number of transactions processed by an application. You also need to define the people who manage these assets and how they are contacted. These are the people who need to be notified if an event occurs on a host or service. Nagios calls these people *contacts*.

Once you have defined your assets, their attributes, and your people to Nagios, then you define the mechanisms for monitoring these assets or hosts and services. Nagios calls these mechanisms *commands*. Commands generally use a plug-in (which we installed in Chapter 1), binary, or script to check a service or host and return its state and status.

The act of monitoring hosts and services using a command is called a *check*. A check does two things. First, it returns the results of its checking to the server—for example, if you were monitoring disk space, then it would return the percentage of disk space free. Second, the check results are used to determine the status of the host or service. If the results of the check vary from the conditions you have set, then the status of the host or service could change; if disk space reaches above a threshold you have set, for instance, the status of a service could change.

This change usually triggers a *notification*. This is a message from Nagios telling you about the change in your host or service. Notifications can be sent via a number of means: via email or Short Message Service (SMS), or you can customize Nagios to send via a variety of other mediums, such as to an Instant Messenger client. These notifications are sent to destination addresses configured in your contact objects and are sent using a particular type of command called a notification command.

So let's look at an example. I have a host called `kitten.yourdomain.com` that runs my company's email and web services, including Postfix, Apache, FTP, and DNS daemons. This host is managed by John, who works for my company's Unix Support team. John carries his Blackberry everywhere with him and is notified of events on the `kitten` host via emails to his Blackberry. John wants to know when any of the services on the `kitten` host are not responding and when the disk space on the host reaches 95 percent.

So how do I set up this monitoring? Well, first I must define a host object to Nagios that will specify the name and IP address of the `kitten` host. Next I define the services (through service objects) I wish to monitor on that host and specify which commands to use to monitor them. I include in the definition of the services being monitored when Nagios should check each service. I also define the conditions to monitor for, when and how often to trigger a notification, and whom to notify. For example, I create a service for the Postfix daemon on the `kitten` host. I tell Nagios that if it can't connect to the Postfix server, it should send a notification. Finally, I define a contact group and a contact object for John; the latter includes details of his email address that Nagios will use to send notifications.

I then start the Nagios server and it will begin monitoring the `kitten` host. If it detects any of the conditions I've defined, it will notify John so he can investigate and fix the problem.

In this chapter, I'll demonstrate how to create all the objects required for an example such as this.

How Is Nagios Configured?

The Nagios server, the web console, and your monitoring configuration are controlled by a series of configuration files that are usually located in the `/usr/local/nagios/etc` directory. There are three types of configuration files. The first are the Nagios server and web console configuration files, which handle the behavior of the server and web console. These files are named `nagios.cfg` and `cgi.cfg`, respectively. I'll look at some of the options in these files that support your monitoring configuration in this chapter. In later chapters I'll go into some of the other options contained in these files in greater depth.

■**Tip** I recommend you read through the sample `nagios.cfg` and `cgi.cfg` files as they are well documented and will offer considerable insight into the functioning of Nagios.

Resource files are the second type of configuration files. They are designed to hold sensitive information, like database connection settings or macros that you want to hide from general view—for example, preventing them from being seen from the web console. I'll discuss them briefly later in the "Defining Commands" section.

Object configuration files are the third type of files. Objects include hosts, services, commands, and other types of objects that can be defined to Nagios. Objects represent the core of your Nagios configuration. Table 2-1 defines all the object types you can use with Nagios and what they do.

Table 2-1. *Nagios Object Types*

Object	Description
host	Hosts are physical devices like servers, routers, and firewalls.
hostgroup	Host groups are collections of hosts that generally have something in common, like their type or location.
service	Services run on hosts and can include actual services like SMTP or HTTP, or metrics such as disk space.
servicegroup	Service groups are collections of services that generally have something in common.
contact	Contacts are escalation or notification points that can potentially be contacted when an event occurs.
contactgroup	Contact groups are collections of contacts. All contacts need to be in a contact group.
timeperiod	Time periods are defined windows of time—for example, during business hours.
command	Commands are called by the check process to perform an action—for example, a command to check the status of a host using the ping command.
servicedependency	Allows a service or services to be dependent on other services.
serviceescalation	Provides a notification escalation process for services.
hostdependency	Allows a host or hosts to be dependent on other hosts.
hostescalation	Provides a notification escalation process for hosts.
hostextinfo	Host Extended Information changes and customizes the way hosts are displayed on the Nagios web console.
serviceextinfo	Service Extended Information changes and customizes the way services are displayed on the Nagios web console.

In Table 2-1, I've referred to the object types by the names used in the configuration files—for example, hostgroup. In this chapter, I'll interchangeably use this object name and the expanded name, host group. The same logic will apply to other object types. In this chapter I'll be principally looking at hosts and host groups, services and service groups, contact and contact groups, time periods, and commands. In subsequent chapters, I'll cover the other object definitions.

Tip This book principally focuses on new installations of Nagios 2.0. But if you're upgrading from a previous version of Nagios, some of the object configuration syntax has changed. I recommend you read the Nagios What's New page at http://nagios.sourceforge.net/docs/2_0/whatsnew.html. Additionally, there are some simple (use at your own risk) tools for migrating your configuration from Nagios 1.2 to 2.0 at http://oss.op5.se/nagios/.

Getting Started with Your Configuration

In order to get started with your Nagios configuration, it is useful to have a basis and a reference to build from. The sample configuration files you've installed provide an excellent basis for building your own configuration, and I highly recommend you use them.

If you installed Nagios from source, you will have installed the sample configuration files. These files are usually installed into the /usr/local/nagios/etc directory. All the installed files have a suffix of -sample on the end of the file. In order to use these files, you should remove the -sample suffix from the file. You can do that with this simple Bash script:

```
puppy# cd /usr/local/nagios/etc
puppy# for i in *-sample; do mv "$i" "${i%*-sample}";done
```

Two particular sample configuration files, minimal.cfg and bigger.cfg, contain examples of all the possible object types you can define to Nagios. The minimal.cfg configuration file is a very simple example of a Nagios configuration file. The bigger.cfg configuration file contains a considerably more detailed Nagios configuration.

■**Tip** If you installed Nagios from an RPM, then you should already have the correctly named configuration files contained in the /etc/nagios directory. The files will have the -sample suffix already removed.

Specifying Your Configuration Files

So that the Nagios server knows about your configuration, you must define your configuration files to the Nagios server. To do this, you specify your configuration files and their location in the nagios.cfg file. To define the configuration files to the Nagios server, use the cfg_file directive. Nagios server configuration directives are divided into two parts: the directive name and the directive setting. These are separated by the = symbol like so:

```
directive=setting
```

Each directive should be on a new line. You can see an example of a Nagios directive here:

```
log_file=/usr/local/nagios/var/nagios.log
```

■**Tip** Directives can be commented out of the nagios.cfg configuration file by prefixing the line with a # symbol. You can also use a # symbol to add comments to your configuration file. The sample nagios.cfg file is heavily commented.

The cfg_file directive tells Nagios the name and location of your configuration files. The setting is the full path to the configuration file being defined. In Example 2-1, you can see the cfg_file section of the sample nagios.cfg file.

Example 2-1. *The cfg_file Directive in nagios.cfg*

```
cfg_file=/usr/local/nagios/etc/checkcommands.cfg
cfg_file=/usr/local/nagios/etc/misccommands.cfg
cfg_file=/usr/local/nagios/etc/minimal.cfg
#cfg_file=/usr/local/nagios/etc/contactgroups.cfg
#cfg_file=/usr/local/nagios/etc/contacts.cfg
#cfg_file=/usr/local/nagios/etc/dependencies.cfg
#cfg_file=/usr/local/nagios/etc/escalations.cfg
#cfg_file=/usr/local/nagios/etc/hostgroups.cfg
#cfg_file=/usr/local/nagios/etc/hosts.cfg
#cfg_file=/usr/local/nagios/etc/services.cfg
#cfg_file=/usr/local/nagios/etc/timeperiods.cfg
#cfg_file=/usr/local/nagios/etc/hostextinfo.cfg
#cfg_file=/usr/local/nagios/etc/serviceextinfo.cfg
```

In Example 2-1, a number of configuration files have been defined but only three of these files—checkcommands.cfg, misccommands.cfg, and minimal.cfg—are not commented out. I'll come back to the first two files later in this chapter, but the third file, minimal.cfg, is a sample configuration file that contains examples of all of the available object types, combined into one file.

You can define as many configuration files as you like to Nagios. Any files you do define, however, must exist; otherwise, the Nagios server will return an error and fail to start. The data in your configuration files also must be valid as it is parsed by the Nagios server prior to the server starting. If the server detects invalid syntax or an illogical or invalid configuration, the Nagios server will fail to start.

Note I'll look at starting and stopping the Nagios server in Chapter 3.

How you group and store your object definitions in your configuration files greatly depends on your requirements. You can specify each object type in a separate file—for example, list all of your host objects in one file. You can also combine all types of objects in a single file, as is done in the sample configuration file, minimal.cfg. Or you could choose a different model and define all objects from a particular site or geographical location in separate files, as I've done here:

```
cfg_file=/usr/local/nagios/etc/india.cfg
cfg_file=/usr/local/nagios/etc/california.cfg
cfg_file=/usr/local/nagios/etc/australia.cfg
```

The cfg_file variables in Example 2-1 that are commented out reflect a configuration model where each object type is contained in a separate file. Throughout this book I'll use this model of configuration. Each object type will have its own separate file—for example, all the hosts contained in one file, hosts.cfg, and all the contacts contained in another file, contacts.cfg. In Example 2-2 I've commented out the sample configuration file (you could also simply delete the line) and uncommented the configuration files I'll be using in this chapter. Later I'll add other configuration files as we explore the remaining object types.

Example 2-2. *Individual Object Types Defined in Separate Files*

```
cfg_file=/usr/local/nagios/etc/checkcommands.cfg
cfg_file=/usr/local/nagios/etc/misccommands.cfg
#cfg_file=/usr/local/nagios/etc/minimal.cfg
cfg_file=/usr/local/nagios/etc/contactgroups.cfg
cfg_file=/usr/local/nagios/etc/contacts.cfg
#cfg_file=/usr/local/nagios/etc/dependencies.cfg
#cfg_file=/usr/local/nagios/etc/escalations.cfg
cfg_file=/usr/local/nagios/etc/hostgroups.cfg
cfg_file=/usr/local/nagios/etc/hosts.cfg
cfg_file=/usr/local/nagios/etc/services.cfg
cfg_file=/usr/local/nagios/etc/servicegroups.cfg
cfg_file=/usr/local/nagios/etc/timeperiods.cfg
#cfg_file=/usr/local/nagios/etc/hostextinfo.cfg
#cfg_file=/usr/local/nagios/etc/serviceextinfo.cfg
```

Now I've uncommented or defined these configuration files to Nagios, I need to create empty files to hold our configuration objects. I do this using the touch command, as you can see here:

```
puppy# cd /usr/local/nagios/etc
puppy# touch contacts.cfg contactgroups.cfg hosts.cfg hostgroups.cfg➡
services.cfg servicegroups.cfg timeperiods.cfg
puppy# ls *.cfg
bigger.cfg          contacts.cfg     misccommands.cfg    services.cfg
cgi.cfg             hostgroups.cfg   nagios.cfg          timeperiods.cfg
checkcommands.cfg   hosts.cfg        resource.cfg
contactgroups.cfg   minimal.cfg      servicegroups.cfg
```

The touch command will create a series of empty files that I can fill with my configuration objects.

■**Caution**   Having the empty files will still not allow the Nagios server to start. It will detect the empty files and determine that no configuration objects have been defined and refuse to start. I'll have to define some objects before I can start the Nagios server.

There is another way to define configuration files to the Nagios server: you can tell Nagios to include all files with a .cfg extension contained in a specified directory using the cfg_dir directive. Example 2-3 shows how to use the cfg_dir directive.

Example 2-3. *The cfg_dir Directive*

```
cfg_dir=/usr/local/nagios/etc/192.168.0
cfg_dir=/usr/local/nagios/etc/192.168.1
cfg_dir=/usr/local/nagios/etc/192.168.2
cfg_dir=/usr/local/nagios/etc/192.168.3
```

In Example 2-3 all files in the directories listed would be parsed by the Nagios server and included in the configuration. This is useful if you have a large number of configuration files and you want to further organize them into categories. For instance, you would create a directory to hold all hosts in a particular subnet while further dividing your objects into types inside configuration files in that directory. Example 2-4 shows a model like this.

Example 2-4. *Categorized Configuration Files*

```
puppy# ls -l 192.168.0
total 16
-rw-r--r--  1 nagios nagios 0 May 12 20:46 firewalls.cfg
-rw-r--r--  1 nagios nagios 0 May 12 20:46 routers.cfg
-rw-r--r--  1 nagios nagios 0 May 12 20:46 servers.cfg
-rw-r--r--  1 nagios nagios 0 May 12 20:46 switches.cfg
```

The 192.168.0 directory contains a series of configuration files that contain the definitions of host objects of different types—for example, firewalls.cfg could hold the object definitions for all the firewalls in the 192.168.0 subnet.

Finally, all configuration files should be owned by the user and group that is running the Nagios server process. In our case, the user and group are both nagios. You should change their ownership prior to attempting to start the Nagios server. The command on the following line changes the ownership of all files ending in .cfg in the /usr/local/nagios/etc directory and all directories below:

```
puppy# chown -R nagios:nagios /usr/local/nagios/etc/*.cfg
```

Defining Nagios Configuration Objects

Inside each configuration file that you specify to Nagios, you define the objects required for your Nagios configuration. Each object definition is created by combining a series of directives. The directives represent the attributes and settings of the object being defined. These directives can either be unique to the type of object being defined—for example, a host object has a directive that defines its address, or generic and applicable to a number of object definitions.

Some directives in an object definition are mandatory. For instance, for a host object definition you must provide a hostname and an address. If you do not provide these mandatory directives in the object definition, the definition will not be valid. An invalid definition will cause the Nagios server to fail when you attempt to start it. Other directives are optional, and excluding them will not impact the validity of the object definition. For each directive I examine, I'll specify whether it is mandatory or optional to a particular object definition.

The directives are contained within an overarching directive called the define directive. Example 2-5 shows the construction of a define directive.

Example 2-5. *The define Directive*

```
define    object_type{
          directive1 setting
          directive2 setting
          directive3 setting
          }
```

As you can see from Example 2-5, the `define` directive consists of the directive name followed by the name of the type of object you wish to define (see Table 2-1 for the available object names). You would replace `object_type` in Example 2-5 with the name of the object type you wish to define—such as `host` for host objects, as you can see in the next few lines:

```
define    host{
              directive1 setting
              }
```

The name of the object type is followed directly (with no space in between) by an opening { bracket. On the following lines, with one directive to a line, are the directives describing that object. These directives consist of the directive name and, separated by spaces or tabs, the directive value. Finally, the `define` directive is closed with a } bracket.

You can also place comments in your object definitions by prefixing them with a ; symbol, as you can see here:

```
define    object_type{
              directive1 setting ; this is a comment
              }
```

Defining Your First Host

In this section I'm going to look at host object definitions and also introduce quite a few of the topics you'll need to understand about Nagios and how it operates. I'll look at each of these topics when introducing the directives related to these topics. Many of these topics will also be used with other object definitions, such as services. Indeed, many of the same directives used to define hosts are also used to define services and other object types.

Host objects represent the physical devices on your network like servers, routers, switches, or other pieces of infrastructure. Another way of looking at host objects is that they are items or assets on your network that can be connected to via some sort of address—for example, an IP address or a media access control (MAC) address. Each host object definition consists of a large number of potential directives, some mandatory and some optional.[1] In Example 2-6 I've provided a typical host definition that contains all of the mandatory directives required for a host definition. You must include at least these directives in your host definition or the definition will be considered invalid.

Example 2-6. *Host Object Definition*

```
define host{
              host_name                kitten.yourdomain.com
              alias                    Primary Sydney Server
              address                  192.168.0.1
              check_period             24x7
              max_check_attempts       1
```

---

1. You can see a full list of the host object directives at http://nagios.sourceforge.net/docs/2_0/xodtemplate.html#host.

```
contact_groups              network_team,field_support
notification_interval       30
notification_period         24x7
notification_options        d,u,r
}
```

Let's look at Example 2-6 and see how it works. First, we've defined a host called kitten. yourdomain.com with an address of 192.168.0.1 that we've described as our Primary Sydney Server. We've defined that it should be checked during a time period called 24x7. If something goes wrong, we want to send notifications during a time period called 24x7 to the network_team and the field_support team. These notifications should be sent every 30 minutes. In this section, I'll look at all the directives that define what I've just described. I'll also look at the further directives available for your host definitions. To do this, I'll step through each major function provided by the directives, starting with some basic directives and moving through checking your host and configuring host notifications and then the remaining host definition directives.

Defining the Hostname and Address

Let's start with some of the basic directives of a host definition, as shown in Table 2-2.

Table 2-2. *Names and Address Directives*

Directive	Description	Macro	Mandatory?
host_name	Name of the host	$HOSTNAME$	Yes
alias	Longer description of the host	$HOSTALIAS$	Yes
address	Address of the host	$HOSTADDRESS$	No (but strongly recommended)

Table 2-2 contains four columns. The first two columns indicate the directive name and description. The third and fourth columns indicate if the directive's value can be used as a macro and whether it is mandatory to the object definition. An object definition must have all the required mandatory directives included in the definition to be valid. An invalid object definition will result in Nagios failing to start. I'll discuss macros in a bit and in the "Defining Commands" section later in this chapter.

The first directive you need to define is the host_name directive. This directive is the name of the host being defined. Nagios calls this the *short name* of the host. It is used in other object definitions to reference the host object. For example, when adding host objects to a host group, you would refer to each host object by the name defined in the host_name directive. It is preferable that you use the actual hostname of the host being defined in this field. This is because if you don't specify an address for the host, Nagios will attempt to use Domain Name Service (DNS) to resolve the contents of the host_name directive to find the address of the host. If DNS is unavailable or you suffer a DNS outage, Nagios will be unable to resolve the address of the host and hence unable to monitor the host or any of its services.

The host_name directive can also be used as a macro. Macros are one of the most useful features in Nagios. Macros are generally used in the commands you use to check hosts and services. Instead of having to specify a particular hostname or address in each command, you specify a macro, which is replaced at the time the command is run with the value required. This allows you to define generic commands that can be used to monitor multiple hosts and services instead of having to define a command to monitor each host or service. I'll discuss macros more in the "Defining Commands" section.

You can identify macros because they are prefixed and suffixed with the $ symbol—for example, the value of the host_name directive is contained in a macro named $HOSTNAME$.

The host_name directive is linked to the next directive, alias, which defines a longer name or description for the host object. This allows you to provide a more descriptive name for the host object. The alias directive is also represented by a macro, $HOSTALIAS$.

Note If you do not specify a value for the alias directive, it defaults to the value of the host_name directive. This includes the value of the $HOSTALIAS$ macro.

The next directive, address, is used to define the address of the host. In most cases this will be an IP address, but it can be any type of address that can be used to check the status of the host. For instance, you could use radio frequency identification (RFID) addresses, a supervisory control and data acquisition (SCADA) address, or a MAC address if you had a command that could check the status of hosts using these types of addresses.

As I discussed earlier, if you don't specify an address for the host and leave this directive blank or exclude it, Nagios will try to use the contents of the host_name directive to determine the address of the host. It will assume the connection is a TCP/IP connection and attempt to resolve the value in the host_name directive using DNS. If it is not a TCP/IP connection, or you do not have DNS resolution on your Nagios server, then you won't be able to check the host's status. This is also true if your DNS name resolution fails. Nagios will then also be unable to check the host. I recommend you always specify an address for your host using this directive.

Tip The host address also has a macro associated with it, $HOSTADDRESS$. This is frequently used in commands to specify the address of your host.

Parents, Host Groups, and Contact Groups

The next directives relate to defining other hosts that your host might be dependent on, any groups of hosts it belongs to, and who to notify in the event that an error is detected on the host. I've displayed the relevant directives in Table 2-3.

Table 2-3. *Names and Address Directives*

Directive	Description	Mandatory?
parents	Specifies the parent hosts of this host	No
hostgroups	Specifies any host groups this host belongs to	No
contact_groups	Contact groups that should be notified for this host	Yes

The first directive in Table 2-3 is the parents directive. The parents directive lets you specify other assets that your host is dependent on to function. This could include a switch, router, or firewall that your host relied on for connectivity. If the parent host is unavailable, all child hosts will also be unavailable. Any parent hosts you define using the parents directive also need to be defined to Nagios using host objects.

You specify any parent hosts in your parents directive using the value of the host_name directive of the parent host or hosts. If one of these intervening hosts is not available when checked by Nagios, all hosts for which that host is a parent will be changed to a state of UNREACHABLE (see the "Host States" sidebar). You can specify multiple parent hosts in the directive by separating them with commas:

```
parents        melb_router,melb_switch1,melb_switch2
```

The next directive is the hostgroups directive. This directive lets you specify the host group or groups that the host you are defining belongs to. Host groups are a means of grouping together like hosts—for example, by type or location. You can specify that the host belongs to multiple host groups by specifying the list of host groups separated by commas:

```
hostgroups        servers,aust_assets
```

The contact_groups directive is a list of the contact groups that should be notified when there is a problem with this host. Contact groups are groupings of the people, or contacts, who may need to be notified when an event or state change occurs. For instance, you could group together all your Network Management staff or all the IT staff in a particular site into contact groups.

You can specify multiple contact groups here by separating each group with commas. You can see that in Example 2-6 where I've specified that the contact groups network_team and field_support should be notified in the event of a problem with the kitten host.

Note All of your contacts should belong to at least one contact group. I'll discuss host and contact groups further in the "Grouping Objects" section.

Checking the Host

Now you have defined the basics of your host, you need to define the directives that relate to checking the host, including the command you want to use to check the host and when and how often it should be checked. You can see these directives in Table 2-4.

Table 2-4. *Host Check Directives*

Directive	Description	Mandatory?
check_command	Command used to check the state of the host	No
check_period	Specifies when to perform checks of the host	Yes
max_check_attempts	The number of check attempts to make before gen- erating a notification	Yes
check_interval	Period in between checks of the host	No
active_checks_enabled	Specifies that active checks are enabled for this object	No
passive_checks_enabled	Specifies that passive checks are enabled for this object	No
check_freshness	Enables freshness checks for this object	No
freshness_threshold	Specifies the freshness threshold for this object	No

The first of these directives is the check_command directive, which tells Nagios what command to use to check the state of the host object. Most host checks are performed to confirm
that the host is active and responding to checks; usually this is done with a ping.

If you do not include the check_command directive in your host object definition or leave
it blank, Nagios will not check the state of the host. Nagios will assume the host is always up.
This is useful for hosts that are often off, such as printers or photocopiers. This prevents you
from receiving false positives for devices that have been deliberately turned off.

Tip The check_command is available as a macro called $HOSTCHECKCOMMAND$.

The check_command directive also has a related directive, host_check_timeout, in the
nagios.cfg configuration file. The host_check_timeout directive controls how long Nagios
will wait for a response from the check command before timing out. By default, it set to
60 seconds:

host_check_timeout=60

If the timeout is reached, Nagios will assume the host is unavailable, put it in a DOWN state,
and log an error indicating that the command timed out. The timeout is mostly designed to
manage runaway checks that have not exited correctly. If necessary you should adjust this
to reflect the network latency in your environment. In most cases the default will be fine.

Note I'll look at commands in the "Defining Commands" section later in this chapter.

The next directive is check_period. This directive tells Nagios when it should check the
host. For example, you may wish to check some hosts all of the time and others only during
set periods. The check_period directive is linked to another object type, the timeperiod object.
The timeperiod object defines periods of time—for example, business hours Monday to Friday

or 24 hours every day of the week. Nagios uses these defined time periods to specify when to monitor or take action on events it detects. In Example 2-6 I've specified a time period called 24x7. I'll demonstrate how to define this period and others later in the "Defining Time Periods" section. The value of the check_period directive should be the value of the timeperiod_name directive from the time period object definition. You can specify more than one time period by separating them with commas.

The max_check_attempts directive tells Nagios how many times to retry checks on a host when a check returns a non-OK state. Until Nagios has retried the checks the requisite number of times it will not generate a notification. For example, Nagios checks the status of the kitten host and determines that it is not responding. Rather than immediately change the status of the host, Nagios rechecks the host the number of times specified in the max_check_attempts directive. If at the end of this rechecking the host is still not responding, then Nagios will change its state and, if configured to, generate a notification.

The setting of the directive is a numeric value. A value of 1 means that if one check fails Nagios will generate a notification immediately. A value of 2 will result in Nagios checking the host twice and if after the second check the result is still not OK, then it will generate a notification. You can specify as many extra checks as you like here. This directive is mandatory and you should always specify a value of at least 1 even if you don't want to check the status of the host. As discussed earlier, if you want to disable host checking you can leave out the check_command directive or leave it blank.

HOST STATES

When Nagios checks a host or service, that check returns the state of that host or service. There are different states for hosts and services. For hosts there are three possible states: OK and two error states, DOWN and UNREACHABLE. The OK state indicates that the host is up and available. The DOWN state indicates that the host is unavailable. For example, if you are using a ping to ascertain the status of the host, this means the ping was not received and the host itself is unavailable or not able to be contacted by the Nagios server. The UNREACHABLE state indicates that for some reason the command was unable to reach the host—for example, the network is down. This doesn't always mean your host is down but generally that the network or some network component between your Nagios server and your host is unavailable. This is also the state used when you have defined dependencies or parents for your hosts. When a host or hosts your host is dependent on has failed, your host is usually marked as UNREACHABLE.

State types add another layer of complexity to your states. State types apply to both host and service states. There are two state types: soft states and hard states. A soft state can almost be described as a "pending" state. Let's look at a brief example. A host object has the max_check_attempts directive set to 3 check attempts. This means that if Nagios checks the host and it returns a state of DOWN, it will retry a check of the host three times. In the period during these checks, Nagios considers the host to be in a soft DOWN state. This means Nagios has not fully determined that it is actually DOWN and is waiting until all the required checks have been performed before finalizing the state of the host. When Nagios has completed all these retry checks and if the host still returns a DOWN state, then this state is now considered a hard DOWN state. This indicates that Nagios now believes that the host is definitely DOWN and that a notification could be generated (if Nagios is configured to do that). If, however, the host recovers from the DOWN state and returns to an OK state during this period of checks, Nagios calls this a soft recovery. The host never reaches the hard state and a notification is not generated. This soft and hard state model helps reduce the number of potential false alarms.

The final directive, `check_interval`, controls how often Nagios performs checks of the host. In most cases you actually don't want to specify this directive at all. In fact, you don't want regular scheduled checks of our host. Why is this so? Well, Nagios has some intelligence built in that only performs checks of the host when they are required.

Let's look at how this works. Generally, you define a host to Nagios and then define the services and attributes of that host that you wish to monitor. Nagios checks these services and notifies you if anything untoward occurs or some condition you have defined is met. Nagios assumes that if a service it is monitoring on that host returns the OK state then the underlying host is also in the OK state. Nagios only checks the host if a service returns a non-OK state. Nagios does this so that it can eliminate the host as a cause for the service returning a non-OK state. It checks the host, and if the host also returns a non-OK state it continues to check the host until the maximum number of checks (as defined by the `max_check_attempts` directive) is reached or an OK state is received. At this stage the host is in a soft error state. If the host is found to be in a non-OK state after all these checks, then a notification will be generated (if this has been configured). The host is now in a hard error state.

Tip While Nagios performs this host check, all other service checking is suspended. This is because Nagios is trying to ensure the state of the host before wasting time processing more service checks.

The `check_interval` directive is measured in minutes—for example, a value of 10 as the interval would result in a check every 10 minutes. A setting of 0 will disable scheduled checking. Additionally, if you do not specify the `check_interval` directive at all, then Nagios assumes that you do not want scheduled host checking.

Tip Remember: don't schedule regular checks of your hosts! Nagios does this automatically for you. Leave the `check_interval` directive out of your host definitions.

Active and Passive Checks

Nagios can perform different types of checks on hosts and services. There are two types of checks: active and passive. An active check is initiated by the Nagios server—for example, pinging a host to determine its state. It requires that Nagios have network visibility of the host or service being checked. This is the type of check most Nagios administrators define for their hosts and services. You define the active check for a host or service by specifying the command you wish to use in the `check_command` directive.

Passive checks are performed by external applications and the results passed back to the Nagios server. Passive checks are submitted using external commands to the Nagios server via the external commands file described in Chapter 1. An example of this might be a check of a process like an end-of-day job or a backup process. A third-party application submits the results of that job or process run—for example, whether the backup succeeded.

Passive checks can also be used for hosts and services of which Nagios does not have visibility or used in a distributed monitoring configuration. In the distributed monitoring configuration, a remote server or servers sends results back to a central server using passive checks.[2]

In the host definition, the `active_checks_enabled` and `passive_checks_enabled` directives control what types of checks are enabled to be performed. You can enable both active and passive checks, though generally you would only use one type of check. Checks are enabled if the directives are set to 1 and disabled if they are set to 0.

Checking the Freshness of Passive Checks

I've just introduced the idea of active versus passive checks. The next two directives in Table 2-4, `check_freshness` and `freshness_threshold`, deal with ensuring the "freshness" of passive checks. Nagios relies on third-party applications or tools to perform or submit the results of passive checks. These tools usually submit the results of their checking on a schedule that is out of Nagios' control. Thus if the passive check does not arrive on schedule, the Nagios server will not be aware of this. The freshness checking function allows Nagios to confirm that the current state of a host or service is the actual state. This will identify whether the passive check has not been received.

So how does Nagios do this? The freshness check takes the form of an active check of the host or service. The active check that will be run is specified by the command defined in the `check_command` directive for that host or service. As a result, you must have a command defined in the `check_command` directive for freshness checking to work.

So in what situations would you use freshness checks? Well, there are two principal situations where freshness checks are useful. The first is a distributed monitoring model where you have a remote server or servers submitting their check results in the form of passive checks to a central server. With freshness checking, Nagios can determine if a remote server fails to send a passive check. If the state of the host or service is "stale," then the central server attempts its own active check of the host or service.

In the second situation, the host or service being monitored is not accessible by the Nagios server. This could either be because of a lack of network visibility of the host or service or because it is not an easily checkable service—for example, a backup job or an end-of-day process. If Nagios detects that the state of the host or service is "stale," an active check is again initiated. But if Nagios potentially cannot see the host or service, what can the freshness check do? Instead of checking the host or service, the active check can run a command that performs an action or changes the state of the host or service. For example, I monitor a service that represents my end-of-day process. At the end of the process a passive check is sent to my Nagios server to indicate that it completed successfully. If the end-of-day process has failed and thus has not sent a passive check result, then my freshness checking would detect this. The resulting active check could be configured to trigger a notification. This can be done simply by defining a command that returns a non-OK state for the host.[3]

So how do we define freshness checking? Well, the first directive, `check_freshness`, enables or disables freshness checking for the host object. A setting of 1 enables the checking and a setting of 0 disables it. The second directive, `freshness_threshold`, determines how fresh the

---

2. See Chapter 8 for a discussion of distributed monitoring.

3. I'll demonstrate how to do this in Chapter 5.

state of the host should be. It is set in seconds. For example, if you set the freshness threshold to 600 seconds, then any state older than 10 minutes will be considered stale and Nagios will be prompted to initiate the active check.

Tip Nagios will perform the active check of the host even if active checks are disabled for the host or even if they are disabled in the Nagios server itself.

Example 2-7 shows these directives, using a modified version of the kitten.yourdomain. com host object.

Example 2-7. *Freshness Checking*

```
define host{
      host_name                       kitten.yourdomain.com
      …
      check_command           notify_outage
      active_checks_enabled   0
      passive_checks_enabled  1
      check_freshness              1
      freshness_threshold          86401
      }
```

In Example 2-7 our host kitten has active checks disabled, passive checks enabled, and freshness checking enabled. I've defined a freshness threshold of 24 hours and one minute. This means any passive check result older than this time will be considered stale and a freshness check initiated. This check will run the command notify_outage. The notify_outage command could set the state of the host to DOWN and thus trigger a notification that would alert you to the stale check.

In order to enable freshness checking, there are some other directives in the main nagios.cfg file that also need to be set. These control freshness checks for hosts. I've listed these directives in Example 2-8.

Example 2-8. *The nagios.cfg Freshness Items*

```
check_host_freshness=0
host_freshness_check_interval=60
```

Note The directive settings in Example 2-8 are the Nagios defaults in the sample nagios.cfg configuration file.

The first directive in Example 2-8 is `check_host_freshness`, which controls whether freshness checks are enabled for hosts. A setting of 1 indicates that freshness checks are enabled and a setting of 0 indicates that they are disabled.

The `host_freshness_check_interval` directive sets the interval between the checks Nagios performs for freshness. This is how often Nagios checks the freshness of passive checks. The default setting is 60 seconds. If the `check_host_freshness` directive is set to disabled, the `host_freshness_check_interval` is ignored.

Notifications

Nagios uses notifications to tell you about problems and issues or changes in the state of your hosts and services. These notifications can be configured to generate in a number of circumstances and can take a number of forms, including email, SMS, or paging alerts. The notifications usually consist of a message containing the name of the host or service involved, the state being reported, and depending on the nature of the check being performed, some information about what has caused the event you are being notified about.

The four directives in Table 2-5 relate to the generation of notifications.

Table 2-5. *Notification Directives*

Directive	Description	Mandatory?
notifications_enabled	Enables notifications for this object	No
notification_interval	Specifies time between notifications being sent out	Yes
notification_period	Specifies when to send notifications about the host	Yes
notification_options	Specifies under what conditions Nagios should send a notification	Yes

The first of the notification directives is `notifications_enabled`, which specifies whether notifications will be enabled for this host. This directive determines whether notifications are sent for this host. A setting of 0 disables notifications and a setting of 1 enables them. If you don't specify this directive, Nagios assumes that notifications are enabled.

The next directive, `notification_interval`, is the time between notifications. The interval is defined in minutes by default. In Example 2-6 I've set it to 30. This means that if a problem is detected, Nagios will send a notification every 30 minutes until the problem is either resolved or acknowledged. If you set this directive to 0, Nagios will only send out one notification.

The `notification_period` directive is similar to the `check_period` directive. Instead of telling Nagios when to check the host, it determines when Nagios will generate notifications. For instance, you may wish to monitor a host all the time but only want to send notifications of problems during business hours. In Example 2-6 I specified that I wanted to send notifications during the same time period as I wanted to check the host, the 24x7 time period. The setting of the `notification_period` directive should be the value of the `timeperiod_name` directive from the time period object definition you wish to use. As with the `check_period` directive, you can specify more than one time period by separating each with a comma:

```
notification_period        business_hours,eod
```

You would need to define both the `business_hours` and `eod` time periods using time period objects.

The next notification-related directive is `notification_options`, which tells Nagios under what conditions to send out notifications for this host. Table 2-6 lists all the possible notification options.

Table 2-6. *Notification Options*

Option	Description
d	Sends notification when the host is DOWN
u	Sends notification when the host is UNREACHABLE
r	Sends notification when the host recovers
n	Sends no notifications
f	Sends notifications when the host starts and stop flapping (see the section "Flapping")

Notifications are generated based on the return status of checks conducted on the host. When Nagios checks the host and it returns a state different from the one that Nagios has currently recorded for it, then it can be configured to generate a notification. Nagios calls this a *state change*. For example, if the host changes state from OK to DOWN, the host can be configured to generate a notification.

■Note I explained at host states in the sidebar "Host States." Services, which I'll look at later in this chapter in the "Defining Services" section, have different states.

Let's now look at each individual notification option. The first notification option, d, tells Nagios to generate a notification when the state of a host is registered as DOWN.

The second notification option, u, tells Nagios to generate a notification when the state of a host is registered as UNREACHABLE. The u option is also used when you configure dependencies or parent hosts. These are hosts that the host you are defining is dependent on to function. An example of this would be a host being dependent on a switch or router to communicate with the Nagios server. If the switch or router fails, then Nagios cannot contact the host. The host is not technically down but rather unreachable. Dependencies are defined using the `parents` directive that I demonstrated earlier in this section.

I recommend that you avoid using the UNREACHABLE notification option, u, unless you have configured parents or dependencies for your hosts. This is because the unreachable notification option can produce incorrect results if your network has latency issues or if you have remote hosts that can be difficult to contact. Even with parents or dependencies configured, enabling unreachable notifications can result in false positives. The u option may require some testing on your behalf to ensure it is suitable for your environment.

The r notification option tells Nagios to generate a notification when a host recovers from a non-OK state. If the host is in a DOWN or UNREACHABLE state and a further check reveals an OK state, then a recovery notification is generated. This is useful to tell you when a host or service is now in the OK state and saves you initiating further troubleshooting activities.

The n notification option is used when you do not want to send notifications about a host. It must be specified on its own and cannot be combined with other notification options.

The last notification option is f. This tells Nagios to generate notifications when a host starts and stops "flapping." Nagios defines flapping as when a host rapidly changes state. This can generate multiple notifications and overwhelm your monitoring system. Flapping is indicative of either some issue on your host or potentially that you have set a threshold for monitoring too low. I'll talk about flapping and flap detection in the "Flapping" section.

You can specify multiple notification options in your host object definition. For example, you can specify that you want notifications when the host is DOWN, UNREACHABLE, or recovered by using the notification_options directive, as you can see on the following line. You separate each option with a comma.

```
notification_options        d,u,r
```

Flapping

As I described earlier, Nagios uses the term *flapping* to describe when a host or a service rapidly changes state. This is often indicative of a problem with the host or service being monitored—for example, a host repeatedly power-cycling or a service restarting and failing over and over. Detecting flapping stops Nagios from sending out large numbers of notifications, potentially overwhelming your notification mechanism, and generally not adding any value to your monitoring.

Nagios checks for flapping whenever a host or service enters a hard state or recovers from a soft state. If you remember, a host or service enters a hard state after a check reveals that it is in a non-OK state after all retry checks are exhausted.[4] A soft state recovery occurs when the state recovers from a non-OK state during the retry checking process.

Nagios does three things when it detects a host or service is flapping. It first logs a message to indicate the host or service is flapping. Next, a comment is added to the host or service indicating that is it flapping.[5] Lastly, notifications for that host or service are suppressed while it is flapping. Additionally, if you have configured it, a notification to tell you that flapping has started can be generated.

When Nagios detects flapping has stopped, it also logs a message indicating this, removes the comment indicating that the host or service is flapping, and stops suppressing notifications. Additionally, if configured, a notification will be generated.

So how does Nagios determine if a host or service is flapping? When you enable flap detection, Nagios keeps a record of the last 21 states of the host or service in an array. It then counts the number of times the states in the array have changed. This is calculated as a percentage. For example, with 21 states recorded we have a possible 20 state changes. For a normal-behaving host or service, it may be that the last recorded 21 states were OK. Hence, the percentage of states change is 0 percent. If, however, during the last 21 recorded states the host or service changed state 9 times, then the percentage of state change is 45 percent. But there is another added layer of complexity in this calculation. The states in this array are weighted—the newest state is considered 50 percent more important than the oldest state. This is because Nagios considers that the newer states are more indicative of the current behavior of the host or service than the older states.

---

4. The number of checks is defined by the max_check_attempts directive.

5. I discuss host and service comments in Chapter 4.

Nagios then checks this percentage against a high and low threshold set either in your server or in the individual host or service definition. If the host or service is currently not flapping when the check occurs and the percentage state change is greater than or equal to the high threshold, Nagios decides the host or service is flapping. If the host or service is currently flapping at the time of the check and the percentage state change is equal to or less than the low threshold, Nagios marks the host or service as not flapping. If neither of these two conditions is met, Nagios does nothing. You can see these flapping status changes represented in Table 2-7.

Table 2-7. *Flapping Detection*

Current Flap State	Percentage of State Change	Resulting Flap State
Not flapping	≥ High threshold	Flapping
Flapping	≤ Low threshold	Not flapping
Either	Between the thresholds	No change

■**Tip** The exact code for the flapping algorithm is contained in the Nagios source package in the file flapping.c, which is contained in the directory base.

The flap detection and the high and low thresholds for flapping can be set in two places. The first place is in the nagios.cfg file. There are three directives in this file that can be set; Example 2-9 shows these directives.

Example 2-9. *The nagios.cfg file and Flapping Directives*

```
enable_flap_detection=0
low_host_flap_threshold=5.0
high_host_flap_threshold=20.0
```

The first directive controls global flap detection. If this directive is set to 1, all of your hosts and services will be checked for flapping unless you explicitly override this in your host or service definitions. The next two directives control the high and low percentage thresholds for flap detection. Example 2-9 shows the default settings for these thresholds that are in the sample nagios.cfg file. Using the thresholds in Example 2-9, Nagios would mark a host as flapping when the state change percentage was equal to or greater than 20 percent. If the host was already flapping and if the state change percentage is equal to or less than 5 percent, then Nagios will mark the host as not flapping.

The second place you can control these directives is in your host definitions. The directives available to you are displayed in Example 2-10.

Example 2-10. *Flapping Directives in Host Definitions*

```
define host{
           host_name                          kitten.yourdomain.com
           ...
           flap_detection_enabled   1
           low_flap_threshold       10.0
           high_flap_threshold      30.0
           ...
           }
```

These directives perform the same function as those in the nagios.cfg file. If you specify these directives in your host or service definition, they will override the values specified in the nagios.cfg file.

Event Handling

Event handlers are optional commands that can be set to run every time the state of a host or service changes. Generally they are used to perform some form of remediation action on a host or service before you are notified. For example, an event handler could be set up to attempt to restart the service if your web server process fails. Event handlers are run every time a host or service enters either a soft or hard error state, or when a host or service recovers from either a soft or hard error state. For example, Nagios would initiate an event handler as soon as

- A soft non-OK state was detected.

- Retry checking was complete and the host changed to a hard non-OK.

- The host recovered during either the soft state retry checking or from a hard non-OK state.

Example 2-11 shows the directives required in your host or service definitions to specify an event handler.

Example 2-11. *Event Handling Directives*

```
define host{
           host_name                          kitten.yourdomain.com
           ...
           event_handler_enabled   1
           event_handler            server-restart
           ...
           }
```

The first directive, event_handler_enabled, tells Nagios that event handlers are enabled for the host or service. The second directive, event_handler, specifies the exact event handler to be used. Event handlers are usually written in languages like shell script or Perl. Generally, the script is configured to take several macros as parameters that allow the script to determine how to respond to the particular state change. For example, you would pass in the current state and state type of a host. In this case, the event handler script can be configured to respond differently to a host in the DOWN state as opposed to the OK state.

■**Note** I'll cover event handler definitions in the "Defining Commands" section later in this chapter.

You can also define global event handlers that run every time any host or service changes state. You can define a separate global event handler for your hosts and your services. These are defined in your nagios.cfg file using the directives in Example 2-12.

Example 2-12. *Global Event Handlers*

```
global_host_event_handler=global-host-events
```

■**Tip** If you also have events handlers defined on your hosts as well as global event handlers, the global event handlers will execute first and then the host event handlers will execute.

Retention of Status

Status and nonstatus retention deals with how Nagios handles retaining information in between restarts of the Nagios server. In normal operation with status retention turned off, the Nagios server forgets the states of the hosts and services it is monitoring and the status of a number of variables, such as whether notifications are enabled. When the Nagios server is restarted, it then has to recheck all hosts and services to learn their current state. This can be time consuming and unnecessary. With status retention enabled, Nagios stores all the current states of the hosts and services being monitored in a file. This file is updated on a defined schedule and the information is reloaded from the file when the Nagios server is restarted. I recommend you enable state retention.

Let's quickly look at how status retention is configured. Status retention is configured both in the nagios.cfg configuration file and in the object definition. Let's first look at the main configuration file directives. You can see them in Example 2-13.

Example 2-13. *State Retention Directives*

```
retain_state_information=1
state_retention_file=/usr/local/nagios/var/retention.dat
retention_update_interval=60
use_retained_program_state=1
```

The first directive controls whether state retention is enabled. A setting of 1 indicates enabled and 0 indicates disabled. The second directive in Example 2-13, state_retention_file, defines the location of the file that will hold the status data. This defaults to /usr/local/nagios/var/retention.dat. You can specify another file location that suits your environment if you wish. The third directive, `retention_update_interval`, controls how often Nagios will save status information. It defaults to 60 minutes. If you set this directive to 0, Nagios will not save the status data on a regular basis but rather will save it before restarting or shutting down the Nagios server.

The last directive controls how the state retention data is used. There are a number of server-wide variables whose state is also retained—for example, the global directive that controls whether notifications are enabled or disabled.[6] If the `use_retained_program_state` is set to 1, Nagios will use this data and maintain the global variable state across server starts, stops, and restarts. A setting of 0 will result in Nagios using the default settings for all these variables as configured in the `nagios.cfg` file.

You also need to define status retention at the object level in your hosts and services. You can see the required directives in Example 2-14.

Example 2-14. *Defining Status Retention in Your Objects*

```
define host{
            host_name                       kitten.yourdomain.com
            …
            retain_status_information       1
            retain_nonstatus_information    1
            …
            }
```

The first directive controls whether status information is retained when the directive is set to 1. State retention must be enabled in the `nagios.cfg` file for this directive to have any effect. The second directive controls the retention of nonstatus information as well. It is enabled by setting the directive to 1. The `retain_status_information` directive must also be enabled, together with state retention, for this directive to have any effect.

So what's the difference between status and nonstatus information? Well, as I discussed earlier state retention also tracks the status of a number of variables as well as the state information of the host or service. One issue with this is that if you make changes to your configuration files, these changes are sometimes not picked up when Nagios is restarted. This is because Nagios is working off the nonstatus data in your state retention file and not the settings in your configuration files. One way to prevent this from happening is to disable the `retain_nonstatus_information` directive by setting it to 0. This means that when Nagios is restarted, it loads the status information about your hosts and services from your state retention file and the configuration settings and variables from your configuration files.

■**Caution** The developer of Nagios reports problems and unexpected results when taking the approach of not retaining nonstatus information. Personally I haven't experienced any issues with this approach, but I recommend you monitor for any unusual results.

---

6. The global variables controlled are notifications, flap detection, use of passive checks, and the enablement of service checking.

State Stalking, Obsession, and Performance Data

The next series of directives deal with the concepts of state stalking, obsession, and performance data. You can see the relevant directives in Table 2-8.

Table 2-8. *Stalking, Obsession, and Performance Data Directives*

Directive	Description	Mandatory?
stalking_options	Specifies whether state stalking is enabled	No
obsess_over_host	Specifies whether checks are obsessed over for this host	No
process_perf_data	Enables the processing of performance data for this host	No

Your checks of hosts and services can return a state, OK for example, in addition to the results of the check such as the information about the host or service you are checking. The check results are only logged if they result in a state change—for example, if a host or service goes from an OK state to a DOWN state. Therefore, if another check occurs and the host is already in a DOWN state, the result of the check is not recorded because the state hasn't changed.

State stalking allows you to record the results of the checks of your hosts and services even if the check doesn't result in a state change. This allows you a greater depth of recording and forensics for events monitored by Nagios. So what is the benefit of this? Nagios only cares about the state of your host or service. It doesn't care how the host or service got into that state. So, theoretically, you could have a series of problems that result in the host or service being in an error state, with only the first problem when the host or service changed into that state being recorded.

This may sound confusing, so let's look at an example. I'm using Nagios to monitor an FTP application. Nagios checks the application, and the results reveal it has failed because the file needed for the application was not present. This changes the state of the service to a non-OK state. Nagios then checks the service again and reports that the application is still failed. But the content of the check result indicates that the error condition is due to a permissions problem. The check remains in an error state and because it remains in the same state it does not log the changed result. Thus, if you wanted to know that the application was in an error state because of two separate events, you would need to enable state stalking.

■Tip Of course, state stalking only works for checks that return different results. If the check returns the same result every time, there is no point in stalking.

You can specify state stalking for all states or a selection of states. For example, for a host you could state stalk only for the DOWN and UNREACHABLE states and use normal monitoring for the OK state. You do this by specifying the stalking_options directive, as you can see in Example 2-15.

Example 2-15. *State Stalking Directive for Hosts*

```
stalking_options      d,u
```

In Example 2-15 I've set the stalking options to d,u. This indicates that state stalking is enabled for DOWN (d) and UNREACHABLE (u) states. If I only wanted stalking on DOWN states, I'd specify the stalking_options directive like so:

```
stalking_options      d
```

With stalking options set to d as we've done here, Nagios will only stalk the host when the host is in a DOWN state.

Unless you require it, I recommend you don't enable state stalking as it will considerably add to the events logged by your Nagios server and skew your reporting figures. Or you should only enable it selectively on hosts and services you explicitly require additional monitoring on.

Host Obsession

Obsessing over hosts is used when you want to run an additional command after every single check of a host. This is used with distributed monitoring to send the results of every check through to central server.[7] Generally, unless you are using distributed monitoring you would not enable host obsession.

Obsession is configured in two places: globally in the nagios.cfg configuration file and locally in your host definition. Let's look at the global configuration first. The directives shown in Example 2-16 control the global settings for host obsession and are contained in the nagios.cfg file.

Example 2-16. *The nagios.cfg Directives for Obsession*

```
obsess_over_hosts=0
ochp_command=obsessive_host_handler
```

■**Note** These two directives are not specified by default in nagios.cfg. If you want to use them, you will have to add them to the file.

The first directive controls whether host obsession is globally enabled. It is disabled by default. To enable it, set it to 1, and to keep it disabled leave the setting of 0. The second directive, ochp_command, is the command that Nagios should run after each host check.

Once you have configured host obsession at the global level, you need to enable it for each individual host you wish to obsess over. You would add the following directive to your host definition to do so:

```
obsess_over_host      1
```

A setting of 1 indicates host obsession is enabled, and a setting of 0 indicates it is disabled.

---

7. I'll discuss distributed monitoring in Chapter 8.

Performance Data

The last directive I'm going to look at involves the processing of performance data. Performance data is made up of two types of data: the performance of the actual check and additional performance information about the host or service being monitored. The first type includes the amount of time taken to execute a check and the latency of the check. This information is available for all checks conducted by Nagios, and you can access it using macros. The second type of performance data is further metrics about the host or service being monitored.

To enable the processing of performance data, you set the `process_perf_data` directive to `1`:

```
process_perf_data    1
```

To disable it, set the directive to `0`.

■**Note** Performance data is an advanced Nagios function that initially you will probably not need to use. I'll look at how you can use performance information in Chapter 7.

Defining Services

After you have defined your hosts to Nagios, the next step is to define the services you want to monitor on those hosts. Services can consist of a wide variety of things, and a large number of plug-ins are available to assist you in monitoring. So what are some of the types of services you can monitor? Well, perhaps the simplest kinds of services are network services—for example, monitoring an SMTP or HTTP daemon. You can also monitor local services on your host system, like disk space or CPU usage. Additionally, you can monitor the services of remote hosts, including Unix or Windows hosts. You can also monitor databases, applications, and even log files. I'll look at how to configure a basic service in this section. I'll discuss monitoring and the types of services you can monitor in more detail in Chapter 5. Chapter 5 will provide examples of many of the possible types of service monitoring.

Like host definitions, service definitions are made up of a number of directives, some mandatory and some optional.[8] The definition in Example 2-17 contains a fully functional service definition in which I've specified all of the mandatory directives for a service. You must include all these directives in the service definition or the definition will be invalid.

Example 2-17. *A Service Object Definition*

```
define service{
            service_description    SMTP
            host_name              kitten.yourdomain.com
            check_command          check_smtp
```

---

8. You can see the full list of service directives at http://nagios.sourceforge.net/docs/2_0/
   xodtemplate.html#service.

```
    max_check_attempts      3
    normal_check_interval   5
    retry_check_interval    1
    check_period            24x7
    notification_interval   60
    notification_period     24x7
    notification_options    w,u,c
    contact_groups          network_team,field_support
    }
```

In Example 2-17 we've defined a service for the host `kitten.yourdomain.com` with a description of `SMTP` that uses a command to check the service called `check_smtp`. This command checks the state of the service during the 24x7 time period every 5 minutes. It also notifies during the 24x7 time period and sends one notification every 60 minutes to the `network_team` and `field_support` contact groups. You'll notice that some of the same directives used for host objects are also used for service objects. You'll also notice some new directives that represent functions unique to service objects. Throughout this section I'll only define any new directives required for services or any directives we've already seen that function differently when used in service definitions. The rest of the directives function as they do for host objects, and you can refer to the definition of them in the "Defining Your First Host" section.

Basic Service Directives

Table 2-9 lists the basic directives required to define a service.

Table 2-9. *Basic Service Directives*

Directive	Description	Mandatory?
service_description	Description of the service	Yes
host_name	Name of the host(s) that the service runs on	Yes
hostgroup_name	Alternative to host_name that allows you to specify one or more host group that this service runs on	Yes
servicegroups	Service group or groups that the service belongs to	No
contact_groups	Contact groups that should be notified for this service	Yes

The first directive, `service_description`, is the name of the service you are defining. It needs to be unique for the host it is defined on. In other words, there can't be two services on the one host with the same service description. Nagios uses the combination of hostname and service description to uniquely identify the service. The description field can include spaces, dashes, and colons, but you should avoid other special characters, including quotation marks, semicolons, and apostrophes, since they can make it difficult to use the service description field as a macro in commands.

Tip You can use the macro $SERVICEDESC$ for the service description.

The second directive in Table 2-9 is host_name. This is the short name of the host that the service resides on. You use the value of the host_name directive from your host definition as the value of this directive. You can specify multiple hosts that this service runs on by separating them with commas:

host_name   kitten.yourdomain.com,puppy.yourdomain.com,duckling.yourdomain.com

This directive indicates that the defined service will run on three hosts: kitten, puppy, and duckling. If you want to define a service that is present on all hosts, you can specify this by setting the host_name directive to * like so:

host_name   *

The next directive, hostgroup_name, provides an alternative to specifying the host_name directive. This allows you to specify a group of hosts that this service runs on like so:

hostgroup_name   servers,aust_assets

This directive tells Nagios that the service you are defining exists on all hosts in the host groups servers and aust_assets. You can specify a single host group, or as you can see, you can specify multiple host groups by separating them with commas.

■**Tip** You should specify either the host_name or hostgroup_name directive but not both!

The servicegroups directive allows you to specify the service's membership in a service group. Service groups allow you to group together like services for display purposes in the web console. I'll discuss service groups in the "Grouping Objects" section. You can specify multiple groups by separating each with a comma:

servicegroups   smtp_servers,au_mail_services

The last directive in Table 2-9 is contact_groups. The contact_groups directive specifies which contact groups should be notified in the event of a notification being generated. It functions exactly as it does with host definitions.

Service Checking

Services have slightly different checking controls than hosts. This is mainly because services are designed to be more regularly checked (remember, you don't generally want to schedule regular host checks) and the associated checking logic required needs to be more flexible.

Service checking is a cycle. Let's step through a simple explanation of that cycle. First, Nagios schedules a check of the service, executes the check, looks for the completed check results, and from those results determines what state the service is in. If the service is in an OK state, it updates the service with that state and schedules the next check of the service. If Nagios finds that the service has changed to a non-OK state, this is initially considered to be a soft non-OK state. The service is then rechecked the number of times indicated in the max_check_attempts directive. If it recovers during this rechecking, Nagios returns to normal checking and does not log or generate a notification. If, at the end of the rechecking, the service is still in a non-OK state, the state of the service is changed to a hard non-OK state. Nagios then logs the hard state change, generates a notification if it is configured to do so, and activates any associated event handlers. Nagios then goes back to checking the service on its normal check schedule and the cycle continues.[9]

I've listed all the service checking–related directives for service objects in Table 2-10.

Table 2-10. *Service Checking Directives*

Directive	Description	Mandatory?
check_command	Command used to check the service.	No
normal_check_interval	Time between regular checks of the service.	Yes
retry_check_interval	Time between retry checks of the service.	Yes
max_check_attempts	Number of check attempts to make before notification.	Yes
parallelize_check	Specifies whether the check is parallelized.	No
is_volatile	Specifies whether the service is volatile.	No
check_freshness	Specifies freshness checks for this object.	No
freshness_threshold	Specifies the freshness threshold for this object.	No
active_checks_enabled	Active checks are enabled for this object.	No
passive_checks_enabled	Passive checks are enabled for this object.	No
check_period	Specifies when to perform checks of the service.	Yes

The first directive in Table 2-10 is the check_command directive. This directive functions identically to its host definition equivalent. It also has a macro associated with it; in this case, the macro for referring to your service commands is $SERVICECHECKCOMMAND$.

As when used in hosts, the check_command directive also has a timeout control directive in the nagios.cfg configuration file. The service_check_timeout directive controls how long Nagios will wait for a response from the service check command before timing out. By default, it is set to 60 seconds, as you can see here:

```
service_check_timeout=60
```

If the timeout is reached, Nagios will assume the service is unavailable, put it in a CRITICAL state, and log an error indicating that the command timed out. The timeout is mostly designed to manage runaway checks that have not exited correctly. If necessary, you should adjust this to reflect the network latency in your environment. In most cases, the default will be suitable.

Service Scheduling

How Nagios schedules checks of services can be quite complicated. In essence Nagios service checking is a lifecycle. The first stage of the cycle is when Nagios is started and service checks

---

9. If you have configured notifications to continue, Nagios will continue to notify on the defined schedule until the state changes.

are initially scheduled. The second stage is scheduling ongoing service checks. The last stage is processing the results of service checks; Nagios calls this stage reaping.

Service checks are submitted into an event queue. Nagios then runs the service checks in parallel, that is, it schedules a check, starts the check and then, without waiting for the check to finish, moves onto the next check.[10] The finished check results are also placed into a queue, and Nagios regularly checks this queue and processes the check results. This is the stage known as reaping.

Service scheduling has a number of directives involved in it, some defined in the service object and some contained in the nagios.cfg configuration file. There are also some reasonably complex calculations involved. I'll take you through how this works in simple terms. A number of other variables are involved, and I recommend you read the relevant Nagios documentation to get a full understanding of how service check scheduling functions.[11]

Initial Service Scheduling

Now, let's look at how service checks get scheduled when you first start Nagios. When Nagios is started up, it schedules an initial check of all defined services. This could potentially result in a large load on your server and hosts. Nagios therefore attempts to schedule these checks in a balanced manner. Nagios balances the load on your local Nagios server and your remote hosts differently. The process of balancing the checks on the Nagios server is called *inter-check delay*. The balancing of remote service checks is called *interleaving*. Let's look at inter-check delay first.

The inter-check delay is managed by a directive in your nagios.cfg called service_ inter_check_delay_period. You can see this directive with its default setting here:

```
service_inter_check_delay_period=s
```

The service_inter_check_delay_period has four possible settings, as shown in Table 2-11.

Table 2-11. *Inter-check Delay Methods*

Setting	Method	Description
n	No	Use no method of scheduling. Schedule all checks immediately.
d	Dumb	Use the "dumb" method of scheduling and leave a delay of 1 second between checks.
s	Smart	Use the "smart" method of scheduling (explained in text that follows).
x.xx	User-supplied	User-supplied delay measured in seconds.

The first scheduling method is n, or no method of scheduling. All checks are scheduled immediately on the local host. I do not recommend that you use this sort of scheduling. The next method is d, or "dumb," scheduling. All checks are scheduled 1 second apart. This is also not a recommended method of scheduling, though it will work better than no method of

---

10. This same principal is applied to most Nagios events, including host checks, log file rotation, and the processing of external commands.

11. http://nagios.sourceforge.net/docs/2_0/checkscheduling.html

scheduling, especially if you have a lot of CPU and memory on your Nagios server. The next method of scheduling is s, or "smart," scheduling, and this is the default and recommended method of scheduling. The last potential method is a user-supplied value (in seconds) for the inter-check delay.

So how does "smart" scheduling work? Well, Nagios performs a simple calculation using the average normal check interval across all your services divided by the total number of services defined. The normal check interval is the period of time between checks when the service is in an OK state. This is defined using the normal_check_interval directive, which I'll discuss later in this section. The calculation is inter-check delay = (average check interval for all services) ÷ (total number of services).

For example, I have an average normal check interval of 5 minutes across 250 services. To find out inter-check delay, I divide 300 (5 multiplied by 60 to represent the check interval in seconds) by 250. This generates an inter-check delay of 1.2 seconds. This would result in checks being scheduled with a delay between them of 1.2 seconds.

Given the complexity of calculating scheduling for potentially thousands of services with varying check intervals, I recommend you use "smart" scheduling rather than any other kind of scheduling.

Tip If you schedule regular host checks for some hosts (which I don't recommend you do as discussed in the "Defining Your First Host" section earlier in this chapter), there is also a host_inter_check_delay directive that performs the same function and has the same options as the related service directive. I recommend this directive also be set to s.

Nagios uses a process called interleaving to schedule checks for remote hosts. Interleaving is controlled by the service_interleave_factor directive, which is contained in the nagios.cfg file. Like the inter-check delay directive, it has options including a "smart" setting. I've shown the directive with its default, "smart," setting here:

```
service_interleave_factor=s
```

So how does Nagios calculate the interleave factor and how does it work? Well, it is calculated using this equation:

```
interleave factor = ceil (total number of services ÷ total number of hosts)
```

Note Ceil indicates that you need to round up the result to the nearest integer.

For example, I have 250 services on 50 hosts. I divide 250 by 50 to achieve an interleave factor of 5. With an interleave factor of 5, when scheduling service checks, Nagios schedules the first check and then skips 5 services and then schedules another check, and so on. When Nagios reaches the end of the list of services, it starts again and schedules the next unscheduled service, skips 5 services, and then schedules the next unscheduled service, and so on until all services have been scheduled. As the list of your services is sorted by host, this should mean that your service checks are evenly balanced and distributed and no single host is heavily loaded.

You can also specify your own service interleave factor. This is a positive value of 1 or greater. A setting of 1 indicates that you do not wish to interleave the services and all checks will be executed simultaneously. You can see this here:

```
service_interleave_factor=1
```

I recommend you leave the value of the service_interleave_factor as s, for "smart" scheduling, as it provides the best possible calculation for ensuring your service checking is balanced and does not overload your Nagios server.

There are three other directives in the nagios.cfg configuration file that can influence startup service checking. The first directive is max_service_check_spread, which controls the maximum period of time over which Nagios will schedule its initial service checks. This directive is specified in minutes. This directive will automatically adjust the spread of your initial service checks so that they occur within the timeframe you specify. You can see an example of this directive on the following line:

```
max_service_check_spread=30
```

This directive will force Nagios to ensure all initial service checks are scheduled within 30 minutes of the server being started.

The second directive is use_retained_scheduling_info, which tells Nagios to retain the scheduling information for hosts and services in between server restarts. Using this option will generally invalidate the use of the max_service_check_spread directive as Nagios will use the stored scheduling information rather than be influenced by the spread directive. You can enable this option by setting it to 1 and disable it by setting it to 0. This directive is enabled by default.

■Tip When you first start adding hosts and services to Nagios, or when you add a large number of hosts and services, you should disable this directive as it can skew the spread of the added service and hosts checks. Reenable it after the new objects have had their initial checks scheduled.

Finally, the third directive in nagios.cfg is called max_concurrent_checks, which is a brute-force method of limiting the number of checks that can be run in parallel. By default this directive is set to 0, which does not limit the numbers of checks that can be run in parallel. You can specify the maximum number of checks to run in parallel. If you set this directive to 1, only one check will be conducted at a time. I recommend you do not do this to avoid the risk of choking your server by only allowing one check at a time. I believe that the "smart" scheduling methods provide the best way of scheduling checks.

■Tip You can also disable parallel service checking for an individual service using the `parallelize_check` directive in the service definition. If you do this, Nagios will halt all other activities to perform the service check. I do not recommend doing this as it can have a serious performance impact on your monitoring.

Ongoing Service Scheduling

Once Nagios has started and is doing routine service checking, service checking is controlled via the `normal_check_interval` and `retry_check_interval` directives. You can see these in Table 2-10. The first directive, `normal_check_interval`, defines the interval between regular or normal checks performed on services. Regular checks are performed when the service is in an OK state or when the service is in a hard non-OK state, that is, the service has been rechecked the number of times specified in the `max_check_attempts` directive. The interval is defined in minutes and the recommended default is 5 minutes, as you can see here:

```
normal_check_interval          5
```

The `retry_check_interval` directive handles retry checking on the service. Retry checking starts if the service goes into a soft non-OK state, that is, the service is being rechecked the number of times specified in the `max_check_attempts` directive. You can see this directive demonstrated on the following line:

```
retry_check_interval          3
```

■Note Obviously if you've set the `max_check_attempts` directive to 1, retry checking will never occur because Nagios will not retry the service but simply change its state.

So why would you want to define two check intervals? Well, the first check interval for "normal" checking is used when the service is OK or when you are sure it is in non-OK state. The "retry" checking interval is used to temporarily either speed up or slow down the rate of your checks while the service is in a soft state. Generally I prefer to speed up the rate of checks when a service is in a soft state to ensure that any problems are identified quickly while still ensuring the problem is not a transitory issue by retrying the service a sufficient number of times.

Service Reaping

The last stage in the service checking process is the receipt and processing of the results of service checks. Nagios calls this process service reaping. This is controlled by another directive in the `nagios.cfg` file called `service_reaper_frequency`:

```
service_reaper_frequency=10
```

The `service_reaper_frequency` directive specifies how often Nagios should process finished service checks. It is specified in seconds and defaults to 10 seconds. This means that every 10 seconds Nagios will process the results of completed service checks.

Volatile Services

You can also define services that are volatile. Volatile services change state frequently—for example, services that reset themselves into an OK state when checked or services that require attention every time they have a problem. So how do these services differ from a normal service? With a normal service, when Nagios checks the service and detects a hard non-OK state change, it logs that state, notifies if it is configured to do so, and activates any associated event handlers. If the service is checked again and it is still in the same hard non-OK state, then Nagios does nothing because generally it only reacts to state changes.[12]

When a volatile service is checked and it is a hard non-OK state, Nagios logs that state, notifies (if it is configured to do so), and activates any associated event handlers. If the service is checked again and it is still in the same hard non-OK state, Nagios repeats the logging, the notification, and the activation of event handlers. It repeats this every time the service is checked and is found to be still in a non-OK state.

A good example of a volatile service is the monitoring of log files. For example, you have defined a service to monitor a log file that receives log entries from an IDS sensor. You configure the service not to use active checks and set the max_check_attempts to 1. You then use a passive command to submit your log entries to the service.[13] When a new log entry is found, this puts the service in a hard non-OK state. This state is logged and then a notification and an event handler could be triggered if they are configured. From then on, every time the service is checked and another log entry is received, that hard non-OK state is logged and Nagios will generate another notification and/or execute an event handler. Thus, you could get a notification for every log entry you wish.

You can indicate that a service is volatile by setting the is_volatile directive in the service definition like so:

```
is_volatile          1
```

The default setting for this directive is 0, which will indicate that the service is not volatile. Generally most services will not be volatile, but it is occasionally a useful tool. I'll discuss the use of volatile services further in Chapter 9 when I look at integrating Nagios with other tools.

Service Freshness

As with host freshness checking, you can specify a check_freshness and freshness_threshold for your services. Freshness checking for services is controlled and operates in exactly the same way as host freshness checking. The major difference is that there are some different directives in the main nagios.cfg file that need to be set for service freshness checking. I've listed these directives in Example 2-18.

Example 2-18. *The nagios.cfg Service Freshness Items*

```
check_service_freshness=1
service_freshness_check_interval=60
```

---

12. Depending on the notification logic, it may still send notifications according to the period defined in the notification_interval directive.

13. I'll discuss how to do this in Chapter 7.

■**Note** The directive settings in Example 2-18 are the Nagios defaults in the sample `nagios.cfg` configuration file.

The first directive in Example 2-18 is `check_service_freshness`, which controls whether freshness checks are enabled for services. A setting of 1 indicates that freshness checks are enabled, and a setting of 0 indicates that they are disabled. The `service_freshness_check_interval` directive sets the interval between the checks Nagios performs for freshness. The default setting is 60 seconds. If the `check_service_freshness` directive is set to disabled, `service_freshness_check_interval` is ignored.

Other Service Checking Directives

Lastly in Table 2-10 there are the directives `max_check_attempts`, `active_checks_enabled`, `passive_checks_enabled`, and `check_period`. All of these directives function as defined in the "Defining Your First Host" section.

Service Status and Notifications

Services, like hosts, have a series of states. These states are different from those of hosts and include two levels of error state that provide you with the ability to use thresholds. I'll examine each of these states in this section.

The normal status for a service is OK. This indicates that the service is functioning normally. There are also three error states: WARNING, CRITICAL, and UNKNOWN. The provision of both the WARNING and CRITICAL states allows you to set thresholds for your services. A WARNING state can be initiated when a service reaches a certain state—for example, the disk space of a host reaching 85 percent. When the service reaches an increased level—for example, the disk space reached 95 percent—the service can be configured to change to a CRITICAL state. These thresholds are created by configuring the check command to trigger each type of state using parameters; I'll discuss that in the "Defining Commands" section. The UNKNOWN state is set when Nagios is unable to determine the state of the service.

Also, as with host objects you can configure how and when services notify contacts of problems and changes in state. Service notifications operate very much like host notifications. Table 2-12 specifies the directives used to control service notifications.

Table 2-12. *Service Notification Directives*

Directive	Description	Mandatory?
notifications_enabled	Enables notifications for this object	No
notification_interval	Time between notifications being sent out	Yes
notification_period	Specifies when to send notifications about the host	Yes
notification_options	Specifies under what conditions Nagios should send a notification	Yes

First, the `notifications_enabled` directive specifies whether this service will send notifications. If it is set to 1, notifications are enabled. A setting of 0 indicates notifications are disabled.

As with host definitions, the `notification_interval` directive specifies the time between notifications. This directive is used when the service is in a non-OK state and a notification has been generated. If the service remains in a non-OK state, Nagios will continue to send notifications, waiting the notification interval between each notification. You can see an example of this directive here:

```
notification_interval    30
```

This directive will send a notification every 30 minutes.

The `notification_period` directive controls when Nagios will send notifications. The value of the directive is one or more time periods—for example, Monday to Friday during business hours, during which time notifications are allowed to be sent. I've used the `notification_period` directive here:

```
notification_period    24x7
```

As you can see, I've specified a time period called 24x7, which would need to be defined using a time period object. Notifications will be sent only the 24x7 time period.

The `notification_options` directive controls for what states Nagios should send notifications. Example 2-19 demonstrates how to use this directive.

Example 2-19. *notification_options Directive for a Service*

```
notification_options    w,c,u,r
```

In Example 2-19 I've specified the notification options w, c, u, and r. In this example Nagios would send notifications when the service was in the WARNING, CRITICAL, and UNKNOWN states. It also sends notifications when the service recovers or returns to the OK state. There are six possible options, listed in Table 2-13.

Table 2-13. *Service Notification Options*

Option	Description
c	Sends notification for critical states
f	Sends notification for flapping
n	Sends no notifications
r	Sends notification for recovery
w	Sends notification for warning states
u	Sends notification for unknown states

Like hosts, services can also flap. By specifying the f value in your `notification_options` directive, you will be notified if the service starts flapping. You can also specify the r option to generate a notification when the service recovers to an OK state from a non-OK state.

You can also specify the n option to configure the service to send no notifications at all. The n option must be specified on its own:

```
notification_options n
```

Service Flapping and Event Handling

Services can also have flap detection configured for them. Flap detection for service objects functions in an identical manner to flap detection for host objects. It does use different directives in the nagios.cfg configuration file, as shown here:

```
low_service_flap_threshold=5.0
high_service_flap_threshold=20.0
```

These two directives control the global low and high thresholds for flap detection for your services. You need to ensure that the enable_flap_detection directive, the global directive that controls flap detection, is enabled if you want flap detection for either hosts or services. You also need to enable flap detection using directives in your service definition, as shown here:

```
define service{
        service_description                         SMTP
        ...
        flap_detection_enabled      1
        low_flap_threshold          10.0
        high_flap_threshold         30.0
        ...
        }
```

Additionally, services can also have event handlers defined for them. As you can with hosts, you can define a global event handler for services that runs every time any service changes its state. This global event handler is defined in your nagios.cfg file using the directive on the following line:

```
global_service_event_handler=global-service-events
```

In addition to a global service event handler, you can define event handlers for each of your services as well. Here's an example:

```
define service{
        service_description         SMTP
        ...
        event_handler_enabled       1
        event_handler               server-restart
        ...
        }
```

Tip If you also have events handlers defined on your services as well as global event handlers, the global event handlers will execute first and then the service event handlers will execute.

Service Stalking and Obsession

Services can be state-stalked and obsessed over in the same way hosts can be. Generally, unless you are using distributed monitoring you would not enable service obsession. Like hosts, obsession is configured in two places: globally in the nagios.cfg configuration file and locally in your service definition. Let's look at the global configuration first. The directives shown here control the global settings for service obsession and are contained in the nagios.cfg file:

```
obsess_over_services=0
ocsp_command=obsessive_host_handler
```

The first directive controls whether service obsession is globally enabled. It is disabled by default. To enable it, set it to 1; to keep it disabled, leave the setting at 0. The second directive, ocsp_command, is the command that Nagios should run after each service check.

Once you have configured service obsession at the global level, you need to enable it for each individual service you wish to obsess over. Add the following directive to your service definition:

```
obsess_over_service        1
```

A setting of 1 indicates service obsession is enabled, and a setting of 0 indicates it is disabled.

You can also stalk service states. This uses the same directive as we defined in the host definition section, stalking_options. Due to services having different states to hosts, the stalking_options directive has different options. Here's an example:

```
stalking_options        w,u,c
```

Here we have enabled state-stalking for WARNING, UNKNOWN, and CRITICAL states. Table 2-14 shows the full list of states you can stalk on.

Table 2-14. *Service State Stalking*

State	State Stalking Option	Description
OK	o	Stalks OK states
UNKNOWN	u	Stalks UNKNOWN states
WARNING	w	Stalks WARNING states
CRITICAL	c	Stalks CRITICAL states

Other Directives

Service definitions can also use a number of other directives. These directives are listed in Table 2-15.

Table 2-15. *Additional Service Directives*

Directive	Description	Mandatory?
`process_perf_data`	Enables the processing of performance data for this service	No
`retain_status_information`	Retains the status of this object between server restarts	No
`retain_nonstatus_information`	Retains nonstatus information for this object between server restarts	No

All of the directives in Table 2-15 I've defined earlier in the "Defining Your First Host" section. There are no significant differences in their operation in a service definition as opposed to a host definition.

Using Templates for Objects Definition

So you've started to define some hosts and services. It becomes an easy process, unless you have thousands of hosts and services. Then you start to notice that the definitions become very repetitive and contain many of the same directives with identical settings repeated over and over again. Thankfully, rather than having you continually cut and paste directives, Nagios offers a solution to this repetition. This solution is achieved using object templates. I'm going to introduce configuration object templates and the concepts of object inheritance and recursion.

A Nagios template is a generic definition for a particular type of object. For example, you might notice that most of the host object definitions for your routers share similar characteristics and therefore have many directives that are set identically for each host. Templates are a way to take advantage of these similarities to reduce your configuration time and effort. With templates, your object definitions inherit directive settings from a template object definition. Example 2-20 contains a template for a host object definition.

Tip Probably the most useful object types to use templates with are hosts, services, and contacts.

Example 2-20. *Host Object Definition Template*

```
define host{
        name                    router_template
        check_command           check-host-alive
        notification_options    d,u,r
        max_check_attempts       5
        register                 0
        }
```

A template for a host object definition, as shown in Example 2-20, closely resembles a normal host object definition but with two additional directives. The first directive, name, is the name of the template definition. The value of this directive is used to refer to the template in other object definitions. The template name needs to be unique for the type of object being defined. In Example 2-20 I've defined a host object template called `router_template`. Due to the requirement for uniqueness there can be only one host object definition called `router_template`. You could, however, have a service object template also called `router_template` because service objects are a different object type.

The next directive is the `register` directive. The `register` directive tells Nagios whether the object definition is a template or the definition of a real object. It has a binary setting, with 0 indicating unregistered and 1 indicating registered. An unregistered object definition will be considered a template and not included in the monitoring configuration. If you do not specify this directive, Nagios will try to include the template into the monitoring configuration and the server probably fail to start when it parses the incorrect syntax.

Tip All objects are registered by default. This means you don't need to specify the `register` directive in all your object definitions; you only need to specify it in template definitions. These have to be explicitly unregistered.

In Example 2-20 I've specified what the template defaults should be for the `check_command`, `notification_options`, and `max_check_attempts` directives. You can specify additional directives that you wish to set defaults for in the template. Now that I've demonstrated how to define a template, how can we use it in an object definition? I've demonstrated this in Example 2-21.

Example 2-21. *Using a Template with an Object Definition*

```
define host{
        host_name               syd_router
        ...
        use                     router_template
        }
```

Example 2-21 is a normal host object definition with one added directive, `use`. The `use` directive allows you to specify the name of a template to be used for this object definition. The value of the `use` directive should be the `name` directive of the template to be applied. Nagios calls this *object inheritance*.

Note It is important to remember that object inheritance is a recursive process. If you want to refer to a template in an object definition, you need to define the template before the object definition in the configuration file. This means you should put all your template definitions at the top of your configuration files before you define your objects!

With the template applied to the host object definition in Example 2-21, the resulting definition of the host object would include the inherited directives from the `router_template` template definition. You can see this actual definition in Example 2-22.

Example 2-22. *The Object Definition with Inherited Directives*

```
define host{
        host_name              syd_router
        check_command          check-host-alive
        notification_options   d,u,r
        max_check_attempts     3
        use                    router_template
        }
```

■Tip If you specify a directive in your object definition that is also specified in a template, the directive in the object definition overrides the template directive. For example, specifying a value for the `max_check_attempts` directive in Example 2-22 would override any setting for this directive in the `router_template` template.

You can also chain together multiple object inheritances. This means that you can create a template or object definition and refer to it in another object definition. You can then create a template from this objection definition and refer to it in further object definitions. This process can become quite complicated, and I'll look at it in Example 2-23.

Example 2-23. *Chaining Object Inheritances*

```
define host{
        host_name              syd_router
        address                192.168.0.1
        check_command          check-host-alive
        notification_options   d,u,r
        max_check_attempts     5
        name                   syd_template
        }

define host{
        host_name              ny_router
        address                192.168.1.1
        max_check_attempts     3
        use                    syd_template
        name                   ny_template
        }

define host{
        host_name              ny_router2
        address                192.168.1.2
        use                    ny_template
        }
```

In Example 2-23 I've defined three host objects.[14] The first is for the host, syd_router. In this object I've defined three directives and created a template called syd_template. You'll note I haven't specified the register directive, which means that the object definition is both a template and a real object I want Nagios to monitor.

Next I've defined a host object called ny_router, which uses the template syd_template and inherits the directives from the previous object. I've overridden one of the directives, max_check_attempts, with a new value. Additionally I've defined a template called ny_template from the ny_router object definition.

Finally I've defined a further host object called ny_router2, which uses the ny_template. This final object would inherit the original directives from the syd_router object and the overridden max_check_attempts directive. It would look like the object definition shown here:

```
define host{
        host_name             ny_router2
        address               192.168.1.2
        check_command         check-host-alive
        notification_options  d,u,r
        max_check_attempts    3
        use                   ny_template
        }
```

■Tip You can use any number of layers of object inheritance in your configuration, but as you can see the inheritance can become quite complicated. It is probably safer to limit your inheritance to a couple of layers.

Finally, in this chapter I'll also provide same sample templates for host, service, and contact object definitions. In Example 2-24 I've specified a generic template for hosts.

Example 2-24. *Generic Host Object Template*

```
define host{
        name                          generic_host_template
        check_command                 check-host-alive
        notification_options          d,u,r
        max_check_attempts            3
        active_checks_enabled         1
        passive_checks_enabled        1
        notifications_enabled         1
        event_handler_enabled         1
        flap_detection_enabled        1
        process_perf_data             1
        retain_status_information     1
        retain_nonstatus_information  1
        register                      0
        }
```

---

14. Ignore the fact that the object definitions don't have all the mandatory directives.

The generic host template is named `generic_host_template` and sets a number of directives. You can see the explanation of what each of these directives do in the "Defining Our First Host" section.

In Example 2-25 I've specified another generic template. This template is for services.

Example 2-25. *Generic Service Object Template*

```
define service{
        name                            generic_service_template
        notification_options            w,u,c
        max_check_attempts              3
        normal_check_interval           5
        retry_check_interval            1
        active_checks_enabled           1
        passive_checks_enabled          1
        notifications_enabled           1
        event_handler_enabled           1
        flap_detection_enabled          1
        process_perf_data               1
        retain_status_information       1
        retain_nonstatus_information 1
        register                        0
        }
```

REGULAR EXPRESSIONS IN OBJECTS

In addition to templates, you can also regular expressions in those directives related to object names—for example, the `host_name` and `service_description` directives. This functionality has two varieties, both of which are enabled using directives in the `nagios.cfg` configuration file. The first directive, `use_regexp_matching`, enables regular expression matching on any name-related directive that contains either the * or ? wildcard characters. To enable this directive, set it to 1. Nagios will only use regular expressions where one of these directives has a ? or * character. For example, specifying `syd*` in the `host_name` directive will tell Nagios to select all hosts that start with `syd`.

The second directive, `use_true_regexp_matching`, enables more advanced regular expression matching. It treats the contents of all name-related fields as a regular expression, not just those that have a * or ? character present. Using this type of regular expression matching you can also negate objects, for example, specify a group of objects excepting one or more objects like so:

```
members                 kitten,puppy,!owlet,!snake
```

This directive would result in the `kitten` and `puppy` hosts being included but the `owlet` and `snake` hosts being excluded.

Be careful when enabling regular expression matching as it can have unexpected results if the value of a directive that is not intended to be a regular expression is interpreted that way. This occurs if you use characters, such as ?, in an object name that Nagios might interpret as a regular expression. This sort of error should show up when you verify or start Nagios and your configuration is checked.

The generic service template is named generic_service_template, and you can see the explanation of the directives in that template in the "Defining Services" section earlier in this chapter.

Tip I strongly recommend that you use templates, even if you have a limited number of hosts and services. Not only will it make creating new objects faster, but if you need to make a global change to a variable, then making the change in one place is much faster than changing it in multiple places.

Contact Objects

Now you know how to define hosts and services, you need to define some contacts. Contacts are the people who will receive notifications about your hosts and services. Like host and service definitions, they are made up a series of directives, some optional and some mandatory.[15] Let's look at an example of a contact definition in Example 2-26.

Example 2-26. *Contact Definitions*

```
define contact{
        contact_name                    jsmith
        alias                           John Smith
        contactgroups           network_team
        service_notification_period     24x7
        host_notification_period        24x7
        service_notification_options    w,u,c,r
        host_notification_options       d,u,r
        service_notification_commands   notify-by-email
        host_notification_commands      host-notify-by-email
        email                           jsmith@yourdomain.com
        pager                           555-5555@pager.com
        address1                        jsmith@icq.com
        address2                        555-999-8888
            }
```

The contact definition in Example 2-26 defines a contact called John Smith. Let's first look at the contact directives involved in defining the basics of the contact; see Table 2-16.

---

15. You can see a full list of the contact object directives at http://nagios.sourceforge.net/docs/2_0/ xodtemplate.html#contact.

Table 2-16. *Basic Contact Directives*

Directive	Description	Macro	Mandatory?
contact_name	Short name of the contact	$CONTACTNAME$	Yes
alias	Alias for the contact	$CONTACTALIAS$	Yes
contactgroups	Contact groups the contact belongs to	None	No

The first directive is contact_name, which is the short name of the contact being defined. This directive is also available as a macro called $CONTACTNAME$. The next directive, alias, allows us to define a longer name for the contact. It is also available as the macro $CONTACTALIAS$.

The last directive in Table 2-17 is the contactgroups directive. This defines any contact groups that the contact may belong to. Contact groups allow us to group together multiple contacts to receive notifications. Every contact that you wish to receive notifications should belong to a contact group. This is because we refer to contact groups using the contact_groups directive rather than referring to contacts directly in our hosts and services when specifying who to notify in the event of problems. So if you wish to receive notifications, you must define at least one contact group and one contact. We discuss defining contact groups in the "Contact Group Objects" section.

The next directives in our contact definition control when and how Nagios notifies the contact of events or problems. These directives are listed in Table 2-17, and I'll look at each of them in turn.

Table 2-17. *Contact Notification Directives*

Directive	Description	Mandatory?
host_notification_period	Time period in which to send host notifications	Yes
service_notification_period	Time period in which to send service notifications	Yes
host_notification_options	States to send host notifications for	Yes
service_notification_options	States to send service notifications for	Yes
host_notification_commands	Commands to use to send host notifications	No
service_notification_commands	Commands to use to send service notifications	No

The first two directives in Table 2-17 are host_notification_period and service_notification_period. These directives control when this contact should receive notifications for hosts and services, respectively. For example, this contact may only be notified during business hours while another contact might be notified after hours. You specify the required time period by specifying the short name of the time period required. You can only specify one time period for each of these directives.

The next two directives in Table 2-17 are host_notification_options and service_notification_options. These control which notifications will be sent to this contact. In your hosts and services, you defined which types of events you wished Nagios to notify on. For example, you may have wished Nagios to only notify when a host was in a DOWN state. This is done in your host and service definitions using the notification_options directive. At the contact level you can further control this by specifying that certain contacts should only receive notifications about particular states. An example of this could be a technician who receives all the notifications for a host while his supervisor only receives DOWN notifications for the host. As a result of setting the notifications options at the contact level, both of these employees could belong to the same contact group but each could be notified for different events or state changes.

■**Caution** When Nagios sends a notification, it considers both the host or service notification options and the contact notification options. Thus, if you have a host that is configured to notify on a DOWN state but no contacts are configured to receive DOWN notifications, then no notification will be sent. You should be careful to ensure a contact is configured to receive all notifications you wish to be notified for.[16]

The last directives in Table 2-17 are host_notification_commands and service_ notification_commands. These allow you to set the commands that will be used to send notifications for this contact. You can specify different commands for your hosts and services. These notification commands take the output of a notification and send them on to the contact. For example, a notification command could take the contents of a notification, format it, and then send it to the contact's email address. These notification commands usually contain one or more macros that let the recipient of the notification know the nature of the event and the host or service involved. You can also specify multiple commands by separating each command with a comma. If you do not specify notification commands, you will not receive notifications.

As with the host and service commands, you can specify a timeout for your notification commands in the nagios.cfg configuration file. Here is the directive with its default setting of 60 seconds:

notification_timeout=60

After 60 seconds without a response, Nagios will kill the notification command and log an error message.

■**Note** I'll look at configuring notification-related commands in the "Defining Commands" section later in this chapter.

The remaining directives in our contact definition are addressing directives. They control the destination of any notifications that Nagios generates. I've listed these directives in Table 2-18.

---

16. You can see a full description of the logic used when a notification is sent at http://nagios. sourceforge.net/docs/2_0/notifications.html.

Table 2-18. *Contact Addressing Directives*

Directive	Description	Macro	Mandatory?
email	Email address	$CONTACTEMAIL$	No
pager	Pager details	$CONTACTPAGER$	No
address*x*	Any additional addresses	$CONTACTADDRESS*x*$	No

The first directive, email, allows you to specify an email address for this contact. The value of the email directive is also contained in a macro called $CONTACTEMAIL$. This macro becomes important when I examine notification commands in the "Notification Commands" section later in this chapter.

The pager directive is very similar to the email directive except that it defines a pager number or the email address of a pager gateway. The value of the pager directive is also available as a macro, this one called $CONTACTPAGER$.

The last directive, address*x*, is actually a series of directives that allow you to define additional addresses that you can use to notify this contact. These could include addresses like cell phone numbers or instant messaging IDs. You can define six additional addresses using the directives address1 to address6, as you can see here:

```
address1    555-999-8888
address2    jsmith_im
address3    jsmith_im2
...
```

You can refer to each of these additional addresses using macros; for address1 you would use the macro $CONTACTADDRESS1$, for address2 you would use the macro $CONTACTADDRESS2$, and so on.

You can also use object templates for your contact objects, and I've included a simple starting template for your contacts in Example 2-27.

Example 2-27. *Starter Contact Template*

```
define contact{
        name                          generic_contact_template
        service_notification_options  w,u,c,r
        host_notification_options     d,u,r
        service_notification_commands notify-by-email
        host_notification_commands    host-notify-by-email
        register                      0
        }
```

Grouping Objects

Nagios allows like objects to be collected into groups. There are three types of groupings: hosts, services, and contacts. We'll cover all three of these objects types in this section.

Host Group Objects

Host group objects allow you to group like or related hosts together to display them in the web console. For example, common host groupings would be all the hosts from a particular site, all the hosts of a particular type, or all the hosts associated with a particular business process. In Example 2-28 I've defined a host group.

Example 2-28. *Host Group Object Definition*

```
define hostgroup{
        hostgroup_name   syd_servers
        alias            Sydney servers
        members          kitten.yourdomain.com,puppy.yourdomain.com,➥
duckling.yourdomain.com
            }
```

Example 2-28 contains all the possible directives used in a host group. The first directive, hostgroup_name, is the name of the host group being defined. This is used when referring to a host group in another object definition—for example, it is used as the value of the hostgroups directive in the host object definition. The next directive, alias, allows you to provide a longer description of the host group.

The final directive, members, can contain the list of hosts that belong to the host group. Multiple hosts can be listed, separated by commas. You can also specify multiple members directives if you have many hosts to make editing your object definitions easier. You can also use the wildcard * symbol to add all hosts defined on your server to a host group.

The members directive is optional; you can specify which host groups your hosts belong to in two places. First, you can list all the host groups that your host belongs to using the hostgroups directive that is part of the host object definition. Here is an example:

```
define host{
        host_name kitten.yourdomain.com
        …
        hostgroups syd_servers
         …
         }
```

On this line we've added the host kitten to the host group syd_servers. We could achieve the same result by using the members directive in a host group object:

```
define hostgroup{
        hostgroup_name   syd_servers
        alias            Sydney servers
        members          kitten.yourdomain.com
          }
```

As you can see, we've also added the host kitten (using the short name of the host defined by the host_name directive) to the syd_servers host group.

■**Tip** To add a host to a host group, you only need to specify the host in one of these two directives: either the `hostgroups` directive in the host object definition or the `members` directive in the host group object.

Service Group Objects

Service group objects allow you to group like or related services together to display them in the web console. For example, a common services grouping would be all services used in a particular business process or a type of infrastructure such as email services. Example 2-29 contains a sample service group.

Example 2-29. *Service Group Object Definition*

```
define servicegroup{
          servicegroup_name      email_services
          alias                  SMTP Services
          members                puppy.yourdomain.com,SMTP,kitten.yourdomain.com,IMAP,➡
kitten.yourdomain.com,POP
          }
```

The directives used to define a service group are similar to those used to define a host group. First, each service group needs a name, specified by the `servicegroup_name` directive. This name is the short name of the service group you would use in the `servicegroups` directive in service object definitions. The next directive is the `alias` directive, which provides a long name for the service group.

The last directive is the `members` directive. This is defined a little differently from other group types and consists of the name of the host that the service runs on, followed by a comma and then the name of the service. In Example 2-29 I've defined three services: SMTP, IMAP, and POP. The SMTP service runs on the `puppy` host and the IMAP and POP services run on the `kitten` host. In Example 2-29 they are all part of the `email_services` service group.

As with host groups, you can define membership in a service group in two places. The first is the `servicegroups` directive in the service definition; the second is the `members` directive in the service group definition. As with host group members, you only need to define the group membership of services in one of these places.

Contact Group Objects

The last type of group is a contact group. A contact group is a little different from host and service groups because it is not designed to pull together like objects for display purposes. Rather, it gathers together contacts for notification and alerting purposes. These contact groups are used in your host and service object definitions to indicate who is notified when an event or error occurs. Both service and host definitions use the `contact_groups` directive to define which contact groups get notified. As we discussed in the "Contact Objects" section, all of your contacts need to belong to a contact group if they wish to receive notifications.

Example 2-30 contains a sample contact group definition.

Example 2-30. *Contact Group Object Definition*

```
define contactgroup{
            contactgroup_name    field_support
            alias                Field Support
            members              jsmith,jbloggs
            }
```

The first directive in Example 2-30, contactgroup_name, is the short name of the contact group being defined. This is what is used as the value in the contact_groups directive in your host and service definitions. The second directive, alias, allows you to define a longer, more descriptive name for the contact group.

Like host and service groups, the members directive allows you to define the contacts you want to belong to this contact group. Also like host and service groups, the members directive is optional. You can either specify the membership of the contact group using this directive or using the contactgroups directive in your contact object definitions.

Defining Time Periods

Time periods define the time frames during which Nagios will perform monitoring or generate notifications. For example, you can define time periods in which Nagios will monitor your hosts and services and apply these to individual hosts and services. Earlier in this chapter I used a time period called 24x7. I've defined that time period object in Example 2-31.

Example 2-31. *24x7 Time Period*

```
define timeperiod{
            timeperiod_name      24x7
            alias                24 hours a day
            sunday               00:00-24:00
            monday               00:00-24:00
            tuesday              00:00-24:00
            wednesday            00:00-24:00
            thursday             00:00-24:00
            friday               00:00-24:00
            saturday             00:00-24:00
            }
```

The first directive, timeperiod_name, in the timeperiod object is the short name of the time period that is being defined. In this case, the name used is 24x7. I can use the value of this directive in a number of places when I specify time periods—for example, in service object definitions as the value of the check_period and notification_period directives, among other places.

The next directive is the alias directive, which defines a longer name for the time period. Both of the alias and the timeperiod_name directives are mandatory to the object definition.

Next you need to define the time period this object covers. The first stage of this is defining which days of the week this time period covers. This is done using directives named for the days of the week, monday through sunday. You can specify any combination of days you wish or all of them. If you do not want the time period to cover a specific day or days, then simply omit that day from the object definition. In Example 2-31 I've specified all of the days of the week.

Next you need to define what time or times of the day are covered by this object. This is done using ranges separated by a – symbol. These ranges are defined in 24-hour time. In Example 2-31 I've defined the full 24 hours of a day using the value of `00:00-24:00`.

The time period definition can also contain multiple separate time periods in a single day. Each time period needs to be separated by commas. Here is an example:

```
monday       00:00-02:00,04:00-08:00,18:00-22:00
```

The time period directive on the previous line would cover the period of Monday midnight to 2 a.m., 4 a.m. to 8 a.m., and 6 p.m. to 10 p.m.

Defining Commands

Nagios commands are defined for several purposes. The first are commands designed to allow you to monitor hosts and services. The second are event handlers that can be optionally set to run when state changes occur. The third are the commands used to send notifications. We refer to these in contact objects using `host_notification_commands` and `service_notification_commands`. Each of these types of commands is defined using command object definitions. I'll cover each type of command and how they function briefly, and go into more detail in Chapter 5.

■**Tip** In the "Specifying Your Configuration Files" section earlier in this chapter, I discussed two files, `checkcommands.cfg` and `miscomands.cfg`. These are part of the sample configuration that comes with Nagios and contain a number of example commands. The `checkcommands.cfg` file contains examples of check commands and the `misccommands.cfg` file contains examples of notification commands. I recommend you review them to learn more about commands.

Check Commands

So how do check commands work? Well, first you specify a check command using the `check_command` directive in your host or service definition. The command is identified in that directive using the short name of the command to be run when a check is performed. Most check commands can also pass variables from the host or service definition to the command object definition, and we'll demonstrate how to do this later in this section.

Next you need to define the command object itself. Inside the command object you define its name and a command line that contains the path to a plug-in or binary that Nagios will execute when the command is run. This includes any options you can set with that plug-in or binary and any variables being passed to the command object.

Command objects are just like any other object definition and contain a series of directives. Command objects contain only two directives and both are mandatory. In Example 2-32 you can see a simple command.

Example 2-32. *Simple Command*

```
define command{
        command_name      check_smtp
        command_line      /usr/local/nagios/libexec/check_smtp -H $HOSTADDRESS$
            }
```

The first directive in our example command, command_name, is the short name of the command you are defining. The value of this directive is also used as the value of the command_name directive in your host and service object definitions.

The second directive of the command definition is command_line. The command_line directive contains the actual command executed by Nagios when the command is used. The command in Example 2-32 would be used to check the status of an SMTP server and would be specified in a service object definition. In Example 2-32 you can see that the check_smtp command executes the Nagios plug-in binary check_smtp located at /usr/local/nagios/libexec/ and passes the value of the $HOSTADDRESS$ macro to the command to populate the –H option. In this case the –H option tells the check_smtp plug-in the IP address of the SMTP server to check.

I introduced macros and specifically the $HOSTADDRESS$ macro in the "Defining Your First Host" section. The $HOSTADDRESS$ macro contains the address, usually the IP address, of the host that the service is running on. Nagios replaces the macro value in the command line with the address of the host. Not all macros can be used in commands. Macros usually have a context in which they work. For example, service-related macros will obviously not contain values when executing a check command from a host object. You can see the context of all the available macros and where they will work at http://nagios.sourceforge.net/docs/2_0/macros.html.

The command_line directive is written as it would appear on an actual command line. So Example 2-32 would look like this if executed on a command line:

```
puppy# /usr/local/nagios/libexec/check_smtp -H 192.168.0.1
```

■**Tip** The command line is not enclosed in any quotation marks and you will need to escape any special characters. Most characters can be escaped with the standard \ character. But if you use a $ in the command line that is not part of a macro, then you need to escape the $ sign with another $, resulting in $$.

Let's look at another example. Example 2-33 contains the command from the sample Nagios configuration that is used to check the status of hosts.

Example 2-33. *Check Host Alive Command*

```
define command{
        command_name   check-host-alive
        command_line   $USER1$/check_ping -H $HOSTADDRESS$ -w 3000.0,80%➥
-c 5000.0,100% -p 1
            }
```

In Example 2-33 I've shown a command called check-host-alive. The command_line directive contains two macros and a plug-in binary called check_ping. I discussed one of the macros, $HOSTADDRESS$, a bit earlier. The other macro, $USER1$, is a user-defined macro. User-defined macros allow you to define macros containing information specific to your environment or that you want to keep confidential. You specify your user-defined macros in resource configuration files.

Note I introduced resource configuration files earlier in this chapter in the "How Is Nagios Configured?" section.

Resource files are designed to hold information you don't want available to anybody except the Nagios server. This includes ensuring they are hidden from the web console. They are principally used to hold user-defined macros. Resource files are defined to Nagios in the nagios.cfg configuration file. This is done in a similar way to object configuration files except that the resource file uses a different directive, resource_file, to define these files to Nagios. For example, in the sample nagios.cfg file a resource file called resource.cfg is defined:

resource_file=/usr/local/nagios/etc/resource.cfg

You can define multiple resource files by specifying multiple resource_file directives.

Tip As the Nagios CGIs will not read the resource files, you can lock them down more securely than your other configuration files. You can change the permissions on these files to 0600.

Inside the resource.cfg sample resource file you can see several $USERx$ macros defined, and I've demonstrated two of these in Example 2-34.

Example 2-34. *User-Defined Macros*

```
$USER1$=/usr/local/nagios/libexec
$USER2$=/usr/local/nagios/libexec/eventhandlers
```

In Example 2-34 you can see that the user-defined macros are constructed with the word USER and a number enclosed in $ symbols. You can define a total of 32 user-defined macros, from $USER1$ to $USER32$. In the case of Example 2-34 I've used our user-defined macros to define the paths to the Nagios plug-ins and event handlers. If you refer to Example 2-33 you can see that I've used the $USER1$ macro to define the directory, /usr/local/nagios/libexec/, where the check_ping plug-in binary is located. This macro allows us to avoid continually having to type the full path to the plug-in binaries.

You can also define arguments that are passed from your host and service object definitions. This allows you to pass arguments from your host and service definitions to the check commands. Here is a check_command directive from a service object definition that is part of the Nagios sample configuration files:

```
define    service{
             ...
             check_command              check_local_users!20!50
             ...
             }
```

The check_command directive indicates that when a check is initiated, the check_local_ user command is executed. When the command is executed, Nagios passes two variables to the command: 20 and 50. The variables to be passed to the command are identified by the ! prefix. They are passed to the command in sequence from left to right. Hence the first variable passed is 20 and the second variable is 50.

Tip If you need to use an ! character in one of your variables, you will have to escape it. This is done by adding a \ character—for example, !value!va\!ue!value.

In Example 2-35 I've shown the corresponding check_local_users command object definition that is also from the sample configuration files.

Example 2-35. *$ARGx$ Macros*

```
define command{
        command_name    check_local_users
        command_line    $USER1$/check_users -w $ARG1$ -c $ARG2$
        }
```

In Example 2-35 there are three macros: $USER1$, $ARG1$, and $ARG2$. I discussed the $USER1$ macro earlier. The $ARG1$ and $ARG2$ macros equate to the first and second variables passed to the command. So if you looked at the command_line directive from Example 2-35 with the macros substituted, you'd see

```
command_line    /usr/local/nagios/libexec/check_users -w 20 -c 50
```

You can specify up to 32 $ARGx$ macros, using the macro names $ARG1$ through $ARG32$. You can also pass in a variety of other macros. This includes many of those I defined earlier in this chapter, such as $HOSTNAME$ or $SERVICEDESC$. You can see a full list of the possible macros in the Nagios documentation at http://nagios.sourceforge.net/docs/2_0/macros.html.

Tip This section should give you an introduction to check commands and their structure. I'll discuss check commands, plug-ins, and macros in more detail in Chapter 5.

Event Handler Commands

The next type of command is an event handler command. I discussed event handling in some detail in the "Defining Your First Host" section. An event handler is executed whenever a state change occurs. Event handlers can be used to initiate actions that fix a problem before notifications are generated—for example, to attempt to restart a service or process. You could also potentially use event handlers to log events to a database or a logging system. They can be executed for hosts and services or configured globally to execute for every state change that occurs.

Event handler commands usually execute shell or Perl scripts and take a series of macros as arguments. I've listed some of the most commonly used macros in Table 2-19.

Table 2-19. *Host and Service Macros for Event Handlers*

Macro	Description
$HOSTSTATE$	Current state of the host
$HOSTSTATETYPE$	Host state type: soft or hard
$HOSTATTEMPT$	Number of retry checks made on the host
$SERVICESTATE$	Current state of the service
$SERVICESTATETYPE$	Current service state type: soft or hard
$SERVICEATTEMPT$	Number of retry checks made on the service

Event handlers normally act in different ways depending on the state and state type of a host or service. For example, you could pass the macros for the host state and state type into a shell script. The shell script would evaluate the value of these macros and act accordingly. Thus, if the host was in a hard DOWN state, you could perform one action and if the host was in another state, you could perform a different action.

Let's look an example of an event handler command:

```
define command{
            command_name       start-smtp-server
            command_line       $USER1$/eventhandlers/start-smtp-server➡
$SERVICESTATE$ $SERVICESTATETYPE$
            }
```

You can see that I've specified a command called start-smtp-server, which calls a script called start-smtp-server. I pass into that script the two macros related to the service state and state type. The script could then perform an action based on the state and state type indicated—for example, starting the SMTP server. I could also use the other user-defined macro from Example 2-34 here to replace the path:

```
command_line $USER2$/start-smtp-server $SERVICESTATE$ $SERVICESTATETYPE$
```

Lastly, event handlers can also be configured to time out using the event_handler_directive in the nagios.cfg configuration file. You can see this directive with its default setting of 60 seconds here:

```
event_handler_timeout=60
```

I'll discuss event handlers in more detail in Chapter 7.

Notification Commands

The last type of command is the notification command. It is these commands that Nagios uses to send you notifications and alerts. For example, a common notification command would send an email message to you with the details of the event. In Example 2-36 I've shown a notification command from the sample configuration files used to send service notifications.

Example 2-36. *Email Notification Command for a Service*

```
define command{
    command_name    notify-by-email
    command_line    /usr/bin/printf "%b" "***** Nagios  *****\n\nNotification Type:➡
$NOTIFICATIONTYPE$\n\nService: $SERVICEDESC$\n\Host: $HOSTALIAS$\n\Address:➡
$HOSTADDRESS$\n\nState: $SERVICESTATE$\n\n\Date/Time: ➡
$LONGDATETIME$\n\n\Additional ➡
Info:\n\n$OUTPUT$" | /bin/mail -s "** $NOTIFICATIONTYPE$ alert ➡
$HOSTALIAS$/$SERVICEDESC$ is $SERVICESTATE$ **" $CONTACTEMAIL$
        }
```

As you can see from Example 2-36, notification commands use the command_name directive to name the command and the command_line directive to define the command to be executed. Notification commands often contain a number of macros that allow you to pass values containing information about the host or service that has generated the event. In Example 2-36, the printf binary is used to generate text that is fed into the mail binary and emailed to a contact. The email generated by the command would tell the recipient the type of notification being sent—for example, a problem or a recovery and variety of information about the service that generated the event. You can see that the last macro used in the command is $CONTACTEMAIL$, which is the email address of the contact for which the email is destined.

You can see other examples of notification commands in the misccommands.cfg and minimal.cfg sample configuration files. There are commands for notifications of host and service events contained in this sample configuration. These commands should work on your system without modification, but you may wish to tweak them further to suit your environment or to send the information you require for your notifications. To do this, you should review the full list of macros available to you and the contexts in which they can be used. The best source for this information is the Nagios documentation at http://nagios.source➡ forge.net/docs/2_0/macros.html. I'll discuss notifications further in Chapter 6.

Checkpoint

- I recommend you define your Nagios configuration objects in separate files using cfg_dir directives in the nagios.cfg file.

- If you don't define an address for a host, then Nagios will assume it is a TCP/IP connection and attempt to resolve the host's address using the host_name directive. If you do not have DNS resolution or if your DNS resolution fails, you will not be able to check your host or the services on that host.

- You generally should not schedule host checks on a regular basis but instead rely on the fact that if your service checks succeed, then the host should be available. If a service check fails, Nagios will check your host.

- If you use state retention, you should consider whether you retain status information as well as nonstatus information. If you retain nonstatus information, you may notice that changes to some configuration variables are not picked up between Nagios server restarts. You can set the `retain_nonstatus_information` directive to 0 to disable the retention of nonstatus information. The Nagios developer has reported some issues with this approach, and you should monitor your environment to ensure it is functioning normally.

- The scheduling of your service checks can be a complicated process. I recommend that you generally use the default "smart" settings and allow Nagios to automatically schedule your checks.

- Object definition can be repetitive and time-consuming, so you should use templates to define your objects wherever possible. They will save you considerable time in defining your objects.

- If you wish your contacts to receive notifications, they must be members of the contact groups that are specified in your host and service object definitions. This means you must specify at least one contact group.

- When defining when notifications are sent, you need to remember that the `notifications_options` directives that control the generation of notifications can be configured in host, service, and contact definitions. Ensure that all of these notification options are correctly configured.

- You can use resource configuration files to hold user-defined macros and other information that you wish to restrict access to from the web console. These files are defined to Nagios using the `resource_file` directive in the `nagios.cfg` file. The resource files can be further secured by limiting their permissions.

Resources

- Nagios Documentation: `http://nagios.sourceforge.net/docs/2_0/`

CHAPTER 3

■■■

Security and Administration

In this chapter I'll look at the security and administration of Nagios, focusing on the security of your web console, the settings and commands used to administer Nagios, and the logging that your Nagios server generates. The security of your Nagios server is important. Your Nagios monitoring environment usually contains a considerable amount of configuration information about your environment, including details of the hosts and services such as IP addresses and running services. This information could prove a boon to an attacker looking for weak points in your environment to compromise. Additionally, securing your Nagios server ensures that it will not be a conduit for an attack.

I'll also look at some of the administration functions of your Nagios server, including starting and stopping your server, managing and rotating the log file, and specifying what Nagios will and will not log.

General Security Guidelines

There are a few basic security guidelines that you should be aware of when running a Nagios server. The first guideline is not so much a guideline as a general series of recommendations to harden and secure your host from intruders.[1] There are a few keys things you can do that will help with this:

- Only install the packages and components you require for your host. Any host build should start from your operating system or distribution's "minimal" build and then add any required packages.

- Update your systems frequently and ensure any known vulnerabilities are addressed using patching, updates, or workarounds. Tools like apt-get or yum will help with this process.

- Remove any unneeded users and groups. Also change the passwords of, and preferably lock, any user accounts that do not need to log in. Remember to choose strong passwords and change them on a regular basis.

- Remove any unnecessary process, daemons, or services. A lot of distributions come with a number of services you probably don't need—for example, unless you need NFS you should disable it and any related services.

---

1. I've written a book specific to securing Linux called *Hardening Linux* (www.apress.com/book/ bookDisplay.html?bID=395), also published by Apress, that may assist with this.

- Firewall your host. Install a firewall such as `iptables` to your host and secure it. Ensure your firewall handles both incoming and outgoing traffic so as to only allow those services and daemons that you actually require to send and receive traffic on your host.

- Secure incoming connections to your host. This includes tools such as `ssh` where you should, for example, disallow `root` logins. This also applies to securing services, such as mail, which you might want to allow through your firewall. Limit access to these services to the resources, hosts, and networks that require them.

- Install a host-based intrusion detection system (HIDS) or an integrity checking application such as Tripwire.[2]

- Look at hardening your host's base operating system and kernel with additions such as Security-Enhanced Linux (SELinux) or Openwall.[3] Also look at tools like Bastille that perform automatic hardening for you.[4]

- Log. Log some more. And then sort, correlate, alert, and, most importantly, review your logs and alerts.

- Review your operating system's or distribution's security announcements and general security lists for vulnerabilities or bugs relevant to your system. Awareness is the first step in prevention.

Do Not Run Nagios As the root User

Do not run Nagios as the `root` user is the second guideline. Nagios does not need the level of privilege provided by the `root` user. Additionally, if your Nagios installation is compromised, an attacker could perform actions as the `root` user and thereby totally compromise your host. To reduce the risk of this occurring, I recommend you run Nagios as another user.

In Chapter 1 we created a user and group for our Nagios server both called `nagios`. We then configured Nagios to run using this user and group. This allows Nagios to drop any privileges after starting and then run as a normal user. You can see which user and group Nagios is configured to run as in the `nagios.cfg` configuration file. Find the following directives:

```
nagios_user=nagios
nagios_group=nagios
```

The settings of these two directives will indicate which user and group Nagios is configured to run as. You should change them to the user and group that you intend Nagios to run as.

Securing and Administering for External Commands

You should also consider whether you intend to use external commands. External commands are checks and commands that can be submitted to the Nagios server through the external command file. We discussed configuring external commands and the external command file in Chapter 1.

---

2. See http://sourceforge.net/projects/tripwire/.

3. See www.nsa.gov/selinux/ and www.openwall.com/.

4. See www.bastille-linux.org/.

The external command file is a named pipe that is created when Nagios is started and removed when Nagios is stopped. External commands can include commands issued from the web console—for example, to turn on or off notifications. It can also receive commands from event handlers or scripts from the command line.

Tip You can see a full list of the possible external commands in the Nagios documentation at `http://nagios.sourceforge.net/docs/2_0/extcommands.html`.

By default, external commands are turned off in your Nagios configuration. This is controlled by the `check_external_commands` directive in your `nagios.cfg` configuration file. By default, this directive is set to 0, which indicates that external commands are disabled. Nagios will not process any commands submitted to the external command file. You can see this here:

```
check_external_commands=0
```

A setting of 1 would be required to enable external commands. If you don't use the web console or event handlers, you should leave external commands disabled.

Two other directives in the `nagios.cfg file` have an impact on external commands:

```
command_check_interval=-1
command_file=/usr/local/nagios/var/rw/nagios.cmd
```

The first directive, `command_check_interval`, specifies how often Nagios should check the external command file for external commands. The setting of -1 (the default) indicates that Nagios will check the file as often as possible. A setting of 1 would result in Nagios checking the command file once every minute.[5] You can also specify a check interval in seconds by suffixing an interval with s as shown here:

```
command_check_interval=30s
```

This directive would result in Nagios checking the external command file every 30 seconds. I recommend you leave this at the default setting of -1 to ensure that Nagios checks the external command file frequently.

The next directive controls the name and location of the external command file. The default filename and location for the Nagios source installation is `/usr/local/nagios/var/rw/nagios.cmd`. As we discussed in Chapter 1, the ownership and permissions of the `/usr/local/nagios/rw` directory and the `nagios.cmd` file are important to both the security and functioning of external commands. To receive external commands from the web console, both the user running the Nagios server and the user running your web server need to have read and write permissions to the external command file and the directory it is contained in.

Why the directory too? Well, the external command file is created when the Nagios server is started and is deleted when the Nagios server is stopped. Therefore, if you want the command file to be owned by the command group we defined in Chapter 1, you need some way of ensuring this ownership is continued between server restarts. To achieve this, you must

---

5. This is true only if the `interval_length` directive has been left as the default length.

enable the group sticky bit on the directory to force new files created in the directory to inherit the group owner of the directory rather than the group owner of the process that created the file.

In Chapter 1, we configured Nagios to use a group called ncmd as the external command group. This group has a membership of the user the Nagios process runs as and the user that the web server runs as—in our case, nagios and apache, respectively. Making this the group of the nagios.cmd file provides the required permissions to both the web server and the Nagios server. We defined this ncmd group to Nagios during the configure process using the --nagios-command-group configure option. We also ran the make step, make install-commandmode. This step changes the ownership of the directory that holds the external command file—in our case, /usr/local/nagios/var/rw—to the user Nagios runs as and the command group we created, ncmd. It also sets the required permissions and sets the group sticky bit on the external command file directory. Here are the resulting directory permissions:

```
drwxrwsr-x  2 nagios ncmd    4096 Jul  3 23:16 rw
```

You could also achieve this same ownership and permissions with the following commands:

```
puppy# chown nagios.ncmd /usr/local/nagios/var/rw
puppy# chmod 2775 /usr/local/nagios/var/rw
```

The external command file, nagios.cmd, will be created when the server starts and will have ownership and permissions like these:

```
prw-rw----  1 nagios ncmd    0 Jul  4 00:31 nagios.cmd
```

With these permissions, the users running both the web server and the Nagios server will have read and write permissions to the command file.

But you can also further reduce the permissions used on the command file directory to secure it. Instead of using the default permissions, override them with this command:

```
puppy# chmod 2710 /usr/local/nagios/var/rw
```

This will result in the following set of permissions:

```
drwx--s---  2 nagios ncmd    4096 Jul  4 02:04 rw
```

You should carefully test that your external commands work after imposing the new permissions.

Additionally, after changing any of the external commands directives, the ownership, and the permissions of the external command file, you should restart the Nagios server and your web server.

Securing the Web Console

The web console is made up of an HTML front-end and a series of CGI programs. These programs can have both an authentication and authorization mechanism applied to them. So why do we need this? Well, first the information contained in the web console could be very useful to an attacker to learn about your hosts and environment. Second, the web console allows you to interact with your hosts and services and turn on and off monitoring among other actions. This can allow an attacker to not only compromise your hosts but also disable any alerting or monitoring that might indicate there is an issue or attack.

Finally, a number of Nagios users place their web-monitoring console on an Internet-facing web server to allow staff to provide remote support. In this position, your Nagios web console can act as a conduit into your network for an attacker.

■**Caution** Personally I don't recommend placing your Nagios server on the Web. If you insist on doing so, you should ensure authentication and authorization are enabled and that you configure Nagios to use SSL for your web traffic to prevent sniffing or eavesdropping on your Nagios traffic.[6]

So what is authentication and what is authorization? Well, authentication is the process of verifying who someone is—for example, in the case of Nagios, using a username and password. Once authenticated, the process of authorization determines what access the authenticated users have to particular resources. We'll configure authentication and authorization using a combination of your web server and the Nagios `cgi.cfg` configuration file. For the purposes of this section I'll assume you're using the Apache web server. If you aren't using Apache, you'll need to adapt the information to your chosen web server.

■**Note** The `cgi.cfg` file contains a number of additional directives other than those that deal with authorization, and I've discussed some of these in other chapters. The file is heavily commented, and I recommend you read it to gain insight into what the other directives do.

Web Console Authentication with Apache

Let's start by configuring authentication on the Apache web server. Nagios uses Apache's inbuilt authentication to authenticate users to the web console. Nagios has two types of users: authenticated users and authenticated contacts. Each of these types of users has different potential levels of authentication and authorization. The first type, authenticated users, have authenticated to the web server with a username and password. The second type, authenticated contacts, are authenticated users whose username matches the short name of a contact. So we have a user, jsmith, who has entered his username and password when prompted and then authenticated to the web server. The authentication credentials are passed to the Nagios server. If the username provided, jsmith, matches the short name of a contact, as defined by the contact_name directive, this authenticated user becomes an authenticated contact.

---

6. Additionally if you wish to place your Nagios Apache web server on the Web, I recommend hardening your web server. A recommended reference is *Hardening Apache* (www.apress.com/book/bookDisplay.html?bID=320).

So what is the difference? Authenticated users are granted some generic rights to view the web console. Authenticated contacts are granted further rights to view and manipulate the hosts and services for which they are contacts. So if they are members of a contact group that is defined using the contactgroups directive to the host or service, they can view and interact with that host or service. Authenticated contacts only have rights to hosts or services that they are contacts for.

Let's begin by defining how we add authenticated users to our web console. In Chapter 1, we configured our Apache web server with Directory directives that specify the location and configuration of the Nagios HTML and CGI files. In Example 3-1, you can see the directives we defined in the httpd.conf file.

Example 3-1. *Nagios Directory Directives*

```
ScriptAlias /nagios/cgi-bin /usr/local/nagios/sbin
<Directory "/usr/local/nagios/sbin">
    AllowOverride None
    Options ExecCGI
    Order allow,deny
    Allow from all
</Directory>

Alias /nagios /usr/local/nagios/share
<Directory "/usr/local/nagios/share">
    AllowOverride None
    Options None
    Order allow,deny
    Allow from all
</Directory>
```

If you refer to the Nagios documentation, you'll notice one major difference between the sample configuration and the configuration in Example 3-1:[7] the AllowOverride directive is not set to AuthConfig. This directive controls what options are allowed in an .htaccess file. An .htaccess file allows you to add additional directives to a particular directory. The .htaccess file is created in a particular document directory, and then the directory is defined to Apache with a Directory directive. The AllowOverride directive lets you specify which additional directives can be used in the .htaccess file. The AuthConfig option allows the use of authentication directives in the .htaccess file.

We're still going to use this Apache authentication to perform our authentication, but we won't place our authentication directives in an .htaccess file. This is because while the prevailing attitude is that you should use .htaccess files to store authentication configuration, it is actually not the ideal approach. There are two reasons for this. The first is performance. Every time a document is loaded, the .htaccess file or files must be loaded also. This adds an overhead to your server. Second, .htaccess files imply exceptions to your server configuration. Authentication and security controls can thus be defined in different places and allowed to override your main server configuration. As a security model, this is not a good idea. Centralized

---

7. See http://nagios.sourceforge.net/docs/2_0/installweb.html.

control over your authentication is a better configuration model.[8] So instead of imbedding our authentication directives in an `.htaccess` file, let's include them inside our existing `Directory` directives, which is the recommended approach.

To use authentication, we're going to rely on Apache Basic authentication (you can also use Apache Digest authentication for your authentication with some caveats that we will discuss in the sidebar "Digest Authentication"). Example 3-2 shows how to enable Apache Basic authentication.

Example 3-2. *Authentication Directives*

```
ScriptAlias /nagios/cgi-bin /usr/local/nagios/sbin
<Directory "/usr/local/nagios/sbin">
    AllowOverride None
    Options ExecCGI
    Order allow,deny
    Allow from all
    AuthName "Nagios Access"
    AuthType Basic
    AuthUserFile /usr/local/nagios/etc/htpasswd.users
    Require valid-user
</Directory>

Alias /nagios /usr/local/nagios/share
<Directory "/usr/local/nagios/share">
    AllowOverride None
    Options None
    Order allow,deny
    Allow from all
</Directory>
```

As you can see, we've added four directives to the first `Directory` directive. The first `Directory` directive defines the location of the CGIs to Apache, and we'll apply a username and password to them. This means that before you can access the CGIs, you must input a username and password. Because we haven't added any authentication directives to the second `Directory` directive, which represents the HTML files, we can still browse to the Nagios server site without authentication being required.

The first directive, `AuthName`, specifies the name or realm of the authentication. The authentication realm names the scope of the authentication. It is also used as the title of the pop-up box in which you enter your username and password when you are prompted to authenticate.

The second directive, `AuthType`, defines the type of authentication being used. For Basic authentication we specify `Basic`. If you wanted to use Digest authentication, you would specify `Digest` here.

The third directive, `AuthUserFile`, specifies the location of the file that holds your usernames and passwords. This file should be located outside of the directory that is protected by the authentication. I recommend you store it in your Nagios configuration file directory. If

---

8. You can read about this in more detail at `http://httpd.apache.org/docs-2.0/howto/htaccess.html`.

you've installed from source, this will be the /usr/local/nagios/etc/ directory. You can call the file by any name. In Example 3-2 we located the file in /usr/local/nagios/etc and called it htpasswd.users.

The fourth and last directive, Require, specifies which users are allowed to be authenticated. In Example 3-2 we've set this directive to valid-user, which indicates that only valid users that exist in the htpasswd.users file can be authenticated. You can also specify a list of individual users in this directive:

```
Require jbloggs jsmith
```

If the Require directive was configured like this, only the jbloggs and jsmith users could be authenticated to the web server. All other users would be rejected.

Once you've defined the authentication directives, you need to create the file to hold your users and passwords. We do this using a command called htpasswd that comes with Apache. Example 3-3 shows this command in action.

■Tip On some systems using Apache version 2, this command may be called htpasswd2. This is true of Gentoo and Debian, among other distributions.

Example 3-3. *Using the htpasswd Command*

```
puppy# htpasswd -c /usr/local/nagios/etc/htpasswd.users jsmith
```

```
New password:
Re-type new password:
Adding password for user jsmith
```

The htpasswd command has two variables: the location of the file that holds our usernames and passwords and the username of the user. It has a single command-line switch, -c, that is relevant to creating users for Nagios.[9] The -c switch is used when you first create a new password file. In Example 3-3 we're creating a new password file with the -c option that will be called htpasswd.users and located at /usr/local/nagios/etc. This is in line with what we configured in Example 3-2 as the name and location of the password file. The next time we run the htpasswd command, we don't need to specify the -c option since we've already created the password file.

Next, in Example 3-3, we've specified the user we're adding, jsmith. Then when we run the htpasswd command, we'll be prompted for a password and then a verification of the entered password. Both passwords must match. If they do, then the command will be successful and the user will be added to the specified password file.

Be sure to add all the users who need access to the Nagios web console. You can either add users who will become authenticated users, or you can use the names of your contacts so as to create authenticated contacts that can interact with the hosts and services they manage. I recommend you use authenticated contacts to make management of your hosts and services easier.

---

9. You can see the other available command-line switches by reading the htpasswd man page.

You can also optionally add authentication for your HTML files as well by adding the required directives to the second `Directory` directive in Example 3-2, as you can see here:

```
Alias /nagios /usr/local/nagios/share
<Directory "/usr/local/nagios/share">
    AllowOverride None
    Options None
    Order allow,deny
    Allow from all
    AuthName "Nagios Access"
    AuthType Basic
    AuthUserFile /usr/local/nagios/etc/htpasswd.users
    Require valid-user
</Directory>
```

These directives will use the same password file as the CGI scripts. You could specify a different password file, but I don't recommend it as doing so probably overly complicates your environment without substantially adding to your security.

Now instead of being prompted to enter your username and password when you use one of the CGI files, you will be prompted to input your password when you browse to the HTML files, as you can see in Figure 3-1.

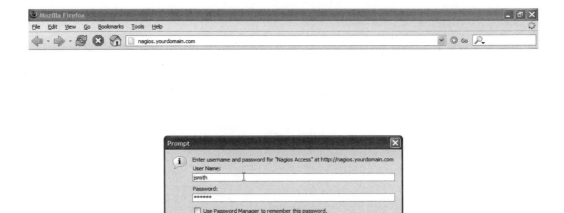

Figure 3-1. *Web console authentication*

DIGEST AUTHENTICATION

The Nagios documentation suggests using Apache Basic authentication. This means your username and password are sent across the network in cleartext. Anyone with a password sniffer can read your username and password. As your username and password is sent with every request, not just when you first authenticate, an attacker doesn't even need to sniff at a particular time. So rather than using the Basic authentication method, you can use Digest authentication. Digest authentication is a more advanced form of Apache authentication that uses MD5 hashes of your password instead of the cleartext password. Digest authentication is still not perfect; a serious attacker with a strong understanding of HTTP traffic can extract the hash and use it to authenticate themselves to the Nagios server. But it is an improvement over Basic authentication.

While Digest is a better choice than Basic authentication, there are three caveats. The first is that Digest authentication is only supported on Apache version 1.3.8 and above and is marked as an experimental module. Personally I haven't experienced any issues with using Digest authentication, and if you take into consideration all three caveats, I recommend using it.

The second caveat is that not all browsers support Digest authentication. The browsers that do support Digest authentication are Opera, Amaya, Mozilla (including Firefox), Netscape, and Microsoft Internet Explorer (with some issues). The third caveat is that Internet Explorer has a known bug in which it does not act in an RFC-compliant manner with Digest authentication. When used with URIs with query strings in them, Digest authentication fails. The Nagios web console uses query strings in its URIs and thus much of the web console fails. This can be worked around, but only in more recent versions of Apache. In Apache 2.0.51 and higher, you can add a `BrowserMatch` directive to your `httpd.conf` configuration file:

```
BrowserMatch "MSIE" AuthDigestEnableQueryStringHack=On
```

After adding the directive and restarting Apache, you should be able to use Digest authentication with Internet Explorer.

Enabling Digest authentication is simple to implement and merely requires some minor changes to the directives you need to use in your `Directory` directive to define authentication. Then instead of using the `htpasswd` command to create passwords, you use the `htdigest` command. You can read about Digest authentication and how to implement it at `http://httpd.apache.org/docs/howto/auth.html#digest`.

■Tip You can also incorporate additional security to your CGIs and external commands by using CGIWrap. Implementing CGIWrap can be very complicated, and a number of issues exist related to CGIWrap and Apache authentication. I don't recommend using it unless you fully understand how CGIs interact with Apache. If you are using virtual hosts, an alternative option is to enable the suEXEC package to protect your CGIs.[10]

---

10. See `http://cgiwrap.unixtools.org/` and `http://httpd.apache.org/docs/suexec.html`.

Nagios Authentication and Authorization

Once you've defined the web console authentication using Apache, you need to configure Nagios to provide further authentication and authorization. This configuration is performed using directives in the cgi.cfg file, which is located with your other configuration files. Nagios authentication and authorization provides access to two facets of the web console: access to view and manipulate the hosts and services you are monitoring and access to the various CGIs that make up the web console.

Tip I'll discuss how to set up authenticated access in this section, and I'll identify exactly what access is required for each of the CGIs in Chapter 4 when we examine the web console in detail.

The first directive we'll look at in the cgi.cfg file is called use_authentication. It controls whether authentication is enabled for the Nagios web console and whether Nagios will use the authentication credentials provided from the web server. The directive looks like this:

```
use_authentication=1
```

A setting of 1 enables authentication and a setting of 0 disables it. The default setting is 1.

Tip I strongly recommend that you do not disable authentication. A Nagios web console without authentication is open to attacks that could disable your monitoring, and it provides considerable information about your environment.

If you've enabled authentication and you haven't defined any users to Nagios, when you try to browse to the Nagios CGIs you will receive an error message indicating that you do not have permission to the resource you are trying to access, as shown in Figure 3-2.

This error indicates that Nagios has authentication enabled but no users have been defined to Nagios. Nagios authentication and authorization is managed by adding users, either authenticated users or contacts, to a series of directives that define various levels of access in the cgi.cfg configuration file. Directives in the cgi.cfg file are constructed in the same way as directives in the nagios.cfg file, as you can see here:

```
directive=setting
```

Each directive consists of a directive name and a setting separated by an = sign. Comments can be added to the file by prefixing them with a # sign. At this point, let's add some users to Nagios and examine some of the additional directives in the cgi.cfg file that control authentication. In Example 3-4 you can see an example of several of the available authorization directives.

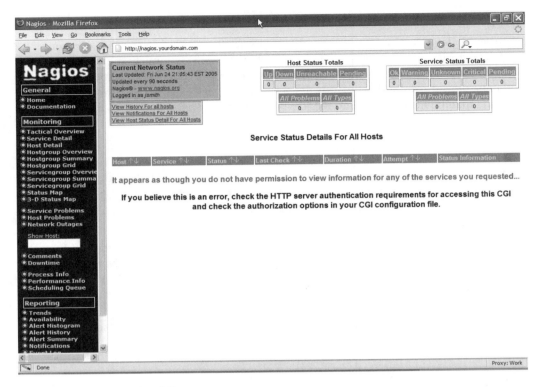

Figure 3-2. *Authentication failure*

Example 3-4. *Authorization Directives*

```
authorized_for_all_hosts=jsmith,jbloggs
authorized_for_all_services=jsmith,jbloggs
authorized_for_system_information=jsmith
```

As you can see in Example 3-4, the setting for each authorization directive consists of a list of users, separated by commas. For example, the authorized_for_system_information directive has a setting of jsmith, which indicates that the user jsmith has permission to view the Nagios process information.

If you wish to specify that all users have access to a particular function, you can use the * symbol:

```
authorized_for_all_services=*
```

This directive setting would provide all authenticated users with access to view information about all services defined on the Nagios server. The * symbol will work for all authorization directives.

Table 3-1 contains the full list of possible authorization directives and describes each one.

Table 3-1. *Authorization Directives*

Directive	Description
`authorized_for_system_information`	Users who can access the Nagios process information
`authorized_for_configuration_information`	Users who can see all configuration information
`authorized_for_system_commands`	Users who can issue commands through the web console
`authorized_for_all_services`	Users who are authorized to all services
`authorized_for_all_hosts`	Users who are authorized to all hosts
`authorized_for_all_service_commands`	Users who can issue service related external commands
`authorized_for_all_host_commands`	Users who can issue host-related external commands

The first directive in Table 3-1, `authorized_for_system_information`, provides access to view information about the Nagios process and the server, such as when the process started and what settings are set on the server. The second directive, `authorized_for_configuration_information`, provides authorization to view all configuration information for your monitoring environment. This includes hosts, services, contacts, and commands, as well as all other object types. The third directive, `authorized_for_system_commands`, controls who has access to start, stop, or restart the Nagios process from the web console.

The next two directives, `authorized_for_all_services` and `authorized_for_all_hosts`, control which users can view all service and host information on the web console. As you may remember, authenticated contacts can view the information about the hosts and services for which they are contacts. These directives allow you to specify users who can view the information of all the hosts and services.

The last two directives in Table 3-1, `authorized_for_all_service_commands` and `authorized_for_all_host_commands`, allow you to specify users who are authorized to issue external commands to services and hosts, respectively. This allows you to perform actions such as disabling active checks of the host or service, or enabling or disabling notifications for the host or service. I'll discuss the possible actions you can perform with external commands in Chapter 4 when we examine the web console in more detail.

■**Note** By default, all of the authorization directives are commented out in the `cgi.cfg` file. You will need to uncomment them and add any required users to the directives.

Default Users

The last directive we'll look at is called `default_user_name`:

```
#default_user_name=guest
```

I've shown this directive commented out, as it is by default in the `cgi.cfg` configuration file. The `default_user_name` directive allows you to provide a username that you can add to the authorization directives that can access the web console without authentication. This still implies that you have the use_authentication directive turned on by setting it to 1. Then you can uncomment the default_user_name directive, disable the web server authentication, and add the default user, in this case guest, to the authorization directives that you want to grant access. For example, if you wished the default user to have access to all of the hosts on the system, you would use the following line:

```
authorized_for_all_hosts=guest
```

Default Authorization

In addition to any authorization directives you define for authenticated contacts, they have access to the hosts and services for which they are contacts. For services, this access includes

- Viewing of service status

- Viewing of service configuration

- Ability to view service history and notifications

- Ability to issue commands to the service

For hosts, this access includes

- Viewing of host status

- Viewing of host configuration

- Ability to view host history and notifications

- Ability to issue commands to the host

Authenticated contacts that have access to a particular host because they are a contact for that host also have the same access to all the services on that host as if they were a contact for that service. For example, if I'm an authenticated contact for the kitten host, I would be able to view the status, configuration, service history, and notifications as well as issue commands to all the services defined on that host.

■Tip By default no one has authorization to the Nagios logs or process information, or the ability to issue commands to the Nagios process. Additionally, the configuration of contacts, contact groups, host groups, time periods, and commands is not available to any user by default. You must explicitly add users to the respective directives to grant them this access.

Nagios Administration

A number of activities are related to the administration of the Nagios server that you must understand if you are going to run a Nagios monitoring environment. The first is starting and stopping the Nagios server. This includes both starting and stopping from the command line and via an init script. In addition, the Nagios server has a logging infrastructure that you should both configure and understand. This is especially important because Nagios communicates much of the status of the server and any error messages encountered via this logging infrastructure. In this section we'll step through both these activities and provide a detailed explanation of this functionality.

Starting and Stopping the Nagios Server

In Chapter 1 I demonstrated how to install Nagios and the related plug-ins, and in Chapter 2 I showed you how to define some of the basics of your monitoring environment, including hosts, services, and contacts. In the first half of this chapter, I explained how to secure the web console. This may seem like a lot of work, but all of these steps are required before you can start the Nagios server. It is especially important to ensure that your Nagios monitoring environment is valid and complete. This requires that the content of your .cfg files is complete and that the syntax of the objects that represent your hosts, services, and the other elements of your monitoring environment is correct. I'll demonstrate how to confirm this in this section when we discuss how to start and stop the Nagios daemon.

Example 3-5 shows the required command to start the Nagios daemon, and I'll explain how this is constructed next.

Example 3-5. *Starting the Nagios Daemon*

```
puppy# /usr/local/nagios/bin/nagios -d /usr/local/nagios/etc/nagios.cfg
```

Let's briefly look at Example 3-5. First, to start Nagios you run the nagios binary. This is located by default in /usr/local/nagios/sbin/ if you performed the source installation and in /usr/bin/ if you installed from RPM. Also, Example 3-5 uses the command-line switch -d. This switch tells Nagios to start the process and daemonize. After the command-line switch the location of the nagios.cfg file is specified. As you should be aware from Chapter 2, this file controls the server's configuration, and when starting, the Nagios server has to load and parse this file.

In Example 3-5 the Nagios daemon loads the configuration specified in the /usr/local/nagios/etc/nagios.cfg file. This includes loading the definitions of any objects configured to the Nagios server.

■**Note** I discussed how configuration files are defined in the nagios.cfg file using the cfg_file directive in Chapter 2.

If you start the Nagios server and the data contained in your object files is incomplete, invalid, or incorrect, the Nagios server will fail to start. You will need to correct the configuration data before the server will start. You can see an example of a failed startup in Example 3-6.

Example 3-6. *Nagios Server Startup Failure*

```
puppy# /usr/local/nagios/bin/nagios /usr/local/nagios/etc/nagios.cfg
Nagios 2.0
Copyright (c) 1999-2005 Ethan Galstad (www.nagios.org)
Last Modified: 04-03-2005
License: GPL

Nagios 2.0 starting... (PID=16053)
Error: Could not find any host matching 'kitten'
Error: Could not expand hostgroups and/or hosts specified in service
(config file '/usr/local/nagios/etc/services.cfg', starting on line 77)
Bailing out due to one or more errors encountered in the configuration
files. Run Nagios from the command line with the -v option to verify your
 config before restarting. (PID=16053)
```

In Example 3-6 you can see that the Nagios server has failed to start because of two errors:

```
Error: Could not find any host matching 'kitten'
Error: Could not expand hostgroups and/or hosts specified in service
(config file '/usr/local/nagios/etc/services.cfg', starting on line 77)
```

These errors indicate issues with your object configuration, most specifically with the configuration of the kitten host. You will also note that Nagios makes a recommendation to run the binary again but this time using the –v command-line switch. This switch allows you to test your configuration for correctness without starting the server, as you can see in Example 3-7.

Example 3-7. *Nagios Server Validation*

```
puppy# /usr/local/nagios/bin/nagios -v /usr/local/nagios/etc/nagios.cfg

Nagios 2.0
Copyright (c) 1999-2005 Ethan Galstad (www.nagios.org)
Last Modified: 04-03-2005
License: GPL

Reading configuration data...

Error: Could not find hostgroup 'syd_servers' specified in host
 'duckling' definition (config file '/usr/local/nagios/etc/hosts.cfg',
 starting on line 32)

***> One or more problems was encountered while processing the config files...

    Check your configuration file(s) to ensure that they contain valid
    directives and data defintions. If you are upgrading from a previous
    version of Nagios, you should be aware that some variables/definitions
    may have been removed or modified in this version. Make sure to read
    the HTML documentation regarding the config files, as well as the
    'Whats New' section to find out what has changed.
```

In Example 3-7 we have run the nagios binary in verification mode, which checks the syntax of all your object configuration files. To do this, you need to specify the –v command-line switch and the location of your nagios.cfg configuration file. This will trigger the syntax check that you can see in Example 3-7 and then exit without trying to start the Nagios server.

In Example 3-7 you can see the error I've highlighted on the following line:

```
Error: Could not find hostgroup 'syd_servers' specified in host 'duckling'
definition (config file '/usr/local/nagios/etc/hosts.cfg', starting on line 32)
```

This indicates that the host group syd_servers, which is specified in a host called duckling, is not defined. To fix the issue, you must define the host group and then try to start the Nagios server again. Nagios detects most object definition errors and will present you with a clear and easy-to-understand error message that should provide the information you need to correct the issue.

In Example 3-7 the check resulted in errors. In Example 3-8 the verification mode is run without any errors being detected.

Example 3-8. *Verification Success*

```
puppy# /usr/local/nagios/bin/nagios -v /usr/local/nagios/etc/nagios.cfg

Nagios 2.0
Copyright (c) 1999-2005 Ethan Galstad (www.nagios.org)
Last Modified: 04-03-2005
License: GPL

Reading configuration data...

Running pre-flight check on configuration data...

Checking services...
        Checked 7 services.
Checking hosts...
        Checked 2 hosts.
Checking host groups...
        Checked 1 host groups.
Checking service groups...
        Checked 4 service groups.
Checking contacts...
        Checked 1 contacts.
Checking contact groups...
        Checked 2 contact groups.
Checking service escalations...
        Checked 0 service escalations.
Checking service dependencies...
        Checked 0 service dependencies.
Checking host escalations...
        Checked 0 host escalations.
```

```
Checking host dependencies...
        Checked 0 host dependencies.
Checking commands...
        Checked 25 commands.
Checking time periods...
        Checked 2 time periods.
Checking extended host info definitions...
        Checked 0 extended host info definitions.
Checking extended service info definitions...
        Checked 0 extended service info definitions.
Checking for circular paths between hosts...
Checking for circular host and service dependencies...
Checking global event handlers...
Checking obsessive compulsive processor commands...
Checking misc settings...

Total Warnings: 0
Total Errors:   0

Things look okay - No serious problems were detected during the pre-flight check
```

This would indicate that the Nagios server should start without issues.

The Nagios binary has one final command-line switch, -s. The -s switch displays the projected scheduling information for your hosts and services. It also makes recommendations about how you should tweak your Nagios configuration to provide better scheduling and performance of your check. As with the -v command-line switch, you need to specify the location of your nagios.cfg file to allow the -s switch to function correctly. You can see an example of the -s switch in Example 3-9.

Example 3-9. *Scheduling Check Using the -s Switch*

```
puppy# ./nagios -s /usr/local/nagios/etc/nagios.cfg

Nagios 2.0
Copyright (c) 1999-2005 Ethan Galstad (www.nagios.org)
Last Modified: 04-03-2005
License: GPL

Projected scheduling information for host and service
checks is listed below. This information assumes that
you are going to start running Nagios with your current
config files.
```

```
HOST SCHEDULING INFORMATION
---------------------------
Total hosts:                      2
Total scheduled hosts:            0
Host inter-check delay method:    SMART
Average host check interval:      0.00 sec
Host inter-check delay:           0.00 sec
Max host check spread:            30 min
First scheduled check:            N/A
Last scheduled check:             N/A


SERVICE SCHEDULING INFORMATION
------------------------------
Total services:                   7
Total scheduled services:         7
Service inter-check delay method: SMART
Average service check interval:   300.00 sec
Inter-check delay:                42.86 sec
Interleave factor method:         SMART
Average services per host:        3.50
Service interleave factor:        4
Max service check spread:         30 min
First scheduled check:            Thu Jun 30 21:14:16 2005
Last scheduled check:             Thu Jun 30 21:18:33 2005


CHECK PROCESSING INFORMATION
----------------------------
Service check reaper interval:    10 sec
Max concurrent service checks:    Unlimited


PERFORMANCE SUGGESTIONS
-----------------------
I have no suggestions - things look okay.
```

As you can see from Example 3-9, the -s switch summarizes and displays all of the host and service scheduling information you have configured as well as any scheduling information that is calculated from your current configuration. This information includes all of the settings for host and service scheduling that I discussed in Chapter 2. For example, under the heading of SERVICE SCHEDULING INFORMATION, the inter-check delay method, the inter-check delay, and the service interleave factor are all displayed. This is a fast and easy way of seeing how your Nagios configuration is likely to perform.

■**Tip** There is also a program called `nagiostats`, which is normally installed into the `/usr/local/nagios/bin` directory, that will provide similar and additional performance and status information about your Nagios server. The `nagiostats` program can output its data to standard out or in the Multirouter Traffic Grapher (MRTG) format, which can then be used to generate graphs.

As you add additional hosts and services, the load on your server increases and the delays in checking your hosts and services potentially become prolonged. Also, the check using the `-s` switch tries to detect opportunities to potentially improve the scheduling settings. If it finds any areas for improvement, these will be displayed under the PERFORMANCE SUGGESTIONS heading shown in Example 3-9. For example, you may see a recommendation for a different service reaping frequency.

■**Caution** This is both a limited checking function and a somewhat arbitrary one. I recommend reviewing any proposed change and testing it before trying it in production.

Nagios init Script

Nagios also has an `init` script that is installed when you install the Nagios package. The `init` script is installed into the `/etc/rc.d/init.d` directory by default. Or you can override the default installation location of the script with the `--with-init-dir` configure variable:

```
puppy# ./configure --with-init-dir=/etc/init.d
```

Here we've overridden the location of the `init` script and specified the directory `/etc/init.d` as if the Nagios server was running Gentoo or a similar distribution.

The Nagios `init` script has a number of options. The basic options are to start, stop, and restart the Nagios server. The following demonstrates starting the Nagios server using the `init` script:

```
puppy# /etc/rc.d/init.d/nagios start
Starting network monitor: nagios
```

Next we show restarting and then stopping the Nagios server on the following lines:

```
puppy# /etc/rc.d/init.d/nagios restart
Running configuration check...done
Stopping network monitor: nagios
Starting network monitor: nagios
puppy# /etc/rc.d/init.d/nagios stop
Stopping network monitor: nagios
```

As you can see from the restart of Nagios using the `init` script on the previous lines, the Nagios server also checks the object definition configuration of your monitoring environment when using the init script. The init script will return an error if the configuration is incorrect. You can see this error here:

```
puppy# /etc/rc.d/init.d/nagios start
CONFIG ERROR!  Start aborted. Check your Nagios configuration.
```

You can also reload your Nagios configuration:

```
puppy# /etc/rc.d/init.d/nagios reload
```

Finally, you can also query the status of the Nagios server using the init script. This will return information about the currently running Nagios process. Here's an example:

```
puppy# /etc/rc.d/init.d/nagios status
  PID TTY          TIME CMD
 5766 ?        00:00:08 nagios
```

Logging

Nagios comes with an extensive logging infrastructure that includes inbuilt log rotation and archiving as well as the ability to log Nagios events to a syslog facility. Nagios logging is configured in the nagios.cfg file using a series of directives. Example 3-10 shows a typical logging configuration.

Example 3-10. *Nagios Logging Configuration*

```
log_file=/usr/local/nagios/var/nagios.log
log_rotation_method=d
log_archive_path=/usr/local/nagios/var/archives
use_syslog=1
log_notifications=1
log_service_retries=1
log_host_retries=1
log_event_handlers=1
log_passive_checks=1
log_external_commands=1
log_initial_states=0
```

The first directive in Example 3-10, log_file, specifies where Nagios will store its primary log file. This directive should be first one in your nagios.cfg file as Nagios needs somewhere to write any errors discovered in the rest of the file. The log_file directive setting in Example 3-10, /usr/local/nagios/var/nagios.log, represents the default log file location when you install from source. You can override this with any location you require.

■**Tip** Nagios logs events using a Unix epoch timestamp, that is the time since the Unix epoch in seconds. These timestamps can be quite hard to read. As a result, the Nagios FAQ contains a short Perl script that converts these timestamps into a more readable format. You can see it at www.nagios.org/faqs/viewfaq. php?faq_id=70.

LOG, STATUS, AND OTHER VAR FILES

By default, there are a number of files contained in the `/usr/local/nagios/var` directory. These contain, among other information, log and status information about your Nagios environment. I've just described the `nagios.log` file that contains log messages generated by the Nagios server. The directory also contains the `status.dat`, `downtime.dat`, `comments.dat`, and `retention.dat` files. The `status.dat` file contains the current status of your hosts and services and is used by the CGI files to display this information. This file is created when Nagios is started and deleted when Nagios is stopped. Its name and location are controlled by the `status_file` directive in the `nagios.cfg` file. The `downtime.dat` file stores data about scheduled downtime for your hosts and services, and the `comments.dat` files contain comments attached to your hosts and services (both of which you can add via the web console, as I'll demonstrate in Chapter 4). Their location and name is defined by the `downtime_file` and `comment_file` directives in the `nagios.cfg` file.

The `retention.dat` file contains your state retention data if the `retain_state_information` directive is set to 1 in the `nagios.cfg` file. We discussed state retention in Chapter 2. The name and location of the retention file is set with the `state_retention_file` directive also in the `nagios.cfg` file. The contents of this file are updated according to the schedule specified in the `retention_update_interval` directive and is retained between server restarts.

Finally, the Nagios lock file and the object cache file are also contained in this directory. The Nagios PID lock file, `nagios.lock`, is generally also contained in this directory depending on how the `lock_file` directive is configured in the `nagios.cfg` configuration file. The object cache file, called `objects.cache` by default, contains a cached version of the object definitions on your server. These definitions are cached when the Nagios server is started. Nagios uses this data in the CGIs rather than the data in the configuration files to avoid inconsistencies if the Nagios configuration files have been changed after Nagios has started. The name and location of the object cache is specified in the `object_cache_file` directive in the `nagios.cfg` file.

The next directive, `log_rotation_method`, tells Nagios how often to rotate log files. Log rotation results in a new log file being created and the old log file being archived. The setting of d indicates that Nagios should rotate logs daily at midnight. Table 3-2 shows the potential log rotation options.

Table 3-2. *Log Rotation Options*

Option	Description
n	No log rotation
h	Hourly at the top of the hour
d	Daily at midnight
w	Weekly on Saturday at midnight
m	Monthly at midnight on the last day of the month

You should set this setting based on the volume and extent of your logging. A setting of daily log rotation is probably suitable for most environments. If you have a large number of hosts and services, you may wish to rotate hourly.

The next directive, `log_archive_path`, tells Nagios where to place the log files it has archived. If you have set `log_rotation_method` to n (indicating no log rotation), this directive is ignored. The default setting for a source installation of Nagios is `/usr/local/nagios/var/archives`.

Tip Your log files will be retained forever. If you only wish to keep a certain subset of your log files, you will need to regularly purge the log archive directory of excess log files. One simple approach is to use a `cron` job to routinely do this. Remember that much of the data used for Nagios reporting is contained in these log files. If you wish to log over periods covered by your archived log files, you will need the data in these files.

The `use_syslog` directive controls whether Nagios will log to the `syslog`. A setting of 1 will enable `syslog` logging and a setting of 0 will disable it. By default, Nagios uses a `syslog` facility of user. On most systems, messages into this facility are placed in your default `syslog` file—for example, on a Red Hat system this would be the `/var/log/messages` file. Unfortunately, this facility is hard-coded into the Nagios source code and cannot be changed. This can make separating out your Nagios `syslog` messages slightly more difficult. If you use a more advanced logging tool such as Syslog-NG,[11] you can select only the Nagios `syslog` messages for processing. In Example 3-11 you can see an example of destination, filter, and log statements from the Syslog-NG tool, which would allow you to log your Nagios `syslog` messages to an individual file. These statements would be placed in your `syslog-ng.conf` configuration file.

Example 3-11. *Nagios syslog-ng Configuration*

```
destination d_nagios { file("/var/log/nagios"); };
filter f_nagios    { facility("user") and program("nagios"); };
log { source(s_sys); filter(f_nagios); destination(d_nagios); };
```

In Example 3-11 all messages coming to the facility user from the program nagios would be placed in a destination file of `/var/log/nagios`.

The next series of directives control what Nagios will log, both to your log file and, if enabled, to `syslog`. Table 3-3 shows the full list of available directives and their descriptions.

Table 3-3. *Directives for Selecting What Nagios Logs*

Directive	Description
`log_notifications`	Log notifications
`log_service_retries`	Log check retries of services
`log_host_retries`	Log check retries of hosts
`log_event_handlers`	Log event handling
`log_passive_checks`	Log passive checks
`log_external_commands`	Log external commands
`log_initial_states`	Log the initial state of hosts and services

---

11. See www.balabit.com/products/syslog_ng/.

Each directive in Table 3-3 is enabled when it is set to 1 and disabled when set to 0. For example, to enable the logging of notifications, you'd set the `log_notifications` directive to

`log_notifications=1`

Let's briefly look at each logging directive and see what it does. The `log_notifications` directive is fairly self-explanatory and generates a log message when a notification is generated.

The `log_host_retries` and `log_service_retries` directives log retries of hosts and services that are in a soft non-OK state. As we described in Chapter 2, this is during the period that Nagios rechecks the host or service the number of times indicated in the `max_check_attempts` directive. During this period, the host or service is a soft non-OK state. When the retry checking is completed, the host or service is marked as being in a hard non-OK state. By default, I don't recommend logging host or service retry checks unless you are debugging a particular check or testing whether an event handler is running correctly.[12]

The `log_event_handlers` directive controls whether the running of host or service event handlers is logged. This is mostly useful when you're first testing event handlers or debugging Nagios. If you extensively use event handlers, your log files may become clogged if you have this option enabled and you may thus wish to disable it.

The next two directives, `log_passive_checks` and `log_external_commands`, are similar. The first logs any passive checks received in the external commands file. The second logs any external commands, such as a change in setting from the web console, received in the external command file. Both of these can be quite useful, but logging passive checks can become cumbersome if you are using distributed monitoring and have a large volume of passive checks being received on your server.[13] The `log_external_commands` directive can also be useful to track if anomalous or malicious external commands are being submitted. Monitoring these log entries might be something you wish to incorporate into any log monitoring you do for security purposes.

The last directive, `log_initial_states`, controls whether the initial states of all your hosts and services will be logged. This is the result of the first check of your hosts and services and the check results will be logged even if the host or service is in an OK state. This directive is usually turned off by default, as you can see in Example 3-10. It is useful if you are tracking the long-term state of hosts and services using your log entries, but generally you should not require this logging data. The only exception to this is if you are using the Availability report from the web console, and if so, I recommend you set this option to 1.

Checkpoints

- Ensure your Nagios server is hardened and secured against threats and vulnerabilities. Firewall your host and verify that any incoming connections are secured.

- Don't run the Nagios server as root. Always choose a different user and group, such as the default of user nagios and group nagios. This will allow the Nagios server to drop privileges when it is started.

---

12. Remember that event handlers are run when a host or service enters a soft non-OK state. See Chapter 2 for details on event handlers.

13. See Chapter 8 for an explanation of distributed monitoring.

- You can use lesser permissions on your external command file directory than the default settings. Examine and test the lesser permissions I've described in this chapter.

- Use your web server's authentication mechanism to secure your web console. If you use Apache then you should consider the use of Digest authentication to provide enhanced authentication to the Nagios CGIs. Remember there are caveats to using Digest authentication that you can read about in the "Digest Authentication" sidebar in this chapter.

- Consider whether you also want to add authentication to the Nagios HTML files as well as the CGI programs.

- Consider adding SSL to secure your web console traffic.

- Consider using CGIWrap and/or suEXEC to further secure your CGI scripts. Be aware that CGIWrap can be complicated and time consuming to install and configure and that suEXEC is generally only effective if you are using virtual hosts.

- Avoid the use of default users in your Nagios CGI configuration. Default users allow unauthenticated users to access your web console. Instead, ensure each of your users is defined and authenticated individually.

- Only grant the authorization that each of your users requires to the Nagios web console. Remember that users who are configured in your web server authentication and who are also contacts for your hosts and services are authenticated contacts. Authenticated contacts have access to those hosts and services they are contacts for. Additional privileges and access should be limited to only those users who require it.

- Make sure the log_file directive is the first directive in your nagios.cfg file to ensure Nagios knows where to log any potential errors.

Resources

- SELinux: www.nsa.gov/selinux/

- Openwall: www.openwall.org

- Bastille: www.bastille-linux.org/

- Tripwire: www.sourceforge.net/projects/tripwire/

- CGIWrap: http://cgiwrap.unixtools.org/

- suEXEC: http://httpd.apache.org/docs/suexec.html

- HOWTO Apache authorization: http://httpd.apache.org/docs/howto/auth.html

- HOWTO Apache .htaccess files: http://httpd.apache.org/docs/howto/htaccess.html

- Nagios cgi.cfg configuration file directives: http://nagios.sourceforge.net/docs/2_0/configcgi.html

- Nagios CGI authentication and authorization: http://nagios.sourceforge.net/docs/2_0/cgiauth.html

- Syslog-NG: www.balabit.com/products/syslog_ng/

CHAPTER 4

■■■

Using the Web Console

The Nagios web console is an optional component of the Nagios monitoring tool. You don't need to use the web console unless you wish to see a visual representation of your hosts and services and to interact with them through this console. Many organizations use the Nagios web console as one of the displays in their network operations center (NOC) or on a projected console to display the current status of your hosts and services.

If you simply want to use the Nagios server for monitoring and notifications, you do not need to configure the web console (which means you can skip the "Configuring Your Web Server for Nagios" section in Chapter 1). Personally, I recommend that you configure the web console (and secure it using the information in Chapter 3) as it provides not only a good interface to the hosts and services being monitored but also an easy mechanism to perform actions on the Nagios server, such as enabling and disabling active checking and notifications.

There are a few issues with the web console, though. The first is that the CGIs are written in C and thus can be slow. This is especially true if you have a large number of hosts and services. The second issue is that Ethan Galstad, the developer of Nagios, has indicated that version 3.0 will likely remove the web console functionality from the server package and replace it with a separate package.[1] He has indicated that this package would preferably be written in Perl or PHP. Galstad has cited a number of reasons for this change:

- He feels the current user interface is a poor design.

- The CGIs need to be recompiled any time the HTML front-end is changed.

- This change makes it easier to support internationalization (or multiple languages).

- It would be problematic to introduce session state tracking in the current CGIs. This process would be considerably easier using a PHP/Perl-developed interface.

It is Galstad's intention that a third party will develop this interface rather than him, but he has offered to assist in the process. Indeed, a couple of front-ends written in PHP have recently started development and at the time of this writing are in Alpha.[2] Unfortunately, at this time these interfaces are both under heavy development and as yet only officially support Nagios version 1.*x*.

In light of this, I am not going to cover the web console in huge detail. This isn't a big issue as generally speaking the web console is intuitive and easy to navigate. I'll cover the highlights

---

1. See www.nagios.org/development/upcoming.php.

2. See http://sourceforge.net/projects/nagios-php/ and www.itgroundwork.com/.

of the web console and its major features with an emphasis on how to use the web console to interact and control the Nagios server using external commands. This should provide a suitable introduction to the web console that will allow you to explore it further from there.

As I've discussed in previous chapters, the web console is made up of an HTML front-end that is combined with a series of CGI programs.

Tip You can find more information about the CGI programs in the Nagios documentation at `http://nagios.sourceforge.net/docs/2_0/cgis.html`.

The HTML front-end of the Nagios web console is divided into two sections. The first section is the menu pane that runs on the left-hand side of the page, and the second section is the main display pane, which occupies most of the page to the right of the menu pane. You can see this in Figure 4-1.

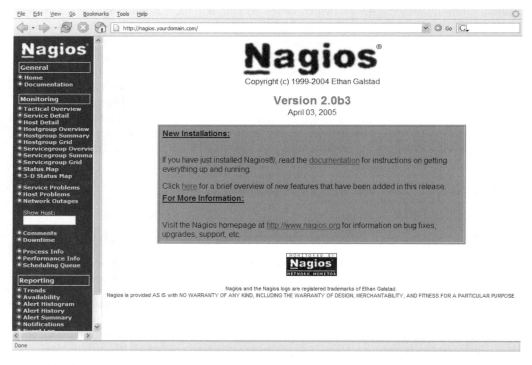

Figure 4-1. *The Nagios web console*

The left-hand menu panel is broken up into four sections. In this chapter, I'll break down my explanation of the web console into these four sections: General, Monitoring, Reporting, and Configuration.

> **Tip** There is also a WAP-based CGI page that allows you to view your hosts and services via your mobile phone or PDA. If your Nagios web console is available from your phone or PDA, you can access this page via the URL `http://nagios.yourdomain.com/cgi-bin/statuswml.cgi`. You will need to replace `nagios.yourdomain.com` with the domain name or location of your web console.

General

The General section contains two links: Home and Documentation. The Home link displays the page shown in Figure 4-1. The Documentation link takes you to a local online version of the Nagios documentation. This is the same documentation available online at `www.nagios.org/docs/`.

Monitoring

The Monitoring section of the menu panel consists of a series of possible views of your monitoring environment. In addition, it contains links to information about the Nagios process, the performance of your host and service checks, and a link to a graphical representation of the queue of checks waiting to be performed. I'll look at each of these possible views and discuss how you can interact with your monitoring environment using them.

> **Tip** The figures in this chapter display only the page described. I've cropped the left-hand menu from these figures.

Tactical Monitoring Overview

The first view we are going to look at is called Tactical Monitoring Overview, shown in Figure 4-2. It is the first item in the Monitoring menu and could be considered an ideal view for a projected status window in an NOC. It displays six major features of your monitoring environment: the status of your monitoring performance, network outages, network health, hosts, services, and the status of your monitoring features, such as whether flap detection, notifications, or checks are enabled. Clicking the Tactical Monitoring Overview link launches the `tac.cgi` CGI program.

First, at the top left of the Tactical Monitoring Overview page (and most of the Monitoring pages) a box is displayed showing the current date and time, a link to the Nagios website, and a line indicating the name of the user who is currently logged into the web console. You can see an example of this box in Figure 4-3.

Located at the top-right corner of the page, the Monitoring Performance box contains the statistics on the execution time and latency of your host and service checks. It also displays the total number of active and passive host and service checks.

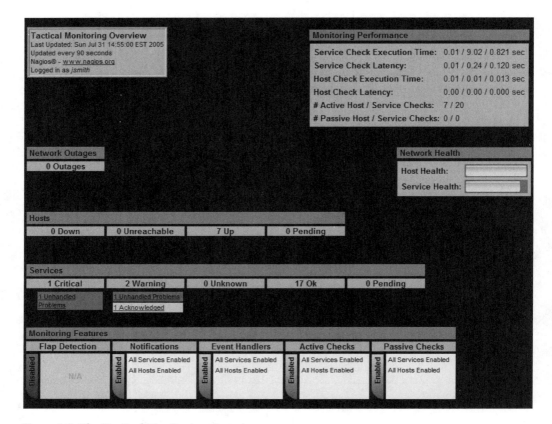

Figure 4-2. *The Tactical Monitoring Overview page*

Figure 4-3. *The status box*

The Network Health and Network Outage boxes are both visual representations of the health of your network and your hosts and services. The Network Outage box indicates whether it appears any network outages have occurred in your environment; clicking on this box takes you to `outages.cgi`, which we will discuss briefly later in this chapter. The Network Health box is a visual representation in the form of two bars—one for hosts and one for services—that indicates the health of your hosts and services. As you can see in Figure 4-2, the Host Health column is full but the Service Health column is only partially full, indicating that one or more services has a problem.

The boxes below this indicate the overall status of your hosts and services. As you will remember from Chapter 2, hosts can have four states: DOWN, UNREACHABLE, UP, and UNKNOWN. On the Hosts box in the Tactical Monitoring Overview page, the totals of the hosts in DOWN,

UNREACHABLE, or UP states are represented together with a total for pending hosts. This indicates hosts for which Nagios has yet to schedule a check or receive a check result. You can see in Figure 4-2 that our environment has seven hosts in the UP state. In the Services box Nagios displays totals for the CRITICAL, WARNING, UNKNOWN, and OK states, together with a total of services in a pending state.

As you can see in Figure 4-2, underneath the Services box in the CRITICAL state column is a link labeled 1 Unhandled Problems. This indicates that one service is in a CRITICAL state. Underneath each status type in the Host and Service status boxes is the total number of each host or service that is in each state. Each total is a link that will take you to a host or service status detail page that contains the list of hosts or services in that state. We'll look at the host and service status detail pages in the "Service Detail" and "Host Detail" sections.

Finally, at the bottom of our Tactical Monitoring Overview page is the Monitoring Features box. This box indicates the status of some of the features of your monitoring environment. These features are flap detection, notifications, event handlers, and active and passive checks. The bar to the left of each feature indicates whether that feature is enabled or disabled globally (either Enabled or Disabled).

Clicking one of these bars will take you to one of the functions of the cmd.cgi CGI program. This CGI program allows you to send external commands to the external command file for processing by the Nagios server. It is by using this program, which is called the External Command Interface, that you are able to interact with the Nagios server from the web console. You pass the cmd.cgi program a variable to dictate which command page to display and hence which command to input. By clicking one of these bars you will invoke one of the feature enable or disable command pages. Which page is invoked depends on whether the feature is currently enabled or disabled. As you can see in Figure 4-2, the Notifications feature is enabled. When I click the Notifications feature bar, it will take me to the page in Figure 4-4, where I can disable notifications.

You are requesting to disable notifications

Figure 4-4. *Disabling notifications via an external command*

In Figure 4-4, you will see that the page is titled External Command Interface and, in red text (the topmost center text), indicates what external command you are requesting to perform (in this case, that notifications be disabled). At this point you must click the Commit button, which will submit the external command to the command file for processing. It will also take you to a new page, which confirms your command has been submitted or, if an error has occurred, displays the related error message. The most common error that occurs here is if the permissions of your command file or command file directory are incorrectly set and the web console is unable to write to the command file. It may take some time for the command to be processed and notifications to be disabled.

Back in Figure 4-2, to the right of the bar that indicates the status of each feature you'll see a series of boxes. These boxes indicate the total number of services and hosts that have been disabled locally for each feature. For example, notifications can be turned off globally for the whole server or locally for an individual host or service. The total number of hosts or services that have had notifications disabled will be displayed in the Notification feature box.

Service Detail

The next menu item, the Service Detail page, displays the details of your services. This page is provided by the status.cgi CGI program. Which page and which services are displayed depends on variables passed to the CGI program by the web console. You can launch this page from the links on the left menu bar or, as we've seen, from the Tactical Monitoring Overview page or from a number of other pages in the web console. If you launch the page from the menu item in the left-hand menu, Nagios will display details of all services on the server.

If you had launched the Service Detail page from the Tactical Monitoring Overview page—for example, by clicking the link below the Service status boxes, as discussed earlier—Nagios will display the list of services in that particular state. In Figure 4-2 underneath the Services status box for the CRITICAL status is a link labeled 1 Unhandled Problems. Clicking this link will display the Service Detail page for those services that are in a CRITICAL state. Figure 4-5 shows the displayed page.

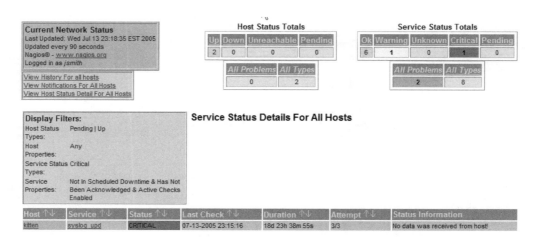

Figure 4-5. *The Service Detail page*

In Figure 4-5 you can see a listing of all the services in a CRITICAL state. There are five major sections on this page. The first section, on the top left, is the descriptive box shown in Figure 4-3 but with the addition of three links below it. The first link allows you to view the history of all hosts. This displays the messages from the nagios.log file. The second link displays the notifications generated for all hosts, and the third link displays the Host Detail page, which I will examine in the next section.

The second and third sections, also on the top of this page, are host and service status boxes containing totals of the hosts and services in each status. You will see these boxes repeated frequently in other pages that are displayed via the items under the Monitoring menu. Each of the status labels in these boxes is a link that displays a list of the hosts or services in that status. For example, in the Host Status Totals box in Figure 4-5, two hosts are listed in the UP state. By clicking the Up label you will be taken to a service detail page for all hosts in the UP state.

The fourth section is a box titled Display Filters that displays the filter conditions for this page. This box only appears if you are displaying a subset of the available hosts or services. If you had launched this page from the left-hand menu item, then this box would not appear. In Figure 4-5 you can see that the Service Status filter shows CRITICAL services only.

The fifth and last section is the list of services in columns. These columns consist of the hostname, service name, status, date and time of the last check, length of time it has been monitored, number of check attempts, and status information returned from the last check.[3] The last column is especially useful as it is the exact data that was returned from the last check of the service. You can see in Figure 4-5 that Nagios reports that No data was received from host! for the syslog_udp service, which indicates that the check either did not receive a response or failed to execute correctly.

You can sort each of these columns, except the Status Information column, in either ascending or descending order by using the arrows next to the column title. The name of the host and the name of the service are also links. The host link will display the Host Information page, which contains detailed information about the particular host. It is provided using the extinfo.cgi CGI program. I'll look at this page in the "Host Detail" section. The service name link will display the Service Information page, which provides detailed information about the particular service. This also uses the extinfo.cgi CGI program. Figure 4-6 shows this page.

As you can see in Figure 4-6, this page contains a considerable amount of information about the syslog_upd service. In the top left is the general descriptive box containing the date, time, and authenticated user with a series of links beneath it that can take you to a variety of other pages. I've listed these links here:

- View Information For This Host

- View Status Detail For This Host

- View Alert History For This Service

- View Trends For This Service

- View Alert Histogram For This Service

- View Availability Report For This Service

- View Notifications For This Service

---

3. This is the number of attempts specified in the max_check_attempts directive.

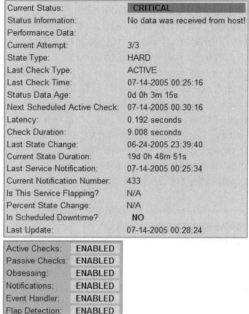

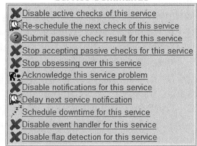

Figure 4-6. *The Service Information page*

The first two links will take you to the Host Information page (which I describe in the "Host Detail" section) and a status detail listing page that will show you details of all the other services on this host. The remaining links will take you to various Nagios reports; we discuss two of these reports in the "Reporting" section later in this chapter.

To the right of this box is some general descriptive information about the service, including its name, the host it is located on, its membership in any service groups, and the address (usually the IP address) of the host the service resides on.

The page also contains three other boxes: Service State Information, Service Commands, and Service Comments. I'll look at each individually.

The Service State Information box contains a variety of information about the current status of the service and some associated performance information. This includes some very useful information such as the Status Information line, which is the data returned from a check of the service, and the State Type line, which indicates whether the service is in a SOFT or HARD state. Beneath the Service State Information box is a list of the Nagios features (enabled or disabled) for this service, such as whether active checks, notifications, or flap detection are enabled.

The Service Commands box contains all of the possible external commands that you can run against this service. Running these commands submits an external command to the external command file to be processed by the Nagios server. This means after submission they may take a short period to execute and for the results of the command to be reflected on the web console. Clicking the links in the Service Commands box will take you to a cmd.cgi page for that particular command, and in some cases you will need to provide additional information to submit the command.

Tip All red entry fields in the web console or the External Command Interface page are required fields. In order to submit commands, you need to fill in these fields.

Most of the commands allow you to enable or disable various Nagios features, such as disabling checks or notifications. Four commands are particularly worth noting: Re-schedule the next check of this service, Submit passive check result for this service, Acknowledge this service problem, and Schedule downtime for this service.

The first command, Re-schedule the next check of this service, allows you to change the time of the next check of this service. You can use this to advance or delay the next check time of the service. On the External Command Interface page that appears when you select this command, you will need to specify the time you want the rescheduled check to run at and then click the Commit button to submit the external command.

The second command, Submit passive check result for this service, provides an interface from the web console to submit a passive check result for this service. We discussed passive checks in Chapter 2. For example, you could reset the status of a service from the web console. In order to submit the result, you need to specify the check results (OK, WARNING, CRITICAL, or UNKNOWN) and the output of the check. You can also specify optional performance data, if necessary, on the External Command Interface page.

The third command, Acknowledge this service problem, appears only when there is a problem with the service. It also only appears when the service has changed from a SOFT non-OK state to a HARD non-OK state after going through the maximum number of check retries. This command is especially important because it allows you to acknowledge a service problem, thus stopping the sending of notifications and indicating that the problem is being worked on. If an existing service acknowledgment is present for a service, then this command changes to Remove problem acknowledgement, which you can use to remove the acknowledgment of the service and resume the sending of notifications.

> **Tip** Many people who integrate their help desk/service desk system with Nagios configure their ticketing system to send an external command acknowledging a problem when a technician or engineer is assigned to a case. We will discuss concepts like this in further detail in Chapter 7.

The fourth and last command we'll discuss, `Schedule downtime for this service`, allows you to schedule downtime for this service from the web console (similar options exist for hosts and host and service groups). Downtime is a period during which Nagios will not send notifications for hosts or services. This could be because the host or service is not available as a result of a scheduled outage, a backup, or the like. Downtime is scheduled using external commands and can be scheduled for hosts and services.

Nagios does not have a downtime calendar or scheduling engine. Downtime is scheduled manually for each individual time period required; for example, you can't specify that Nagios observe downtime for a particular host every day between 1 a.m. and 4 a.m. You can only specify that Nagios observe downtime for that host on a particular day—for example, Wednesday July 27, 2005, between 1 a.m. and 4 a.m. You need to repeat this schedule for every day that the downtime is required.

> **Tip** Downtime scheduling is one of the weaker points of Nagios. We'll discuss some options and ways to interact with Nagios to do regular downtime scheduling in Chapter 7.

As a result of the complications of scheduling downtime, the web console is a commonly used interface to schedule ad hoc downtime. You can see the External Command Interface page for scheduling downtime in Figure 4-7.

As you can see in Figure 4-7, you need to specify additional details for the external command to schedule downtime. Some of the fields have already been filled, including the hostname, service name, and the author (the user who is authenticated to the web console is used for this value). You also need to specify a mandatory comment describing this downtime.

The next option, `Triggered By`, controls what Nagios calls triggered downtime. This allows you to trigger downtime for a host or service based on the downtime of another host or service. Thus, you can specify that the downtime for this service or host start when downtime starts on another host or service. We'll come back to triggered downtime in a moment when we look at the different types of downtime.

You are requesting to schedule downtime for a particular service

Command Options	Command Description
Host Name: `kitten` Service: `syslog_udp` Author (Your Name): `jsmith` Comment: Triggered By: `N/A` Start Time: `07/27/2005 16:19:34` End Time: `07/27/2005 18:19:34` Type: `Fixed` If Flexible Duration: `2` Hours `0` Minutes [Commit] [Reset]	This command is used to schedule downtime for a particular service. During the specified downtime, Nagios will not send notifications out about the service. When the scheduled downtime expires, Nagios will send out notifications for this service as it normally would. Scheduled downtimes are preserved across program shutdowns and restarts. Both the start and end times should be specified in the following format: **mm/dd/yyyy hh:mm:ss**. option, Nagios will treat this as "flexible" downtime. Flexible downtime starts when the service enters a non-OK state (sometime between the start and end times you specified) and lasts as long as the duration of time you enter. The duration fields do not apply for fixed downtime.

Please enter all required information before committing the command.
Required fields are marked in red.
Failure to supply all required values will result in an error.

Figure 4-7. *Scheduling service downtime*

Downtime comes in two types: fixed and flexible. Fixed downtime is a fixed period, from 1 a.m. to 4 a.m. for example, during which Nagios will not send notifications for the host or service. Flexible downtime is more powerful. In flexible downtime you specify a range of time during which time you believe the host or service will become unavailable. For example, if you believe your downtime will occur sometime between 7 a.m. and 8 a.m. you would specify this range of time. You then need to specify the period of time the downtime will take. Nagios monitors for the host or service to become unavailable during the time range you specify, and if it then does become unavailable, it puts the host or service into downtime for the period you specified. So why use flexible downtime? Well, flexible downtime takes into consideration the fact that not all of your downtime activities will take place at an exact time—for example, an end-of-day process that starts during a period rather than an exact time. Another example is when rebooting a server you may not be sure how long it will take to become available again.

This also ties into triggered downtime. Let's look at an example. I specify a flexible downtime range of 8 a.m. to 9 a.m. and for a period of two hours for a particular service. This means that Nagios will monitor between 8 a.m. to 9 a.m. for the service to become unavailable and, when the service does become unavailable, it starts the two-hour scheduled downtime. I then use this scheduled downtime as the trigger for downtime in other services and hosts. This is done by selecting the downtime instance we have just defined in the `Triggered By` box in the External Command Interface page. You need to do this for all the services and hosts on which you want downtime to be triggered. I also specify the length of the downtime for these services and hosts. When the downtime starts for the original service, then the downtime for the other hosts and services is also triggered and Nagios puts all the services and hosts into downtime for the period you specified.

So how do we schedule downtime using the interface in Figure 4-7? There are four options that need to be filled in. The first two options are compulsory: the start and stop time for the downtime. You need to complete these options for both fixed and flexible downtime. For fixed downtime this is the actual time frame the downtime will occur over. For flexible downtime, Nagios expects that the host or service will become unavailable during this time frame. The next option is a dropdown box allowing you to specify whether this is fixed or flexible downtime. The last option is only valid if you select flexible downtime in the Type drop-down box and specify the length of time of the flexible downtime.

Note Downtime information is stored in a file defined by the `downtime_file` directive in the `nagios.cfg` configuration file. By default, this is the `/usr/local/nagios/var/downtime.dat` file.

Downtime can only be scheduled for current and future periods. If you try to schedule downtime in the past, Nagios will disregard the downtime and will not report an error. Additionally, if you schedule more than one period of downtime for a host or service where the two periods overlap, Nagios will consider the host or service as being in downtime until the last period of downtime is completed.

Tip You can see what downtime has been scheduled in the comments section for your host or service. I'll look at comments later in this section.

The Service Comments box contains a list of all the comments that apply to this service. It also has two actions: adding a comment and deleting all comments. These comments can consist of a number of comment types. The types of comments include user, acknowledgment, and scheduled downtime. User comments are comments added by you to the service using the Add New Comments link, which submits an external command to add the comment. Acknowledgment comments are adding by submitting an acknowledgment external command, as we discussed earlier. Scheduled downtime comments are added when you schedule downtime for the service, and they disappear when the downtime is complete.

In the comment box you can see the time of the entry, the author of the comment, the comment itself, an ID for the comment, whether the comment is persistent (which indicates whether the comment will be saved between server restarts), the type of comment, and when the comment expires. You can also see a rubbish bin icon, which you can click to delete a particular comment.

You can add a user comment to the service by clicking the Add New Comments link. This will take you to the External Command Interface page for comment addition. The hostname, the service, and the author of the comment (it uses the currently authenticated user signed into the web console) are automatically filled in. There is also a check box labeled Persistent, which is checked by default. If you deselect the box, then the comment will only stay on the server until Nagios is next restarted. After the restart, the comment will be deleted. You then need to click the Commit button to submit the external command and add the comment.

You can also delete all comments on the service by clicking the `Delete all comments` link.

Host Detail

The Host Detail page is very similar to the Service Detail page but focuses on hosts rather than services. It is accessible via the Host Detail link on the left-hand menu, from the Hosts box on the Tactical Monitoring Overview page, or from a variety of other pages in the web console. Figure 4-8 shows the Host Detail page.

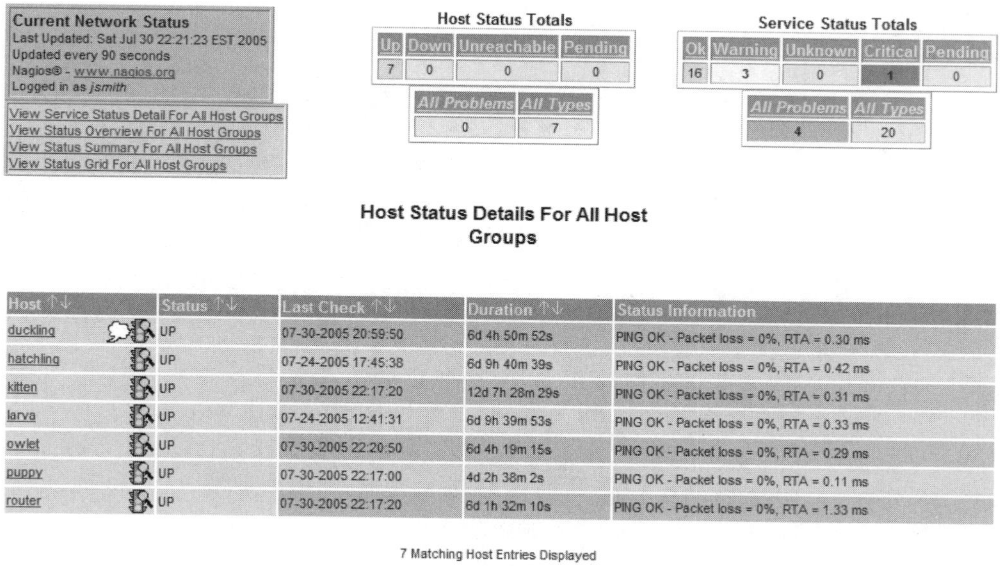

Figure 4-8. *The Host Detail page*

The Host Detail page displays a list of all the hosts on your server. The top of the page contains items similar to the ones on the Service Detail page, including the current network status and the host and service status totals boxes. You can click the host and service status descriptions—for example, UP, OK, WARNING or CRITICAL—in the totals boxes to take you to the Host or Service Detail pages for any hosts and services in that particular status.

The main portion of the page shows a list of all the hosts on your system. The list has columns displaying the hostname, current status, the time of the last check, and the duration that Nagios has been monitoring the hosts. You can sort these columns in an ascending or descending order by clicking the up and down arrows next to the column title. A series of icons appears next to the hostname field that report different conditions about the host—for example, a traffic light icon is a link to a listing of all services on the host. Also displayed is the status information for the host, which consists of the response to the command specified in the check_command directive in the host object definition. By default this is usually the check-host-alive command, which uses the check_ping plug-in to send ICMP pings to your hosts to detect if they are up. The results of the ping are reported in this column.

Clicking on the hostname of the host in the first column will take you to the Host Information page for that particular host. This page is very similar to the Service Information page we discussed in the "Service Detail" section earlier in this chapter; you can see it in Figure 4-9.

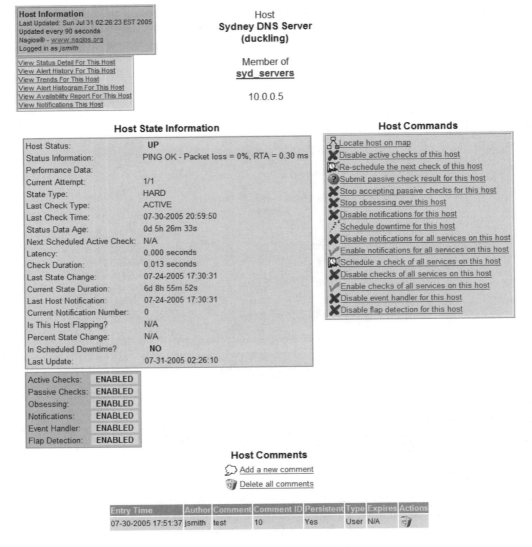

Figure 4-9. *The Host Information page*

Like the Service Information page, this page contains three major sections: the Host Status Information box, the Host Commands box, and the Host Comments section. The Host Status Information box contains a series of useful details about the host, including when it was last checked, the check result, the host's status, and, at the bottom of the box, which Nagios features are enabled for this host.

The Host Commands box provides a series of external commands that you can execute related to hosts. This includes many of the same commands you can execute for services. You can also issue commands that impact the services on the host—for example, disabling notifications or service checks for all services on the host. You can also schedule downtime for the host in a nearly identical manner to how you schedule downtime for services. There is one additional function that is invoked when scheduling downtime for hosts: the ability to also schedule downtime on any child hosts of the host. This can be done using triggered or normal downtime for the child host or hosts. Enabling or disabling notifications commands for hosts also have an option to allow you to change the notification behavior of any child hosts.

The Host Comments box contains comments about the current host and functions, similar to the service comments we discussed in the "Service Detail" section earlier in this chapter.

Host and Service Group Views

The next six menu items display different views of your host and service groups. There are three basic types of view: Overview, Summary, and Grid. There is an Overview view for host groups and for service groups, and a Summary view for host groups and service groups and so forth. All pages are provided by the `status.cgi` CGI program, and the page and view displayed depend on variables passed to the CGI program.

The first view is the host or service group overview. It displays each host or service group defined on your Nagios server, the hosts contained in it, and the status of the services defined on each hosts. You can see the Hostgroup Overview view in Figure 4-10.

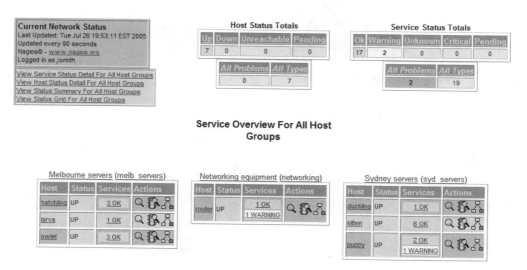

Figure 4-10. *The Hostgroup Overview page*

The Hostgroup Overview page shows each of your host groups and the hosts it contains, together with a list of the states of the services on each host. For example, in Figure 4-10 you can see the host group networking, which contains the host router and which in turns contains one service in the OK state and one service in the WARNING state. For each host in the host groups, you can link to a variety of other pages, including the Service Detail page for that host. Using the symbols next to each host, you can view other information. The magnifying glass symbol takes you to the Host Information page, the traffic light symbol takes you to the Service Status detail page for that host, and the map symbol takes you to the Status Map menu item (which we cover briefly later in this chapter). The Servicegroup Overview page is identical except that your hosts and services are collated in service groups instead of host groups.

The second type of host or service group view is the Summary view. This presents a view of your hosts and services displayed in three columns: by group, by totals of hosts for each group, and by total of services for each group. You can see an example of the service group version of this view in Figure 4-11.

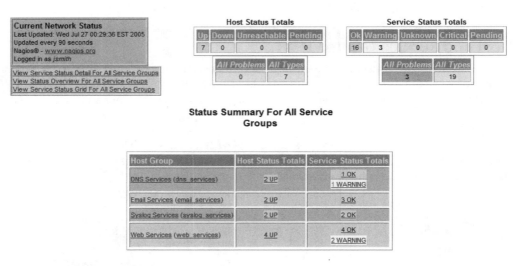

Figure 4-11. *The Servicegroup Summary page*

In Figure 4-11 you can see that you can click on the description and name of the service group. Clicking on the description of the service group, for example DNS Services, will take you a page showing the Servicegroup Overview page for that particular service group. Clicking on the service group name, in this example dns_services, will take you to the Servicegroup Commands page, which allows you to issue commands that will affect all hosts and services in that service group. You can issue the following service group commands:

- Schedule downtime for all hosts in this servicegroup

- Schedule downtime for all services in this servicegroup

- Enable notifications for all hosts in this servicegroup

- Disable notifications for all hosts in this servicegroup

- Enable notifications for all services in this servicegroup

- Disable notifications for all services in this servicegroup

- Enable active checks of all services in this servicegroup

- Disable active checks of all services in this servicegroup

All of these commands will submit an external command that will be processed via the Nagios server. The command will affect all of the hosts or services in a particular service group. For most of the commands, you will need to fill in additional information before you can submit the command. For example, in Figure 4-12 you can schedule downtime for all services in a particular service group.

External Command Interface
Last Updated: Wed Jul 27 01:47:33 EST 2005
Nagios® - www.nagios.org
Logged in as *jsmith*

You are requesting to schedule downtime for all services in a particular servicegroup

Command Options

Servicegroup Name:	dns_services
Author (Your Name):	jsmith
Comment:	
Start Time:	07/27/2005 01:47:33
End Time:	07/27/2005 03:47:33
Type:	Fixed
If Flexible, Duration:	2 Hours 0 Minutes
Schedule Downtime For Hosts Too:	☐

Commit   Reset

Command Description

This command is used to schedule downtime for all services in a particular servicegroup. During the specified downtime, Nagios will not send notifications out about the services. When the scheduled downtime expires, Nagios will send out notifications for the services as it normally would. Scheduled downtimes are preserved across program shutdowns and restarts. Both the start and end times should be specified in the following format: **mm/dd/yyyy hh:mm:ss**. If you select the *fixed* option, the downtime will be in effect between the start and end times you specify. If you do not select the *fixed* option, Nagios will treat this as "flexible" downtime. Flexible downtime starts when a service enters a non-OK state (sometime between the start and end times you specified) and lasts as long as the duration of time you enter. The duration fields do not apply for fixed downtime. Note that scheduling downtime for services does not automatically schedule downtime for the hosts those services are associated with. If you want to also schedule downtime for all hosts in the servicegroup, check the 'Schedule downtime for hosts too' option.

Please enter all required information before committing the command.
Required fields are marked in red.
Failure to supply all required values will result in an error.

Figure 4-12. *Scheduling downtime for all services*

To schedule the downtime, you need to add some further information: the service group name, your name, a comment for the downtime, and the time period of the downtime required. You can then click Commit and submit the command to schedule the downtime. The Hostgroup Summary view is identical except that your hosts and services are collated in host groups instead of service groups.

The third type of host or service group view is the Grid view. This displays a view of your host or service groups laid out in a grid. You can see the host group version of this view in Figure 4-13.

From this view you can click on the hostname for each host to take you to the Host Information page or alternatively on the service name of each service on the host to take you to the Service Information page. Each host list also has three actions you can execute by clicking on the symbols after each host and service listing. The magnifying glass symbol takes you to the Host Information page, the traffic light symbol takes you to the Service Status detail page for that host, and the map symbol takes you to the Status Map menu item (which we cover briefly later in this chapter). The Servicegroup Grid view is identical except that your hosts and services are collated in service groups instead of host groups.

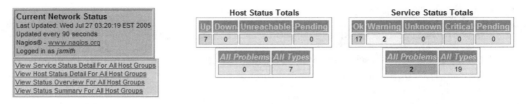

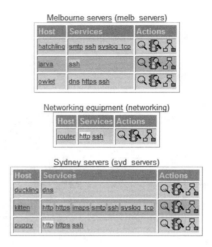

Figure 4-13. *Host group grid view*

Process Information

The next menu item, the **Process Information** page, contains a series of information about the Nagios server process and the settings of the Nagios server itself. It also provides the ability to interact with the Nagios process and server settings from the web console. You can see the Process Information page in Figure 4-14.

On the left side of the page you can see a variety of information about the running Nagios process and the settings of the server. This includes information like the start time and PID of the Nagios process. Below this is a series of lines that detail the settings of the Nagios server. These include, among other things, whether notifications are enabled, whether service checks are being executed, whether host and service obsession are enabled, and whether performance data is being processed.

On the right side of the page is a series of links that execute external commands that can manipulate the Nagios process and server settings. These commands are submitted to the external command file and processed by the Nagios server. As they are submitted and processed, they can take a short period of time to take effect. Using the external commands you can shut down or restart the Nagios process and control most of the settings of the Nagios server, such as enabling or disabling notifications, service checks, event handlers, and flap detection.

When you click the link it calls the `cmd.cgi` program with a parameter specifying the command you wish to run. Figure 4-15 shows the `cmd.cgi` page for disabling notifications.

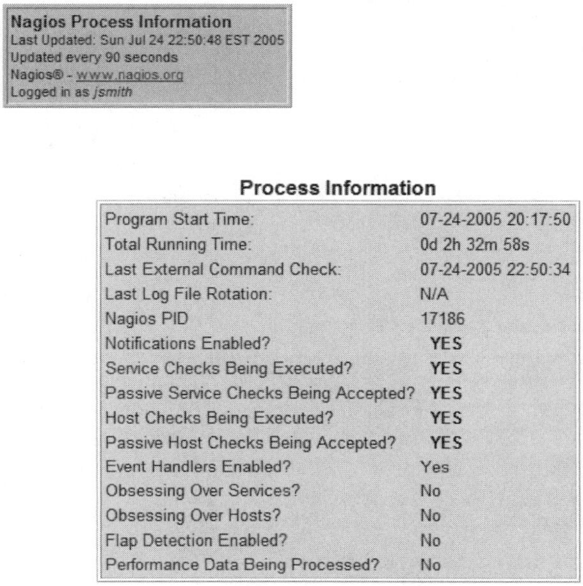

Nagios Process Information
Last Updated: Sun Jul 24 22:50:48 EST 2005
Updated every 90 seconds
Nagios® - www.nagios.org
Logged in as *jsmith*

Process Information

Program Start Time:	07-24-2005 20:17:50
Total Running Time:	0d 2h 32m 58s
Last External Command Check:	07-24-2005 22:50:34
Last Log File Rotation:	N/A
Nagios PID	17186
Notifications Enabled?	YES
Service Checks Being Executed?	YES
Passive Service Checks Being Accepted?	YES
Host Checks Being Executed?	YES
Passive Host Checks Being Accepted?	YES
Event Handlers Enabled?	Yes
Obsessing Over Services?	No
Obsessing Over Hosts?	No
Flap Detection Enabled?	No
Performance Data Being Processed?	No

Process Commands

- Shutdown the Nagios process
- Restart the Nagios process
- Disable notifications
- Stop executing service checks
- Stop accepting passive service checks
- Stop executing host checks
- Stop accepting passive host checks
- Disable event handlers
- Start obsessing over services
- Start obsessing over hosts
- Enable flap detection
- Enable performance data

Figure 4-14. *The Process Information page*

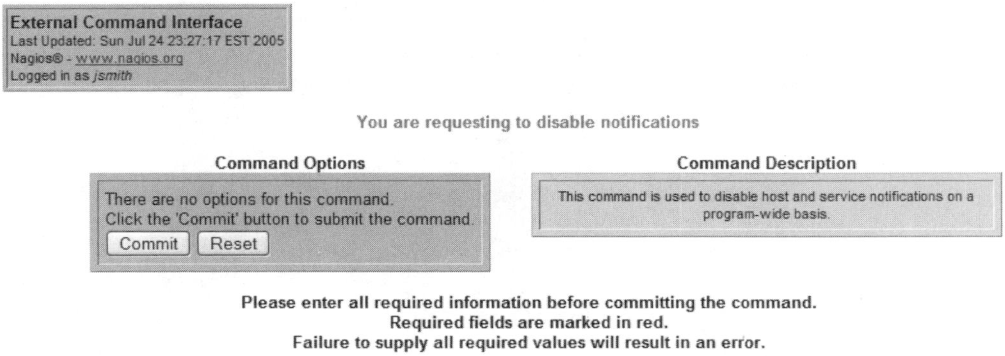

External Command Interface
Last Updated: Sun Jul 24 23:27:17 EST 2005
Nagios® - www.nagios.org
Logged in as *jsmith*

You are requesting to disable notifications

Command Options

There are no options for this command.
Click the 'Commit' button to submit the command.

Commit   Reset

Command Description

This command is used to disable host and service notifications on a program-wide basis.

Please enter all required information before committing the command.
Required fields are marked in red.
Failure to supply all required values will result in an error.

Figure 4-15. *Disabling notifications*

To submit the external command, you need to click the Commit button. For some external commands, you will need to add additional information or variables. The Reset button is used to reset the entry fields for these variables. After you click the Commit button, the command will be submitted. If an error occurs with the command submission, Nagios will report it on the page displayed.

Scheduling Queue

The **Scheduling Queue** menu item displays a list of the scheduled checks awaiting execution by the Nagios server. The entries are sorted in ascending order of the next check time, as shown in Figure 4-16.

Check Scheduling Queue
Last Updated: Mon Jul 25 12:22:40 EST 2005
Updated every 90 seconds
Nagios® - www.nagios.org
Logged in as *jsmith*

Entries sorted by **next check time** (ascending)

Host ↑↓	Service ↑↓	Last Check ↑↓	Next Check ↑↓	Active Checks	Actions
kitten	http	07-25-2005 12:18:05	07-25-2005 12:23:05	ENABLED	✖ 📠
kitten	ssh	07-25-2005 12:18:21	07-25-2005 12:23:21	ENABLED	✖ 📠
owlet	dns	07-25-2005 12:18:37	07-25-2005 12:23:37	ENABLED	✖ 📠
hatchling	smtp	07-25-2005 12:19:08	07-25-2005 12:24:08	ENABLED	✖ 📠
kitten	https	07-25-2005 12:19:24	07-25-2005 12:24:24	ENABLED	✖ 📠
kitten	syslog_tcp	07-25-2005 12:19:40	07-25-2005 12:24:40	ENABLED	✖ 📠
owlet	https	07-25-2005 12:19:56	07-25-2005 12:24:56	ENABLED	✖ 📠
hatchling	ssh	07-25-2005 12:20:27	07-25-2005 12:25:27	ENABLED	✖ 📠
router	syslog_tcp	07-25-2005 12:20:31	07-25-2005 12:25:31	ENABLED	✖ 📠
kitten	imaps	07-25-2005 12:20:43	07-25-2005 12:25:43	ENABLED	✖ 📠
kitten	syslog_upd	07-25-2005 12:20:59	07-25-2005 12:25:59	ENABLED	✖ 📠
router	https	07-25-2005 12:21:03	07-25-2005 12:26:03	ENABLED	✖ 📠
owlet	ssh	07-25-2005 12:21:15	07-25-2005 12:26:15	ENABLED	✖ 📠
router	http	07-25-2005 12:21:34	07-25-2005 12:26:34	ENABLED	✖ 📠
hatchling	syslog_tcp	07-25-2005 12:21:46	07-25-2005 12:26:46	ENABLED	✖ 📠
kitten	smtp	07-25-2005 12:22:02	07-25-2005 12:27:02	ENABLED	✖ 📠
duckling	dns	07-25-2005 12:22:03	07-25-2005 12:27:03	ENABLED	✖ 📠
router	ssh	07-25-2005 12:22:12	07-25-2005 12:27:12	ENABLED	✖ 📠
larva	ssh	07-25-2005 12:22:18	07-25-2005 12:27:18	ENABLED	✖ 📠

Figure 4-16. *The Scheduling Queue page*

The checks are listed one per line with columns displaying the host, service, last and next check time, and whether active checks are enabled for each check. Of these columns you can sort the queue entries in ascending or descending order by host, service, and the last and next check time by clicking the up and down arrows on top of the columns.

The last column allows you to perform actions on each check. The two actions possible for each check are to disable active checks for the service being checked and to reschedule the service check. Both of these actions submit external commands to the Nagios server for processing. For the disable service check command, you will need to specify the host and service being disabled on the page that appears and then click the Commit button to submit the command. To reschedule a service check, you must specify the host and service being rescheduled as well as the time you want the service check to run. There is also an option available to force checks, which forces a check to be submitted even if service checks are disabled for this service. Once you have entered this information, you can click the Commit button to submit the command.

Other Items in the Monitoring Menu

You'll note there are a few menu items I have not touched on in this chapter. In this section I will just briefly discuss these options to let you have some idea of what they are. The two most obvious items I've not discussed are **Status Map** and **3-D Status Map**. These options allow you to display your hosts in a map layout, the first in a flat map layout that you can customize to display in a number of different configurations. The second provides a Virtual Reality Modeling Language (VRML) map layout. You will need to install a VRML plug-in for your browser, such as Corona or Octaga, to be able to view these status maps.[4]

In addition, there are the **Service Problems** and **Host Problems** menu items, which display lists of only those of your services or hosts that currently have a problem. Related to these is the **Network Outages** menu item, which displays a list of the hosts that are causing network outages, ranked by the severity of the network outage. So how does Nagios do this? Well, it uses the parent-child relationship that you can create for your hosts using the parents directive we discussed in Chapter 2. Nagios determines the effect of a network outage by checking a host that has child hosts to see if it is in a DOWN or UNREACHABLE state. If it is in either of those states, it checks the parent and child hosts of that host. If the parent hosts are up and all of the child hosts are in a DOWN or UNREACHABLE state, Nagios assumes that this host has caused a network outage and reports it. It determines the severity of the outage by the number of child hosts that are DOWN or UNREACHABLE as a result of the outage. If one or more of the parent hosts is in a DOWN or UNREACHABLE state, Nagios assumes this host is not the cause of the network outage and checks upward on the parent host until it find what it considers the source of the network outage. This is not a perfect mechanism and is not a true root cause analysis tool, but it tries crudely to determine which hosts are creating the most problems on your network. Additionally, it is generally only useful on larger networks where you have multiple routers, switches, firewalls, or bridges that allow you to configure a true representation of parent-child relationships.

Beneath these three menu items is a box that allows you to enter a hostname and press **Enter**. This will bring up the Service Detail page for that particular host.

Also available are the **Comments** and **Downtime** menu items, which provide an interface directly to add or delete comments or downtime to your hosts and services, respectively. This provides for fast entry or deletion of comments or downtime, and may be a useful interface for systems administrators or help desk staff.

Lastly, there is the **Performance Info** menu item, which displays a series of performance metrics for your Nagios, including many of the same statistics displayed by the nagiostats program we discussed in Chapter 3.

---

4. Find these at www.parallelgraphics.com/products/cortona/ or www.octaga.com/download_octaga.html.

ADDITIONAL CGI PROGRAMS

There are also two other CGI programs that you can incorporate into your web console. These are daemonchk.cgi and traceroute.cgi. Both CGI programs are located in the contrib directory of the Nagios source package. The daemonchk.cgi program checks the status of the Nagios daemon and the traceroute.cgi program allows you to traceroute to a host defined to Nagios, respectively. At the time of this writing, the daemonchk.cgi program does not yet work with Nagios 2.x. To use the programs you will need to compile them in the contrib directory (there is a Makefile in this directory so just type make while in the directory). You can then move the compiled CGI programs into your CGI program directory. In a Nagios source-based installation, this defaults to the /usr/local/nagios/sbin directory. You can then call them from your web browser by navigating to the URL of the CGI program.

Reporting

The Reporting menu contains a series of reports about your hosts, services, and the alerts, events, and notifications that have been generated on your Nagios server. These include reports detailing the availability of your hosts, services, host groups and service groups, reports demonstrating state trending for your hosts and services, and reports on the alerts generated by your host and services. I've listed all the reports available in the web console in Table 4-1.

Table 4-1. *Web Console Reports*

Report Name	Description
Trends	Trend state history for hosts or services
Availability	Percentage availability for a host, host group, service, or service group
Alert Histogram	Event histogram showing alerts for hosts or services
Alert History	History of all alerts for all of your hosts and services
Alert Summary	Configurable summary reports on alerts
Notifications	Configurable notification report
Event Log	Report showing all Nagios log events from the nagios.log file

In this section I'll examine two of the reports in Table 4-1, the Availability and Event Log reports, and allow you to explore the others yourself. Generally, the reports are intuitive and easy to produce, and you should have no trouble displaying the information you require.

The Availability Report

Probably the most useful report available in the web console is the Availability Report. This sort of reporting is used by most organizations to report on the uptime and outages of their hosts and services. In the Availability Report, Nagios presents availability in terms of a percentage over a time period you can specify—for example, the percentage availability of a host over the last month. You can access the report by clicking the Availability link, which executes the avail.cgi CGI program.

To display availability over periods of time, you need to keep your log files for those periods. Additionally, the Nagios server needs to have been running and logging the state of the objects, such as a host or service, during the period you want to measure availability for. For any period for which Nagios does not know the state of the object, it is reported as being in an undetermined state. Generally, in order to report on availability you will need to have enabled log rotation using the `log_rotation` directive and keep your archived log files in the path indicated by the `log_archive_path` directive. Both of these directives are specified in the `nagios.cfg` file, and I discussed how to configure them in Chapter 3.

In addition, you need to be authorized to display the data about the hosts and services in your environment. If you are an authenticated contact, you can see the availability for the hosts and services for which you are a contact. For you to see availability for all hosts, your username must be added to the `authorized_for_all_hosts` directive in the `cgi.cfg` file. For you to see availability for all services, your username must be added to the `authorized_for_all_services` directive, also in the `cgi.cfg` file.

You can see the first page used to define the Availability Report in Figure 4-17.

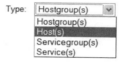

Figure 4-17. *Availability Report Step 1 page*

On this page is Step 1 of defining your Availability Report, which allows you to select whether you wish to display availability statistics for a host or hosts, service or services, or one or more host or service groups. You can only select one type of report. In Figure 4-17 I've selected `Host(s)`. You then click the Continue to Step 2 button, which will display the page in Figure 4-18.

Figure 4-18. *Availability Report Step 2 page*

On this page you can select all hosts or specify a host. If you had selected another type of object, you could select all of those objects or a specific object; for example, if you had selected service groups, you could select all service groups or a specific service group. I've selected all hosts.

Tip If you've selected host or service objects to report on, you will see a tip on the screen telling you that if you want to output the availability data in CSV format you should select all hosts or services. Outputting the data in CVS format allows you to manipulate the data using other tools, such as producing graphs using Microsoft Excel. We will demonstrate this later in this section.

Once you have selected all hosts, click the Continue to Step 3 button to display the selection page shown in Figure 4-19.

Host Availability Report
Last Updated: Thu Jul 14 23:46:35 EST 2005
Nagios® - www.nagios.org
Logged in as *jsmith*

Step 3: Select Report Options

Report Period:	Last Month
If Custom Report Period...	
Start Date (Inclusive):	June / 1 / 2005
End Date (Inclusive):	June / 30 / 2005
Report time Period:	None
Assume Initial States:	Yes
Assume State Retention:	Yes
Assume States During Program Downtime:	Yes
Include Soft States:	No
First Assumed Host State:	Unspecified
First Assumed Service State:	Unspecified
Backtracked Archives (To Scan For Initial States):	4
Output in CSV Format:	☐
	Create Availability Report!

Figure 4-19. *Availability Report Step 3 page*

In Step 3 of defining your Availability Report, you need to define the final options for your report. First you need to select the report period. You do this in the Report Period box. You can select a variety of ranges such as the current day, the last week, the last month, the last year, or a custom-defined period. If you select the custom-defined period, you need to specify the date range in the Start and End Date boxes beneath the Report Period box.

You can also select the particular time period your Availability Report covers. This can be any of the time periods defined using time period objects; for example, in Chapter 2 we defined a time period called 24x7. This will limit the period your report covers to the time period within the report period; you could view availability within business hours for the last month, for instance.

The options below the time period box control how the availability data is interpreted. There are seven options, listed in Table 4-2 along with their defaults.

Table 4-2. *Availability Data Interpretation*

Option	Default	Description
Assume Initial States	Yes	Use an assumed state if initial state can't be detected.
First Assumed Host State	Unspecified	Specify the initial host state.
First Assumed Service State	Unspecified	Specify the initial service state.
Assume States During Program Downtime	Yes	Use the assumed state for periods when Nagios was not monitoring.
Assume State Retention	Yes	Specify whether state retention is enabled.
Include Soft States	No	Calculate availability including soft states.
Backtracked Archives (To Scan For Initial States)	4	Specify how many log files to check back for initial states.

So what do these options do and why do we need them? Well, Nagios does its best to tell you about the availability of your hosts and services. As discussed earlier, it bases this information on the entries in the current and archived log files on your server. If Nagios was not running or if during the period being reported on the data is not available on a particular object or objects, the state of those object or objects will be reported as undetermined. To calculate that availability, Nagios needs to find a log entry that indicates the state of the object or objects at the start of the time frame you are reporting on. Nagios needs this initial state of the object being monitored as a baseline to start calculating availability. If Nagios can find this in the archived log files, it will work off this state. If Nagios cannot find the state, you must help it to determine that state.

The first option in Table 4-2, Assume Initial States, allows you to assist Nagios in specifying that initial state. It can either be set to Yes or No. The first option tells Nagios that if it cannot find the initial state of the object being reported on it should assume the state. This assumed state is specified using the First Assumed Host State and First Assumed Service State options further down the page. You can set a variety of states as the first assumed state. These include the current state and the UP, DOWN, and UNREACHABLE states for hosts and current state, and the OK, WARNING, UNKNOWN, and CRITICAL states for services. For both hosts and services, the current state indicates the state that the host or service is in at the time you are running the report.

The Assume States During Program Downtime option is linked to the previous setting of assumed states. This option, if set to Yes, specifies that Nagios should use the assumed states you have specified for an object or objects if the logs indicate a period of program downtime when the Nagios server not running.

The Assume State Retention option should be set to Yes if you have state retention enabled on your server (we discussed state retention in Chapter 2).

The next option, Include Soft States, tells Nagios to include any changes in state on your objects that resulted in a soft state being set. For example, Nagios would normally only indicate an object is unavailable if it is in a hard DOWN state. If this option is enabled, Nagios would include any outages where the object was in a soft DOWN state also. I recommend leaving this option set to No as soft states are usually not actually indicative of a real outage.

The last option in Table 4-2, Backtracked Archives (To Scan For Initial States), indicates how many log files to backtrack looking for the initial state of the objects being reported on. It defaults to 4.

The last option on the Step 3 page is Output in CSV Format. If you check this box, Nagios will output your availability data to the screen in CSV (Comma-Separated Values) format. This is a commonly used data format that can be readily imported into tools like Microsoft Excel or Crystal Reports. You will need to select the resulting output on the screen and then copy and paste it into a file to collect the data.

After selecting the required options, you need to click the Create Availability Report button to generate your Availability Report. If you haven't selected CSV output, then a page similar to Figure 4-20 will be displayed.

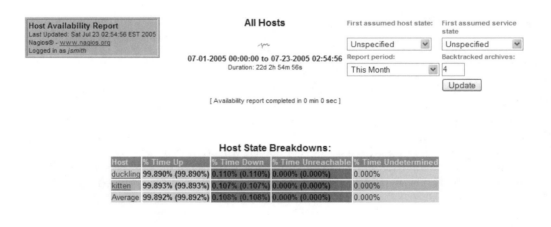

Figure 4-20. *The Availability Report page*

The Availability Report page has a number of components. It displays the variables used to configure the report, such as the time frame covered and the time taken to generate the report. Additionally, there are four dropdown boxes that allow you to update some of the options used to configure the report: First assumed host state, First assumed service state, Report period, and Backtracked archives. You can change any of these options and then click the

Update button to regenerate the report with the new option values. All these options function the same way as their equivalents in Table 4-2.

The actual content of the report depends on what object or objects you are reporting on. In Figure 4-20 I've displayed the availability for all hosts being monitored on the server during this month. Each of the hosts is displayed with percentages totals next to them for each of the four possible states they could have been in: UP, DOWN, UNREACHABLE, and Undetermined.

Tip If you see that all of your objects are showing 100 percent of time in an undetermined state, this is generally because Nagios is unable to determine the initial state of your object or objects. You need to use assumed initial states or increase the number of backtracked archives to attempt to determine the initial state. This problem also occurs with reports generated using the Trends report.

If we had displayed host groups, the report would show our hosts displayed by the host groups they belong to. The same concept also applies if you had reported on services or service groups. You can also drill down further into your availability data by clicking on the objects being reported on; in Figure 4-20, for example, you can click on either the duckling or kitten hosts and display a more detailed breakdown of the host status, a breakdown of the availability of the services on that host, and any availability-related log entries for that host, such as any state changes that have influenced the overall availability figure.

CUSTOM CGI HEADERS AND FOOTERS

You also have the capability on the web console to add custom headers and footers to the Nagios web pages. You can create these headers and footers by placing files in the ssi directory. The ssi directory is located in the directory containing your HTML files. If you've installed from source, this is the /usr/local/nagios/ share directory. The content of these files is inserted into the output of the CGI programs. In the case of headers, the content is inserted just after the opening <BODY> tag, and for footers just before the closing </BODY> tag. If the files are not executable, they are not processed in any way and thus need to output content that your web browser can understand, such as HTML, JavaScript, or the like. So putting the HTML <p>This is a test header</p> into a file would output the string This is a test header. You can also make the header and footer files executable. If you do, Nagios will process the content of the files prior to inserting the output. This allows you to design your own CGIs to insert other information into the web console, such as displaying other graphs or data. The header or footer executable files will execute within the Nagios CGI environment and thus can parse all the Nagios information, such as authentication or query information.

There are two types of headers and footers. The first type is common headers and footers, which appear on every CGI page. These are created by placing the required output in two files, called common-header.ssi and common-footer.ssi, respectively. This content will be placed in the output of all CGI files. The second type of headers and footers are local to specific CGI files. These are created by using files named cgi-footer.ssi and cgi-header.ssi and replacing the cgi with the name of the CGI program where you wish to insert the header or footer. For example, to display a header on the Tactical Monitoring Overview CGI you would create a file called tac-header.ssi. You can use any combination of common and specific headers and footers, or none at all.

The Event Log Report

The next report we are going to look at is the Event Log report, which displays a breakdown of the log entries in the current log file, `nagios.log`. The report, which you access by clicking the `Event Log` link in the left-hand menu, will display a screen similar to Figure 4-21.

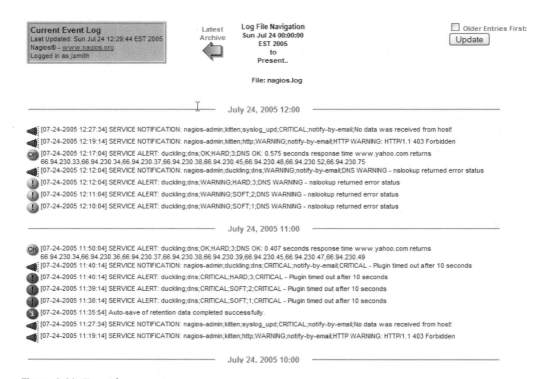

Figure 4-21. *Event log report*

On this screen you can see all of the events listed in the current log file. Each log entry is displayed on a separate line and is broken up into hourly blocks. The log entries are sorted by the most recent event to the oldest. You can change this sort order by selecting the Older Entries First check box and clicking the Update button. This reverses the sort order and displays the last log entries first. You can also backtrack through your log files to show older entries by clicking the backward-facing arrow labeled Latest Archive.

Configuration

The last item on the left-hand menu is the **View Config** menu item. This allows you to display the configuration of your hosts, services, and other objects. As I discussed in Chapter 3, you need to be authorized to these configuration objects. If you are an authenticated contact, you automatically have access to view the configuration of those hosts and services for which you are a contact. No other users have access to any other configuration objects unless their user-name is added to the `authorized_for_configuration_information` directive in the `cgi.cfg` file like so:

`authorized_for_configuration_information=jsmith,jbloggs`

On the previous line we've indicated that the users `jsmith` and `jbloggs` would be able to access all configuration information.

In Figure 4-22 you can see the View Config page.

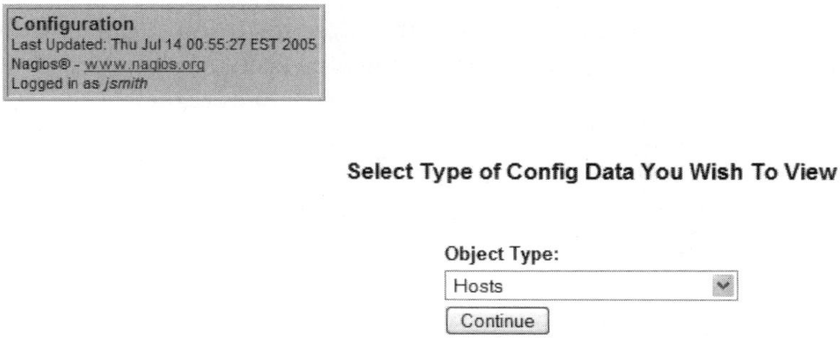

Figure 4-22. *The View Config page*

The View Config page contains a dropdown list that lets you select the particular type of object configuration you want to view. You select the required object type and click Continue. For example, if you have selected `Timeperiods` objects and you are authorized to view all objects, you would see a page similar to Figure 4-23.

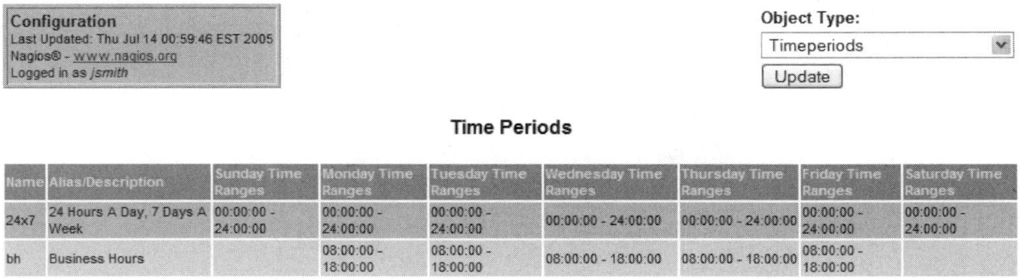

Time Periods

Name	Alias/Description	Sunday Time Ranges	Monday Time Ranges	Tuesday Time Ranges	Wednesday Time Ranges	Thursday Time Ranges	Friday Time Ranges	Saturday Time Ranges
24x7	24 Hours A Day, 7 Days A Week	00:00:00 - 24:00:00	00:00:00 - 24:00:00	00:00:00 - 24:00:00	00:00:00 - 24:00:00	00:00:00 - 24:00:00	00:00:00 - 24:00:00	00:00:00 - 24:00:00
bh	Business Hours		08:00:00 - 18:00:00	08:00:00 - 18:00:00	08:00:00 - 18:00:00	08:00:00 - 18:00:00	08:00:00 - 18:00:00	

Figure 4-23. *Display object configuration*

Checkpoints

- Any entries fields in red in the web console or the External Command Interface page are mandatory fields and need to be filled in.

- In your Availability Report, if all your hosts and services are reported as being in an undetermined state, then Nagios probably can't find an initial state for them. You will need to specify the initial state.

- You can add your own content to the Nagios web console using headers and footers. This can include your own CGI programs.

- You can only view the object configuration you are authorized for. If you are an authenticated contact you can view those hosts and services for which you are a contact. For any other objects, you need to be added to the `authorized_for_configuration_ information` directive in the `cgi.cfg` file.

CHAPTER 5

■■■

Monitoring Hosts and Services

At the heart of the Nagios solution are the mechanisms and methods used to monitor your assets, such as hosts and services. As I've discussed in earlier chapters, Nagios uses commands that call plug-ins, binaries, or scripts to query hosts and services for information. This information is returned in the form of check results that Nagios uses to update the status of your hosts and services.

This chapter focuses on how to use Nagios to monitor your hosts and services. I cover how to monitor local services on your Nagios server, as well as network services like daemons and servers. I also discuss remote monitoring of items like memory and disk space and logs. You'll also learn how to monitor your hosts and services where you have limited access to these devices—for example, through a firewall.

I don't look at every available plug-in but rather focus on some key plug-ins and, in the process, explain the model and approach Nagios takes to monitoring and how to do particular types of monitoring, depending on the target host or service you are attempting to monitor. Also, I don't look at every possible way to monitor hosts and services. Several methods are available, and I focus on the key ones that will enable you to quickly and effectively start monitoring hosts and services.

The chapter concentrates on details of monitoring Unix-like and Windows platforms and will touch on monitoring network devices.[1] There are obviously a lot of other types of devices you can monitor, such as environmental and power equipment. I don't directly cover these, but the key to remember about Nagios monitoring is that anything with an address can be monitored. All you require is a mechanism that returns the required check data: the host and service name, status, and any output and/or performance data that the check returns. Nagios can then process this check result and perform all the normal actions, such as notifications. For most services you wish to monitor, a plug-in will be available, as part of the Nagios standard plug-ins package, from sites like Nagios Exchange, or on the Internet. Or, since the data required to submit a check to Nagios is simple, you can easily design a plug-in using Perl, C, or even a shell script to monitor a device or service that a plug-in does not exist for.[2]

---

1. This includes Unix-like systems like Linux and BSD. I will refer to these generically, if not entirely accurately, as Unix in this chapter.

2. I discuss plug-in development in Chapter 10.

Introduction to Monitoring

Before looking at how to monitor particular services and metrics, let's briefly discuss how commands and plug-ins work. Some of this information I've already covered in Chapter 2, but I'll refresh your memory here. Commands can be used to monitor both hosts and services. Commands are defined using command objects and then referenced using the check_command directive in host and service object definitions.

■Tip You can see sample commands in the checkcommands.cfg and misccommands.cfg (or the minimal.cfg and bigger.cfg) sample configuration files that come with Nagios. Some of these commands may not be functional since the sample files are not always updated when the plug-ins are, but they should provide an excellent basis for creating commands.

Monitoring Hosts

As I discussed in Chapter 2, typically we only want to monitor hosts when absolutely required. This is because if services are responding to checks, then Nagios assumes the host is available. If Nagios does need to check the host, it generally uses some type of network ping to check if the host is up. Example 5-1 shows the command check-host-alive, which is the default command used in the host object check_command directives in the sample configuration files.

Example 5-1. *The Sample Host Check Command*

```
define command{
        command_name    check-host-alive
        command_line    $USER1$/check_ping -H $HOSTADDRESS$ -w 3000.0,80% ➡
-c 5000.0,100% -p 1
}
```

The command in Example 5-1 runs the check_ping plug-in and inputs the macro value $HOSTADDRESS$ (which generally represents the IP address of the host as defined by the address directive in your host object configuration) to the -H option.[3] The plug-in takes three additional options: -w, -c, and -p. The -w and -c options specify the thresholds that will trigger the WARNING and CRITICAL status, and the -p option specifies the number of packets to be sent to the host. The thresholds consist of two values separated by a comma. The first value is the round-trip time in milliseconds for the ping, and the second value is the percentage of packet loss that will trigger a change in status.

■Caution You should always use full paths to the binaries, scripts, or plug-ins that your command executes, either expressed as the full path or using $USERx$ macros. This reduces the risk that someone could insert a malicious replacement binary or plug-in earlier in the path and execute that instead of the real target.

---

3. I discussed the $HOSTADDRESS$ macro in Chapter 2.

The thresholds are triggered in order and are an escalation. The WARNING status comes first and then the CRITICAL status. Your threshold values need to reflect this escalation. We can see this in Example 5-1; to trigger a WARNING status, 80 percent of packets would need to be lost, and to trigger a CRITICAL status, 100 percent of packets would need to be lost. For most plug-ins, if you try to specify a value for the WARNING threshold that precludes a logical escalation to the CRITICAL threshold, the plug-in will fail with an error message. An example of this would be if I reversed the values in Example 5-1 and specified that the CRITICAL status be triggered by 80 percent packet loss and the WARNING status by 100 percent of packet loss. The check_ping plug-in would then fail with an error like so:

```
puppy# check_ping -H 10.0.0.4 -w 3000.0,100% -c 5000.0,80% -p 1
<wpl> (100) cannot be larger than <cpl> (80)
check_ping: Could not parse arguments
```

Note You will also see that the command in Example 5-1 used a user macro, $USER1$, which in this case contains the path to the Nagios plug-in being used. You configure any user macros in your resource configuration files as I discussed in Chapter 2.

So how is this command used in a host object definition? Example 5-2 shows a partial host object definition.

Example 5-2. *Host check_command Directive*

```
define host{
            host_name           puppy
            check_command       check-host-alive
            …
}
```

In Example 5-2, when Nagios needs to check the host, it executes the check-host-alive command that returns the results of the check, including the status response and the ping results. This is a very simple check. If required, I could also edit the command definition and the check_command directive to add arguments to specify different criteria for the thresholds and settings of the plug-in.

Monitoring Services

The basic configuration for checking services is very similar to the configuration required to monitor hosts. Example 5-3 shows a typical service check command.

Example 5-3. *Typical Service Check Command*

```
define command{
        command_name     check_tcp
        command_line     $USER1$/check_tcp -H $HOSTADDRESS$ -p $ARG1$
}
```

The command in Example 5-3 uses one of the most basic plug-ins for Nagios, check_tcp. This plug-in simply connects to a TCP port on a particular IP address and returns a status code depending on the result of the connection; for example, it returns the OK status if a connection is accepted and the CRITICAL status if the connection is refused. It also returns the response time of the connection. Here's an example of the output of a plug-in:

```
TCP OK - 0.002 second response time on port ➥
22|time=0.001755s;0.000000;0.000000;0.000000;10.000000
```

The first portion of the output is the check status, OK, and the textual data returned by the plug-in and displayed in the web console as I described in Chapter 4. The plug-in can also return optional performance data. The performance data is one or more metrics about the host or service being measured. It is included in the output of the check separated from the plug-in response by a pipe symbol, |.

Note I examine performance data in Chapter 6.

The check_tcp plug-in has a number of options, but in this case I've only specified two. First, I passed the macro $HOSTADDRESS$ to the -H option to specify the IP address of the port being checked. Second, I passed the argument $ARG1$ to the -p option, which indicates what port number to try to connect to. Arguments are passed from the check_command directive defined in your service object definition. You can define up to 32 arguments, named $ARG1$ to $ARG32$. Example 5-4 shows a service object definition that uses the command defined in Example 5-3.

Example 5-4. *Service check_command Directive*

```
define service{
          service_description      syslog
          host_name                owlet
          check_command            check_tcp!514
          …
}
```

In Example 5-3 when the service is checked, it executes the check_tcp command and passes an argument to the check command with a value of 514. The value would replace the $ARG1$ argument in the check command when the command was run. This would result in the check command checking port 514 of the owlet host the service was defined on.

You see that arguments are prefixed by the ! symbol. Here a service object definition passes three arguments:

```
define service{
          service_description      syslog
          check_command            check_tcp!514!60!20
          …
}
```

> ■**Note** I will look at the `check_tcp` plug-in in more detail in the "Monitoring Network-Based Services" section.

These values would replace the arguments $ARG1$, $ARG2$, and $ARG3$ if I had specified them in the command object. As you can see from this, arguments are parsed in sequence and the sequence must be replicated in the command object. For example, the three values 514, 60, and 20 would be passed to the command object in that order. You can see this in the command object definition here:

```
define command{
        command_name      check_tcp
        command_line         $USER1$/check_tcp -H $HOSTADDRESS$ -p $ARG1$ ➥
-w $ARG2$ -c $ARG3$
}
```

You must also ensure that if you specify values for arguments that a corresponding argument is specified in the command object. If it is not, then the check command will probably fail because it has received an invalid or bad argument. For example, if you pass three values from the `check_command` directive to the command, there must be three arguments defined in the command, $ARG1$, $ARG2$, and $ARG3$, to receive those values.

> ■**Note** Nagios also uses commands to send notifications and execute event handlers. I look at both these types of commands in more detail in Chapter 6.

Local Unix Monitoring

The first type of monitoring we'll examine is monitoring services and metrics on a local Unix-like host. These services include disk space, memory, CPU usage and the status of applications, processes, and other aspects of your Unix-like hosts. Indeed, using Nagios you can monitor almost any aspect of your hosts, either through one of the provided plug-ins or by writing your own. As I demonstrate in Chapter 10, developing your own plug-ins or monitoring scripts is relatively simple. All Nagios requires is that the plug-in or script returns a status code, the result of the check, and potentially some performance information.

> ■**Note** At this point you can only perform these checks on your local Nagios server as I haven't yet demonstrated a mechanism to execute checks and send check results from a remote host to your Nagios server. I will demonstrate this in the "Remote Monitoring" section.

To explain how plug-ins work, I'm going to examine one plug-in in detail: check_disk. I'll also provide details on other useful plug-ins. I've chosen these plug-ins to give you an idea of how plug-ins work and how you configure them, and as a broad sample of some of the functionality available to you in the standard plug-in package.

The check_disk plug-in monitors the disk space available on a particular path or device and measures it against two thresholds, one that triggers the WARNING status and another that triggers the CRITICAL status. It also returns statistics on the disk space being used. For example, if you are using the web console, the plug-in will display the disk space statistics for the path or paths being monitored in the Status Information box of the Service Detail page.

Example 5-5 shows an example of a check_disk command.

Example 5-5. *Check Local Disk Command*

```
define command{
        command_name    check_local_disk
        command_line    $USER1$/check_disk -w $ARG1$ -c $ARG2$ -p $ARG3$
}
```

As you can in Example 5-5, the check_local_disk command has configured the check_disk plug-in to take three arguments: $ARG1$ passed to the -w option, $ARG2$ passed to the -c option, and $ARG3$ passed to the -p option. These options specify the thresholds required to trigger the WARNING and CRITICAL states, respectively, and the path that the plug-in is monitoring. The type of threshold is dependent on the value of the argument passed. Example 5-6 shows a service objection definition that would pass the required arguments to the check_local_disk command.

Example 5-6. *Local disk check_command Directive*

```
define service{
                service_description    check_local_disk
                check_command          check_local_disk!10%!5%!/
                ...
}
```

In Example 5-6, I've passed the value 10% to the -w option, which indicates that Nagios should change the service into a WARNING state when there is less than 10% of disk space left. I have passed the value 5% to the -c option, which indicates that Nagios should change the service into a CRITICAL state when there is less than 5% of disk space left. I have passed the value / to indicate that it is the disk space of the root directory of the host that is being monitored.

For the check_disk, and most of the other plug-ins that provide thresholds, the thresholds need to make sense. In Example 5-6 the WARNING threshold is 10% and the CRITICAL threshold is 5%. This means that the threshold logically escalates—if the disk space went from 10% free to 5% free, this would escalate the status of the service from OK to WARNING and finally to CRITICAL. If you try to input values that do not make sense here, the check will fail with an error message. For example, if you reversed the values and specified that the WARNING status would be triggered at 5% and the CRITICAL status at 10%, then the check would fail because it does not make sense for the value required to trigger the CRITICAL status to be larger than the value required to trigger that WARNING status.

Additionally, the check_disk thresholds can actually consist of multiple types of values. In Example 5-6 I've specified percentage values for the threshold, but you can also input the actual size of the disk in a variety of units. For example, here I've specified a service object definition that utilizes units of size:

```
define service{
                service_description    check_local_disk
                check_command          check_local_disk!150!50!/
                ...

}
```

The default unit of measure is in megabytes, so this service object definition would trigger a WARNING status if the disk space dropped to 150MB free and a CRITICAL status if the disk space dropped to 50MB free. I demonstrate a little later how to change the default unit of measure.

The check_disk plug-in is typical of most plug-ins in the Nagios plug-in package. As a result, there a few things about it that are common to most plug-ins. First, all well-written plug-ins generally contain built-in help text that describes their functions and potential options that can be displayed via the command line. Let's look at part of the check_disk plug-in's help text by executing it from the command line like so: .

```
puppy# cd /usr/local/nagios/libexec
puppy# ./check_disk --help
check_disk (nagios-plugins 1.4.1) 1.57
Copyright (c) 1999 Ethan Galstad <nagios@nagios.org>
Copyright (c) 1999-2004 Nagios Plugin Development Team
        <nagiosplug-devel@lists.sourceforge.net>
...
```

Tip Rather than having to define commands in command objects and test them by updating the Nagios configuration, you may often find it easier to run a plug-in from the command line. Plug-ins are usually binaries or scripts, and thus it is possible to run them from the command line to test them or to check arguments and variables. I recommend doing this before you define the command in Nagios. This allows you to test the command without actually having to wait for scheduled checks to execute or generate false positives or incorrect data if the command you are testing fails.

The --help option (you can also usually use the option -h to display the help text) should be present in all plug-ins contained in the Nagios plug-in package and in any plug-ins designed in accordance with the developer guidelines.[4] In the case of the check_disk plug-in, the --help option displays a full list of the possible command-line options as well as examples of how to use them. Table 5-1 lists all these options.

---

4. See http://nagiosplug.sourceforge.net/developer-guidelines.html.

Table 5-1. *check_disk Options*

Option	Description
-h, --help	Displays help
-V, --version	Displays the version
-v, --verbose	Displays command-line debugging details (will probably be truncated in the web console)
-w, --warning=*value*	The WARNING status threshold
-c, --critical=*value*	The CRITICAL status threshold
-u, --units=*value*	Specifies the unit being measured
-k, --kilobytes	Equivalent to kB units
-m, --megabytes	Equivalent to MB units
-p, --path=*value*, --partition=*value*	The path or partition being monitored (can be used multiple times)
-x, --exclude_device=*value*	Ignore a particular device; cannot be used with -p option
-X, --exclude-type=*value*	Ignore filesystems of a particular type
-C, --clear	Clears the thresholds presently on the command line
-M, --mountpoint	Displays the mount point instead of the partition
-l, --local	Only checks the local filesystems
-e, --errors-only	Displays only devices which have errors
-t, --timeout=*value*	Specifies the number of seconds before the connection times out; defaults to 10 seconds

Some of these options are fairly easy to understand. The -h option I've already discussed. The -V option displays the version of the plug-in. The -v option makes the plug-in more verbose. You can repeat this option to increase the verbosity, that is, -vv. As the results of a check are displayed in the web console, the more verbose you make them, the more likely they will be truncated since there is only a limited space to display results.

I've already discussed using the -w and -c options and the fact that you can set thresholds in percentages and integers representing physical disk space. You can also influence what units those integers are measuring. By default, check_disk uses MB units. But you can also set it to kBs, GBs, and TBs by using the -u option as you can see here:

```
puppy# ./check_disk -w 10 -c 5 -p / -u GB
DISK OK - free space: / 15 GB (83%);| /=3GB;15;16;0;17
```

In this example I've set the units being measured in the -w and -c options in gigabytes. If I specified a value of 1 for the -w option, the plug-in would trigger the WARNING status if less than 1GB of disk space was free on the device or partition being monitored. There are also two options, -k and -m, that are shorthand for kilobytes and megabytes and that you can use instead of -u kB or -u MB, respectively.

I used the next option, -p, earlier to identify the path or partition being monitored. The -p option can also be repeated multiple times on the command line to monitor multiple points, as you can see here:

```
puppy# check_disk -w 10% -c 5% -p / -p /tmp -p /var
```

In this check, the check_disk plug-in will monitor the root partition, /, as well as the /tmp and /var partitions. If you specify a partition that does not exist, the plug-in will return a CRITICAL result. You can also not specify the -p option and the plug-in will monitor and return results for all devices on the host.

You can also exclude particular types of filesystems and even whole devices using the -X and -x options. The -X option allows you to exclude types of filesystems, as shown here:

```
puppy# check_disk -w 10% -c 5% -X tmpfs
```

As you can see, I'm monitoring all devices on the host except ones with a filesystem type of tmpfs.

The -x option is similar except that it excludes whole devices or partitions, such as /dev/hda1 or /var. It cannot be used if you also specify the -p option:

```
puppy# check_disk -w 10% -c 5% -x /var
```

Here the plug-in will monitor all partitions on the host except the /var partition. You can specify the -x option multiple times to exclude multiple partitions or devices.

What if you want to measure different partitions with different thresholds? Well, combining -p options with the -C option allows you to do this. Let's look at an example:

```
puppy# check_disk -w 10% -c 5% -p / -p /tmp -p /var -C -w 150 -c 50 -p /home
```

In this check, the plug-in will monitor the /, /tmp, and /var partitions and issue a WARNING or a CRITICAL status when disk space gets lower than 10% and 5%, respectively. I've then specified the -C option, which tells the plug-in that we want to set new thresholds. After the -C option, I've specified new thresholds for the /home partition. For that partition the WARNING or CRITICAL status should be generated when disk space gets lower than 150MB and 50MB, respectively.

The -M option will result in the plug-in returning the mount points of the devices instead of the partition. The -l option will cause the plug-in to only return local filesystems. The -e option will cause the plug-in to only report partitions with non-OK status.

The last option in Table 5-1, -t, allows you to control the timeout the plug-in uses. If the plug-in has not received a result from its check in this time period, then it aborts itself and returns an error. This option defaults to 10 seconds, which should be more than adequate for most plug-ins. This option is present in most plug-ins.

Table 5-2 lists some other plug-ins that you might be interested in using to monitor local resources.

Table 5-2. *Other Local Service Monitoring Plug-ins*

Plug-in	Description
check_file_age	Checks the age and size of a file
check_load	Checks and returns load statistics for the host
check_log	Checks a log for a particular entry
check_mailq	Checks thresholds for numbers of items in mail queues for a number of Mail Transfer Agents (MTAs)
check_procs	Checks thresholds for the number of processes or for a particular process or processes
check_swap	Checks the free swap space
check_users	Checks a threshold of number of users logged on

In Table 5-2 I've listed a few of the available stock plug-ins for monitoring host-based services. Let's take a brief look at each of them and what they can do.

The check_file_age plug-in allows you to specify WARNING and CRITICAL thresholds for the age and size of a file that Nagios can monitor. If the age or size of the file exceeds the thresholds set, then Nagios will return a WARNING or CRITICAL status. Here's an example of this plug-in:

```
puppy# ./check_file_age -w 600 -c 1200 -f /var/log/messages
CRITICAL - /var/log/messages is 1270 seconds old and 1978757 bytes
```

On the previous line I've tested the age of the file, /var/log/messages. The age of the file is measured in seconds and two thresholds have been set using the -w and -c options. The check will trigger a WARNING status if the file is older than 600 seconds and a CRITICAL status if the file is older than 1,200 seconds. The check result in this example is CRITICAL as the file is 1,270 seconds old. There are another set of thresholds, using the -C and -W options, that you can set instead of, or in addition, to the -w and -c options, which check the size of the file. If the file size exceeds the size specified in the -W threshold, the WARNING status will be set, and if it exceeds the size in the -C option, the CRITICAL status will be set.

The next plug-in in Table 5-2 is the check_load plug-in, which allows you to monitor and specify WARNING and CRITICAL thresholds for the load on your host using the same load average format as that used by the uptime and w commands. You can see an example of the plug-in here:

```
puppy# ./check_load -w 10,15,20 -c 15,20,25
OK - load average: 0.00, 0.00, 0.00|load1=0.000;10.000;15.000;0;➥
load5=0.000;15.000;20.000;0; load15=0.000;20.000;25.000;0;
```

The check_load plug-in uses the -w and -c options to specify thresholds that will trigger WARNING or CRITICAL status if the load averages exceed the values set in the thresholds.

The check_log plug-in allows you to monitor log files for a particular entry to appear. The check is not overly sophisticated but will work for basic purposes. The check_log plug-in works by specifying two files: the file containing the log entries and a file to store previously checked messages and a pattern. The plug-in uses the grep command to search the log file, so the pattern used to select messages should be compatible with grep. You can see the plug-in in action here:

```
puppy# ./check_log  -F /var/log/messages -O /var/log/nagioslog/messages -q sshd
```

On this line I've specified the log file, /var/log/messages, using the -F option. I've also specified a file to store the already checked log messages, /var/log/nagioslog/messages, using the -O option. The pattern to be matched, sshd, is specified using the -q option.

Every time the plug-in is executed, the contents of the /var/log/messages file will be scanned for the pattern, and if it is found, the associated message will be returned in the check result. The messages from the log file will then be copied to the file specified in the -O option. This means only new messages since the last run of the plug-in will be returned in check results.

Additionally, the first time you run the plug-in, it will not return any results but will merely initialize the check by creating the old log file. It will only be on subsequent executions of the plug-in that any new matched log messages will be returned.

■**Tip** In the `contrib` directory of the Nagios plug-in package, there is a more advanced variation of this plug-in called `check_log2.pl` that might be worth reviewing. Additionally, if this plug-in interests you, in Chapter 9 I discuss integrating `syslog` and Nagios.

The `check_mailq` plug-in checks the status of your mail queues and works with a number of Mail Transfer Agents (MTAs), including Sendmail, Postfix, Exim, and qmail. On the following line you can see the `check_mailq` plug-in used to check the mail queues of a Sendmail mail server:

```
puppy# ./check_mailq -w 100 -c 200 -M sendmail
OK: mailq is empty|unsent=0;100;200;0
```

The `-w` and `-c` options set `WARNING` and `CRITICAL` thresholds for the number of messages in the queue, and the `-M` option allows you to specify which MTA to check the queues for.

One of the more useful plug-ins is the powerful `check_procs` plug-in. By default this plug-in returns the number of running processes on your host but with a few arguments it is capable of a lot more functionality. The most obvious is to see whether a particular process is running and to issue alert if it is not. In addition, it is capable of monitoring processes against a number of threshold metrics including number of processes running, CPU used, two types of memory use, and time elapsed. On the following line you can see the plug-in being used to check against thresholds for the number of running processes:

```
puppy# ./check_procs -w 5 -c 10 --metric=PROCS
PROCS CRITICAL: 67 processes
```

The `-w` and `-c` options set thresholds for triggering the `WARNING` or `CRITICAL` status. The `--metric` option specifies what metric is being tested by the plug-in. If the option is not specified, the default behavior of the plug-in is to test the threshold against the number of running processes. You can also specify this behavior by using the `--metric=PROCS` option, as I have in the example. The other possible metrics you can test against are `VSZ` for virtual memory size, `RSS` for resident set memory size, `CPU` for percentage of CPU used, and `ELAPSED` for time elapsed in seconds for the process. You can see an example of using this plug-in to test against the CPU metric here:

```
puppy# ./check_procs -w 10 -c 20 --metric=CPU
CPU OK: 66 processes
```

In the previous example, if any of the processes on the `puppy` host are using more than 10 percent of the CPU, the `WARNING` status will be triggered. If the processes are using more than 20 percent of the CPU, the `CRITICAL` status will be triggered.

The `check_procs` plug-in is also capable of selecting particular processes based on who the process is running as, its status flags, its arguments, and the command run by the process.

Using the `check_swap` plug-in, you can check the free space, both in terms of actual memory and as a percentage, available in your swap partitions. Here is an example of how you'd use the `check_swap` plug-in:

```
puppy# ./check_swap -w 20% -c 10%
SWAP OK - 100% free (512 MB out of 512 MB) |swap=511MB;102;51;0;511
```

In this example the check_swap plug-in will test the percentage of swap space available. If the free swap space drops below 20 percent, the WARNING status will be triggered; if the free swap space drops below 10 percent, the CRITICAL status will be triggered.

The last plug-in in Table 5-2 is the check_users plug-in, which allows you to specify a threshold for the maximum number of users who are logged on. You can see an example of this plug-in here:

```
puppy# ./check_users -w 5 -c 10
USERS OK - 1 users currently logged in |users=1;5;10;0
```

The check_users plug-in on this line triggers the WARNING status if more than 5 users are logged on and the CRITICAL status if more than 10 users are logged on.

■**Tip** A large number of other plug-ins are available in the default plug-ins package; for example, to monitor databases there are plug-ins for MySQL, Oracle, and PostgreSQL. On the NagiosExchange site and in the
contrib directory in the Nagios plug-ins package you can find a large range of other plug-ins that could be
useful. I recommend you review these as well.[5]

Monitoring Network-Based Services

One of the easiest things to monitor with Nagios are network-based services like servers and daemons. A number of stock plug-ins exist to monitor services like LDAP, SSH, FTP, SMTP, or ICMP (which is typically used by Nagios host object checks to confirm that a host is available). These plug-ins connect to the network-based service and return a status code, usually an OK if the connection is accepted or a CRITICAL status if the connection is refused. They can also return some information, such as the banner of the network-based service, along with perform-ance information, such as the response time in seconds of the service. I'll look at several of these stock plug-ins and explain how they can be used to monitor your network-based services.

■**Tip** Remember that a network-based service can be anything that can be, and has value to be, monitored! You can monitor anything that has some form of network address that Nagios can contact. This could
be a server or a router but it could also be a piece of facilities management infrastructure equipment, such
as an air conditioner, a temperature sensor, or a UPS. It could even be a piece of industrial equipment such
as a SCADA system or an industrial lathe.

Let's start by looking at a commonly used plug-in, the check_ssh plug-in, that monitors sshd daemons. In Example 5-7, I've demonstrated how to use this plug-in in a command object.

---

5. See www.nagiosexchange.org/.

Example 5-7. *The check_ssh Plug-in*

```
define command{
             command_name      check_ssh
             command_line      $USER1$/check_ssh -H $HOSTADDRESS$
}
```

The check_ssh plug-in connects to a specified host address provided by the $HOSTADDRESS$ macro. The check returns the status of the sshd daemon and its response to the connection attempt, usually the banner for the daemon. On these lines you can see an example of running this plug-in from the command line and the response to that connection:

```
puppy# ./check_ssh -H 10.0.0.15
SSH OK - OpenSSH_4.2 (protocol 2.0)
```

The check_ssh plug-in also has a number of options, in addition to the -H option, that you can pass to it. I've listed all of these options in Table 5-3.

Table 5-3. *check_ssh Options*

Option	Description
-p, --port=*value*	Specifies the port number (default: 22).
-4, --use-ipv4	Uses IPv4 networking.
-6, --use-ipv6	Uses IPv6 networking.
-r, --remote-version=*value*	Checks the remote version of the daemon.
-t, --timeout=*value*	Specifies seconds before the connection times out. Defaults to 10 seconds.
-v, --verbose	Displays command-line debugging details (will probably be truncated in the web console).
-h, --help	Displays help.
-V, --version	Displays the version.

The -p option allows you to specify an alternative port for the sshd daemon; it defaults to the standard ssh port of 22. The -4 and -6 options allow you to specify whether you want to use IPv4 or IPv6 networking. If you do not specify either option, the check_ssh plug-in uses IPv4 networking by default.

The -r option lets you test the content of the banner returned by the check. You can specify a string that the plug-in will test against the banner response it receives from the check. The following lines demonstrate how to do this:

```
puppy# ./check_ssh -H 10.0.0.15 -r OpenSSH_4.3
SSH WARNING - OpenSSH_4.2 (protocol 2.0) version mismatch, expected 'OpenSSH_4.3'
```

Here I've specified that I want the check_ssh plug-in to compare the response from the check to the string OpenSSH_4.3. The check has resulted in a WARNING status because the actual string returned was OpenSSH_4.2.

So how would we represent this in a command and service object? Well, let's look at a command object:

```
define command{
            command_name       check_ssh
            command_line       $USER1$/check_ssh -H $HOSTADDRESS$ -r $ARG1$
}
```

As you can see, this is a simple expansion of Example 5-7 but we're passing the value of $ARG1$ to the -r option. Now let's see the corresponding service object:

```
define service{
            service_description    sshd
            check_command    check_ssh!OpenSSH_4.1
            …

}
```

As you can see, I've defined the value I want tested in the -r option, prefixed with a ! symbol, which will be passed to the command object as $ARG1$.

The last four options in Table 5-3 are standard to most plug-ins, and I've described their functions earlier in this chapter.

Also earlier in this chapter I introduced the check_tcp plug-in. This is another example of a network monitoring plug-in and is used extensively both on its own and as a basis for other plug-ins. It allows you to monitor network-based services via TCP or UDP ports. This also enables you to monitor network-based services for which a specific plug-in does not exist—for example, if you wished to monitor a syslog daemon, a tftp server, or a proprietary daemon that uses a specific port. In Example 5-8 I've used the check_tcp plug-in from the command line to monitor a syslog daemon or other service running on port 514.

Example 5-8. *The check_tcp Plug-in*

```
puppy# ./check_tcp -H 10.0.0.15 -p 514
TCP OK - 0.000 second response time on port ➥
514|time=0.000483s;0.000000;0.000000;0.000000;10.000000
```

In Example 5-8 I've specified an IP address for the -H option and a port number for the -p option. You can also see the check result that has returned the OK status, the response time, and, after the | symbol, the performance data from the check. The OK status is returned when the plug-in successfully connects to the targeted server or daemon.

The check_tcp plug-in also has some standard plug-in options. These include the -V option to display the version, the -h option to display the plug-in's help text, and the -v option to display verbose check results. You can also use the -t option to specify the timeout for the plug-in. This option defaults to 10 seconds.

There are some additional options for the check_tcp plug-in, shown in Table 5-4.

Table 5-4. *check_tcp Options*

Option	Description
-4, --use-ipv4	Uses IPv4
-6, --use-ipv6	Uses IPv6
-w, --warning=*value*	Response time in seconds that triggers a WARNING status
-c, --critical=*value*	Response time in seconds that triggers a CRITICAL status
-s, --send=*value*	Sends specified string to the server
-e, --expect=*value*	Specifies a string to expect in the server response
-q, --quit=value	Sends the specified string to the server to ensure connection is closed
-M, --mismatch=*ok|warn|crit*	Specifies what status to return if a mismatch is detected
-r, --refuse=*ok|warn|crit*	Specifies what status to return if the connection is refused (defaults to CRITICAL)
-j, --jail	Hides output from TCP socket
-m, --maxbytes=*value*	Closes connection once more than this number of bytes are received
-d, --delay=*value*	Specifies seconds to wait between sending the string and polling for a response
-S, --ssl	Uses SSL for the connection
-D, --certificate=*value*	Specifies the minimum number of days a certificate has to be valid

The first two options, -4 and -6, control whether the plug-in will use IPv4 or IPv6 networking. The check_tcp plug-in uses IPv4 connections by default.

The next two options, -w and -c, control whether the WARNING or CRITICAL status is generated when the response time of the connection exceeds specified thresholds. The thresholds are measured in seconds. You can see an example of this here:

```
puppy# ./check_tcp -H 10.0.0.15 -w 1 -c 2 -p 514

TCP OK - 0.000 second response time on port ➥
514|time=0.000440s;1.000000;2.000000;0.000000;10.000000
```

On the previous line I've specified that the WARNING status be triggered if the response time of the TCP connection to port 514 takes longer than 1 second and the CRITICAL status if it takes longer than 2 seconds.

The next option, -s, allows you to send a string to the TCP port you are connecting to. This can be used to incite some response from the remote service.

You can also specify a string you expect in response to a connection using the check_tcp plug-in using the -e option. Finally, you can also send a string to ensure the connection is correctly closed using the -q option.

Let's look at the expect option, -e, which allows you to specify a string that you expect the remote service to respond with. Example 5-9 demonstrates this.

Example 5-9. *The check_tcp Expect Option*

```
puppy# ./check_tcp -H 10.0.0.15 -e SSH-2.0-Sun_SSH_1.0 -p 22

TCP OK - 0.011 second response time on port 22 [SSH-2.0 Sun_SSH_1.0] ➡
|time=0.011059s;0.000000;0.000000;0.000000;10.000000
```

In Example 5-9 I've specified that the response to the TCP connection on port 22 should be SSH-2.0-Sun_SSH_1.0. This is not a precise match and in fact is quite granular. The plug-in will try to match anything in the string specified in the -e option with the response. So in Example 5-9 the plug-in would return a match if the -e option had been SSH, Sun, or 1.0.

By default, the -e option returns a WARNING status if the response does not match the string specified in the -e option. But you can modify this behavior using the -M option. When you specify -M crit, the behavior of the plug-in would change to return the CRITICAL status when a mismatch is detected. You can also specify the -M ok option to return the OK status when a mismatch is detected.

Using the -r option, you can also change what status is returned when a connection is refused. By default for a refused connection the status returned is CRITICAL. To change the status returned for a refused connection to the WARNING status, specify the -r warn option.

The next option, -d, allows you to specify a value in seconds to wait between opening the connection and polling for the response.

The last two options in Table 5-4 allow you to work with SSL connections. The first option, -S, tells the check_tcp plug-in to use an SSL connection. The second option, -D, tests the validity of any certificate being used by the SSL connection. To use the -D option, you need to specify the minimum number of days that the certificate must be valid for. Here's an example:

```
puppy# ./check_tcp -H 10.0.0.15 -p 443 -S -D 100
Certificate will expire on 04/25/2006 03:5.
```

On these lines I've checked a connection to an HTTPS server using an SSL connection. I also asked the plug-in to check the expiry of the certificate and ensure it will be valid for at least another 100 days.

You will note the check only returned the certificate validity period. It did not return the check results. You would need to define a separate check without the -D option to monitor the availability or status of the service like so:

```
puppy# ./check_tcp -H 10.0.0.15 -p 443 -S
TCP OK - 0.097 second response time on port 443 ➡
|time=0.096874s;0.000000;0.000000;0.000000;10.000000
```

A number of plug-ins are based on the check_tcp plug-in. This is achieved by symlinking the check_tcp plug-in to create other plug-ins. The check_tcp plug-in detects the name of the plug-in symlink and from that knows what its behavior is. For example, the check_udp plug-in is a symlink of the check_tcp plug-in. When the check_udp plug-in is run, check_tcp detects the name of the symlink being executed and hence knows to use UDP connections instead of TCP connections. A number of other symlinked plug-ins monitor services like POP, IMAP, NNTP, FTP, and Jabber. You can see these other plug-ins by reviewing the contents of your plug-in directory and examining the symlinked entries.

There are a large number of stock plug-ins that monitor network-based services, and I've listed a selection of them in Table 5-5. You can see further examples in the directory you installed your plug-ins to, usually /usr/local/nagios/libexec. Several additional plug-ins are available in the contrib directory of the Nagios plug-in package and on the Internet, especially the Nagios Exchange site.[6]

Table 5-5. *Other Network-Based Monitoring Plug-ins*

Plug-in	Description
check_dhcp	Checks that a DHCP server is offering IP addresses
check_dns	Checks that your DNS servers is resolving addresses
check_fping	Checks your hosts using the fping command
check_http	Checks the status of web pages including SSL
check_imap	Checks the status of an IMAP server
check_ldap	Checks the status of an LDAP server
check_nntp	Checks the status of an NNTP server
check_ntp	Checks the status of an NTP server
check_pop	Checks the status of a POP server
check_rpc	Checks if RPC services are running
check_smtp	Checks the status of your SMTP server

Some of the plug-ins in Table 5-5 are symlinked from the check_tcp plug-in as I described earlier and thus have very similar, if not identical, options to that plug-in. This makes them very easy to configure and utilize. Others, like the check_smtp plug-in, which monitors the status of an SMTP service, are stand-alone plug-ins.

The first plug-in in Table 5-5, check_dhcp, checks the status of a DHCP server and ensures it is serving out IP addresses. You can see an example of using this plug-in here:

```
puppy# ./check_dhcp -s 10.0.0.1
DHCP ok: Received 1 DHCPOFFER(s), 1 of 1 requested servers responded, ➥
max lease time = 86400 sec.
```

The check_dhcp plug-in uses the -s option to specify the DHCP server you wish to query. You can also add the option -r to request a specific IP address from the DHCP pool. The plug-in queries the DHCP server and requests an IP address. If the request is satisfied and the IP address offer made, then the plug-in will return the OK status. If the offer is refused, the plug-in will return the CRITICAL status.

The second plug-in in the table, check_dns, confirms your DNS servers are resolving addresses. It works by specifying a DNS server to query and an address or hostname to resolve like so:

```
puppy# ./check_dns -H www.apexmail.com -s 10.0.0.5
DNS OK: 0.471 seconds response time www.apexmail.com ➥
returns 209.87.135.202|time=0.470644s;;;0.000000
```

---

6. See www.nagiosexchange.org/Check_Plugins.21.0.html.

The hostname you wish to resolve is specified in the -H option while the -s option holds the IP address of the DNS server that you wish to resolve the address. The -s option is optional; if you omit it, the plug-in will attempt to resolve the hostname using the default DNS server or servers for your Nagios server. If the resolution occurs, the plug-in will return an OK status; if it fails, it returns a CRITICAL status. It will also return the resolved IP address of the hostname and some performance data about the response time of the DNS query.

The check_fping plug-in is very similar to the check_ping plug-in used for host status checks except that it utilizes the fping command instead of the ping command. You can use it like so:

```
puppy# ./check_fping -H 10.0.0.15
FPING OK - 10.0.0.15 (loss=0%, rta=0.310000 ms)|loss=0% ➥
;;;0;100 rta=0.000310s;;;0.000000
```

The fping command is a more advanced version of ping and generally performs a faster check of the target host than the ping command.[7]

The check_http plug-in is a powerful plug-in that allows you to query the status of web servers and pages. You can see a basic use of the check_http plug-in here:

```
puppy# ./check_http -H 10.0.0.15
HTTP OK HTTP/1.1 200 OK - 1068 bytes in 0.005 seconds ➥
 |time=0.004829s;;;0.000000 size=1068B;;; 0
```

Using the check_http plug-in, the remote web server is specified using the -H option. The check result includes the OK status if the web server responds correctly, or the CRITICAL result if it does not respond or the connection is refused. If the web server responds with an error message instead, then the WARNING status is set. The check result also includes the amount of data returned and the response time for the return of that data. You can use the -w and -c options to specify thresholds for this response time.

A number of other options are available for the plug-in. For example, you can also check the status of an SSL site by adding the option, --ssl, to the plug-in command line. You can override the default ports of 80 or 443 using the -p option, and you can specify an IPv4 or IPv6 connection using the -4 and -6 options, respectively.

You can also query the site or server for specific data to be returned, including using regular expressions to do this using the -s, -r, and -R options. You can also authenticate to a site using Basic authentication with the -a option.

■Tip The check_http plug-in has a number of features, and I recommend you check the help text for the plug-in for further details.

The check_ldap plug-in allows you to query the status of an LDAP server, including searching for a specific attribute in the LDAP database.

---

7. There is also a plug-in called check_icmp that allows ICMP checks to be performed.

The check_imap and check_pop plug-ins let you check the status of IMAP and POP servers. They are both symlinked to the check_tcp plug-in and use the same options as that plug-in. Another similar plug-in is the check_nntp, which is also symlinked to the check_tcp plug-in and again uses the same options.[8]

The check_rpc plug-in provides the ability to check the status and registration of RPC commands on a remote host. You can see this command being used to check the status of the nfs command on this line:

```
puppy# ./check_rpc -H 10.0.0.15 -C nfs -p 2049 -t
```

The check_rpc checks the status of a remote server specified in the -H option. You specify the RPC command to be checked using the -C option. These are commands like nfs, ypbind, portmap, or mountd, among others. You can also specify the port to connect to test if the RPC command is running using the -p option and specify whether to make a TCP or UDP connection using the -u and -t options. By default, the plug-in makes UDP connections.

The last plug-in in Table 5-5, check_smtp, checks the status of an SMTP server. You can see it here:

```
puppy# ./check_smtp -H 10.0.0.15 -S
SMTP OK - 0.020 sec. response time|time=0.020409s;;;0.000000
```

The check_smtp plug-in checks the SMTP server specified in the -H option. In the previous example, I have also specified the -S option, which sends the STARTTLS command to the SMTP server. The response from the server consists of the OK status if the server responds together with the response time of the connection. You can set thresholds for this response time in seconds using the -w and -c options. If the thresholds are exceeded, then the WARNING or CRITICAL status is triggered.

A number of other options are available for the check_smtp plug-in. First, you can override the default SMTP port of 25 using the -p option. You can also control whether the connection is made using IPv4 or IPv6 with the -4 and -6 options, respectively.

You can also send SMTP commands to the server using the -C option and specify an expected response to those commands using the -R option. Additionally, as with the check_tcp plug-in, you can specify a string you expect the SMTP server to reply with, such as a banner, using the -e option.

Remote Monitoring

So far I've looked at two types of monitoring: plug-ins that can monitor local services like disk space and memory and plug-ins that can monitor network-based services. The first type of monitoring is useful, but as the plug-ins can only be run on the local Nagios host they are of limited value. To make full use of them on remote systems, you need a mechanism to transmit the results from the plug-ins back to the Nagios server. The second type of monitoring is more useful but is only effective for those services that are network facing.

So how do we monitor services running on remote hosts that are not network facing? For example, in the "Local Unix Monitoring" section I looked at the check_disk plug-in. How do

---

8. There are other similar plug-ins like this, such as check_ftp, check_spop, check_simap, and check_nntps.

we use this plug-in on a remote host to provide details of the disk usage on that host and pass the results back to the Nagios server?

Well, there are several ways to achieve this, and there are issues and challenges with each of these ways. The key issues and challenges involve security and securing both your connections and the hosts themselves while still allowing Nagios to monitor and collect any required information. There is also the issue that at least one of these methods requires the deployment of a tool, or what could be considered an "agent," on your remote hosts. This obviously introduces the challenge of maintaining that agent, updating its configuration, and ensuring it gets deployed on all required hosts.

Thus I recommend you read about the methods detailed in this section and then look at each potential remote host and select the monitoring method most suited for that host. One of your key objectives should always be the security of the host in addition to achieving your monitoring objectives. In this section, I'll show you a number of methods to monitor services on your remote hosts. These include monitoring via the nrpe daemon, SSH, and SNMP. You can select one or more of these methods to achieve your monitoring objectives.

Note   You can also monitor remote hosts via the NSCA daemon; I discuss that in more detail in Chapter 8 when I look at distributed monitoring, redundancy, and failover.

Monitoring via NRPE

The first method to remotely monitor the services on your hosts I'm going to demonstrate uses a tool written by Nagios developer Ethan Galstad called NRPE. NRPE has two components: a plug-in called check_nrpe and a daemon called nrpe. The plug-in is installed on your Nagios server and then the nrpe daemon is installed on the remote host. You use the check_nrpe plug-in on the Nagios server to query the nrpe daemon running on the remote host.

The check_nrpe plug-in works by passing the name of a check command to be executed to the nrpe daemon on the remote host and returns the result of that check command to the Nagios server. On the Nagios server, the check_nrpe plug-in is defined in a command object. This command object, together with the command to be executed on the remote host, is specified as the value of the check_command directive in a service object. When the service check is performed, the check command is run and the check_nrpe plug-in passes the name of the command to be executed on the remote host to the nrpe daemon. The nrpe daemon has a configuration file, nrpe.cfg, which contains definitions for all check commands that you wish to execute on the remote host. The nrpe daemon then executes the defined command and returns the results of that command to the check_nrpe plug-in and from there to the Nagios server.

Let's look at a practical example. I have a remote host called owlet. I want to monitor the disk space used on this remote host. First I define a command object called check_nrpe that uses the check_nrpe plug-in. Next I define a service object, like the partial one you can see on the next lines, that contains a check_command directive that calls that check_nrpe command object and passes to it the value check_disk.

```
define service{
            service_description    disk
            host_name                   owlet
            check_command         check_nrpe!check_disk
            ...
}
```

The `check_nrpe` daemon contacts the `nrpe` daemon on the remote host using a TCP connection on port 5666 and tells it to execute the `check_disk` command definition. The `check_disk` command definition in the `nrpe.cfg` file contains a binary or plug-in to be executed. The plug-in in that command definition is executed, the disk space is checked, and the result returned to the Nagios server. The status of the `disk` service on the `owlet` host is then updated based on the check result.

Note You will need to ensure your Nagios server can see the remote host on port 5666. This means any intervening firewalls or network devices must allow traffic on this port between the Nagios server and the remote host.

You can execute any command, binary, or script on the remote host that will return data that Nagios can receive and process. Any plug-in, binary, or script you wish to execute on the remote host needs to be compiled and/or installed on the remote host; for example, if you wished to execute the `check_disk` plug-in you would need to compile and install this plug-in on the remote host.

Installing and Compiling NRPE

To get started with NRPE we first need to download, compile, and install the NRPE package. You will need to compile and install the `check_nrpe` plug-in on your Nagios server and the `nrpe` daemon on your remote hosts. The compilation process for the package will create both the `check_nrpe` plug-in and the `nrpe` daemon. At the time of this writing the latest version of the NRPE package was 2.0. Use the following lines to download and unpack the NRPE package:

```
puppy# wget http://prdownloads.sourceforge.net/nagios/nrpe-2.0.tar.gz
puppy# tar -zxf nrpe-2.0.tar.gz
puppy# cd nrpe-2.0
```

Caution You should ensure that the `check_nrpe` plug-in located on your Nagios server and the `nrpe` daemon located on your remote hosts are from the same version of the NRPE package. There have been many changes to the NRPE package between versions, and this can cause difficulties in connections and functionality. If you upgrade the `check_nrpe` plug-in on the Nagios server, you need to ensure that you upgrade the version of the `nrpe` daemon deployed on your remote hosts, and vice versa. I recommend the use of a software distribution tool like cfengine for this.[9]

---

9. See www.cfengine.org/.

The NRPE package comes with a `configure` script that you can use to start the compilation process. I've shown a typical `configure` script on the following line:

```
puppy# ./configure --enable-ssl
```

I've only specified one option, `---enable-ssl`, in the `configure` script. This enables native SSL/TSL support in the NRPE package using the OpenSSL package. This can be used to encrypt and secure the connections between your Nagios server and the remote host. I strongly recommend that for security reasons you enable this functionality. If you do not enable it, an intruder could either eavesdrop on or subvert the connections between your Nagios server and the remote host.

Note You will need a recent version of OpenSSL (0.9.7a or more recent) installed on both the Nagios server and remote host for SSL/TLS functionality to operate. You will also need to specify the `--enable-ssl` option in the `configure` script on both hosts. If you do not use this option on both hosts, the SSL handshake will fail.

This native SSL/TLS functionality is provided by utilizing the Anon-DH function with SHA1 and AES-256 bit encryption. The Anon-DH function does not require pregenerated keys or certificates but instead dynamically creates keys when the `nrpe` daemon is started. This is authentication encryption at its most basic, and as such there is a risk of man-in-the-middle attacks. But the risk is limited and this solution should provide adequate protection for most circumstances. If you do not feel this is suitable protection for your environment, you have the option of deploying a tool such as Stunnel to encapsulate your NRPE traffic in a more secure SSL tunnel.

Note More detail about encryption and NRPE is contained in the `README.SSL` file in the NRPE package.

Table 5-6 lists a number of other `configure` options.

Table 5-6. *NRPE configure Options*

Option	Description
`--prefix=prefix`	Specifies an alternative prefix
`--with-ssl-lib=directory`	Specifies the location of the SSL libraries
`--with-ssl-inc=directory`	Specifies the location of the SSL includes
`--with-kerberos-inc=directory`	Specifies the location of the Kerberos includes
`--with-nrpe-user=value`	Sets the NRPE username (defaults to nagios)
`--with-nrpe-group=value`	Sets the NRPE group name (defaults to nagios)
`--with-nrpe-port=value`	Sets the NRPE port number (defaults to 5666)
`--enable-command-args`	Allows the passing of arguments to remote hosts

The first option in Table 5-6 is --prefix, which allows you to specify an alternative prefix for the nrpe daemon. The --prefix controls the paths that are defined in the nrpe daemon configuration file, nrpe.cfg. The default prefix if this option is not set is /usr/local/nagios.

The next three options let you specify the location of your SSL and Kerberos libraries and includes. You should only need these if NRPE is unable to find these libraries or includes by default.

The next three options control the configuration of the nrpe daemon. The first two options, --with-nrpe-user and --with-nrpe-group, enable you to specify the user and group used to run the daemon. If you do not specify these options, they both default to nagios. This user and group must exist for the daemon to start. The --with-nrpe-port option allows you to override the default TCP port of 5666 with an alternative port number. Unless you need to change this, I recommend leaving it as the default.

The last option is particularly interesting as it controls whether you want to compile in support for the passing of arguments to your remote hosts. By default, the check_nrpe plug-in simply sends the name of the command it wishes the nrpe daemon to run to the remote host. The nrpe daemon executes the command and sends back the results. Any arguments required for the command need to be hard-coded into the nrpe.cfg file on the remote host. This obviously limits the flexibility of the commands you can execute on the remote host.

So why do we care if arguments do or don't get sent to the remote host? Especially as this would make command configuration and execution much easier? Well, there is a security risk involved in enabling arguments. Arguments allow you to pass strings of data other than the check command to be executed to the nrpe daemon. These strings of data could contain commands or meta-characters that could be used to subvert the nrpe daemon and submit malicious commands on the remote host.

There are a couple of ways to mitigate this risk. The first is to ensure that you use SSL or, even more effective, encapsulate your NRPE traffic in a Stunnel-generated tunnel. The second is to use a host firewall and lock down the source and destination of all traffic on port 5666 (or the port you intend to use for NRPE). Let's look at a quick example using iptables:

```
owlet# iptables -A INPUT -p tcp -m tcp --dport 5666 -s 10.0.0.15 -j ACCEPT
owlet# iptables -A OUTPUT -p tcp -m tcp --sport 5666 -d 10.0.0.15 -j ACCEPT
```

On these lines I've locked down the NRPE traffic entering and leaving the remote host on port 5666 to only that traffic from and destined to host 10.0.0.15. This means that our Nagios server at 10.0.0.15 is the only host on our network that can send the owlet host NRPE traffic. You can obviously vary this to suit your environment.

Overall, if you don't absolutely need to use arguments with NRPE, I recommend you leave this option disabled when you compile the package. In case you do want to use arguments, I recommend you apply the mitigants I've suggested. Later in this section I'll briefly examine how to use arguments with NRPE.

Note The nrpe daemon does reject some special characters: | ` & > < ' " \ [ ] { } and the ! symbol, which is used to separate arguments. This is designed to further lessen the risk of a malicious argument being executed. Any command or argument received with these characters in it will be rejected.

Once you have configured the NRPE package, you need to make it, as shown here:

```
owlet# make
```

The NRPE package does not have an automatic installation script. Once the make process is complete, you will need to manually install the required files. In light of this, I'm going to examine the next steps required on the Nagios server and the remote host in separate sections.

NRPE on the Nagios Server

The first step required on the Nagios server is to install the check_nrpe plug-in, located in the src directory of the NRPE package, into your plug-in directory:

```
puppy# cp src/check_nrpe /usr/local/nagios/libexec
```

Next you need to define a command for the check_nrpe plug-in. I've displayed a sample check_nrpe command in Example 5-10.

Example 5-10. *Sample check_nrpe Command*

```
define command{
        command_name    check_nrpe
        command_line    /usr/local/nagios/libexec/check_nrpe -H $HOSTADDRESS$ ➥
                                -c $ARG1$
 }
```

The check_nrpe plug-in is very simple. It has five potential options. Here's an example of running the plug-in from the command line:

```
puppy# ./check_nrpe -H 10.0.0.15 -c check_disk
```

On this line you can see the check_nrpe plug-in is being executed with two of the five potential options, -H and -c. The -H specifies the IP address of a remote host that is running the nrpe daemon. The -c specifies the command that is to be executed on the remote host. You will need to define this command in the nrpe.cfg file on the remote host.

There are three other options you can use with the check_nrpe plug-in. These options are -t, -p, and -a. The -t option specifies the timeout for the NRPE command. It defaults to 10 seconds. The -p option allows you to specify a port other than 5666 to connect to. The last option, -a, enables you to specify arguments (as discussed earlier) to the remote host. Multiple arguments can be specified and each must be separated by a space. This option must always be the last option on the command line. An example of using the -a option when executing check_nrpe from on the command line is

```
puppy# ./check_nrpe -H 10.0.0.15 -c check_disk -a /dev/hda1
```

To use the check_nrpe plug-in with arguments, you also need to define a command object that will accept arguments like so:

```
define  command{
                command_name    check_nrpe
                command_line        /usr/local/nagios/libexec/check_nrpe ➥
-H $HOSTADDRESS$ -c $ARG1$ -a $ARG2$
}
```

You can then represent this check command in the check_command directive in a service object like so:

```
define service{
            service_description    disk
            check_command        check_nrpe!check_disk!/dev/dha1
            ...
}
```

Tip Arguments are passed to the check_nrpe command just like for any other plug-in via $ARGx$ macros.

NRPE on the Remote Host

First, in order to run the nrpe daemon on your remote hosts, you will need a user and group for the daemon to run as. You will not, and should not for security reasons, be able to run the nrpe daemon as the root user. I generally use nagios as both the user and group, which is the user and group that the configure script defaults to in the compilation process, but you can choose a user and group that suits you. If you specify a different user and group, be sure to specify them in the configure script before compiling the nrpe daemon. I've created a user and group on the following lines:

```
owlet# groupadd nagios
owlet# useradd -g nagios nagios
```

Note You will only need to do this on the remote host. The nrpe daemon does not need to run on the Nagios server and hence does not require a user or group to be created.

Next, after you have compiled the nrpe daemon, install it somewhere appropriate on your host. I usually create a directory structure under /usr/local/ (or you can use your Unix platform's equivalent directory) like so:

```
/usr/local/nagios
/usr/local/nagios/etc
/usr/local/nagios/bin
/usr/local/nagios/libexec
```

I then copy the nrpe binary into the /usr/local/nagios/bin directory. The nrpe binary is created during the compilation process in the src directory of the NRPE package.

```
owlet# cp src/nrpe /usr/local/nagios/bin
```

I also copy the nrpe.cfg file. It is created in the root directory of the NRPE package. I usually place this in the /usr/local/nagios/etc directory.

```
owlet# cp nrpe.cfg /usr/local/nagios/etc
```

In order for the nrpe daemon to work, you also need to change the ownership of the nrpe.cfg file so that the user and group that is running the nrpe daemon can read the file:

```
owlet# chown nagios:nagios /usr/local/nagios/etc/nrpe.cfg
```

You should change its ownership to the user and group you have specified that nrpe should run as, in our case nagios and nagios.

After you have installed the nrpe daemon, you must download and install the Nagios plug-ins or other binaries or scripts that you wish to use on the remote host. For the Nagios plug-ins, you can use the instructions for installing the Nagios plug-in package in Chapter 1 to do this. By default I generally install the plug-ins into the /usr/local/nagios/libexec directory.

■Tip If you don't want to install all the plug-ins, you can install individual plug-ins by running the configure script, changing into the plugin directory in the Nagios plug-in source package, and typing make plugin for each plug-in you want to compile. Replace plugin with the name of the plug-in you wish to compile; for example, make check_disk.

Once you have installed the daemon and any required plug-ins, you need to configure the nrpe.cfg file. Example 5-11 shows a typical nrpe.cfg configuration file.

Example 5-11. *Sample nrpe.cfg Configuration File*

```
server_port=5666
#server_address=10.0.0.15
allowed_hosts=127.0.0.1,10.0.0.31
nrpe_user=nagios
nrpe_group=nagios
dont_blame_nrpe=1
debug=0
command_timeout=60
#include=<somefile.cfg>
#include_dir=<somedirectory>
command[check_disk1]=/usr/local/nagios/libexec/check_disk -w 20 -c 10
#command[check_disk2]=/usr/local/nagios/libexec/check_disk -w $ARG1$ ➡
-c $ARG2$ -p $ARG3$
```

Let's look at each of the options in Example 5-11. The first two options, server_port and server_address, allow you to specify the port and address the nrpe daemon will listen on. This defaults to all interfaces on port 5666. By default the server_address option is commented out. You can comment out options by prefixing them with a # symbol.

The next option, `allowed_hosts`, specifies the IP addresses that are allowed to contact the `nrpe` daemon and transmit command requests. The loopback address, `127.0.0.1`, is included by default and you need to specify the IP addresses of any Nagios server that need to be able to connect to the `nrpe` daemon. Multiple IP addresses should be separated by commas.

Note If you run the `nrpe` daemon under `inetd` or `xinetd`, the `allowed_hosts` option has no effect and you don't need to specify it.

The next two options specify the user and group that the `nrpe` daemon will run as. These both default to `nagios`.

The `dont_blame_nrpe` option is used in conjunction with NRPE arguments. If you want to use arguments with NRPE, then in addition to specifying the `--enable-command-args` configure option, you need to change this option to 1. It defaults to 0.

The `debug` option turns on extended `nrpe` daemon debugging information. This information is logged to `syslog`. Changing this option to 1 turns on debugging and 0 turns it off. This option is very useful if you are having issues with `nrpe` and need to see exactly what is occurring on the remote host.

The `command_timeout` option specifies the maximum amount of time that `nrpe` will let a plug-in execute before killing it. It defaults to 60 seconds.

The `include` and `include_dir` options allow you to include additional files or directories of files into your `nrpe` configuration. The `include_dir` option will include all files with a `.cfg` extension to the `nrpe` configuration. Both of these options are most useful for allowing you to include additional command definitions.

The last option is the `command`, which allows you to specify commands that the `nrpe` daemon will execute. The option is constructed like so:

```
command[command_name]=command_line
```

The `command_name` on the previous line should be replaced with the name of the command that you wish to define. This is the name used as the value of the `-c` option of the `check_nrpe` plug-in on the Nagios server. As you can see in Example 5-11, I've defined a command called `check_disk1`. On the next line you can see how I would call that command using the `check_nrpe` plug-in:

```
puppy# ./check_nrpe -H 10.0.0.15 -c check_disk1
```

The `command_line` portion of the command definition should be the command line that the `nrpe` daemon will execute on the remote host. It can use one of the standard plug-ins, a script, or a plug-in you have developed yourself as long as it returns the response code and additional data that the Nagios server requires.[10] You can add as many commands as you like to the `nrpe.cfg` configuration file (or include them from other files using the `include` and `include_dir` options).

---

10. I will discuss plug-in development in Chapter 10.

If you have enabled arguments with NRPE, then you can also specify arguments in the command_line portion of the command definition. You can see this in the last line in Example 5-11, which I have repeated here:

```
command[check_disk2]=/usr/local/nagios/libexec/check_disk -w $ARG1$ -c $ARG2$ ➥
-p $ARG3$
```

You can pass the arguments from the service object definition's check_command directive like so:

```
define service{
            service_description    disk
            check_command     check_nrpe!check_disk2!5!10!/
            ….
}
```

From the service object definition, you need to define a command object definition like so:

```
define command{
            command_name check_nrpe
            command_line     $USER1$/check_nrpe -H $HOSTADDRESS$ -c $ARG1$ ➥
            -a $ARG2$ $ARG3$ $ARG4$
}
```

The $ARGx$ macros are replaced with the arguments check_disk2, 5, 10, and /. You can specify up to 16 $ARGx$ arguments in NRPE commands.

Or you can see the same command executed from the command line like so:

```
puppy# /usr/local/nagios/libexec/check_nrpe -H 10.0.0.15 -c check_disk2 -a 5 10 /
```

■Tip I recommend testing all of your check_nrpe commands on the command line before adjusting your Nagios configuration. They are much easier to troubleshoot this way. Also remember if you are having issues, you should turn on debugging using the debug option in the nrpe.cfg file on the remote host.

Finally, I need to decide how the nrpe daemon will run. You can either run it using inetd or xinetd or as a local listening daemon. If you intend to run it via inetd or xinetd, then you should follow the instructions contained in the README document included in the root directory of the NRPE package. I generally recommend running the daemon as a local listening daemon and not through inetd or xinetd.

You can see running the nrpe daemon as a local daemon on the following line:

```
owlet# /usr/local/nagios/bin/nrpe -c /usr/local/nagios/etc/nrpe.cfg -d
Aug 10 21:07:37 owlet nrpe[18728]: Starting up daemon
```

As you can see, I've specified two options to the nrpe daemon: -c and -d. The -c option specifies the location of the nrpe.cfg file. The -d option tells the nrpe daemon to run as a stand-alone daemon. You could also specify the -i option if you wish to run the nrpe daemon with inetd or xinetd.

■**Tip** Also contained in the root directory of the NRPE source package is a series of `init` files for a number of different platforms. You can use these to automatically start, stop, or restart the `nrpe` daemon.

Now you have the `nrpe` daemon running, you can query plug-ins or other binaries and scripts from the Nagios server and hence monitor your remote hosts.

Indirect Monitoring with NRPE

Using the `nrpe` daemon is not limited to checking local resources on a single remote host. You can use the `nrpe` daemon as a relay service to check services on remote hosts that are contactable from the host running the `nrpe` daemon. Nagios calls this indirect monitoring. For example, I have a Nagios server called `puppy`. It needs to monitor the `kitten` and `owlet` hosts that are located behind a firewall. I deploy the `nrpe` daemon on the `kitten` host and open the TCP port 5666 on my firewall to allow NRPE traffic between the `puppy` and `kitten` hosts. I can now use the `check_nrpe` plug-in on the `puppy` host to monitor the `kitten` host. But I can also monitor the `owlet` host by executing plug-ins on the `kitten` host. I can monitor network-facing services on `owlet` using the appropriate plug-ins, like `check_tcp`. Or I can query an `nrpe` daemon on a remote host, use the `check_by_ssh`, or the SNMP protocol to check internal facing resources on that host. In this model I only need to open one hole in my firewall: a connection between the `puppy` and `kitten` hosts on port 5666. The `kitten` host will perform all other monitoring and pass the check results back to the Nagios server on `puppy`.

■**Tip** Indirect monitoring can become quite complicated with multiple `nrpe` daemons deployed to relay results back to one or more Nagios servers. I recommend using it carefully as it can add substantial delays in your check processes and add multiple points of failure in your monitoring environment. You can also read about indirect monitoring in the Nagios documentation at `http://nagios.sourceforge.net/docs/2_0/ indirectchecks.html`.

You can see a diagram of how this works in Figure 5-1 (see the following page).

Let's quickly look at how this might be achieved. On the following lines are partial host and service objects for the `owlet` host and a `syslog` service I wish to monitor on this host:

```
define host{
          host_name        owlet
          address          10.0.0.5
          ...
}

define service{
          service_description    syslog
          host_name              owlet
          check_command          check_kitten_nrpe!check_owlet_syslog
          ...
}
```

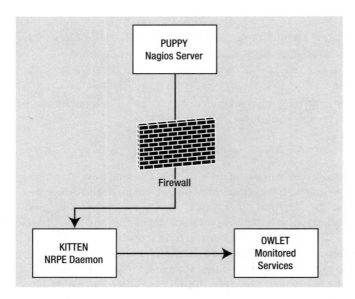

Figure 5-1. *Indirect NRPE monitoring*

As you can see, I've defined a host object for the owlet host that has an IP address of 10.0.0.5. I've also defined a service called syslog on that owlet host. The check_command directive for that service executes a command called check_kitten_nrpe and passes the argument check_owlet_syslog to that command. You can see the check_kitten_nrpe check command here:

```
define command{
            command_name    check_kitten_nrpe
            command_line    $USER1$/check_nrpe -H $HOSTADDRESS:kitten$ -c $ARG1$
}
```

This check command executes the check_nrpe plug-in and connects to an nrpe daemon on the kitten host. I've defined the address of the kitten host using an on-demand macro. On-demand macros allow you to reference the details of other host and service objects. I need this macro because it is the owlet host that is executing the service check and hence the only host address it is aware of is its own.

■**Tip** I explain on-demand macros in more detail in Chapter 6.

The name of the command to execute, check_owlet_syslog, is passed as the value of the -c option. On the following line you can see the check_owlet_syslog command that would be defined in the nrpe.cfg file on the kitten host:

```
command[check_owlet_syslog]=/usr/local/nagios/libexec/check_tcp -H 10.0.0.5 -p 514
```

You can see that the check_owlet_syslog command executes the check_tcp plug-in (which would need to be compiled and installed on the kitten host) and checks port 514 on the owlet host at IP address 10.0.0.5. The check command would complete and the nrpe daemon on the kitten host would return the check result to the Nagios server on the puppy host. The Nagios server would then update the status of the syslog service on the owlet host.

If I want to monitor an internal resource, rather than a network-facing resource, on a remote host, I could daisy-chain together several NRPE requests. In the following examples, the nrpe daemon would be running both on the kitten and owlet hosts:

Tip I could also use the check_by_ssh or check_snmp plug-ins to perform these checks rather than having the nrpe daemon running on both hosts. You can read about both of these plug-ins later in this chapter. Simply replace the check_nrpe plug-in with one of these plug-ins and its required arguments.

```
define service{
            service_description     disk
            host_name               owlet
            check_command           check_kitten_nrpe!check_owlet_disk
            ...
}
```

The disk service definition executes the check_kitten_nrpe check command that I defined earlier but passes in a new command called check_owlet_disk. This NRPE command is configured as

```
command[check_owlet_disk]=/usr/local/nagios/libexec/check_nrpe -H 10.0.0.5 ➡
 -c check_disk
```

The check_owlet_disk command runs the check_nrpe plug-in on the kitten host. The check_owlet_disk command uses the check_nrpe plug-in to contact an nrpe daemon running on the owlet host and executes the check_disk NRPE command on that host. This command would check the status of the disk or disks on the owlet host.

The check results are then returned to the kitten host and from there to the puppy host. This would result in an update on the Nagios server to the disk service running on the owlet host.

Or I could simplify this service check greatly by using arguments to pass the required variables. In the following lines you can see the service object, check command, and NRPE command all modified to use arguments where possible instead of hard-coding the required command and addresses:

```
define service{
            service_description     syslog
            host_name               owlet
            check_command           check_kitten_nrpe!check_tcp!514
            ...
}
```

```
define command{
              command_name    check_kitten_nrpe
              command_line    $USER1$/check_nrpe -H $HOSTADDRESS:kitten$ ➥
                                      -c $ARG1$ -a $HOSTADDRESS$ $ARG2$
}
```

```
command[check_tcp]=/usr/local/nagios/libexec/check_tcp -H $ARG1$ -p $ARG2$
```

In these object definitions I've again created a syslog service on the owlet host. This service uses a modification of the check_kitten_nrpe check command that I created earlier in this section to perform service checks and passes the arguments, check_tcp and 514, to that check command. The check command calls the check_nrpe plug-in to connect to the kitten host (again using an on-demand macro to retrieve that host's IP address) and passes the name of the command to be executed in the $ARG1$ macro, in this case check_tcp. Also passed is the host address of the owlet host using the $HOSTADDRESS$ macro and the argument 514 in the $ARG2$ macro.

The check_tcp NRPE check command on the kitten host is executed. The values of the -H and -p options are populated using the IP address of the owlet host and the port number 514. The check is executed by the nrpe daemon and the check results returned to the Nagios server to update the status of the syslog service.

You can perform host checks on remote hosts in the same way as monitoring services by requesting that the nrpe daemon on the remote host execute a host check using the check_ping plug-in. The following lines show examples of the host, check command, and NRPE check command objects required to achieve this. These examples also use arguments to make the checks easier to manage:

```
define host{
              host_name owlet
              address  10.0.0.5
              check_command check_kitten_nrpe!check_ping
              …
}
```

```
define command{
              command_name check_kitten_nrpe
              command_line    $USER1$/check_nrpe -H $HOSTADDRESS:kitten$ ➥
                                      -c $ARG1$ -a $HOSTADDRESS$
}
```

```
command[check_ping]=/usr/local/nagios/libexec/check_ping -H $ARG1$ ➥
-w 3000.0,80% -c 5000.0,100% -p 1
```

In these object definitions I've defined a host object for the owlet host that has an IP address of 10.0.0.5. The check command for that host executes a command called check_kitten_nrpe and passes the argument check_ping to the command. The check_kitten_nrpe command sends the argument check_ping as the name of the NRPE command to be executed on the kitten host and the IP address of the owlet host as an argument for that check command using the -a option.

The NRPE check command, check_ping, executes the check_ping plug-in and receives the IP address of the owlet host as the value of the $ARG1$ macro. The check is performed, the result is returned to the puppy host and the Nagios server updates the status of the owlet host.

Monitoring via SSH

The previous method of checking hosts using the NRPE package does have some issues. Probably most significant are that you need to open a port in your host or network firewalls to allow connections to be made, that passing arguments to your check commands is a security risk, and that Anon-DH with AES is not an ideal encryption model to prevent man-in-the-middle attacks and compromises of your hosts.

With this in mind, let's look at another method of remote monitoring. This time I'm going to use an SSH connection to execute commands on remote hosts and receive the replies. This partially addresses the concerns raised with using NRPE. First, most environments tend to have SSH already enabled on their hosts, and it is generally allowed through host and network firewalls. Second, addressing the two other concerns with using NRPE, it uses the ssh command and sshd daemon as its back end, which provides a somewhat better level of connection security.

The solution, however, is not perfect and has a risk of its own. The principal risk is how it authenticates the SSH connection. Normally an SSH connection is authenticated via a username and password. Obviously inputting a password every time a check occurs is not feasible, so a public/private key combination with a null passphrase is used. The risk exists that, if someone compromises your private key, they could use it to compromise the security of your hosts. You can, however, limit the potential commands that can be run using that public/private key combination to mitigate the risk somewhat.

To perform checks via SSH, the check_by_ssh plug-in is used. This plug-in comes with the default Nagios plug-in package that I installed in Chapter 1.

■**Note** To use the check_by_ssh plug-in, you need OpenSSH (or your platform's SSH equivalent) installed on both your Nagios server and all remote hosts you wish to monitor by this mechanism. The sshd daemon must also be running on all remote hosts and must allow connections from your Nagios server so that the checks can be performed.

In Example 5-12 I've demonstrated the check_by_ssh plug-in.

Example 5-12. *The check_by_ssh Plug-in*

```
puppy$ check_by_ssh -H 10.0.0.15 ➡
-C "/usr/local/nagios/libexec/check_disk -w 10 -c 5 -p /"
admin@10.0.0.15's password:******
DISK OK - free space: / 77 MB (52%);| /=70MB;137;142;0;147
```

You can see from Example 5-12 that the check_by_ssh plug-in allows you to execute a command on the remote host and receive output from that command. The command is specified by the -C option and can consist of any plug-in, script, or binary that is installed on the remote host. This is much the same functionality as the nrpe daemon, and you will need to install any required plug-ins or scripts on the remote host. So in Example 5-12 the check_disk plug-in from the standard Nagios plug-in package would need to be installed on the remote host.

In Example 5-12 I've enclosed that command in quotation marks to ensure it is cleanly submitted on the remote host. This prevents any characters from being incorrectly interpreted by the shell on the remote host.

You can also see that the plug-in has prompted me for a password on the remote host. The username it is using to connect to the remote host has defaulted to the admin user, which is the user my shell session is logged on as. You can override this by specifying another option, -l:

```
puppy$ check_by_ssh -H 10.0.0.15 -l nagios ➥
-C "/usr/local/nagios/libexec/check_disk -w 10 -c 5 -p /"
nagios@10.0.0.15's password:
DISK OK - free space: / 77 MB (52%);| /=70MB;137;142;0;147
```

As you can see, it isn't going to be overly practical for our Nagios server if I have to input a password every time a check is performed. So instead I need to use OpenSSH's public/private key authentication mechanism.[11] How does this work? Well, I generate a pair of keys: one public and one private. The private key stays on our Nagios server and the public key is placed in an authorized_keys file on the remote host. The public/private key combination is then used to authenticate our host when the check_by_ssh plug-in connects and submits the required command.

■Note There is not enough space, nor is it appropriate, to fully discuss public key encryption here, but you can read about it in more detail at http://en.wikipedia.org/wiki/Public-key_cryptography.

Let's start by generating some keys to use. Using a command from the OpenSSH package called ssh-keygen, I generate the keys on Nagios:

```
puppy$ ssh-keygen -t dsa
Generating public/private dsa key pair.
Enter file in which to save the key (/home/nagios/.ssh/id_dsa):
Enter passphrase (empty for no passphrase):
Enter same passphrase again:
Your identification has been saved in /home/nagios/.ssh/id_dsa.
Your public key has been saved in /home/nagios/.ssh/id_dsa.pub.
The key fingerprint is:
0a:16:d0:c3:11:19:74:6a:a6:b2:5b:05:78:88:e4:db nagios@puppy.yourdomain.com
```

For this purpose I am generating DSA keys, which means I will be using SSH Protocol 2 connections (SSH Protocol 1 connections can only use RSA keys).[12] I recommend using DSA

---

11. There is a useful HOWTO on this at www.puddingonline.com/~dave/publications/
    SSH-with-Keys-HOWTO/document/html/SSH-with-Keys-HOWTO.html.

12. See http://en.wikipedia.org/wiki/Digital_Signature_Algorithm.

and Protocol 2 as it is more secure than RSA and Protocol 1. I indicate this to the ssh-keygen command by specifying the -t dsa option.

Next the ssh-keygen command will ask us where to store the key, defaulting to the home directory of the current user in a directory called .ssh. This user should be the user you intend to run the check_by_ssh plug-in as. This would normally be the user that the Nagios server runs as, in our case nagios. This will result in the private key being stored in a file called id_dsa and the public key in a file called id_dsa.pub in the directory /home/nagios/.ssh.

You will also be prompted to enter a passphrase for the keys. To use these keys in Nagios, you need to hit Enter at both of these prompts. This will generate a null passphrase key and will stop Nagios from being prompted to enter a passphrase when you're trying to connect.

As I stated earlier, this is one of the key risks of using the check_by_ssh plug-in. Without a passphrase, the only security for the connection is ensuring that the public/private key pair are safe (especially the private key). If someone has your public and private keys, not only will they be able to use your check_by_ssh plug-in but they will also be able to connect to the remote host via SSH without having to input a password. This is obviously a huge risk. I recommend considering carefully whether the use of this plug-in is worth taking this risk.

Once you've generated my keys, you need to distribute the public key to all the remote hosts you want to connect to. The public and private keys must be kept safe and protected. Ensure that only the Nagios server user owns these files and can read them. You can do this by changing the file's ownership and permissions like so:

```
puppy# chown nagios:nagios /home/nagios/.ssh/id_dsa /home/nagios/.ssh/id_dsa.pub
puppy# chmod 0600 /home/nagios/.ssh/id_dsa /home/nagios/.ssh/id_dsa.pub
```

The public key needs to be added to all the remote hosts that you wish to connect to with the check_by_ssh plug-in. Place the key in the .ssh directory under the home directory of the user that will be executing the check or command in the authorized_keys file. For example, if you are executing checks using the nagios user, then the public key needs to be placed in the file /home/nagios/.ssh/authorized_keys.

You can transfer the file to the remote host using the scp command like so:

```
puppy$ scp id_dsa.pub owlet:/home/nagios/.ssh/id_dsa.pub
```

Note There is another file in the .ssh directory that is important here called known_hosts. This file also contains a copy of the public key of all remote hosts that have tried to connect to this host via ssh. This file is updated when an initial connection is made and you will be prompted as to whether you wish to add the public key to this file; in this case, when you initiate the scp command above you will see this prompt. This is not an authorization function but rather an identification function. The file is checked when subsequent connections are made to confirm that it is the same public being used. If the public key changes, connections will fail and you will need to update the known_hosts file with the new key.

And then add it to the authorized_keys file like so:

```
owlet$ cd /home/nagios/.ssh
owlet$ cat id_dsa.pub >> authorized_keys
owlet$ rm id_dsa.pub
```

If the .ssh directory and the authorized_keys file do not exist, you will need to create them. You will also need to set permissions for this directory and file:

```
owlet$ cd /home/nagios
owlet$ chmod go-w . .ssh .ssh/authorized_keys
```

Tip If you are having trouble connecting to the remote host, the permissions of this directory and files can often be the issue.

Finally, you need to confirm that your sshd daemon is configured to allow public key authentication. You should confirm the following three settings are present in your sshd_config file (usually located in the /etc/ssh directory):

```
RSAAuthentication yes
PubkeyAuthentication yes
AuthorizedKeysFile     .ssh/authorized_keys
```

By default, in most SSH installations all these settings will usually be present and set this way in most sshd configurations. If they are not present, you will need to add them and then restart the sshd daemon.

Now that I've configured public key authentication, I can use it with the check_by_ssh plug-in. Let's see how to do this via the command line:

```
puppy$ check_by_ssh -H 10.0.0.15 -l nagios -i /home/nagios/.ssh/id_dsa ➥
-C "/usr/local/nagios/libexec/check_disk -w 10 -c 5 -p /"
DISK OK - free space: / 77 MB (52%);| /=70MB;137;142;0;147
```

Here I've specified the -i option and used it to specify the private key from the public/private key pair I've just generated. It does not prompt you for a password as the authentication is handled by the public/private keys.

The check_by_ssh plug-in also has another method of operation called passive mode. Passive mode allows you to execute multiple checks using one check_by_ssh command. Let's look at an example of how this works from the command line in Example 5-13.

Example 5-13. *check_by_ssh in passive mode*

```
puppy$ check_by_ssh -H 10.0.0.15 -l nagios -i /home/nagios/.ssh/id_dsa -n owlet ➥
-s check_disk:check_user -C "/usr/local/nagios/libexec/check_disk -w 10 -c 5 -p /" ➥
 -C "/usr/local/nagios/libexec/check_user -w 20 -c 10" -O /tmp/owlet_output
```

The command in Example 5-13 looks quite complicated but is in fact quite simple. I'm connecting to the remote host at IP address 10.0.0.15 using public/private key authentication to connect with user nagios. First, I need to specify the -n option. This option must contain the short name of the host being monitored. This is the value of the host_name directive in the host object definition.

The next option is -s. This option specifies a list of the services being checked, each separated by a colon. In this example I've specified the check_disk and check_user services.

The services in the -s option must match services defined on the host being monitored, and when you specify them, use their name from the service_description directive.

You then need to specify -C options, representing the commands to be executed on the remote host, one for each of the services being checked. These command options should be specified in the same order as the services defined in the -s option. So the check_disk command is defined first, followed by the check_user command.

Using passive mode the check_by_ssh plug-in does not return its results directly to the Nagios server but rather to a file. I've specified the -O option that specifies where the output of the checks should be stored—in this case to a file named owlet_output in the /tmp directory. Here are the contents of this file:

```
puppy# cat /tmp/owlet_output
[1124286516] PROCESS_SERVICE_CHECK_RESULT;owlet;check_disk;0; ➥
DISK OK - free space: / 77 MB (52%);| /=70MB;137;142;0;147
[1124286516] PROCESS_SERVICE_CHECK_RESULT;owlet;check_user;0; ➥
USERS OK - 0 users currently logged in |users=0;10;20;0
```

These results are in the form that Nagios uses for submission to the external command file. To get the results of the check into Nagios, you'll need to submit the contents of this file to the external command file. You can do this by using the echo command; I've done this very crudely on the following line:

```
puppy# echo /tmp/owlet_output >> /usr/local/nagios/var/rw/nagios.cmd
```

More sophisticated methods of submitting the results could include building this into a script executed by a cron job or as part of an event handler script attached to the service.[13]

As the results of the check are being submitted into the external command file, the services they are being submitted for should be configured to accept passive check results.

One potential way of using passive mode is to configure a host and a series of services for that host. One of those services executes all of the checks for all the other services using the check_by_ssh plug-in in passive mode. This first service is the only service configured to perform active checks. The other services are configured to only accept passive check results and not perform any active checks themselves. The checks are performed by the first service and the results submitted to the Nagios server for all the services to be checked.

■**Note** You must specify the -n, -s and -O options in the correct order for the check_by_ssh plug-in to operate in passive mode.

You can further secure the check_by_ssh plug-in by editing the authorized_keys file to allow the public key to execute only one command. I restrict the command that can be executed by prefixing the key for the Nagios server in the authorized_keys file with a command option, as shown here:

```
command="/usr/local/nagios/libexec/check_disk" ssh-dss AAAAB3NzaC1yc2…
nagios@puppy.yourdomain.net
```

---

13. See Chapter 6.

> **■Note** I've truncated this example of a key and only left the first and last sections of the key. Your normal key will be much longer.

The `command` option tells `sshd` to only allow the `/usr/local/nagios/libexec/check_disk` command to be executed.

> **■Tip** One way of limiting the command to be executed and still performing more than one check is to configure a script in the `command` option.

There are some additional options you can use with the `check_by_ssh` plug-in, and I've listed these in Table 5-7. They are fairly self-explanatory.

Table 5-7. *Additional check_by_ssh Options*

Option	Description
`-h, --help`	Displays help.
`-V, --version`	Prints the version.
`-t, --timeout=value`	Timeout for the plug-in. Defaults to 10 seconds.
`-p, --port=value`	Specifies a port number.
`-4, --use-ipv4`	Uses an IPv4 connection.
`-6, --use-ipv6`	Uses an IPv6 connection.
`-1, --proto1`	Specifies that `ssh` use Protocol 1.
`-2, --proto2`	Specifies that `ssh` use Protocol 2.
`-S, --skiplines=n`	Ignores the first *n* lines of standard error (can be used to bypass a banner).
`-f`	Forks `ssh` rather than creating a `tty` session.
`-w, --warning=value`	Specifies response time in seconds that triggers a `WARNING` status.
`-c, --critical=value`	Specifies response time in seconds that triggers a `CRITICAL` status.

The first three options in Table 5-7 are the standard help, version, and timeout options that all correctly developed plug-ins should have.

The next option, `-p`, is used to specify a different port to connect to rather than the default SSH port of 22.

The next four options are optional and control how the plug-in will connect. The `-4` and `-6` options control whether the connection will occur via IPv4 or IPv6, respectively. The plug-in defaults to IPv4 connections. The `-1` and `-2` options control which variation of the SSH protocol the plug-in will use. The default for the plug-in is `-2` for SSHv2.

The `-S` option allows you to ignore a number of lines of standard error that you could use to bypass a banner.

The `-f` option forks the `ssh` session used by the plug-in rather than creating a `tty` session. It is optional.

The last two options, `-w` and `-c`, allow the specification of a threshold for connection time, measured in seconds, that will result in the WARNING or CRITICAL status being set if these thresholds are exceeded.

Monitoring via SMNP

The last method of monitoring services on your remote hosts that we'll look at uses Simple Network Management Protocol (SNMP), which is common to most Unix and networking devices. Indeed, of all the monitoring mechanisms in this chapter, this one is the most useful for monitoring network devices such as routers, firewalls, and switches. Nagios is generally not an ideal solution for monitoring more than basic availability such as an ICMP response or the presence of active ports on network devices, but SNMP monitoring can provide more sophisticated monitoring. SNMP can also be enabled and used to monitor Windows-based hosts.

■**Tip** Cisco has one of the most detailed and clear explanations of the workings of SNMP available at `www.cisco.com/warp/public/535/3.html`.

SNMP is a TCP protocol that allows the exchange of management information between hosts. I'll provide a simple explanation of SNMP and show you how to monitor devices and services using it. This will represent a basic introduction to using SNMP with Nagios, and you can take the use of SNMP monitoring in Nagios much further with some additional experimentation.

■**Caution** This is a much abbreviated description of SNMP and how to use it with Nagios. I recommend you read more widely on SNMP. Several excellent books are available on the topic, including one I particularly recommend, *Essential SNMP* (O'Reilly, 2005).[14]

Hosts running SNMP are generally called *network elements* or *managed devices*. They have a software component called an agent running on the device. This agent collects and holds data about that managed device. The agent can be contacted via the network and can send, receive, and change that data. The SNMP protocol traditionally uses TCP port 161 to communicate.

■**Tip** On a Unix-like host, the snmpd daemon needs to be running and on Windows hosts the SNMP Service generally needs to be running for a device to be queried via SNMP. For other devices, like network devices, check their documentation for instructions on how to enable SNMP.

---

14. See www.oreilly.com/catalog/esnmp2/.

To tell the agent what data to hold and collect, the agent is loaded with one or more management information bases (MIBs). MIBs are hierarchical collections of information that detail the attributes and characteristics of a device. These attributes and characteristics, called *managed objects*, include such items as the name of the host, its memory usage, and the status of its hardware. Many hardware vendors ship MIBs for their devices, like a Cisco PIX MIB or an IBM AIX MIB.

The hierarchical information contained in MIBs is represented as a tree with the managed objects as the branches and leaves on that tree. The data items on these branches and leaves are known as *object identifiers* (OIDs). OIDs can be represented as a series of numbers separated by full stops, like this: 1.3.6.1.4.1.9. Each number represents a branch or leaf in the tree, and it is viewed in a descending order from left to right.

Each of these numbers also represents a word. Our example of 1.3.6.1.4.1.9 can be represented textually as iso.org.dod.internet.private.enterprises.cisco. This OID is the top of the branch that is assigned to the Cisco Corporation. Further branches and leaves beneath this OID would represent the objects and characteristics of objects that Cisco makes or sells. For example, one of the characteristics of a Cisco device would be represented by the OID of 1.3.6.1.4.1.9.9.41.2.0.1, which can be textually represented as the rather long-winded

iso.org.dod.internet.private.enterprises.cisco.ciscoMgmt.ciscoSyslogMIB.cisco ➥
SyslogMIBNotificationPrefix.ciscoSyslogMIBNotifications.clogMessageGenerated

This SNMP OID is the OID for a syslog message generated by a Cisco device. You could query this OID and return a generated syslog message or information about that message. Obviously, frequently referring to an SNMP OID like this would be annoying, and several aliases and shortcuts are possible, in addition to referring to the OID in its numeric form, that I'll briefly look at in a moment.

Each of these managed objects, such as 1.3.6.1.4.1.9.9.41.2.0.1, can have instances, or *variables*, that represent some form of data about the device being monitored. It is these variables that are monitored by tools such as Nagios. For example, a variable could contain the status of an interface, the number of packets that have traversed a switch port, or the amount of disk space used on a drive. Some of these variables represent single items of data, and others are arrays.

Each of these variables is capable of one or more interactions: reads, writes, and traps. A read interaction reads the contents of a variable and a write interaction changes the contents. The last type of interaction, the trap, is a reporting event that is generated by the managed device and can be sent to monitoring systems.

■Note   I discuss using Nagios to receive SNMP traps in Chapter 9.

Nagios only uses read interactions to query devices and return information. To query SNMP-enabled devices, Nagios uses a plug-in called check_snmp. This plug-in requires a prerequisite package called Net-SNMP. The Net-SNMP package is available from the http://net-snmp.sourceforge.net site.

■**Tip** The Net-SNMP site also contains quite a bit of useful information about SNMP and how to use it.

To install Net-SNMP, first download the current release from the Net-SNMP Sourceforge site located at `http://net-snmp.sourceforge.net/download.html`. Then unpack it and run the `configure` script.

```
puppy# wget http://optusnet.dl.sourceforge.net/sourceforge/net-snmp/ ➡
net-snmp-5.3.pre4.tar.gz
puppy# tar -xzf net-snmp-5.3.pre4.tar.gz
puppy# cd net-snmp-5.3.pre4
puppy# ./configure
```

During the `configure` process, you will be prompted to answer a number of questions. The default answers should be suitable for most installations, and the information provided about each option is extensive and clear if you wish to not use the default answers.

After configuring Net-SNMP, you need to compile and install it like so:

```
puppy# make
puppy# make install
```

■**Tip** The Net-SNMP package is also available as a series of installable packages on many distributions, and you may be able to install it via your distribution's package management system, such as `yum`, `apt`, or the like. On Red Hat, SuSE, Debian, and Mandrake distributions, the required packages are called `net-snmp`, `net-snmp-libs`, and `net-snmp-utils`. You may also require some additional prerequisites for the Net-SNMP packages, but your package management system should identify these for you.

The Net-SNMP package provides a number of commands that you can use to interact with SNMP-enabled devices. The key command required to use the `check_snmp` plug-in is `snmpget`. This command performs read interactions with SNMP-enabled devices and returns information from them that can be used by Nagios.

Additionally, the Net-SNMP package comes with a command called `snmpwalk` that allows you to return some or all of the possible OIDs on an SNMP-enabled device. This greatly assists in finding out what variables are available on SNMP-enabled devices and which you can potentially use with Nagios to monitor characteristics of your devices. The `snmpwalk` command queries an SNMP-enabled device and can be configured to return all the available variables and their current values. This is particularly useful because finding the right OID to query can be a difficult process and many devices lack extensive or even adequate documentation on their available SNMP variables.

The following shows how you'd use the snmpwalk command:

```
puppy# snmpwalk -v 1 -c public 10.0.0.1
SNMPv2-MIB::sysDescr.0 = STRING: Linux router 2.4.20 #640 ➥
Wed Jun 8 13:27:20 CEST 2005 mips
SNMPv2-MIB::sysObjectID.0 = OID: NET-SNMP-MIB::netSnmpAgentOIDs.10
SNMPv2-MIB::sysUpTime.0 = Timeticks: (783455470) 90 days, 16:15:54.70
...
```

On these lines, I've queried an SNMP-enabled device at the IP address 10.0.0.1 using the snmpwalk command. I've specified two options in the command: -v and -c. The -v option controls which version of the SNMP protocol I'm querying the device with. There are three versions of the SNMP protocol: SNMPv1, SNMPv2, and SNMPv3, represented by the values 1, 2, and 3, respectively. Each has an increasing level of complexity and security, and each is supported by a varying range of devices. SNMPv3 is relatively new and is often not supported by older or legacy devices. SNMPv1 and v2 both have limited security, and I recommend that you use SNMPv3 if you can.

The -c option allows you to specify an SNMP community string. The SNMP community string is a text string that acts as a token password for SNMP-enabled devices. There are two types of communities: read and read-write. The read community only allows read interactions to take place. The read-write community allows both read and write actions to take place. By default, most SNMP-enabled devices have a read community string of public and a read-write community string of private. If you do not specify the correct community string for the device and type of action you are querying, the query will fail. This does not provide a large amount of security as most SNMP-traffic is very easy to sniff and the community string can be quickly determined, but it does limit the potential for malicious activity. You will need to know the value of the read community string for all devices that you wish to query using the check_snmp plug-in.

■Caution Writable SNMP variables can be quite dangerous; for example, if the status of an interface on your device is writable it could be changed from up to down, rendering the interface inaccessible. You should ensure that writing to variables using SNMP is disabled for those devices that do absolutely not require it.

The snmpwalk command I demonstrated earlier will return all of the OID variables available to be queried on the 10.0.0.1 host. For most devices, that will be probably be quite a large list.

■Tip If you are querying this device for the purposes of selecting variables to monitor, I recommend you pipe the output to a file for later review.

You can see one of these variables that was returned when I ran the snmpwalk command:

```
SNMPv2-MIB::sysUpTime.0 = Timeticks: (783455470) 90 days, 16:15:54.70
```

The OID variable on this line holds the uptime of the device being queried. So what happened to our long OID variable? Well, when you use the snmpwalk command, the default output from the command is an abbreviated OID variable that contains the name of the MIB that defined the variable, in this case SNMPv2-MIB, and is known as the symbolic name of the variable. The symbolic name is the last part of the variable name, in this case sysUpTime.0.

So instead of the complicated full OID value, you can use this abbreviated value when you are using the check_snmp plug-in to query an SNMP-enabled device. You can use the snmpwalk to display the full list of these abbreviated OID variables that are available on your devices and then use these in conjunction with the check_snmp plug-in.

After the symbolic name is the type of variable—in this case a timetick—that represents a hundredth of a second since some event—in this case since the device started. There are a variety of other variable types like gauges, integers, network addresses, and counters. After the variable type is the data returned for the variable—in this case the time the device has been up.

Tip There are a number of other places where you can find out what variables are available for specific devices. Cisco has made available a tool to search for specific OIDs at http://tools.cisco.com/Support/ SNMP/do/BrowseOID.do?local=en. You can also find a search interface for OIDs at www.alvestrand.no/ objectid/top.html.

As I stated earlier, Nagios can query variables on SNMP-enabled devices using the check_ snmp plug-in. This plug-in connects to the SNMP-enabled devices and queries a variable or variables you specify and then returns the data to the Nagios server in the form of a check result. Let's look at an example of the check_snmp command in action. In Example 5-14 I've used the plug-in to return the status of a network interface on a device.

Example 5-14. *Using the check_snmp Plug-in*

```
puppy# check_snmp -H 10.0.0.4 -C public -o IF-MIB::ifOperStatus.1
SNMP OK - up(1) | RFC1213-MIB::ifOperStatus.1=up(1);;;;
```

In Example 5-14 I've specified the IP address I'm connecting to using the -H option. I've specified the read community string for the device at 10.0.0.4 of public. I've also specified the particular OID I want to read using the -o option. In this case, the OID is IF-MIB::ifOperStatus.1 (which I could also specify as its numeric OID equivalent of .1.3.6.1.2.1.2.2.1.8.1, although it is considerably easier to use the abbreviated OID name). You can also specify multiple OIDs on a single -o option by separating each with a comma like so:

```
puppy# check_snmp -H 10.0.0.4 -C public ➥
-o IF-MIB::ifOperStatus.1,IF-MIB::ifOperStatus.2
SNMP OK - up(1) up(1) | RFC1213-MIB::ifOperStatus.1=up(1);;;; ➥
RFC1213-MIB::ifOperStatus.2=up(1);;;;
```

Both Example 5-14 and the command on the previous line returned data from the SNMP-enabled device that was queried. First, because it was able to connect and retrieve the variable data, the plug-in returned an OK status code. It has also returned the status of the interface, up(1), and in the second example the status of both interfaces. Additionally, the check_snmp plug-in returns performance data after the | symbol.

The check_snmp plug-in has three modes of operation: 1) query variables, 2) query variables, and then compare the results to a string or regular expression, and 3) query a variable and measure against a threshold. The first mode I've just demonstrated in Example 5-14. This mode simply returns information about the variable and an OK status if it connects. This is only marginally useful.

The second mode of the plug-in allows you to trigger an alert on specific values using either the exact string returned or a regular expression. In Example 5-15 I've again used the check_snmp plug-in to check the state of an interface.

Example 5-15. *Using check_snmp with an Evaluation String*

```
puppy# check_snmp -H owlet -o IF-MIB::ifOperStatus.1 -s "up(1)"
SNMP OK - up(1) | RFC1213-MIB::ifOperStatus.1=up(1);;;;
```

I've added the -s option to the check_snmp plug-in the command line. The -s option lets you specify an exact string that you expect in the check result. If this string is not present, the check will return a CRITICAL status. In Example 5-15 I've specified that if the check_snmp plug-in does not return the string up(1) for the required OID, indicating in this case that an interface being polled is up, then it should return a CRITICAL status.

■**Tip** You will notice I've enclosed within quotation marks the string to be compared against. This will ensure it is passed correctly to the device and not incorrectly interpreted by the shell or device.

If you want to match more than just an exact string, you can also specify a regular expression.[15] There are two types of regular expression you can use. The first type is specified using the -r option. It tests the check results using a case-sensitive regular expression. The second type is specified using the -R option and tests the check results with a case-insensitive regular expression. Let's look at this second type of regular expression:

```
puppy# check_snmp -H owlet -o IF-MIB::ifOperStatus.1 -R 'up\(1\)|testing\(1\)'
SNMP OK - up(1) | RFC1213-MIB::ifOperStatus.1=up(1);;;;
```

Here I've used a regular expression to check the interface status of a device. Instead of just testing to see if it is up as I did in Example 5-15, I now use a regular expression to test if it is in either the up(1) or the testing(1) status. If the interface is in either status, the plug-in will return an OK status. If the interface is not in either status, the plug-in will return a CRITICAL status. Using regular expressions allows you to perform powerful queries of remote devices.

The last mode of operation for the check_snmp plug-in allows you to specify integer values or ranges with thresholds that will trigger a WARNING or CRITICAL status. Here's an example:

```
puppy# check_snmp -H 10.0.0.1 -o HOST-RESOURCES-MIB::hrSystemProcesses.0 ➥
-w 25 -c 30
SNMP OK - 23 | HOST-RESOURCES-MIB::hrSystemProcesses.0=23;;;;
```

---

15. You can see information about regular expressions at www.regular-expressions.info/.

In this example, if the value of the HOST-RESOURCES-MIB::hrSystemProcesses.0 variable goes above 25, a WARNING status will be triggered; if it goes over 30, a CRITICAL status will be triggered. Single integers are always considered upper limits. This does limit the flexibility of the thresholds, but it still can be effective.

To make it more effective, you can also specify ranges of values by separating integers with a colon. Ranges are inclusive. If you specify the range in the format minimum:maximum, an OK state is returned if the value is between the range specified. A non-OK state is generated for values outside the range. If you specify the range as maximum:minimum, then the non-OK state will be generated when the value is within the range specified. You can omit upper or lower ranges by omitting one half of the range like so:

```
puppy# check_snmp -H 10.0.0.1 -o HOST-RESOURCES-MIB::hrSWRunPerfMem.50 ➡
-w 500: -c 400:
```

If you are checking multiple OIDs (which are separated by commas as demonstrated earlier in this section), you also specify multiple ranges by separating the ranges with commas.

■**Tip** The Nagios plug-in package comes with several plug-ins that use these SNMP-based checks. These include check_ifoperstatus and check_ifstatus, which both check the operational status of network interfaces on a target host using SNMP. There are also a number of additional SNMP-related plug-ins and scripts located in the contrib directory of the Nagios plug-ins package. Additionally, there is a Sourceforge project called Nagios-SNMP (http://sourceforge.net/projects/nagios-snmp/) and a project located at www.manubulon.com/nagios/. These projects are both developing a series of SNMP-based plug-ins for monitoring a variety of devices and attributes. These are all worth investigating.

The check_snmp plug-in also has some additional options that you see if you execute the plug-in with the -h option.

This has been a very brief introduction to using SNMP to perform Nagios checks. Indeed, some of the information may appear quite complicated, and it's true that the full-blown SNMP protocol can be quite complicated. But it is essential to remember that, for the purposes of using it with Nagios, all SNMP and the check_snmp plug-in do is allow you to query the status of some aspect of a device, such as its disk space, and return that value to the Nagios server. This is no different in function from any of the other mechanisms you can use to monitor your hosts and services, except that it utilizes a slightly more complicated method.

Monitoring Windows

Up until now I've looked at monitoring network-based services and on Unix-like hosts. You can also use Nagios to monitor Windows-based hosts, including Windows NT, 2000, and 2003 servers. You can monitor a variety of things on Windows-based hosts such as the status of services; disk, memory, and other performance metrics; event logs; and other information.

Like Unix hosts, a number of methods and tools are available for monitoring Windows-based hosts. Generally, monitoring Windows-based hosts operates in a similar model to using the nrpe daemon. A client is installed on the Windows host, and the Nagios server uses a plug-in, such as the check_nrpe or check_nt plug-in, to query the client and receive the data. Most of the clients available run as a service on your Windows hosts.

Tip You can also use SNMP to monitor Windows-based hosts. This uses the same methods I described in the "Monitoring via SNMP" section. You would need to have SNMP running on your Windows-based hosts and use the check_snmp plug-in to perform the checks.

Currently four clients are available for monitoring Windows-based hosts:

- **NSClient**: This client is designed to run with the check_nt plug-in. It is no longer developed but is still available from http://nsclient.ready2run.nl/.

- **NSClient++**: This more advanced version of the NSClient agent is still under development and is available from http://nscplus.sf.net/. It can use either check_nt or check_nrpe as the querying plug-in.

- **NRPE_NT**: This is a Windows version of the Unix nrpe daemon. It works with the check_nrpe plug-in and is available from www.miwi-dv.com/nrpent/.

- **NC_Net**: This is also designed to use the check_nt plug-in and requires the .NET Framework. It is available from www.shatterit.com/nc_net/.

Each of these clients offers a slightly different set of features and functions, and each has a slightly different mode of operation. For the purposes of this book I'll look at the NSClient++ client as a tool to monitor your Windows-based hosts. I'm choosing NSClient++ because of its continued development and my experiences with its stability and functionality.

Tip I recommend you examine all of the clients currently under development to select one that best suits your environment. Most of them offer similar functionality and support most versions of Windows.

NSClient++

The NSClient++ client runs as a service on your Windows-based hosts and comes with a series of modules and functions that allow a variety of monitoring checks to take place. These modules are implemented as DLLs. You can also develop your own modules in languages like C++ to provide additional functionality.

NSClient++ can operate in two modes. Each mode is provided by a separate DLL module, which I'll cover in the "Configuring NSClient++" section. The first mode replicates the functionality of NSClient, one of the precursors to this client, and uses the check_nt plug-in on your Nagios server to query your host. The second mode is a Windows implementation of the nrpe daemon I discussed earlier in this chapter. It binds to a port on the Windows-based hosts, usually port 5666, the same port used by NRPE. The Nagios server then connects to the service running on that port using the check_nrpe plug-in.

This NRPE mode can execute functionality provided by other modules you can load into NSClient++, such as modules that monitor disk space, CPU, and the event log. These are called internal checks. Or you can define your own checks using scripts, batch files, or executables, as you can with NRPE on a Unix-based host. These are called external checks.

Installing NSClient++

The NSClient++ client is very easy to install and requires downloading the installation package, creating a directory and running the installation process. You can download NSClient++ from `http://nscplus.sourceforge.net/`; the current version at the time of this writing was 0.2.4g. This section documents this version.

Download the zip file and unpack it into a directory onto your target host. I usually create a directory in the root of my system drive, usually the host's C drive, called `NSClient++`. Unzip the package maintaining the directory structure contained within the package.

The package contains a directory called `docs`, which contains the NSClient++ documentation. It contains a directory called `modules` that contains the modules you can use to monitor your host. The package also contains the `NSCLient++.exe` file, which runs the NSClient++ service, and the `NSC.ini` file, which is the configuration file for the client. This file needs to be edited before the NSClient++ client can be run.

To install the service itself, you need to execute an installation function using the `NSClient++.exe` command. Start by running a command shell. On most Windows-based hosts this can be done by clicking Start ➤ Run and entering `command` in the Run box. This will launch a command-line window. Change into the directory you created for NSClient++ using the `cd` command and then execute the following executable:

```
C:\cd NSClient++
C:\NSClient++\NSClient++.exe /install
```

This executable will install the NSClient++ service onto your Windows-based host. You must be logged onto the host as the Administrator (or have Administrator-level privileges) to install the service.

▌Tip The ease of NSClient++ installation means that it is easy to develop a package that can be deployed across a large number of servers using a software deployment tool like Radius.

If you wish to uninstall the NSClient++ package, you also use this executable but with the option `/uninstall`, as shown here:

```
C:\NSClient++\NSClient++.exe /uninstall
```

You can start and stop the NSClient++ service using this executable. You can start the service by running the executable with the following option:

```
C:\NSClient++\NSClient++.exe /start
```

You can then stop the service using the /stop option like so:

C:\NSClient++\NSClient++.exe /stop

The installation process will also set the service to start automatically when the Windows host is started.

■**Tip** You can also start and stop the NSClient++ service using the Services dialog box on your Windows host.

Configuring NSClient++

Before you start the NSClient++, you need to edit its configuration file, NSC.ini. This is because by default none of the available modules for monitoring functions on your host is enabled and the client is configured to only accept connections from the IP address 127.0.0.1. This will prevent your Nagios server from making connections to the client. Example 5-16 shows a sample of the NSC.ini file.

■**Tip** Any line that starts with a ; is not interpreted by NSClient++ and is considered commented out.

Example 5-16. *Sample NSC.ini Configuration File*

```
[modules]
FileLogger.dll
CheckSystem.dll
CheckDisk.dll
;NSClientListener.dll
NRPEListener.dll
;SysTray.dll
;CheckEventLog.dll
;CheckHelpers.dll

[log]
;debug=1
;file=NSC.log
;date_mask=%Y-%m-%d %H:%M:%S

[Settings]
;obfuscated_password=JwOKAUUdXlAAUwASDAAB
;password=secret-password
;allowed_hosts=127.0.0.1
```

```
[NRPE]
port=5666
command_timeout=60
allow_arguments=0
allow_nasty_meta_chars=0
use_ssl=1

[NRPE Handlers]
;command[check_users]=/usr/local/nagios/libexec/check_users -w 5 -c 10
;# Or simplified syntax:
;test=c:\test.bat foo $ARG1$ bar
;check_disk1=/usr/local/nagios/libexec/check_disk -w 5 -c 10
;# Or even loopback (inject) syntax (to run internal commands)
;# This is a way to run "NSClient" commands and other internal module commands
; such as check eventlog etc.
;check_cpu=inject checkCPU warn=80 crit=90 5 10 15
;check_eventlog=inject CheckEventLog Application warn.require.eventType=error
warn.require.eventType=warning critical.require.eventType=error
critical.exclude.eventType=info truncate=1024 descriptions
;check_disk_c=inject CheckFileSize ShowAll MaxWarn=1024M MaxCrit=4096M
;File:WIN=c:\ATI\*.*
;# But be careful:
; dont_check=inject dont_check This will "loop forever" so be careful with the
; inject command...
;# Check some escapings...
; check_escape=inject CheckFileSize ShowAll MaxWarn=1024M MaxCrit=4096M ➥
; "File: foo \" WIN=c:\\WINDOWS\\*.*"
```

I'll step through each of the configuration blocks in the NSC.ini file and specify what each item does. In the process of walking through this file, I'll also demonstrate how to use NSClient++ to monitor various aspects of your Windows-based hosts.

■Tip Anytime you make a change to the NSClient++ configuration, it is a good idea to restart the NSClient++ service.

Modules

The first configuration block in the NSC.ini configuration file in Example 5-16 is the [modules] block. Much of the functionality of NSClient++ is provided through modules in the form of DLLs that are enabled in NSC.ini. The modules are specified in the [modules] configuration block, which consists of a list of modules. In the default configuration, each of the modules is commented out with a ; symbol. You will need to uncomment all of the modules you wish to activate. Table 5-8 lists all currently available modules and provides a brief description of their functions.

■**Caution** You should only enable the modules you require. If you do not require a module, do not enable it. This limits the risk of unneeded modules causing functionality and security issues.

Table 5-8. *NSClient++ Modules*

Module Name	Description
FileLogger.dll	Provides logging for NSClient++
CheckSystem.dll	Provides monitoring checks for system-related items
CheckDisk.dll	Provides monitoring checks for disk and file size
CheckEventLog.dll	Provides event log checking function
NSClientListener.dll	Enables NSClient-like functionality
NRPEListener.dll	Provides nrpe daemon functionality
SysTray.dll	Provides a system tray icon when the NSClient++ service is running
CheckHelpers.dll	Provides some check tools

The first module in Table 5-8, FileLogger.dll, provides logging for NSClient++. You need to enable it for the client to log anything. You can see more information in the "Logging" section.

The next three modules provide a variety of check commands that can be executed via check commands from your Nagios server. CheckSystem.dll provides a variety of system-related checks like memory, CPU, service status, and uptime. CheckDisk.dll provides check functions for disk and file sizes on your host. The last module, CheckEventLog.dll, provides monitoring of your Windows event log. I'll look at some of the commands provided by these modules later in this section.

The NSClientListener.dll module provides NSClient-like functionality. NSClient is a precursor to NSClient++ that performs a number of checks for Windows-based hosts. The NSClient package is not currently supported; continued development of it has ceased, and I've experienced issues with installing it on newer releases of Windows, such as Windows 2003. This module allows you to mimic the functionality of the NSClient package and use its check features. You can see a list of the NSClient check features supported in NSClient++ in Table 5-9.

Table 5-9. *NSClient Checks*

Check	Description
CLIENTVERSION	Returns the NSClient version
CPULOAD	Returns the average CPU load over a specified period
UPTIME	Returns the uptime of the host
USEDDISKSPACE	Checks the size and percentage of disk used
MEMUSE	Checks the memory use
SERVICESTATE	Checks the state of one or more services
PROCSTATE	Checks if one or more processes are running
COUNTER	Checks the performance counters of a host

On the Nagios server, a plug-in called check_nt is used to initiate the NSClient check functions. The check_nt plug-in is distributed with the standard Nagios plug-in package that you learned how to install in Chapter 1. Example 5-17 shows the execution of this plug-in from the command line.

Example 5-17. *The check_nt plug-in*

```
puppy# /usr/local/nagios/libexec/check_nt -H 10.0.0.100 -p 1248 ➥
-s password -v MEMUSE -w 80 -c 90
```

The check_nt plug-in has a number of options. The first two options in Example 5-17, -H and -p, specify the IP address and port of the host being checked. The next option, -s, specifies an optional password that is needed to connect to the NSClient client on the Windows host. This password is defined in the NSC.ini configuration file in the password option in the [Settings] block.

The -v option specifies exactly what check function is to be executed on the remote host. These are the functions listed in Table 5-9. Some of these functions have options; for example, the MEMUSE check has the -w and -c options, which specify the WARNING and CRITICAL thresholds, respectively, for memory use. You can see a full list of the check_nt check functions and their options by reading the help text of the plug-in using the -h option like so:

```
puppy# ./check_nt -h
```

If you have enabled the NSClientListener.dll module, there are also some configuration options you may require in the NSC.ini file in the [NSClient] configuration block. These options are described at http://nscplus.sourceforge.net/Configuration/index.html.

I recommend that you do not use the NSClient-like functionality to perform your checks but instead use the inbuilt nrpe daemon. The inbuilt nrpe daemon is more powerful and flexible and is also able to use SSL to secure the check requests and replies.

This nrpe daemon functionality is also enabled by a module, NRPEListener.dll. It must be enabled to use NRPE handlers and allow checks from your Nagios server using the check_nrpe plug-in. I'll look at configuring NSClient++ using NRPE checks in the "NSClient++ and NRPE" section.

The SysTray.dll module, when enabled, provides a system tray icon on your Windows host that is present when the NSClient++ service is running.

The last module in Table 5-8, CheckHelpers.dll, provides some additional commands that allow you to submit perform multiple checks using one check request from the Nagios server. It also provides commands that allow you to control the check responses that are sent in response to a particular check command—for example, ensuring a check always returns an OK state.

Logging

NSClient++ has an inbuilt logging function that can log and track activities conducted by the client. This logging function is controlled by the settings in the [log] section of the NSC.ini file and using the FileLogger.dll module. By default, this module is disabled when NSClient++ is installed and no logging of the client occurs. To enable logging, FileLogger.dll needs to be enabled by removing the ; prefix from it in the NSC.ini configuration file. You can see in Example 5-16 that the DLL is enabled and logging will take place.

Additionally, there are three options in the [log] options block that influence how logging occurs. The first is the debug option, which controls whether debug information is included with logging data. If this is set to 1, debugging is enabled and debug information will be logged to the client's log file. The second option, file, controls the name and location of the client log file. By default, this is set to NSC.log. As no directory has been specified, the log file will be created in the directory where you installed the client, for example C:\NSClient++\NSC.log. You could also specify another location like so:

```
file=c:\logfiles\nsclient++.log
```

The last logging directive, date_mask, controls how the date and time will be written to the log file. The standard format is 2000-01-01 01:01, representing Year-Month-Day Hour-Minute-Second.

Settings

The [Settings] configuration block contains some general configuration options for the NSClient++ client, as shown here:

```
[Settings]
;obfuscated_password=JwOKAUUdXlAAUwASDAAB
password=secret-password
allowed_hosts=127.0.0.1
```

The first two options in the block, obfuscated_password and password, relate to the NSClient-like functionality that NSClient++ is able to replicate. These options are where the password used by the check_nt plug-in's -s option is set.

To generate an obfuscated password you can run the NSClient++ executable with the -encrypt option:

```
C:\NSClient++\NSClient++.exe -encrypt
Enter password to encrypt (has to be a single word): goldfish
obfuscated_password=MgcGEUEb
```

■**Caution** This is very simple obfuscation and should not be relied on for serious security.

The next option, allowed_hosts, specifies a list of hosts or IP addresses that are allowed to connect to the NSClient++. You should only list those hosts and IP addresses that are allowed to query the client, that is, your Nagios servers. By default, this option is set to 127.0.0.1. If you do not specify any hosts or IP addresses, anyone can connect to this client. I do not recommend using this configuration.

NSClient++ and NRPE

The easiest way to use NSClient++ to perform checks on your Windows-based hosts is to use its NRPE-style functionality. The NSClient++ service includes an nrpe daemon that can be queried with the check_nrpe plug-in. This works in much the same way as the Unix-based nrpe daemon I discussed earlier in this chapter in the "Monitoring via NRPE" section. Commands to be executed are configured in the NSC.ini configuration file, much like NRPE commands using the nrpe daemon on a Unix-based host are stored in the nrpe.cfg configuration file. Commands can either come from modules, what NSClient++ describes as internal commands, or you can execute commands, scripts, or batch files, which are called external commands. They are then executed using a command defined on the Nagios server that uses the check_nrpe plug-in, like the command demonstrated in Example 5-10 earlier in this chapter.

NSClient++'s NRPE daemon is enabled by uncommenting the NRPEListener.dll module in the [modules] configuration block in the NSC.ini file. There are also some configuration options that control the functioning of the daemon. These options are contained in a configuration block labeled [nrpe]. Additionally, the] commands that you can execute are specified in the [NRPE Handlers] block. I'll look at some commands in the "Windows Checks" section later in this chapter.

I have listed all the options for the nrpe daemon in Table 5-10.

Table 5-10. *NSClient++ NRPE Configuration Options*

Option	Default	Description
port	5666	Indicates the port that NSClient++'s NRPE will listen for requests on
allowed_hosts		Contains a list of the IP addresses that are allowed to query the nrpe daemon
use_ssl	1	Toggles whether SSL encryption is enabled
command_timeout	60	Specifies the length of time after which an NRPE command will time out
allow_arguments	0	Allows check requests to contain arguments
allow_nasty_meta_chars	0	Allows NRPE commands to contain meta-characters

Each of the options in Table 5-10 controls the settings of the NSClient++'s nrpe daemon. The first option, port, specifies what port the daemon will listen on. This defaults to 5666. If you have a host-based firewall on your Windows host, such as the Windows Firewall, you will need to allow access to this port from your Nagios server or servers.

■**Tip** You can see more information on customizing the Windows Firewall at www.microsoft.com/windowsxp/using/security/internet/sp2_wfintro.mspx.

The next option, allowed_hosts, controls which hosts can connect to the client's nrpe daemon and execute check requests. It consists of a list of hosts or IP addresses. If you specify more than one host or IP address, they should be separated with commas. The default setting for this option is to specify the localhost address of 127.0.0.1. You should change this option to specify all the Nagios servers that will need to query this host like so:

allowed_hosts=127.0.0.1,10.0.0.1,10.0.0.2

I recommend you set this option to only those Nagios servers that will be querying the client using the nrpe daemon.

The next option, use_ssl, enables SSL support for the client. By default, it is set to 1, which enables support. To disable support, set the option to 0. I strongly recommend you leave SSL enabled to prevent an attacker from eavesdropping or subverting the communication between the Nagios server and the client.

The command_timeout option specifies the maximum time in seconds that a command can execute on the client. It is set to a default of 60 seconds. After this time, the command is stopped. This only applies to external commands, which as I described earlier are scripts or batch files you can execute. The internal commands, which are provided by the NSClient++ modules, are not affected by this option.

The last two options, allow_arguments and allow_nasty_meta_chars, control how commands can be configured. The first option, allow_arguments, is very similar to the nrpe daemon's dont_blame_nrpe option and prevents command arguments from being passed to internal commands only. You can still use them in external commands, as I'll demonstrate shortly. The allow_nasty_meta_chars option controls whether commands can contain meta-characters that could be interpreted by the host. By default it is set to 0, which restricts most meta-characters. Set it to 1 to enable meta-characters.

Note NSClient++ is under development and changes can occur to the available configuration options. I recommend checking the documentation available with the package for any changes.

Windows Checks

As I've discussed, you can use either the NSClient-like mode and the check_nt plug-in or the nrpe daemon and the check_nrpe plug-in to monitor your Windows hosts using NSClient++. I recommend using the nrpe daemon, and I'll demonstrate how to use this mode in this section. The nrpe daemon mode] works by executing commands defined in the [NRPE Handlers] configuration block in the NSC.ini configuration file. The commands are executed by running the check_nrpe plug-in on the Nagios server.

In Example 5-18 you can see two commands from the [NRPE Handlers] section of the NSC.ini configuration file.

Example 5-18. *NSClient++ NRPE Handlers*

```
[NRPE Handlers]
check_batch=c:\tools\monitor.bat
check_cpu=inject checkCPU warn=80 crit=90 5 10 15
```

Commands are created by specifying a command name and then, separated by an = symbol, the actual command to be executed. The commands in Example 5-18 represent the two types of commands: external and internal.

External Commands

External commands are batch files, executables, and scripts that can be run and will return information about the status of your hosts and services. The first command in Example 5-18 is an external command. Called `check_batch`, it executes a batch file called `monitor.bat` that is located in the `C:\tools` directory. To execute this script, you would need to create the `monitor.bat` batch file and code it to perform the checks you require and then return the results in the form of a Nagios check result that the `check_nrpe` plug-in and the Nagios server can process.

From the Nagios server, this command would be executed using the `check_nrpe` plug-in. Example 5-19 shows the execution of the command from the command line using this plug-in.

Example 5-19. *The check_batch Example Command*

```
puppy# ./check_nrpe -H 10.0.0.10 -p 5666 -c check_batch
```

In Example 5-19 I'm querying a host running NSClient++ at IP address 10.0.0.10 on port 5666. Using the `-c` option, I've specified the name of the command to be run, `check_batch`, which I defined in Example 5-18.

Tip Running the command from the command line is the fastest and easiest way to test that it works and that you receive the correct response from the remote host.

To use this command from the Nagios server itself, you'd define a command object for the `check_nrpe` plug-in as we did earlier in this chapter in Example 5-10. Then you'd create a service object for the service you wish to monitor on your Windows host. In the service object, the `check_command` directive would execute the appropriate command—in this case the `check_nrpe` command from Example 5-10—and then pass in the command name you wish to execute on the remote host like so:

```
define service{
...
check_command    check_nrpe!check_batch
...
                 }
```

You can also specify arguments to be passed to the NRPE commands on your Windows hosts. To do so, enable the `allow_arguments` option in the `[nrpe]` configuration block by setting it to 1. You can then add arguments to commands in the `[NRPE Handlers]` block like so:

```
check_batch=c:\tools\monitor.bat $ARG1$ $ARG2$ $ARG3$
```

In this example, I've added three arguments to the `check_batch` command. I've specified them in the form of $ARGx$ macros, as we'd do on the Nagios server. Indeed, this is reflected on the Nagios server like so:

```
puppy# ./check_nrpe -H 10.0.0.10 -p 5666 -c check_batch -a CPU MEMORY DISK
```

As you can see, I've used the -a option to specify a list of arguments to pass to the check_batch command when the check_nrpe plug-in is executed from the command line—in this case, the arguments: CPU, MEMORY, and DISK. If I were specifying these arguments in a Nagios command object rather than on the command line, I'd do so like this:

```
define command{
        command_name    check_batch
        command_line    /usr/local/nagios/libexec/check_nrpe -H $HOSTADDRESS$ ➥
                                -c check_batch -a $ARG1$ $ARG2$ $ARG3$
        }
```

Finally, you can pass the required arguments from the check_command directive in a service object definition like so:

```
define service{
…
check_command    check_batch!CPU!MEMORY!DISK
…
        }
```

Here I've defined a partial service object definition that contains a check_command directive that will call the check_batch command object and pass the three arguments of CPU, MEMORY, and DISK to it.

■Note External commands can be used to run a number of types of function, including executables, batch files, and scripts of various kinds, including VBScript, WMI, Windows Scripting Host, Active Directory Service Interfaces (ADSI), and Office automation. All external commands simply need to return check results such as hostname, service description, return code, and plug-in output that Nagios can interpret and process. I'll discuss how to design your own plug-ins in Chapter 10.

Internal Commands

Internal commands are provided via the modules and include checks like CPU, memory, disk and file sizes, and the event log. To enable particular internal command checks, you need to enable the related module. If you do not need the particular internal command, do not enable the parent module. Each of the modules provides one or more internal commands. You can see a full list of the internal commands listed by the module that provides them in Table 5-11.

Table 5-11. *Internal Check Commands by Module*

Module	Command	Description
CheckDisk.dll	CheckFileSize	Checks the size of one or more files or directories
	CheckDriveSize	Checks the size of one or more disk drives
CheckEventLog.dll	CheckEventLog	Checks event log messages
CheckSystem.dll	CheckCPU	Checks CPU load

Module	Command	Description
	CheckUpTime	Checks system uptime
	CheckServiceState	Checks the state of a service
	CheckProcState	Checks the state of a process
	CheckMem	Checks the memory usage
	CheckCounter	Checks the status of a counter
CheckHelpers.dll	CheckAlwaysOK	Alters the return code of another check to always return the OK status
	CheckAlwaysCRITICAL	Alters the return code of another check to always return the CRITICAL status
	CheckAlwaysWARNING	Alters the return code of another check to always return the WARNING status
	CheckMultiple	Runs multiple checks and returns the worst state

As I mentioned earlier, NSClient++ internal commands use a special function, called inject, to submit the commands for processing. A sample internal command is shown in Example 5-20.

Example 5-20. *Sample Internal Command*

```
check_disk_c=inject CheckDriveSize MaxWarnUsed=90% MaxCritUsed=95% ShowAll Drive=c:\
```

The internal command is constructed by specifying the name of the command, in this case check_disk_c, and separated by an = symbol, the command itself. The first part of the command is the inject statement, followed by the name of the internal command to be executed, here CheckDriveSize, and then any arguments to be submitted with that internal command. This internal command can then be executed using the check_nrpe plug-in on the Nagios server.

Let's look at some of these internal commands and how they can be used to monitor your Windows hosts. I'll only look at several of the available commands, but the documentation and examples available with the NSClient++ package more than adequately explain how you can use the commands I don't demonstrate.

CheckDisk.dll

The first module in Table 5-11 is CheckDisk.dll, which provides two internal commands, CheckFileSize and CheckDriveSize. The CheckFileSize command checks the size of a particular file, files, or directories, and CheckDriveSize checks the size of your disk drives. Both checks can be configured to use a variety of thresholds. I am going to look at how to use the CheckDriveSize command to monitor your disk space.

Example 5-20 shows the CheckDriveSize command. Let's break this example down. After the command name and the inject statement is the internal command name and its arguments. The CheckDriveSize command has a number of arguments. The first arguments allow you to set the thresholds that the check will be monitoring for. Table 5-12 lists these arguments.

Table 5-12. *CheckDriveSize Thresholds*

Threshold	Description
MaxWarnFree	Maximum allowed free space to trigger a WARNING status
MaxCritFree	Maximum allowed free space to trigger a CRITICAL status
MinWarnFree	Minimum allowed free space to trigger a WARNING status
MinCritFree	Minimum allowed free space to trigger a CRITICAL status
MaxWarnUsed	Maximum allowed used space to trigger a WARNING status
MaxCritUsed	Maximum allowed used space to trigger a CRITICAL status
MinWarnUsed	Minimum allowed used space to trigger a WARNING status
MinCritUsed	Minimum allowed used space to trigger a CRITICAL status

Like the check_disk plug-in I demonstrated earlier in this chapter, the CheckDriveSize command has two levels of thresholds. First, you can set a threshold that triggers the WARNING status for the service; then you can set a threshold that will trigger the CRITICAL status. In the CheckDriveSize command, there are also two types of thresholds that you can set: free space and used space. You can set thresholds for both the maximum and minimum for both of these types of thresholds. So in Example 5-20, the CheckDriveSize command is checking how much used space is allowed in the C: drive using the MaxWarnUsed and MaxCritUsed arguments. Like with the check_disk plug-in, you need to specify these thresholds in pairs, both WARNING and CRITICAL thresholds, for the check to function correctly.

The CheckDriveSize command can measure the threshold in bytes, kilobytes, megabytes, or gigabytes, if you append the value of the threshold with the characters B, K, M, or G, respectively. Or as I've done in Example 5-20, you can measure the threshold in terms of the percentage free on the drive or drives by using the % symbol. So to measure the threshold for a WARNING status for the maximum disk space used in gigabytes, you'd set the MaxWarnUsed argument to

```
MaxWarnUsed=2G
```

This would trigger a WARNING status if more than 2GB of disk space was used on a specified drive or drives.

You can also select a particular drive or check all drives on a host. In Example 5-21 I've selected drive C. I can also select all drives by adding the argument CheckAll like so:

```
check_disk_all=inject CheckDriveSize MaxWarnUsed=90% MaxCritUsed=95% ➡
ShowAll CheckAll
```

Note The ShowAll argument tells the internal command to return data even if NSClient++ cannot determine the state of the item being checked.

I can execute this command using the check_nrpe command on the Nagios server. The following shows an example of a partial service object that executes this command:

```
define service{
        host_name             owlet
        service_description   disk
        check_command         check_nrpe!check_disk_all
        ...
        }
```

On a system with two drives, C and E, this would return plug-in output like this:

```
WARNING: C:\: Total: 9.77G - Used: 8.96G (91%) - Free: 830M (9%) > warning, ➥
E:\: 4.93G|C:\;91%;90;95; E:\;50%;90;95;
```

The plug-in output returns the WARNING status for the service because more than 91 per-cent of the C disk drive is being used. Performance data is also returned after the | symbol. As I've specified in the ShowAll argument, the E drive is also listed.

You can also select drives of a particular type by using the FilterType argument. There are four types of drives you can filter by: FIXED, CDROM, REMOVABLE, and REMOTE. Fixed drives are your host's internal disk drives; CD-ROM drives are self-explanatory; and removable drives include USB, FireWire, and other removable media drives. The last type of drive, remote drives, are network-attached drives or shares. For example, to check all fixed disk drives you'd use the following command:

```
check_disk_fixed=inject CheckDriveSize MaxWarnUsed=90% MaxCritUsed=95% ➥
                        ShowAll CheckAll FilterType=FIXED
```

Finally, it is possible to use arguments with the CheckDriveSize internal command. To do so, you need to enable the allow_arguments option in the NSC.ini file:

```
check_disk=inject CheckDriveSize Drive=$ARG1$ MaxWarnUsed=$ARG2$ ➥
MaxCritUsed=$ARG3$ ShowAll
```

We can then pass these arguments from a partial service object definition like so:

```
define service{
        host_name             owlet
        service_description   disk
        check_command         check_nrpe!check_disk!c:\\!80%!95%
        ...
        }
```

Tip You notice that I've specified the c:\ with two backslashes as c:\\. This is because the backslash character is interpreted by Nagios and needs to be escaped. You will need to escape any other meta-characters used in commands either directly or passed in as arguments.

You can see that each argument is prefixed with a ! character. These arguments would be passed to the check_nrpe command object definition, which would be defined like so:

```
define command{
        command_name    check_nrpe
        command_line    /usr/local/nagios/libexec/check_nrpe -H $HOSTADDRESS$ ➥
                            -c $ARG1$ -a $ARG2$ $ARG3$ $ARG4$
        }
```

You will notice the argument numbering is different between the command defined in the NSC.ini configuration file and the command object definition. This isn't a concern as NRPE passes the arguments in the order they are specified—in this case, the command name to be executed, the drive to be checked, and the WARNING and CRITICAL thresholds. So when NSClient++ receives the first command argument, the command name, it will use it to select the check_disk command to execute. It will then use the remaining three arguments to populate the required arguments for that command.

CheckSystem.dll

The last module I'm going to look at is CheckSystem.dll, which provides a number of useful system commands that perform checks of CPU, memory, uptime, and the status of processes and services. It also provides a very useful command called CheckCounter that allows you to check the value of one or more of the numerous Windows performance counters. You can find information and examples of the other commands in the NSClient++ documentation available with the package.

The first internal command from the CheckSystem.dll module we'll look at is the Check➥ ServiceState command, which allows you to check the state of one or all of your Windows services. You can see a typical use of this command in Example 5-21.

Example 5-21. *CheckServiceState Command*

```
check_service_lms=inject CheckServiceState lanmanserver
```

■**Tip** You can specify as many services to check as you need on the command line by separating each with a space character.

The check command, check_service_lms, created in Example 5-21 uses the Check➥ ServiceState internal command to check whether the lanmanserver service on the host is running. On the following lines, you can see the execution of Example 5-21 from the command line of a Nagios server using the check_nrpe plug-in:

```
puppy# ./check_nrpe -H 10.0.0.10 -p 5666 -c check_service_lms
OK: All services are running.
```

The message that All services are running in response to the command indicates that the service is running. If the service is not running, the command will return the CRITICAL status and an error message like so:

```
CRITICAL: lanmanserver: stopped (critical)
```

You could also use arguments, if you have them enabled, to pass in the name of the service to be checked.[16] Here I've shown a similar command but with an argument specified:

```
check_service=inject CheckServiceState $ARG1$
```

The following line shows how you can use this command by passing in the name of the service to be checked to the -a option:

```
puppy# ./check_nrpe -H 10.0.0.10 -p 5666 -c check_service -a lanmanserver
```

You can also specify multiple services to be checked via the -a option like so:

```
puppy# ./check_nrpe -H 10.0.0.10 -p 5666 -c check_service -a "lanmanserver wscsvc"
```

■Tip For all the services I'm checking, I use the service name of the service, not the display name that is shown in the Services tool on a Windows host. You can find the service name of a service by checking its properties in the Services tool. Also, tools are available that will list the service names of your services.

By default, when you execute the command in Example 5-21 and the service being checked is running, then the message All services are running will be returned. But you can override this behavior by adding another argument, ShowAll, like so:

```
check_service_lms=inject CheckServiceState ShowAll lanmanserver
```

This will return a message in response to the check_nrpe plug-in request explicitly stating that the service being checked is running:

```
OK: lanmanserver: started
```

Using the CheckServiceState command, you can also check if a particular service or services is stopped rather than started by specifying a service name and adding the stopped argument:

```
check_service_lms2=inject CheckServiceState ShowAll lanmanserver=stopped
```

This will check if the lanmanserver service is stopped. If it is not stopped, then the command will return a CRITICAL state:

```
puppy# ./check_nrpe -H 10.0.0.10 -p 5666 -c check_service_lms2
CRITICAL: lanmanserver: started (critical)
```

■Tip Related to the CheckServiceState command is the CheckProcState command, also available from the CheckSystem.dll module. This allows you to check the state of a process. The check is constructed in a very similar way to the CheckServiceState command and will allow you to monitor those applications that use processes rather than services.

---

16. This is if the allow_arguments option is enabled in the NSC.ini configuration file.

The next internal command we'll look at from the `CheckSystem.dll` module is `CheckCounter`. It can be used to check the contents of a Windows performance counter. Windows performance counters contain information output from a variety of applications and tools, such as Microsoft SQL Server, Microsoft Exchange Server, or another application installed on your host that has been configured to output to a performance counter. You can see a typical `CheckCounter` internal command in Example 5-22.

Example 5-22. *The CheckCounter Internal Command*

```
check_cnt_conns=inject CheckCounter "Counter=\TCP\Connections Established" ➥
MaxWarn=4 MaxCrit=8
```

In Example 5-22 I'm checking a counter called `\TCP\Connections Established` that contains the number of TCP connections being made to the host. I've specified the counter using the `Counter` argument, and separated the argument and the counter name using a = symbol. I've also enclosed both the `Counter` argument and the counter name in quotation marks because the counter name contains a space. It is generally a good idea to do this as most counters contain space or other special characters. If you do not enclose the counter, either in the `NSC.ini` configuration file or in the `check_nrpe` command, then the internal command may misinterpret the characters in the counter name and fail.

I've also specified two other arguments, `MaxWarn` and `MaxCrit`. These specify two maximum thresholds—in this case for the maximum number of connections, one threshold for `WARNING` status and one threshold for `CRITICAL` status. These same thresholds can be used for any counter. The `CheckCounter` command also has two opposite thresholds called `MinWarn` and `MinCrit` that allow you to specify minimum thresholds for counter values.

In Example 5-22, if the value of the counter is 4 or greater, a check of the internal command would result in a `WARNING` status. If the value of the counter is 8 or greater, a `CRITICAL` status would result. You can see this command executed from the Nagios server command line on the following lines:

```
puppy# ./check_nrpe -H 10.0.0.10 -p 5666 -c check_cnt_conns
WARNING: \TCP\Connections Established: 6 > ➥
warning|\TCP\Connections Established;6;4;7;
```

As you can see, the check of the command returned a `WARNING` status because the number of connections is 6, greater than the `WARNING` threshold of 4 set in Example 5-22.

Returning the entire counter name can also be cumbersome, so the `CheckCounter` internal command allows us to alias a counter name like so:

```
check_cnt_conns=inject CheckCounter ➥
"Counter:TCPConns=\TCP\Connections Established" MaxWarn=4 MaxCrit=8
```

Once you add the `TCPConns` alias after the `Counter` argument, separated by a : symbol, the check will change the counter name so as to return the following result:

```
WARNING: TCPConns: 6 > warning|TCPConns;6;4;7;
```

■**Note** As you can see, the check has returned performance data. This data can be used in a variety of ways to provide more advanced reporting on your hosts. I discuss using this data in Chapter 6.

You can also use arguments to specify a particular counter and thresholds like so:

```
check_cnt=inject CheckCounter "Counter=$ARG1$" MinWarn=$ARG2$ MinCrit=$ARG3$
```

On the Nagios server, you can pass these arguments to the check_cnt command like so:

```
puppy# ./check_nrpe -H 10.0.0.10 -p 5666 -c check_cnt ➡
-a "\TCP\Connections Established" 4 8
WARNING: \TCP\Connections Established: 6 > ➡
warning|\TCP\Connections Established;6;4;7;
```

You can get a list of all performance counters on your Windows hosts using the NSClient++.exe executable. To do this, run NSClient++.exe using the /listpdh option like so:

```
C:\NSClient++\"NSClient++.exe" /listpdh
```

Checkpoint

- Always use full paths in your command_line directives. This will reduce the risk of someone inserting a malicious object ahead of the real object and execute that instead.

- If you are using the check_by_ssh command, ensure that you protect your public and private keys from compromise. Treat them carefully and make sure that any files holding them have suitably restrictive permissions.

- Performing checks with SNMPv1 and v2 has limited security. If you can use SNMPv3, which contains a higher level of security including authentication, I recommend you use this version of the protocol.

- If you use NSClient++ for monitoring your Windows hosts, I recommend you use its NRPE-like daemon mode. It is the most powerful, flexible, and secure of the monitoring alternative in the client.

Resources

Following is a series of books and sites that should assist you in developing checks for your hosts and services.

Books

- Mauro, D., and Schmidt, K., *Essential SNMP*, O'Reilly, 2005.

Sites

- NRPE: http://prdownloads.sourceforge.net/nagios/nrpe-2.0.tar.gz

- SNMP: www.cisco.com/warp/public/535/3.html

- Net-SNMP: http://net-snmp.sourceforge.net

- Cisco OID Object Navigator: `http://tools.cisco.com/Support/SNMP/do/BrowseOID.do?local=en`

- Searchable OID Register: `www.alvestrand.no/objectid/top.html`

- Nagios-SNMP: `http://sourceforge.net/projects/nagios-snmp/`

- Nagios SNMP plug-ins: `www.manubulon.com/nagios/`

- NSClient: `http://nsclient.ready2run.nl/`

- NSClient++: `http://nscplus.sf.net/`

- NRPE_NT: `www.miwi-dv.com/nrpent/`

- NC_Net: `www.shatterit.com/nc_net/`

CHAPTER 6

■■■

Advanced Commands

A significant part of Nagios monitoring configuration are the commands used to monitor your environment. In Chapter 2 I provided a basic introduction to monitoring your hosts and services with command objects. In Chapter 5 I discussed using plug-ins with the check command and how to use these commands to monitor your environment. This chapter covers some of the more advanced uses and types of commands. I expand on the use of command objects, including additional information on macros, event handlers, external commands, notifications, and performance data.

I'll look at how to use some advanced features of macros to enhance their functionality in your commands. I'll explore in more detail the use of event handlers to perform actions based on the state of a host or service. Additionally, I'll look at how notifications are constructed and how they can be better managed, and provide you with more detail about external commands. Finally, I'll look in greater depth at performance data, which is gathered using check commands, and show you how to use this data.

All of this information builds on your existing configuration and will assist you in the remaining chapters in this book when I look at concepts like distributed monitoring and integration of Nagios with other tools.[1]

Macros

One of the most powerful features of Nagios is the ability to add macros to your command definitions. Macros can be added to command object definitions and allow those definitions to be more flexible. The macros placed in your command definitions are replaced when the command is executed with actual values from object definitions. I've already demonstrated how to use some of these macros in Chapters 2 and 5, such as the $HOSTNAME$ and $HOSTAD-DRESS$ macros, which contain the hostname and host address of a particular host object. When a command that contains these macros is executed, these macros are replaced with the hostname and address of the relevant host object.

---

1. See Chapters 8 and 9.

META-CHARACTERS IN MACRO VALUES

During the replacement of macros with actual values, Nagios tries to protect you from some potentially dangerous data in the form of shell meta-characters. It does this by stripping out these characters when the replacement occurs in notifications, event handlers, and other commands like performance data processing commands. It does not do this for host and service check commands. This stripping out of meta-characters reduces the risk that the data contained in the macro will be interpreted by the shell. If these characters were interpreted, this could allow an attacker to execute malicious commands using Nagios.

The characters that are stripped out are defined in the directive `illegal_macro_output_chars`, which is specified in the `nagios.cfg` configuration file. By default, the characters that are stripped out are

`` `~$&|'"<> ``

The characters are only stripped out from some macros. These macros are `$HOSTOUTPUT$`, `$HOSTPERFDATA$`, `$HOSTACKAUTHOR$`, `$HOSTACKCOMMENT$`, `$SERVICEOUTPUT$`, `$SERVICE`➡ `PERFDATA$`, `$SERVICEACKAUTHOR$`, and `$SERVICEACKCOMMENT$`.

Macros can be used in a wide variety of commands, including

- Host and service check commands

- Host and service notifications

- Host and service event handlers

- Host and service obsession commands

- Host and service performance data processing commands

Although macros can be used in all of these command types, not all macros can be used in all commands. Nagios calls this *macro context*. Macro context means that not all macros make sense in the context of certain types of commands. For example, the `$HOSTNAME$` macro can be used in all types of command objects, but the `$SERVICECDESC$` macro can only be used in service check, service notification, service obsession, and service performance data processing commands. It cannot be used in a host check command. This is because in a host check command the `$SERVICEDESC$` macro has no context since no service is being referenced.

There are far too many macros to list in this book, but I've covered some of the significant ones in this and other chapters. You can also see a full list in the Nagios documentation at `http://nagios.sourceforge.net/docs/2_0/macros.html`. This list also documents the context of all the available macros and in what types of commands they can be used.

On-Demand Macros

The only macros that do not have a context are a special kind of macro called *on-demand macros*. On-demand macros reference values from host or service objects in a command that is not being executed for that host or service. For example, if I needed it I could reference the IP address of the `kitten` host in a check of the `puppy` host. Let's look at an example of how an on-demand macro might work. In Example 6-1 I've defined a command object.

Example 6-1. *A Command Object Using On-Demand Macros*

```
define command{
                command_name      check_host
                command_line      /usr/local/nagios/libexec/check_host ➡
-H $HOSTADDRESS$ -G $HOSTADDRESS:gateway$
                }
```

The command in Example 6-1 contains one normal and one on-demand macro. If the command in Example 6-1 was executed on the puppy host, the value of the $HOSTADDRESS$ macro would be replaced with the address of the puppy host. The value of the second macro, $HOSTADDRESS:gateway$, would be replaced with the address of the gateway host. On-demand macros behave like normal macros except that they reference the value of another object by specifying the name of that object in the on-demand macro.

On-demand macros come in two forms. The first form is for host-based macros, such as $HOSTADDRESS$, and the second form is for service-based macros such as $SERVICEDESC$. The first form of on-demand macro is created by specifying a host macro and adding the name of the host object to be referenced. These are separated with a colon symbol. Hence the macro $HOSTADDRESS:gateway$ refers to the address of the host object gateway and the macro $HOSTADDRESS:kitten$ refers to the address of the host object kitten. I could also create an on-demand host macro from any of the available host macros—for example, to refer to the host state of a particular host I would construct a macro like $HOSTSTATE:host_name$, where host_name would be replaced with the name of the host being referenced.

The second form of on-demand macro is for service object–based macros. In this case, the other services are referenced by specifying the name of the service macro, then the hostname of the host the service is running on, and finally the service description. Each item is separated by a colon symbol. For example, the service state of the dns service running on the owlet host can be referenced with the following macro:

```
$SERVICESTATE:owlet:dns$
```

One of the potential uses for on-demand macros include designing commands to monitor clusters, such as being able to collectively reference values about multiple hosts that make up a cluster in a single command using on-demand macros. Another use might be to reference values from multiple hosts or services in an event handler to perform linked or escalating actions. An example is when a service is in a particular state that could also impact other services or hosts. You can run an event handler and pass the values, such as IP addresses or names, of these additionally impacted objects and perform some action(s) on them as well.

Macros As Environmental Variables

Finally, macros are also available as environmental variables. This is a new feature that has been introduced in Nagios 2.0. Almost all macros are available as environmental variables. The only exceptions are on-demand macros and the $USERx$ macros.[2]

You can identify the Nagios macro environmental variables as they are prefixed with the word NAGIOS and an underscore character, like so: NAGIOS_. Thus, the $HOSTNAME$ macro is

---

2. The $USERx$ macros are not available for security reasons as they often contain sensitive information.

available as an environmental variable called NAGIOS_HOSTNAME. These environmental variables can be used in any script, such as those executed by commands, event handlers, or notifications. It is important to remember that the environmental variables are also subject to macro context. The variables available will be dependent on the object that the command, event handler, or notification that is being executed. For example, only host-based macros will be available as environmental variables if a command is being run for a host object.

In Example 6-2 I've shown a simple shell script that shows how a script executed by the Nagios process might use these environmental variables.

Example 6-2. *Macros As Environmental Variables*

```
#!/bin/sh

if [ $NAGIOS_SERVICESTATETYPE = "HARD" ]; then
      echo "The service state type is HARD"
else
      echo "The service state type is SOFT"
fi

exit 0
```

In Example 6-2, instead of having to pass in the $SERVICESTATETYPE$ macro to the shell script, I've referred to it using the environmental variable that contains it.

Event Handlers

Event handlers can be powerful and useful tools. Event handlers are optional commands that can be configured to run whenever a host or service state change takes place. There are two types of event handlers: local and global. Local event handlers are specified in host and service object definitions, and global event handlers are defined using the global_host_event_handler and global_service_event_handler directives in the nagios.cfg configuration file. Local event handlers only apply to state changes on the host or service they are defined in. Global event handlers apply to every host or service state change.

■**Tip** If you specify both global and local event handlers, the global event handler runs first and then the local event handler executes.

Event handlers are executed when a host or service is in a SOFT state, when it first goes into a HARD state, and when it recovers from either a SOFT or HARD state.[3] Unlike notifications, event handlers cannot be configured to selectively execute on particular states or state types. They execute for all state changes of the types just listed.

---

3. See Chapter 2 for details of HARD and SOFT states.

Event handlers are principally useful for two purposes. First, they can be used to perform some action in the event of a particular type or kind of state change on a specific host or service. For example, if a daemon or service returns a CRITICAL state, an event handler could restart that service or daemon. Or if disk space on a host reached a WARNING threshold, an event handler could delete temporary files or perform some other form of file maintenance.

Second, event handlers can perform some global action, such as forwarding information about events that have triggered event handlers to another enterprise monitoring system like HP OpenView or BMC Patrol. You could also forward the events to a database or some other processing engine.

Let's look at how an event handler is defined in a host or service. In Example 6-3 I've created a service object definition and added the relevant event-handling directives. The same directives are also used in host object definitions.

Example 6-3. *Service with Event Handler Enabled*

```
define service{
            host_name                   kitten
            service_name                smtpd
            …
            event_handler_enabled  1
            event_handler               service-restart
            …
            }
```

The first directive, event_handler_enabled, specifies whether an event handler is enabled for this object. If this directive is set to 1, the event handler is enabled; if it is set to 0, the event handler is disabled.[4] The event_handler directive specifies the specific event handler that is executed when a state change occurs. If event handlers are enabled for a host or service and no event handler is specified, Nagios takes no action. In this case I've defined an event handler called service-restart.

Each event handler is defined using a command object definition. Here, I've defined an event handler using a command object:

```
define command{
        command_name    service-restart
        command_line    /usr/local/nagios/libexec/eventhandlers/service-restart ➥
$SERVICEDESC$ $SERVICESTATE$ $SERVICESTATETYPE$
        }
```

The command I've defined, called service-restart, executes a shell script also called service-restart, which I've placed in a directory called eventhandlers underneath the /usr/local/nagios/libexec/ directory.

■**Tip** You can write an event handler in a number of languages such as (but not limited to) shell script, Perl, Python, or Ruby.

---

4. I usually configure this directive in an object template to globally activate it.

Three macro values are passed to the shell script: $SERVICEDESC$, $SERVICESTATE$, and $SERVICESTATETYPE$. These three macros contain the name of the service, the current state of the service, and whether it is a SOFT or HARD state. Example 6-4 shows an example of this shell script.

Example 6-4. *service-restart Shell Script*

```
#!/bin/sh

# $1 $SERVICEDESC$ Macro
# $2 $SERVICESTATE$ Macro
# $3 $SERVICESTATETYPE$ Macro

case "$3" in
                HARD)
                                case "$2" in
                                OK)
                                # The service is okay - don't do anything.
                                ;;
                                WARNING)
                                UNKNOWN)
                                # The service is in WARNING - don't do anything.
                                # Or the service is in an UNKNOWN state.
                                ;;
                                CRITICAL)
                                # Try to restart the service if it is in a HARD state.
                                /etc/rc.d/init.d/"$1" restart
                                ;;
                                esac
esac
exit 0
```

In Example 6-4 I've demonstrated an event handler written in shell script. It performs actions based on the state and state type. In this example, only one action is taken: if the event handler is activated by a HARD CRITICAL state, it tries to restart the service, based on its name drawn from the service description, using its init script. The script does this using two case statements. The first case statement takes actions based on the particular state type received. In Example 6-4 the action will only occur if the state type is HARD. The second case statement executes based on the actual state received. In Example 6-4 I've only added an action for the HARD CRITICAL state. You could add other actions for the other state types and states depending on your requirements.

One of the most important things to consider about event handlers is that the event handler runs with the permissions of the user and group that is running the Nagios process. In the case of my installation, this would be the user nagios and a group also called nagios. This means you cannot perform any action with an event handler that the user and group that Nagios is running as does not have permission to do. For example, you will not be able to bind a privileged port or to restart a service that requires higher permissions or root access. Thus, you will need to provide the user or group that Nagios is running as with the required permissions to perform any actions your event handlers need to take. Another possible way to overcome this is to use the sudo command to allow the user Nagios is running as to temporarily adopt the required privileges.[5]

Example 6-4 is a very simple example of how to use an event handler. You can also add more complicated logic to an event handler by adding a number of other macros. An example often cited is the use of the $HOSTATTEMPT$ and $SERVICEATTEMPT$ macros. These macros contain the current retry attempt number of the host or service check. You can thus configure an event handler to execute a different action depending on the number of the retry check. For instance, you can take an escalating series of actions to try to resolve the issue. Using our previous example of restarting a service, you could attempt to reload the service, then fully start and stop it, and if that still failed you could then increase the debug value for the service and email any resulting logs to a technician.

Event handlers can be complicated to implement, and you should consider turning on logging of a few items: service and host retries and event handlers. This logging is enabled through three additional directives in the nagios.cfg configuration file. The required logging directives are listed on the following lines and are enabled by setting them to 1:

```
log_service_retries=1
log_host_retries=1
log_event_handlers=1
```

Note This logging can be quite intensive and can generate a considerable amount of logging data. I recommend you only leave them enabled while you are testing your event handlers.

Notifications

Notifications are commands that Nagios uses to notify a contact of issues and problems. Notifications occur whenever a host or service changes to a HARD state that is specified in the notification_options directive. For example, if a host changes to the DOWN state and the notification_options directive in the host object definition is configured to generate a notification for this state, Nagios will execute a notification command or commands. You can see a partial service object definition in Example 6-5.

Example 6-5. *Sample Service Definition for Notifications*

```
define   service{
              host_name               puppy
              service_desc            vpnd
              ...
              notification_options    c,w,u
              contact_groups          field_support
              }
```

---

5. See www.sudo.ws/.

Based on the `notification_options` directive in the service object definition I've just defined, if the service was in the `CRITICAL`, `WARNING`, or `UNKNOWN` state, a notification would be generated.

The notification would be sent to the contacts contained in the contact group defined in the service object; in Example 6-5 it would be the contact group `field_support`. The particular notification command or commands executed are specified in the contact object definitions that are in the contact group. They are specified in that contact object using either the `host_notification_commands` or `service_notification_commands` directive, depending on whether it is a host or service that has changed state. These two directives are specified in the contact object definition.

■**Tip** You can read about the lifecycle of notifications in more detail at `http://nagios.sourceforge.net/docs/2_0/notifications.html`.

As notifications are constructed using command object definitions, they can use all the macros available to the context they are executed in—for example, if notifying about a service, the host- and service-related macros are available. If notifying about a host only, the host-related macros are available.

Notification commands can use binaries or scripts to transmit the information you wish to a contact or contacts. Notifications can be sent via a number of mechanisms such as email, pager, SMS,[6] or even an instant messaging service such as Jabber or ICQ.

In Example 6-6 you can see one of the notification commands that comes with the Nagios sample configuration: the `notify-by-email` command. This command is designed to send notifications about service objects via email to a contact.

Example 6-6. *The notify-by-email Command*

```
define command{
            command_name    notify-by-email
            command_line    /usr/bin/printf "%b" "***** Nagios ➡
*****\n\nNotification Type: $NOTIFICATIONTYPE$\n\nService: $SERVICEDESC$\nHost: ➡
$HOSTALIAS$\nAddress: $HOSTADDRESS$\nState: $SERVICESTATE$\n\nDate/Time: ➡
$LONGDATETIME$\n\nAdditional Info:\n\n$SERVICEOUTPUT$" | /bin/mail -s ➡
"** $NOTIFICATIONTYPE$ alert - $HOSTALIAS$/$SERVICEDESC$ is $SERVICESTATE$ **" ➡
$CONTACTEMAIL$
            }
```

In Example 6-6 you can see that the `notify-by-email` command uses the `printf` command to echo text and macros to the `mail` command. You can put text, macros, and three special characters—\t, \r, and \n—into the `command_line` directive of the notification command. The special characters allow you to format the notification output: the \t character inserts a tab character, the \r character inserts a carriage return, and the \n symbol inserts a new line.

---

6. Short Messaging Services

Let's have a quick look at some of the macros in the command. Probably one of the most important is the $NOTIFICATIONTYTPE$ macro. This macro contains the type of notification being sent. There are five types of notifications. The most common type is the PROBLEM notification type, which is generated when a host or service has entered a non-OK state, such as a host being in a DOWN state. The next type of notification is a RECOVERY. The RECOVERY type notification is generated when a host or service has returned to an UP or OK state, respectively. The ACKNOWLEDGEMENT notification type is created by acknowledging a problem using the web console or via an external command. The last two notification types are the FLAPPINGSTART and FLAPPINGSTOP notification types. These notifications are generated if Nagios detects that flapping has started or stopped on a host or service. If the notification_options directive in your host or service object definition has the f option specified, these notification types will be generated.

Also present is the $LONGDATETIME$ macro, which is one of a number of date and time macros available in Nagios. It outputs dates in a similar format to Sun Jan 1 00:00:00 AEST 2000. This is dependent on what global date format you have selected. I've listed the other date and time macros and their descriptions and formats in Table 6-1.

Tip The global date format for Nagios is set using the date_format directive in the nagios.cfg configuration file. There are four possible settings: us, euro, iso8601, and strict-iso8601. See http://nagios.sourceforge.net/docs/2_0/configmain.html#date_format for the details of each format.

Table 6-1. *Date and Time Macros*

Macro	Format	Description
$SHORTDATETIME$	1-1-2000 00:00:00	Short date format
$DATE$	1-1-2000	Date only
$TIME$	00:00:00	Time only
$TIMET$	N/A	The time_t time format representing seconds since the Unix epoch

The last macro in Example 6-6 is the $CONTACTEMAIL$ macro. This macro contains the email address of the contact that is to receive the notification. This is being used as the target of the notification mechanism, in this case the sending of the notification using the mail command.

So what does a notification like Example 6-6 look like? In Example 6-7 you can see a sample of a service notification generated by the notify-by-email notification command.

Example 6-7. *Problem Notification Email*

```
***** Nagios  *****

Notification Type: PROBLEM

Service: local_disk
Host: Melbourne Server
Address: 10.0.0.70
State: CRITICAL

Date/Time: Thu Oct 20 23:30:43 EST 2005

Additional Info:

Connection refused by host
```

In addition to email notifications, Nagios comes with a notification command called notify-by-epager, which is designed to send notifications via pager. In addition, there are two other default commands, host-notify-by-email and host-notify-by-epager, designed to send notifications via email and pager for hosts. Example 6-8 shows the host-notify-by-email notification command.

Example 6-8. *host-notify-by-email Notification Command*

```
define command{
            command_name    host-notify-by-email
            command_line    /usr/bin/printf "%b" "***** Nagios ➥
*****\n\nNotification Type: $NOTIFICATIONTYPE$\nHost: $HOSTNAME$\nState: ➥
$HOSTSTATE$\nAddress: $HOSTADDRESS$\nInfo: $HOSTOUTPUT$\n\nDate/Time: ➥
$LONGDATETIME$\n" | /bin/mail -s "Host $HOSTSTATE$ alert for $HOSTNAME$!" ➥
$CONTACTEMAIL$
            }
```

This is similar in function to the notify-by-email command for services but contains different macros, the $HOSTSTATE$ and $HOSTOUTPUT$ macros, for example, that will report the host status and output in the notification.

Obviously, being able to send notifications via email is extremely useful as many potential mechanisms for notifications can use email as an input, such as most SMS gateways. But in addition to email and pager notifications there are a variety of other mechanisms you can use to send notifications.

■**Tip** The NagiosExchange site has a list of scripts and tools that allow you to send notifications using a variety of mechanisms. You can see these at www.nagiosexchange.org/Notifications.35.0.html?&tx_netnagext_pi1[page]=0%3A10.

Sending Notifications via Instant Messenger

One of the more useful mechanisms for sending notifications is via instant messenger infrastructure. There are a number of different instant messaging services, such as MSN, ICQ, Yahoo, AIM (AOL Instant Messenger), and the open source service, Jabber. In this section I'll cover using Jabber to send notifications in the form of instant messages. I'm choosing Jabber for several reasons:

- It is an open source service and therefore it is easy to integrate with.

- A number of add-on tools for Jabber server integration already exist.

- You can use publicly available Jabber servers or you can run your own internal Jabber server.

The Jabber instant messaging server is based on the Extensible Messaging and Presence Protocol (XMPP), which describes a series of XML-based streaming protocols for instant messaging. I'm going to use a Perl-based program called sendxmpp to send our notifications using Jabber.

In order to run sendxmpp you require four prerequisites. The first is Perl, the second is the sendxmpp program itself, and the third is a CPAN module called Net::XMPP, which provides the back-end functionality that allows the script to work. The fourth is a Jabber account. You can either run your own Jabber server or get a free Jabber account from one of a number of Jabber servers worldwide.[7]

■Tip You can find a tutorial on setting up your own Jabber server at http://linuxgazette.net/112/tomar.html.

You will need Perl and the Net::XMPP module in order to run this program. You can install the Net::XMPP module via CPAN, as you can see in Example 6-9.

Example 6-9. *Installing Net::XMPP via CPAN*

```
puppy# cpan
cpan> install Net::XMPP
```

Alternatively, you can download the module from the CPAN site at http://search.cpan.org/dist/Net-XMPP/lib/Net/XMPP.pm and install it from source. Once you have downloaded the package, you can unpack and compile it as shown on the following lines:

```
puppy# wget http://search.cpan.org/CPAN/authors/id/R/RE/REATMON/Net-XMPP-1.0.tar.gz
puppy# tar -zxf Net-XMPP-1.0.tar.gz
puppy# cd Net-XMPP-1.0
puppy# perl Makefile.PL
puppy# make
puppy# make install
```

---

7. See www.xmpp.net/ for a list of publicly available Jabber servers.

Next download the sendxmpp source package from www.djcbsoftware.nl/code/sendxmpp/ and unpack it:

```
puppy# wget http://www.djcbsoftware.nl/code/sendxmpp/sendxmpp-0.0.8.tar.gz
puppy# tar -zxf sendxmpp-0.0.8.tar.gz
puppy# cd sendxmpp-0.0.8
```

Then you need to make and install the script like so:

```
puppy# perl Makefile.PL
puppy# make
puppy# make install
```

The sendxmpp binary is installed into the /usr/bin/ directory; a man page for the binary is also installed.

The sendxmpp command is very easy to use. First, I create a configuration file, called .sendxmpprc, that will contain the Jabber account, server, and password that will be used to send the notifications. This file needs to be owned by the user executing sendxmpp and have permissions of 0600 to protect the password contained in it. As the Nagios server will be executing sendxmpp through a notification command, my configuration file will need to be owned by the user and group running my Nagios server process. In my case, this is the user and group nagios. In Example 6-10 I've shown a typical configuration file.

Example 6-10. *A .sendxmpprc Configuration File*

```
nagiosbook@jabber.org password
```

The file is constructed by specifying your username at the Jabber server you wish to sign on to, for example nagiosbook@jabber.org. Then specify the password for this account. You can also specify a port number for the server you wish to connect to, if your server uses an unusual port. You can see this on the following line:

```
nagiosbook@jabber.org:443 password
```

On this line I've overridden the default Jabber port, which is 5222 for non-SSL traffic and 5223 for SSL traffic, with port number 443.

I normally locate this file in the /usr/local/nagios/etc directory and change its ownership and permissions to suit Nagios like so:

```
puppy# chown nagios:nagios /usr/local/nagios/etc/.sendxmpprc
puppy# chmod 0600 /usr/local/nagios/etc/.sendxmpprc
```

Next let's look at how the sendxmpp command itself works. The sendxmpp command is very similar in function to the mail command. You can either pipe in a message to be sent, or execute the command and input the message required from STDIN and terminate it with Ctrl+D. In Example 6-11 I've demonstrated sending an instant message using sendxmpp.

Example 6-11. *Sending a Message with sendxmpp*

```
puppy# ls -l | /usr/bin/sendxmpp -f /usr/local/nagios/etc/.sendxmpprc -s ➥
"This is a test message" \ jamtur01@jabber.org.au
```

In Example 6-11 I've piped the content of a directory listing using the `ls` command to the `sendxmpp` command. This will send the directory listing of the current directory to a Jabber server as an instant message. In Example 6-11 you can see that the `sendxmpp` command itself is constructed like so:

```
puppy# sendxmpp [options] recipient
```

I've used two options in Example 6-11. The first option, `-f`, tells `sendxmpp` where to find the configuration file to be used for the message being sent. By default this file is `~/.sendxmpprc`. I've overridden this to point to the configuration file I've just created. The second option, `-s`, specifies a subject for the instant message.

There are a number of other options you can use with `sendxmpp`, and I've listed the most useful in Table 6-2.

Table 6-2. *sendxmpp Options*

Option	Description
`-u, --username` *user*	Overrides the user in the configuration file
`-p, --password` *password*	Overrides the password in the configuration file
`-j, --jserver` *server*	Overrides the server in the configuration file
`-t, --tls`	Uses SSL/TLS for connections
`-h, --help, --usage`	Shows usage message
`-v, --verbose`	Uses verbose output
`-d, --debug`	Shows debugging information

The first three options, `-u`, `-p` and `-j`, allow you to override the values for the user, password, and server specified in the `.sendsmpprc` configuration file.

The `-t` option enables a SSL/TLS connection between your host and your Jabber server. I recommend that if your Jabber server supports SSL/TLS, you use this to protect your notifications from eavesdropping. You will need to install the `IO::Socket::SSL` CPAN module to enable this functionality (and CPAN may prompt you to install some additional modules).

The `-h` option displays some simple help text, and the `-v` and `-d` display verbose logging and complete debugging information for the command.

■**Caution** The `-d` option will display all information about the sending process, including any passwords.

Once you have installed `sendxmpp`, a Nagios notification command object is needed to utilize this command and send notifications via Jabber. In Example 6-12 you can see a suitable command for sending notifications for services.

Example 6-12. *Notification Command for sendxmpp*

```
define command{
            command_name    notify-by-im
            command_line    /usr/bin/printf "%b" "***** Nagios ➥
 *****\n\nNotification Type: $NOTIFICATIONTYPE$\n\nService:➥
 $SERVICEDESC$\nHost: ➥
$HOSTALIAS$\nAddress: $HOSTADDRESS$\nState: $SERVICESTATE$\n\nDate/Time: ➥
$LONGDATETIME$\n\nAdditional Info:\n\n$SERVICEOUTPUT$" | /usr/bin/sendxmpp -f ➥
/usr/local/nagios/etc/.sendxmpp -s "** $NOTIFICATIONTYPE$ alert - ➥
$HOSTALIAS$/$SERVICEDESC$ is $SERVICESTATE$ **" $CONTACTADDRESS1$
            }
```

The command, notify-by-im, in Example 6-12 is very similar to the notify-by-email command present in the Nagios sample configuration. Instead of the notification being piped to the mail command, it is being piped to the sendxmpp command. The destination address for the instant message is the value of the macro, $CONTACTADDRESS1$. This macro would be defined in a contact object definition using the address1 directive, as you can see in Example 6-13.

Tip It should be easy to create a host-notify-by-im notification command by modifying the sample host-notify-by-email notification command.

Example 6-13. *Contact Object Definition*

```
define contact{
      contact_name                    test01
        …
      service_notification_commands   notify-by-im
      address1                        test01@jabber.org
      }
```

Note There is an add-on for sending notifications via ICQ at NagiosExchange (www.nagiosexchange.org/ Notifications.35.0.html?&tx_netnagext_pi1[p_view]=184). There is also an alpha version of a tool to send Nagios notifications via AIM at http://os.cyberheatinc.com/nim.php.

Notification Aggregation and Suppression

One of the issues with Nagios notifications is that if the notification logic is fulfilled, a notification will be generated and sent. Nagios considers each notification to a particular contact to be an individual instance. It counts the number of notifications sent (for purposes like escalations), but it does not make any assertions about how many notifications it has sent to a particular contact. This can result in large volumes of notifications being sent to a contact or contacts if a network outage or a major service outage occurs. This means a contact could be flooded with emails, pages, or SMS. This can reduce the value of notifications.

To deal with this potential problem, you can choose from a number of possible solutions, including aggregating notifications, throttling the volume of notifications sent, or suppressing notifications. You can do this by developing your own scripts and tools or by using an already developed tool for the purpose. I've included a Perl script, called `throttling_notifications.pl`, with the electronic resource for this book that will perform throttling of email notifications.[8] The `throttling_notifications.pl` script acts as a layer between your notification command and the notification mechanism—in this case, any mechanism that takes an email address as its input.

With regard to already developed tools, at the time of this writing only two tools are currently maintained and compatible with Nagios 2.0 for managing notifications like this. The first is called NAN, or the Nagios Notification Daemon, and it is available from `http://os.cyberheatinc.com/nan.php`. The NAN daemon works by acting as a filtering layer between Nagios and the notification mechanisms. It controls two functions: when to send notifications and how often. NAN can limit the number of notifications sent, concatenate a series of notifications together, and control how often notifications are sent. NAN does this by inserting itself between Nagios and the notification mechanism. Instead of the notification command calling the notification mechanisms, Nagios calls the NAN daemon and passes the notification to the daemon. The NAN daemon processes the notification according to predefined rules, and performs the notification by calling the required notification mechanism. The NAN daemon consists of two components: the server and a client application. The client application receives the notifications, and the server processes them and sends them on using the notification mechanisms.

■**Note** The NAN daemon and client are written in Perl.

The second tool is called NANS, or Netsaint Aggregate Notification System.[9] It is available from `www.nachtwache.org/projects/netsaint/utilities/nans/`. It is also another notification filter, again written in Perl, which sits between Nagios and its notifications mechanisms. It functions in much the same way as NAN but also includes the ability to perform regular aggregate reporting of the current count of notifications generated and summary reporting detailing all hosts and services in particular states.

External Commands

Integrating Nagios with other applications is made considerably easier with the functionality provided by external commands. External commands allow you to submit commands to the Nagios server that perform a variety of functions, ranging from controlling server settings to manually submitting host and service check results to the server. It is this last function, submitting host or service check results, that offers significant advantages for integration with

---

8. You can download this from the Source Code section of the Apress website.

9. Netsaint is the former name for Nagios.

other applications. You can take information, such as an SNMP trap or a log entry, and submit it to Nagios as a passive check result. This result can be monitored and notified on, depending on the information contained within it. In this section, I'll look at how to submit external commands and how you can interact with them.

■**Tip** You'll learn about integrating Nagios with other tools in Chapter 9.

External commands are not enabled by default on your Nagios installation. Enabling them requires some changes to your nagios.cfg configuration file and configuration of an external command file. First, you will also need to enable the check_external_commands directive in the nagios.cfg file by setting it to 1 to ensure that the Nagios server will process external commands. You also need to configure the command_file and command_check_interval directives:

```
check_external_commands=1
command_file=/usr/local/nagios/var/rw/nagios.cmd
command_check_interval=-1
```

The command_file directive specifies the location of the external command file; by default this is /usr/local/nagios/var/rw/nagios.cmd. I discussed configuring and securing the external command file in Chapter 3.

The command_check_interval controls how often the command file will be checked for external commands. The default setting is –1, which specifies that the command file will be checked as often as possible. You can specify an alternative value in seconds.

■**Tip** The external command file will also be checked immediately after an event handler is executed.

Once you have enabled external commands, you need to understand how they are constructed. The external command is made up of three elements: a timestamp, a command name, and a series of arguments for that command. The command name and arguments are separated by a semicolon like so:

```
[time] command_name;command_arguments
```

The timestamp is specified in time_t format. This format is the time in seconds since the Unix epoch started. You can generate this timestamp on the command line using the date command like so:

```
puppy# date +%s
```

```
1129109677
```

The timestamp is enclosed in square brackets, [1129109677], and separated from the command_name element with a space. The command_name element is the name of the external command that you wish to submit to the external command file. A large number of commands are available to you. Three major categories of external command exist: commands that change the configuration of the server; commands that interact with hosts, services, and other objects including enabling and disabling checks, submitting check results, and scheduling downtime; and commands that relate to adaptive monitoring.

■**Tip** You can see a full list of commands at `www.nagios.org/developerinfo/externalcommands/` `commandlist.php`.

Let's look at some examples of each type of command and how they function. One of the more useful combinations of commands allows you to globally enable and disable active host and service checks. Here is an example of the command to globally disable active service checks:

```
[1129109677] STOP_EXECUTING_SVC_CHECKS
```

The `STOP_EXECUTING_SVC_CHECKS` command requires no command arguments. It simply tells the Nagios server to stop executing active service checks.

You need to get this external command into the external command file to be processed by the Nagios server. The external command file is a named pipe created by Nagios when it starts and removed when it stops.[10] As a result, when the Nagios server is active, you simply need to echo the timestamp, the command name, and any arguments to the pipe. You can do this from the command line like so:

```
puppy# echo "[1129109677] STOP_EXECUTING_SVC_CHECKS" >> ➥
/usr/local/nagios/var/rw/nagios.cmd
```

Here I've enclosed the external command in quotation marks and used the Unix command `echo` to send it to the external command file. The command will be processed whenever Nagios next checks the external command file. Depending on the interval set for this, it may take some time for the command to be processed and the change to be reflected on the Nagios server.

■**Note** There is also an opposite command called `START_EXECUTING_SVC_CHECKS`, which enables active service checks on the Nagios server.

As you can see, it is easy to submit an external command from the command line, and by extension, it is also easy to submit a command via a shell script. In Example 6-14 I've shown a simple shell script to submit an external command.

---

10. See Chapters 1 and 3 for more details.

Example 6-14. *Submitting an External Command via a Shell Script*

```sh
#!/bin/sh

cmd_file=/usr/local/nagios/var/rw/nagios.cmd
time=`date +%s`

/bin/echo "[$time] START_EXECUTING_SVC_CHECKS" >> $cmd_file

exit 0
```

In Example 6-14 I've defined two variables: `cmd_file` for the location of the command file, and `time`, which executes the `date` command and returns the current time in `time_t` format. The `echo` command sends the `$time` variable combined with the command `START_EXECUTING_SVC_CHECKS` to the command file. When processed, this command will enable active service checks if they have been disabled. It will have no effect if active service checks are already enabled.

I could also use the more advanced version of `echo`, the `printf` command, to send the external command to the command file. Here I've replaced the `echo` command portion of Example 6-14 with `printf`:

```
/usr/bin/printf "[%lu] START_EXECUTING_SVC_CHECKS\n" $time >> $cmd_file
```

As you can see, I've passed the same external command to the external command file using the `printf` command.

■**Tip** The `echo` and `printf` commands may be located in different directories on your distribution. Additionally, for security reasons I recommend you always specify full directory paths to any binaries you execute.

A large number of the functions and settings of the Nagios server can be controlled or changed with the use of external commands, including enabling and disabling active and passive host and service checks, notifications, event handlers, host and service obsession, and a variety of other functions. You can even restart or shut down the Nagios process with external commands.[11]

Processing Checks Results with External Commands

One of the primary functions external commands are used for is to submit passive check results from external sources to Nagios. This is primarily done using two commands: `PROCESS_HOST_CHECK_RESULT` and `PROCESS_SERVICE_CHECK_RESULT`. Let's look at how to submit a passive service check using the `PROCESS_SERVICE_CHECK_RESULT` external command. This command requires a timestamp, the command name, and a series of command arguments. It is constructed as you see here:

---

11. See the `RESTART_PROCESS` and `SHUTDOWN_PROCESS` external commands.

```
[time] PROCESS_SERVICE_CHECK_RESULT;<host name>;<service description>;➡
<return code>;<output>
```

First is the timestamp, contained in block brackets, then the command name followed by a semicolon. Next are the command arguments for that external command. To submit service check results, you need to specify the hostname and service description of the service object you're submitting check results for, with each argument separated by a semicolon. Then you must specify the service return code, which is a numeric representation of the service state: 0 for OK, 1 for WARNING, 2 for CRITICAL, and 3 for UNKNOWN. Finally, you need to specify the results of the check itself—for example, the plug-in output, including any optional performance data.

Here's an example of this external command:

```
[1129191361] PROCESS_SERVICE_CHECK_RESULT;puppy;vpnd;0;VPN Daemon active
```

This example contains the timestamp and the name of the external command being submitted. The command arguments follow: the host and service description for which the result is being submitted; the service return code, in this case 0 for OK; and then the output of the check, VPN Daemon Active.

In Example 6-15 I demonstrate how to submit the external command to the external command file. In this example, to get the current time I use the date command enclosed in back ticks. The printf command places the generated time in the formatted output.

Example 6-15. *Submitting External Commands*

```
puppy# /usr/bin/printf "[%lu] PROCESS_SERVICE_CHECK_RESULT;puppy;vpnd;0;➡
OK - VPN daemon active\n" `date +%s` > /usr/local/nagios/var/rw/nagios.cmd
```

I can do the same with a host check result using the PROCESS_HOST_CHECK_RESULT external command. On the following line is an example of how this external command might look:

```
[1129191361] PROCESS_HOST_CHECK_RESULT;puppy;0;OK - Host alive
```

With this command you only need to specify the hostname, the return code for the host status (0 for UP, 1 for DOWN, and 2 for UNREACHABLE), and the output of the check result, again with optional performance data.

A number of other external commands interact with hosts and services, including commands that reschedule host and service checks, acknowledge problems with hosts and services, add and delete comments, and work with host and service groups.

External Commands for Adaptive Monitoring

Finally, there is a special type of external command that allows a form of adaptive monitoring to be utilized. Adaptive monitoring allows you to change some of the settings and monitoring characteristics of your host and service objects during operation without requiring a restart of the Nagios server.

There are a limited number of settings you can change. For hosts and services these are

- The check command and its arguments (specified by the check_command directive)

- The event handler and its arguments (specified by the event_handler directive)

- The check interval (specified by the check_interval directive)

- The maximum check attempts (specified by the max_check_attempts directive)

You can also change the global host and service event handlers, which are controlled by the global_host_event_handler and the global_event_service_handler directives in the nagios.cfg configuration file.

An example of the use of adaptive monitoring would be to change the max check attempts or the arguments of a check command being used for a host or service in response to a particular state or output from a check. For example, I'm monitoring a particular service and I detect a particular state that might indicate the service check is timing out. I can initiate an event handler that would change the arguments of the check command to expend the timeout on the check, thus allowing the service sufficient time to return a response.

The changes to these settings take place during runtime and are reset back to their normal settings when Nagios is reloaded or restarted. In Example 6-16, I demonstrate how to change the check command used by a particular service.

Example 6-16. *Changing the Service Check Command Using Adaptive Monitoring*

```
puppy# /usr/bin/printf "[%lu] CHANGE_SVC_CHECK_COMMAND;puppy;vpnd;check_vpnd2\n"➥
`date +%s` > /usr/local/nagios/var/rw/nagios.cmd
```

You can see that I've again used the printf command to echo the external command to the external command file. The CHANGE_SVC_CHECK_COMMAND command takes a number of arguments: the hostname, the service description, and the new check command that you wish the service to use. In Example 6-16 the check command for the vpnd service on the puppy host is changed to check_vpnd2.

When you change the check command, you can add arguments for that new command. If you don't wish to change the command, you can change the arguments used by the existing command. You can do this by listing the new or changed arguments after the new or existing command name and separating them with bang, !, symbols, as shown here:

```
puppy# /usr/bin/printf ➥
"[%lu]CHANGE_SVC_CHECK_COMMAND;puppy;vpnd;check_vpnd2!eth0!eth1\n" ➥
`date +%s` > /usr/local/nagios/var/rw/nagios.cmd
```

You can see in the previous line that I've changed the check command for the vpnd service on the puppy host to check_vpnd2 and passed the two arguments, eth0 and eth1, to the new command. Each argument is separated by a ! symbol.

■**Note** Any new check command and event handler you specify must already be defined to Nagios. If you try to change to a command that does not have a command object definition in Nagios, the external command will fail.

Another of the useful changes you can make using adaptive monitoring is to change the value of the check_interval and max_check_attempts directives for hosts and services. On the following lines are two external commands. The first command changes the maximum service check attempts for the vpnd service on the puppy host to 4. The second command changes the check interval of the puppy host from 30.

```
[1129191361] CHANGE_MAX_SVC_CHECK_ATTEMPTS:puppy:vpnd:4
[1129191361] CHANGE_NORMAL_HOST_CHECK_INTERVAL:puppy:30
```

Tip You can also read about Adaptive Monitoring at http://nagios.sourceforge.net/docs/2_0/adaptive.html.

Performance Data

Performance data is optional data related to the performance of checks or statistical information returned by the check itself. The most common use for this data is to feed it to an external program, such as RRDtool, to provide graphs and statistical analysis or more sophisticated reporting than Nagios is capable of providing. In this section I'll demonstrate the different types of performance data, how to process that data, and some potential uses for the data.

Performance data comes in two forms: internal Nagios performance data and information that checks and plug-ins are configured to collect. This could include statistical information about a host or service.

The first form of performance data, internal Nagios data on the performance of a check, includes the length of time taken to execute the check and the latency of the check, that is, how much later than scheduled the check occurred. This data is available as a series of Nagios macros, such as $SERVICEEXECUTIONTIME$ and $SERVICELATENCY$. This data can be used to graph the timing of the execution of checks and the latency of your checks.

There are four macros that display the internal performance data related to the execution of your checks. The first two are the $HOSTEXECUTIONTIME$ and $SERVICEEXECUTIONTIME$ macros, which contain the length of time the check of the host or service took to execute. The second two are the $HOSTLATENCY$ and the $SERVICELATENCY$ macros. These contain the latency value of your host or service check. Latency is the length of time after a check was scheduled that it actually executed. For example, if a check is scheduled to be executed at 18:23:45 and is actually executed at 18:24:00, the latency of the check is 15 seconds. In other words, the check was executed 15 seconds after it was scheduled to be executed.

The second form of performance data are metrics that can be gathered by plug-ins. This could include data like CPU utilization, disk space used, memory used, or any other metrics that a plug-in can be programmed to collect. These metrics are returned to Nagios in the output from host and services checks. In check results, the performance data is specified after the plug-in output, separated from the output by a pipe, |, character. You can see some sample output in Example 6-17.

Example 6-17. *Sample Output Showing Performance Data*

```
HTTP OK HTTP/1.1 200 OK - 721 bytes in 0.093 seconds|time=0.093398s;;;0.000000 ➥
size=721B;;;0
```

The first portion of the output is the text output of the plug-in. This is returned to the Nagios server and can be displayed in the web console. It can also be referred to using the macros, $HOSTOUTPUT$ or $SERVICEOUTPUT$, depending on the type of check being executed. The second portion of the output, after the pipe character, is the performance data or metrics collected by that plug-in. You can refer to the performance data using the $HOSTPERFDATA$ or $SERVICEPERFDATA$ macros, depending on whether it is data from a host or service check.

■Note Not all plug-ins return performance data, but only those that are programmed to return some form of performance data. If the plug-in does not return any performance data, no data will be present in the output and the $HOSTPERFDATA$ or $SERVICEPERFDATA$ macros will be empty.

Processing Performance Data

To use performance data, you need to configure Nagios to process this information. This tells Nagios what to do with the performance data, including what to do when performance data is received. There are two methods of processing performance data. In the first method, a command is executed to process performance data. In the second method, a template is defined and the data in the template is written directly to a file or named pipe. I'll examine both methods in this section.

To enable performance data processing, a number of directives need to be configured and some commands created. The first directive controls the processing of all host and service checks for performance data. It is defined in the nagios.cfg configuration file, as shown here:

```
process_performance_data=1
```

Set the directive to 1 to process performance data and 0 to disable it. Enabling this directive tells Nagios to process performance data.

Additionally, as discussed in Chapter 2, there is a directive present in your host and service object definitions, process_perf_data, that also needs to be enabled for performance data to be processed. Set the directive to 1 to enable the processing of performance data for particular hosts and services. I generally define this directive in my host and service templates to avoid having to repeat it multiple times in host and service object definitions.

Processing Performance Data Using Commands

The first method of processing performance data uses two commands, one for hosts and one for services, to process performance data after each check result is received. The commands to be executed are specified by two directives contained in the nagios.cfg configuration file. You can see these two directives on the following lines. The values of the directives are the default settings from the sample Nagios configuration.

```
host_perfdata_command=process-host-perfdata
service_perfdata_command=process-service-perfdata
```

Note There is also a timeout directive for the execution of performance data processing commands. It is the `perfdata_timeout` directive. By default, it is set to 5 seconds. If the command takes longer than the timeout to execute, Nagios will kill the command.

Both of these directives are commented out in the sample Nagios configuration. You don't need to specify both commands unless you want to process performance data from both host and service checks. If you only wish to process performance data from one type of check, only uncomment the directive for the required check type, hosts or services. You can specify your own performance processing commands by changing the value of these directives. The commands you specify in these directives will need to be defined in your Nagios configuration.

Let's look at one of these sample commands. In a default Nagios installation, these commands are defined in the sample configuration file, `misccommands.cfg`, in the `/usr/local/nagios/etc` directory. In Example 6-18 I show the sample `process-service-perfdata` command.

Example 6-18. *Sample process-service-perfdata Command*

```
define command{
          command_name    process-service-perfdata
          command_line    /usr/bin/printf "%b" ➥
"$LASTSERVICECHECK$\t$HOSTNAME$\t$SERVICEDESC$\t$SERVICESTATE$\t$SERVICEATTEMPT$➥
\t$SERVICESTATETYPE$\t$SERVICEEXECUTIONTIME$\t$SERVICELATENCY$\t$SERVICEOUTPUT$➥
\t$SERVICEPERFDATA$\n" >> /usr/local/nagios/var/service-perfdata.out
          }
```

In Example 6-18 the command appends the values of a number of macros to a file using the `printf` command, each separated by the `\t` character, which represents the tab character, to a file located at `/usr/local/nagios/var/service-perfdata.out`. Also specified after the `printf` command is the `\n` character, which also appends a new line to the output. The macros include the $SERVICEOUTPUT$ macro, which contains the output of the plug-in, and the $SERVICEPERFDATA$ macro, which contains the performance data. You can see an example of the output that this command writes to the `service-perfdata.out` file on the following lines:

```
1129557936    puppy https  OK    1    HARD   0.427  0.221  HTTP OK ➥
HTTP/1.1 200 OK - 1098 bytes in 0.408 seconds   time=0.408291s;;;0.000000 ➥
size=1098B;;;0
```

This output consists of the values of all the macros listed in Example 6-18, separated by tab characters. You can specify your own command to write the data to a file or process it in some other way. I'll demonstrate some different ways to do this when I look at what we can do with this data later in this section.

Processing Performance Data to File or Pipe

In the second method, Nagios writes performance data to a file or named pipe based on a template specified in the `nagios.cfg` configuration file. This method does not require specifying or executing a command. Nagios writes the data directly to the file or named pipe. You need to define separate files or pipes and templates for host and service performance data. The performance data files are specified with two directives in the nagios.cfg configuration file. You can see these directives in Example 6-19.

Example 6-19. *Directives to Specify Performance Data Files*

```
host_perfdata_file=/tmp/host-perfdata
service_perfdata_file=/tmp/service-perfdata
```

By default, these directives are commented out in the sample configuration file. You will only need to uncomment the required directive or directives for the type of performance data you want to collect, host or service or both. You can specify as the destination file any file or named pipe that the user that is running the Nagios server process has permission to write to. The files specified in Example 6-19 are the default settings from the sample configuration, and you can change them as required.

Next, to determine what is written to the file or pipe, you must specify two more directives that define a template for the performance data being outputted. The templates specify the exact data and format of that data as it is written to the file or files. The required directives are the host_perfdata_file_template for the host performance data template and the service_perfdata_file_template for the service performance data template. You can see samples of both these directives in Example 6-20.

Example 6-20. *Performance Data File Templates*

```
host_perfdata_file_template=[HOSTPERFDATA]\t$TIMET$\t$HOSTNAME$➡
\t$HOSTEXECUTIONTIME$\t$HOSTOUTPUT$\t$HOSTPERFDATA$
service_perfdata_file_template=$SERVICEOUTPUT$\t$SERVICEPERFDATA$
```

The templates can contain macros, three special characters—\t for a tab, \r for a carriage return, and \n for a new line and any plain text you wish to specify. A new line will be automatically added after each performance data entry written to the file.

In Example 6-20, in the host_perfdata_file_template, you can see a series of macros that are separated by tab characters, using \t, that will be written to the host performance data file. Also note the $HOSTOUTPUT$ and $HOSTPERFDATA$ macros containing the output of the plug-in and the performance data, if any, generated by the host check. This will result in output that resembles the following line:

```
[HOSTPERFDATA]  1129561681    puppy   0.013   PING OK - Packet loss = 0%, ➡
RTA = 0.25 ms
```

The service_perfdata_file_template directive only contains two macros and simply outputs the plug-in output and the performance data, if any, for the plug-in.

Next there are two additional directives that relate how the performance data is written to files. These are the host_perfdata_file_mode and the service_perfdata_file_mode directives. They have two options: w for write mode and a for append mode. For normal files you would generally use the append, or a, option to append the performance data entries to the file. For a named pipe the write, or w, option might be more appropriate. Examples of these directives are

```
host_perfdata_file_mode=a
service_perfdata_file_mode=a
```

Finally, four other directives are related to this second method of performance data processing. These directives are optional and allow the regular processing of the performance data files using commands defined in Nagios. This is an easy way to execute actions to process the performance data in your files. You could also schedule actions with `cron` or another scheduling tool.

The first two directives specify how often the files can be processed, and the second two directives specify the names of the commands used to do the processing. I've specified these four directives in Example 6-21.

Example 6-21. *Performance Data File Processing Directives*

```
host_perfdata_file_processing_interval=60
service_perfdata_file_processing_interval=0
host_perfdata_file_processing_command=process-host-perfdata-file
service_perfdata_file_processing_command=process-service-perfdata-file
```

The first two directives, `host_perfdata_file_processing_interval` and `service_perfdata_file_processing_interval`, control how often, in seconds, that the performance data files will be processed. In Example 6-21 I'm processing the host performance data file every 60 seconds. The setting of service performance data file processing interval to 0 disables regular processing of this file.

The second set of directives, `host_perfdata_file_processing_command` and `service_perfdata_file_processing_command`, specify the names of the command object definitions used to process the performance data files. Hence in Example 6-21 every 60 seconds Nagios will run the `process-host-perfdata-file` command. You need to define these commands as object definitions in your Nagios configuration.

Using Performance Data

Performance data can be used for a number of purposes. Most of the uses for performance data combine the data about the particular check, such as its execution time, and one or more metrics collected by the plug-in. This allows you to create collections of statistical and trending data and report on them—for example, to report on the CPU usage of a host. These collections can be in the form of a database, or they could be written out using a tool like RRDtool into graphs. In this section I'll demonstrate how to insert this performance data into a MySQL database and how to graph it using RRDtool.

Inserting Data Into MySQL

One of the ways you can use performance data is to populate a database with Nagios data. This data can then be queried, collated, reported on, or graphed. In this section I'll demonstrate a simple way to populate a MySQL database using performance data command processing. I'll populate this database and some tables I'll create with a selection of the potential data available in Nagios. You can add or customize the data being collected and stored by modifying the instructions in this section.

■**Tip** There is also an open source package currently in beta called Nagios-DB that uses the new Nagios Event Broker functionality (which I discuss in Chapter 10) to populate a database.[12] This may also be worth investigating if you wish to log Nagios data to a database.

First, you will need to have the MySQL database server installed and running on your host. You can create a database to hold the performance data. To do this you need to connect and log on to the MySQL server as shown here:

```
puppy# mysql -u root -p
```

```
password:
```

```
mysql> CREATE DATABASE nagios_db;
mysql> exit
```

Sign on to the MySQL server as the root user and enter the required password. Then execute the CREATE DATABASE command to create a database called nagios_db. You can see the created database by using the SHOW DATABASES command like so:

```
mysql> SHOW DATABASES;
```

```
+-------------+
| Database    |
+-------------+
| mysql       |
| nagios_db   |
| test        |
+-------------+
3 rows in set (0.00 sec)
```

Next you need to add tables to hold the performance data from Nagios. You can do this by executing a script I've created called create_nagiosdb. This script is demonstrated in Example 6-22.

Example 6-22. *create_nagiosdb Script*

```
USE nagios_db;
CREATE TABLE service_data
(
  timet INT,
  host_name VARCHAR(75),
```

---

12. See http://sourceforge.net/projects/nagios-db.

```
 service_description VARCHAR(75),
 service_state_id INT,
 service_state VARCHAR(8),
 service_output VARCHAR(255),
 service_perf_data VARCHAR(255),
 KEY (host_name),
 KEY (service_description)
);

CREATE TABLE host_data
(
 timet INT,
 host_name VARCHAR(75),
 host_alias VARCHAR(75),
 host_state_id INT,
 host_state VARCHAR(8),
 host_output VARCHAR(255),
 host_perf_data VARCHAR(255),
 KEY (host_name)
);
```

The script in Example 6-22 creates two tables, service_data and host_data. The service_
data table contains fields for the time, hostname, service description, service state ID, service
state, output of the service check, and performance data, if any, generated by the service check.
I've keyed this table on the host_name and service_description fields. The host_data table
contains the time, hostname, alias of the host, host state ID, host state, output of the host
check, and performance data, if any, generated by the host check. This table is keyed on the
host_name field.

To execute this script and create the tables, pipe it into the mysql command as you can
see here:

```
puppy# mysql -u root -p < create_nagiosdb
```

```
password:
```

You will be prompted for the root user's password and then the required tables will be
created. You can confirm the tables are created and have the correct fields using the SHOW
TABLES and DESCRIBE commands in MySQL. First, select the nagios_db database like so:

```
mysql> use nagios_db;
```

```
Database changed
```

Next list all the tables in the database like so:

```
mysql> SHOW TABLES;
```

```
+---------------------+
| Tables_in_nagios_db |
+---------------------+
| host_data           |
| service_data        |
+---------------------+
2 rows in set (0.00 sec)
```

If both the host_data and service_data tables are present, the script has succeeded.
You can also check the content of the tables using the DESCRIBE command, as you can see in
Example 6-23.

Example 6-23. *Show the Contents of a Table*

```
mysql> DESCRIBE host_data;
```

```
+----------------+--------------+------+-----+---------+-------+
| Field          | Type         | Null | Key | Default | Extra |
+----------------+--------------+------+-----+---------+-------+
| timet          | int(11)      | YES  |     | NULL    |       |
| host_name      | varchar(75)  | YES  | MUL | NULL    |       |
| host_alias     | varchar(75)  | YES  |     | NULL    |       |
| host_state_id  | int(11)      | YES  |     | NULL    |       |
| host_state     | varchar(8)   | YES  |     | NULL    |       |
| host_output    | varchar(255) | YES  |     | NULL    |       |
| host_perf_data | varchar(255) | YES  |     | NULL    |       |
+----------------+--------------+------+-----+---------+-------+
7 rows in set (0.03 sec)
```

In Example 6-23 you can see the field definitions of the host_data table.

Next you need to create a user and assign a password to that user to allow you to access
this database. Do this using the GRANT command as shown on the following line:

```
mysql> GRANT ALL PRIVILEGES ON nagios_db.* TO nagios@localhost ➥
identified by 'password' with grant option;
```

Replace the password value with a suitable password for your database. This creates a user
called nagios that has all privileges to the nagios_db database.

Next you must define one or more commands that will process the performance data.
I'm using the first method of processing performance data that I described in the "Processing
Performance Data Using Commands" section. These commands are defined in the nagios.cfg
configuration file in two directives. You can see these directives on the following lines:

```
host_perfdata_command=process-host-perfdata
service_perfdata_command=process-service-perfdata
```

The two commands, `process-host-perfdata` and `process-service-perfdata`, need to be defined using command object definitions to Nagios. I usually define these commands in the `misccommands.cfg` configuration files. You can see the `process-service-perfdata` command in Example 6-24.

Example 6-24. *The process-service-perfdata Command*

```
define command{
        command_name    process-service-perfdata
        command_line    $USER1$/serviceperf_mysql.pl $TIMET$ '$HOSTNAME$' ➥
'$SERVICEDESC$' $SERVICESTATEID$ $SERVICESTATE$ '$SERVICEOUTPUT$' ➥
'$SERVICEPERFDATA$'
        }
```

The `process-service-perfdata` command in Example 6-24 passes a number of macros, contains the data required to populate the `service_data` table in the `nagios_db` database, to a Perl script called `serviceperf_mysql.pl`. You will note that several of the macros that might contain strings of data rather than single data items have been encapsulated in single quotation marks to ensure they are correctly passed to the script.

You can see the `process-host-perfdata` command in Example 6-25. It is constructed in a very similar way to the command in Example 6-24 and passes slightly different macros to another Perl script called `hostperf_mysql.pl`. Again, some of the macros are enclosed in single quotation marks.

Example 6-25. *The process-host-perfdata Command*

```
define command{
        command_name    process-host-perfdata
        command_line    $USER1$/hostperf_mysql.pl $TIMET$ '$HOSTNAME$' ➥
'$HOSTALIAS' $HOSTSTATEID$ $HOSTSTATETYPE$ '$HOSTOUTPUT$' '$HOSTPERFDATA$'
        }
```

Next you need to define the Perl scripts that will process the performance data. Example 6-26 contains the `serviceperf_mysql.pl` script. This script uses the DBI package to connect to your MySQL database and insert the performance data into the appropriate table, in this case the `service_data` table.

Example 6-26. *The serviceperf_mysql.pl Program*

```perl
#!/usr/bin/perl -w

use strict;
use DBI;
```

```
my $timet = $ARGV[0];
my $hostname = $ARGV[1];
my $servicedesc = $ARGV[2];
my $servicestateid = $ARGV[3];
my $servicestate = $ARGV[4];
my $serviceoutput = $ARGV[5];
my $serviceperfdata = $ARGV[6];

my $dsn = 'DBI:mysql:nagios_db:localhost';
my $db_user_name = 'nagios';
my $db_password = 'password';

my $dbh = DBI->connect($dsn, $db_user_name, $db_password)
        or die "Couldn't connect to database: " . DBI->errstr;

my $sth = $dbh->prepare( q{
        insert into service_data
        (timet, host_name, service_description, service_state_id, service_state,➡
service_output, service_perf_data)
                    values
                    (?, ?, ?, ?, ?, ?, ?)
            });

$sth->execute($timet, $hostname, $servicedesc, $servicestateid, $servicestate,➡
$serviceoutput, $serviceperfdata);

$dbh->disconnect;
```

You will need Perl and the DBI module in order to run this program. You can install the DBI module via CPAN, as shown in Example 6-27.

Example 6-27. *Installing DBI via CPAN*

```
puppy# cpan
cpan> install DBI
```

Or you can download the module from the CPAN site at http://search.cpan.org/~timb/ DBI-1.48/DBI.pm and install it from source. Once you have downloaded the package, unpack and compile it as you can see on the following lines:

```
puppy# wget http://search.cpan.org/CPAN/authors/id/T/TI/TIMB/DBI-1.48.tar.gz
puppy# tar -zxf DBI-1.48.tar.gz
puppy# cd DBI-1.48
puppy# perl Makefile.PL
puppy# make
puppy# make test
puppy# make install
```

The DBI module allows you to connect to a database using Perl. You need to provide some connection information in the Perl script in Example 6-26. You will have to change the following lines to the values you used when the MySQL database and associated user and password was created.

```
my $dsn = 'DBI:mysql:nagios_db:localhost';
my $db_user_name = 'nagios';
my $db_password = 'password';
```

The script uses these values to connect to the MySQL database. The script takes the required performance data from the command line and assigns them to variables. It inserts each of these variables into the service_data table and disconnects from the database.

It should be easy to modify this script (and the script that creates the MySQL tables) to add whatever macro, plug-in, or performance data you require into a MySQL database.

Note I've provided a copy of the serviceperf_mysql.pl script with the electronic resources for this book. You can also find a Perl script to process the host performance data generated by the process-➥ host-perfdata command. It is called hostperf_mysql.pl and is contained in the additional resources file for this book available for download at the Apress website with the source code for this book.

Inserting Performance and Output Data into RRDtool

In Chapter 4 I demonstrated some of the reporting and graphing capabilities of the Nagios server. They are not very sophisticated and only provide very limited reporting on elements such as Availability and Alert History. To generate more sophisticated reporting requires outputting data from Nagios to another tool. For this purpose I'm going to demonstrate the use of the RRDtool. RRDtool is an open source tool for logging and data graphing. RRD is an acronym for Round Robin Database, and it stores the data in a compact form that allows for easy growth and displays elegant graphs. It is ideal for logging and graphing many forms of time-based data. RRDtool can be run from the shell or called via a Perl module.

Tip You can find an excellent tutorial on using RRDtool at http://people.ee.ethz.ch/~oetiker/webtools/rrdtool/tut/rrdtutorial.en.html.

RRDtool requires you to specify the data format of any data you input into it for logging or graphing. To make this process easier, I'm also going to use a package called Nagiosgraph that helps integrated Nagios with RRDtool by providing many of the data formats for common plug-ins. I'll demonstrate how to install and utilize this package in this section too.

Installing RRDtool

Let's start by installing the RRDtool package. You can download RRDtool from http://people.ee.ethz.ch/~oetiker/webtools/rrdtool/pub/rrdtool.tar.gz.

> **Tip** RRDtool is also available as an RPM package from http://dag.wieers.com/packages/rrdtool/ if you prefer to install it this way. This may be easier if you are not used to installing and compiling packages.

Unpack the package and changing into the resulting directory:

```
puppy# tar -zxf rrdtool.tar.gz
puppy# cd rrdtool-1.2.11
```

> **Note** At the time of this writing, the current version of RRDtool was 1.2.11.

Before you compile and install RRDtool, you may require some additional prerequisites for installation. These include

- cgilib
- zlib
- libPNG
- Freetype
- libart

Instructions for installing these prerequisites are contained in the file rrdbuild.txt in the doc subdirectory of the RRDtool package.

Once you have installed any required prerequisites, you can run the configure script that is the first step in compiling RRDtool. The configure script comes with a number of options, which you can see if you run the configure script with the --help flag. The most important is the --prefix flag, which specifies where RRDtool is to be installed. By default, this is /usr/local/rrdtool-version, where version is the current version of RRDtool. You can override this to a more suitable installation location if you prefer:

```
puppy# ./configure --prefix=/usr/local/rrdtool --enable-perl-site-install
```

On this line I've configured RRDtool and installed it underneath the directory /usr/local/rrdtool. I've also specified the --enable-perl-site-install option to tell the configure script to make best efforts to install the Perl packages into your default Perl installation. If you do not specify this option, the Perl packages will also be installed under the /usr/local/rrdtool directory path, and if you wish to refer to them in a Perl script, you will need to include this path.

Next you need to compile and install RRDtool using the make command:

```
puppy# make && make install
```

> **Tip** Installing RRDtool also installs a Perl module for integrating RRDtool into your Perl applications. It is called RRDs and can be referenced in your Perl code by including it with the use function like so: use RRDs;.

Installing Nagiosgraph

To aid in the integration of Nagios and RRDtool, I'm also going to make use of another open source add-on for Nagios called Nagiosgraph. Nagiosgraph provides an automated mechanism of adding performance and check output data into RRDtool. It is also extensible and allows you to specify additional performance and output data that can be logged and graphed.

You can download the Nagiosgraph add-on from Sourceforge at http://sourceforge.net/ projects/nagiosgraph/. Nagiosgraph's only prerequisites are Perl and the CGI and RRDs Perl packages. The RRDs package has been installed with RRDtool earlier. The CGI package can be installed from CPAN as demonstrated in the following lines:

```
puppy# cpan
cpan> install CGI
```

Or you can download it from CPAN as a tarred zip file at http://search.cpan.org/CPAN/ authors/id/L/LD/LDS/CGI.pm-3.11.tar.gz. Unpack the source package and compile it as shown here:

```
puppy# tar -zxf CGI.pm-3.11.tar.gz
puppy# cd CGI-pm-3.11
puppy# perl Makefile.PL
puppy# make && make install
```

After installing the prerequisites, download and unpack the Nagiosgraph package as you can see here:

```
puppy# wget http://optusnet.dl.sourceforge.net/sourceforge/nagiosgraph/➥
nagiosgraph-0.6.tar.gz
puppy# tar -zxf nagiosgraph-0.6.tar.gz
```

The package does not require compilation as it only consists of a configuration file, Perl script, CGI file, and the map file that contains the data formats for a variety of Nagios output data. You need to copy these files into a suitable location. I usually install them into my Nagios directory structure at /usr/local/nagios/nagiosgraph. Here I've created the directory and copied the required files:

```
puppy#  mkdir /usr/local/nagios/nagiosgraph
puppy# cp nagiosgraph.conf /usr/local/Nagios/nagiosgraph/
puppy# cp insert.pl /usr/local/Nagios/nagiosgraph/
puppy# cp map /usr/local/Nagios/nagiosgraph/
puppy# cp show.cgi /usr/local/nagios/nagiosgraph/
```

I then need to change the ownership of the copied files to allow them to be used by the Nagios server:

```
puppy# chown -R nagios:nagios /usr/local/nagios/nagiosgraph
```

Configuring Nagiosgraph

After installation, the first step in configuring Nagiosgraph is to edit the nagiosgraph.conf configuration file. Example 6-28 shows a sample nagiosgraph.conf file.

Example 6-28. *Sample nagiosgraph.conf File*

```
debug = 2
colorscheme = 1
heartbeat = 600
logfile = /usr/local/nagios/var/nagiosgraph.log
rrddir  = /usr/local/nagios/nagiosgraph/rrd
mapfile = /usr/local/nagios/nagiosgraph/map
perflog = /usr/local/nagios/var/perfdata.log
```

In Example 6-28 there are seven directives. The first is debug, which controls the verbosity of information that Nagiosgraph generates. It ranges from 0 for no debug information to 5 for the maximum debugging level. The default is 2.

The colorscheme directive controls the color scheme of any generated graphs. There are eight possible variations, specified by using the range 1 to 8. I recommend you experiment with this to find the best color combination for you.

The heartbeat directive specifies the maximum number of seconds that may pass between two updates of an RRD database before the value of the database is assumed to be unknown. See the RRD documentation for more details on how this might affect you. The Nagiosgraph developer recommends a setting of at least twice the check interval for your services.

The next four directives control the location of a number of the files the Nagiosgraph application requires. The first directive, logfile, controls the location and name of the Nagiosgraph log file. I normally store it with my Nagios logs in /usr/local/nagios/var/. This file needs to be writable by the Nagios server and the web server. I already have a user and group combination that allows this access for my external command file using the combination of the nagios user and the ncmd group that I created in Chapter 1. Here I've created this log file and changed the log file ownership to this user and group:

```
puppy# touch /usr/local/nagios/var/nagiosgraph.log
puppy# chown nagios:ncmd /usr/local/nagios/var/nagiosgraph.log
```

The second directive, rrddir, controls the location of the RRD databases that will contain the data logged by RRDtool. I normally create a directory called rrd under the /usr/local/nagios/nagiosgraph/ directory:

```
puppy# mkdir /usr/local/nagios/nagiosgraph/rrd
```

This directory needs to be readable by the Nagios server and your web server. To achieve this, change the ownership of the directory. I've used the same permissions as the Nagiosgraph log file:

```
puppy# chown nagios:ncmd /usr/local/nagios/nagiosgraph/rrd
```

The mapfile directive controls the location of the map file that contains the mapping of the Nagios data to the RRD data format. In this configuration, it is located at /usr/local/nagios/nagiosgraph/map.

The last directive, perflog, specifies the location of the performance data file being loaded by Nagiosgraph into RRDtool. I'll configure Nagios to put the right data in this file later in this section. In this case I've defined a file called perfdata.log in /usr/local/nagios/var.

Next, the location of this configuration file needs to be specified in the inset.pl and show.cgi files. In both the insert.pl and show.cgi files, change the following line to reflect the location of the nagiosgraph.conf file:

```
my $configfile = '/usr/local/nagios/nagiosgraph/nagiosgraph.conf';
```

Configuring Nagios

Now that Nagiosgraph is configured, the Nagios server needs to be configured to output the required data. This is done using the performance data directives and command object definitions I've discussed in this chapter. Data is sent from Nagios to Nagiosgraph using the performance data file method. First, the process_performance_data directive is set to 1 to enable the processing of performance data:

```
process_performance_data=1
```

The Nagiosgraph tool only logs and graphs service data, so only the service_perfdata_file directive needs to be set to the name and location defined in the perflog directive in the nagiosgraph.conf file. In this case:

```
service_perfdata_file=/usr/local/nagios/var/perfdata.log
```

Also required is the service_perfdata_file_template directive that specifies what data will be written to the performance data log file. I've specified the required data template for Nagiosgraph in Example 6-29.

Example 6-29. *Nagiosgraph service_perfdata_file_template Directive*

```
service_perfdata_file_template=$LASTSERVICECHECK$||$HOSTNAME$||$SERVICEDESC$➥
||$SERVICEOUTPUT$||$SERVICEPERFDATA$
```

Also needed are the service_perfdata_file_mode and service_perfdata_file_processing_interval directives. The first directive should be set to a, for append mode. The second directive controls how often performance data is processed by the command in the service_perfdata_file_processing_command directive. A setting of 30 seconds should be suitable for most environments.

```
service_perfdata_file_mode=a
service_perfdata_file_processing_interval=30
```

The last directive, service_perfdata_file_processing_command, specifies which command will be used to process the performance data file. On the following line, the process-service-➥perfdata-file command is used:

```
service_perfdata_file_processing_command=process-service-perfdata-file
```

To complete the Nagios configuration, the process-service-perfdata-file command must be defined in Nagios. In a configuration file, like misccommands.cfg, create the command object definition shown in Example 6-30.

Example 6-30. *The process-service-perfdata-file Command*

```
define command {
                command_name   process-service-perfdata-file
                command_line   /usr/local/nagios/nagiosgraph/insert.pl
                }
```

Now when Nagios executes checks, performance data is added to the /usr/local/nagios/ var/perfdata.log file, as specified in the service_perfdata_file directive and in the format defined in the service_perfdata_file_template directive. Every 30 seconds, as defined in the service_perfdata_file_processing_interval directive, Nagios will execute the process-➥ service-perfdata-file command that I've specified in the service_perfdata_file_processing_ command directive. This will execute the insert.pl script and populate the RRD databases.

Nagiosgraph populates the RRD databases by reading the map file and mapping output or performance data from Nagios into RRD databases and metrics. For example, the output from the check_ping command has two metrics that Nagiosgraph can map: the percentage of packets lost and the Round Trip Average (or RTA) for the ping. The default map file that comes with the package already contains a data mapping for the check_ping command that maps both these metrics. Both of these metrics are added to an RRD database called ping.

An RRD database will be generated for each host and service. The databases will be stored in the directory specified in the rrddir directive in the nagiosgraph.conf file. In our case this is the /usr/local/nagios/nagiosgraph/rrd directory. In Example 6-31 I've listed the contents of this directory on my Nagios installation.

Example 6-31. *The rrd Directory*

```
puppy# ls -la /usr/local/nagoios/nagiosgraph/rrd
total 628
drwxr-xr-x  2 nagios nagios   4096 Oct 24 00:09 .
drwxr-xr-x  3 nagios nagios   4096 Oct 24 00:41 ..
-rw-rw-r--  1 nagios nagios  24096 Oct 24 11:21 kitten_http_http.rrd
-rw-rw-r--  1 nagios nagios  24096 Oct 24 11:21 kitten_smtp_smtp.rrd
-rw-rw-r--  1 nagios nagios  24096 Oct 24 11:20 puppy_https_http.rrd
-rw-rw-r--  1 nagios nagios  71152 Oct 24 11:21 puppy_local_load_load.rrd
-rw-rw-r--  1 nagios nagios  71152 Oct 24 11:21 puppy_local_users_procs.rrd
```

In Example 6-31 you can see the list of my RRD databases generated by Nagiosgraph and RRDtool. The filenames are constructed using the name of the host and the service description of the service being graphed.

Displaying the Graphs

So how do I now display the required graphs? Well, there are two possible ways. The first is to integrate them into the web console using the notes_url directive in a Service Extended Information object, serviceextinfo. I discussed these objects in Chapter 6. The second is to call the graphs directly using the supplied CGI program, show.cgi.

For both methods, I need to define the nagiosgraph directory to the web server. This is a simple process of adding a ScriptAlias for the nagiosgraph directory to your Apache httpd.conf file. Add the following directive to the httpd.conf file:

```
ScriptAlias /nagiosgraph/ /usr/local/nagios/nagiosgraph/
```

For clarity I recommend adding it near the rest of your Nagios configuration.[13] You will need to restart the web server to activate this configuration change.

In the first method of displaying the Nagiosgraph graphs, the show.cgi file is called directly from your web browser by browsing to a URL like this one:

```
http://nagios.yourdomain.com/nagiosgraph/show.cgi?host=puppy&service=http
```

Replace the hostname and domain with the names of your own web server and the reference to the host and service, puppy and http in the example URL, with a host and service that you have graphed on your Nagios server. You can also see some additional options that you can pass to the URL later in this section.

In the second method of displaying the graphs, I use a serviceextinfo object that needs to be defined. Example 6-32 shows a sample object.

Example 6-32. *Nagiosgraph serviceextinfo Object*

```
define serviceextinfo {
            service_description        http
            host_name                  puppy
            notes_url         /nagiosgraph/show.cgi?host=puppy&service=http
            icon_image        graph.gif
            icon_image_alt  View graphs
            }
```

The key directives in Example 6-32 are notes_url, icon_image, and icon_image_alt. notes_url defines a URL that calls the show.cgi program and passes in two variables: the hostname and service description of the service. This tells Nagiosgraph which graph to display. icon_image specifies the image file that is displayed in the web console as the icon that links to the graph. This icon will be displayed in both the Service Detail and Service Information pages of the web console.[14] You should use a 40×40-pixel icon in GIF or GD2 format and copy it into the /usr/local/nagios/share/images/logos directory. The icon_image_alt directive specifies the text description of the ALT tag for the image.

Another alternative is to use macros as the values for the hostname and service description like so:

```
notes_url       /nagiosgraph/show.cgi?host=$HOSTNAME$&service=$SERVICEDESC$
```

This allows you to specify a Service Extended Information object for multiple hosts or for one or more host groups. In the following serviceextinfo object, I've specified multiple hosts in the object:

```
define serviceextinfo {
            service_description        http
            host_name                  puppy,kitten,duckling
            notes_url         /nagiosgraph/show.cgi?host=$HOSTNAME$&service=$SERVICEDESC$
            icon_image                 graph.gif
            icon_image_alt             View graphs
                }
```

---

13. I configure the Apache web server for Nagios in Chapter 1.

14. See Chapter 4 for further details.

You can also replace the host_name directive with the hostgroups directive to allow you to specify one or more host groups.

Additionally, in the notes_url directive or when you call the show.cgi program directly, you can pass a number of additional options to the show.cgi program that let you further customize the graphs that are displayed. These allow you to select specific metrics from an RRD database. For example, as I mentioned earlier, the output of a check_ping command has two possible metrics: percentage of packets lost and the RTA in milliseconds. Nagiosgraph stores both of these in the same RRD database called ping. If you displayed the ping RRD database for the puppy host, as you can see here:

```
notes_url        /nagiosgraph/show.cgi?host=puppy&service=ping
```

then both metrics would be displayed in a single graph. If, however, you only want to select one of these metrics to graph and display, you can add the db option to the URL like so:

```
notes_url➥
/nagiosgraph/show.cgi?host=$HOSTNAME$&service=$SERVICEDESC$➥
&db=ping,losspct
```

The db option selects the database named ping and the metric called losspct and displays it in a graph. If you wish to display separate graphs for each metric in a database, you can specify more than one db option, as you can see in the URL on the following line:

```
notes_url /nagiosgraph/show.cgi?host=$HOSTNAME$&service=$SERVICEDESC$&db=ping,➥
losspct&db=ping,rta
```

This URL would display the losspct and the rta metrics in separate graphs.

You can also change the size of the graphs being displayed using the geom option. You can see this option here:

```
notes_url        /nagiosgraph/show.cgi?host=puppy&service=ping&geom=400x200
```

The geom option would change the size of the graphs displayed to 400 by 200 pixels.

Finally, you can specify the rrdopts option in the URL. This allows you to specify options that further control the display of the graphs. The options that can be specified are the same ones that can be used with the rrdgraph binary that RRDtool uses to format graphs. You can read about rrdgraph and its potential options at http://rrdtool.paracoda.com/doc/rrdgraph.en.html.

Creating Additional Graphs

Nagiosgraph creates the RRD databases based on information stored in the map file in the /usr/local/nagios/nagiosgraph directory. The map file consists of a series of Perl-compatible regular expressions that map data from Nagios output or performance data and uses it to create RRD databases and metrics. There is one regular expression for each service being logged by RRD. There are already a number of output or performance data regular expressions defined that you can use as examples in this file. Indeed, some of your output or performance data may already match data mappings present in the file. At the time of this writing, these include output from the check_ping command, SMTP, NTP, and HTTP servers and a variety of others.

You can see one of these regular expressions in Example 6-33.

■Tip You can read about Perl regular expressions at `http://www.perl.com/doc/manual/html/pod/perlre.html`. Or Jeffrey Friedl's *Mastering Regular Expressions* (O'Reilly, 1997; `www.oreilly.com/catalog/regex/`) is a good reference.

Example 6-33. *Map File Regular Rxpression*

```
/output:PING.*?(\d+)%.+?([.\d]+)\sms/
and push @s, [ ping,
                [ losspct, GAUGE, $1       ],
                [ rta,      GAUGE, $2/1000 ] ];
```

Example 6-33 looks complicated, but in fact it is very simple and is based on a template. This template appears on the following lines.

```
/output|perfdata:<servicetype> <key>=<value> <key2=value2> .../
and push @s, [ <databasename>,
                [ <key>,  GAUGE|DERIVE, <value>  ],
                [ <key2>, GAUGE|DERIVE, <value2> ];
```

In Example 6-33 the data specified is the output from a command performing a `ping` of a host. The regular expression matches the output or performance data. The first part of the regular expression is the type of data being graphed, output, or performance data, as you can see in the template. In Example 6-33 this is identified as `output`. To use performance data, specify `perfdata` instead. Then, separated from the type of data by a colon, is the output or performance data itself. You can see this data here:

```
PING OK - Packet loss = 0%, RTA = 0.00 ms
```

Nagiosgraph breaks the output or performance data into chunks and feeds this data into RRDtool to be logged and graphed. It breaks this into a series of key and value pairs. To do this it uses regular expression variables, which capture the value data by enclosing it in brackets. In Example 6-33 two variables are captured in this way: the percentage of packet loss and the RTA.

```
PING.*?(\d+)%.+?([.\d]+)\sms/
```

On this line you can see that the bracketed items are the percentage loss, expressed using the regular expression \d+, and the RTA in milliseconds using the expression [.\d]+.

These values are then passed into the `push` statement on the following line. A database name is then specified, in this case ping. Metrics are created from the captured data. The two metrics created are GAUGE measures, one called `losspct` and the second called `rta`. You can see the `losspct` measure here:

```
[ losspct, GAUGE, $1       ],
```

As you can see, the regular expression variable, in the form of $1, is specified as the value of the `losspct` metric.

> ■**Tip** GAUGE-based metrics show the value of the metric at that given point in time, with each additional measurement extending the graph.

The second variable, the rta metric, is output from Nagios measured in milliseconds. After being captured in the Nagiosgraph regular expression as variable $2, it is divided by 1000, as shown here:

```
[ rta,     GAUGE, $2/1000 ] ];
```

This converts the value from milliseconds to seconds, which will then be graphed by RRDtool. You can specify as many metrics in each database as required.

Using this information and the example contained in the map file, you should be able to create data mappings for any incoming output or performance data.

Once you have edited your map file, you can confirm that any regular expressions that you have added are correct by using the perl binary with the -c flag (which checks the syntax of a Perl script) like so:

```
puppy# perl -c map
map syntax OK
```

Finally, if you need more assistance mapping data, the Nagiosgraph package contains a file with further information called README.map.

> ■**Tip** There are other tools that provide similar functionality to Nagiosgraph, with varying levels of compatibility with Nagios 2.0. These include Perfparse (http://perfparse.sourceforge.net/), add-ons from www.hannes-schulz.de/?doc=proj&proj=nagios#nagios_addons, rrdgraph (http://magoazul.com/proj/nagios/), Nagiostat (http://sourceforge.net/projects/nagiostat), and APAN (http://apan.sourceforge.net/). The last two, Nagiostat and APAN, do not support version 2.0 of Nagios at this stage. You can see a more complete list at www.nagiosexchange.org/Charts.42.0.html.

Checkpoints

- Remember that for some types of commands Nagios strips out the meta-characters specified in the illegal_macro_output_chars directive in the nagios.cfg configuration file to prevent them from being interpreted by the shell. This could lead to your commands failing or providing unexpected output.

- Notifications can use a wide variety of mechanisms from traditional email and pagers to SMS, instant messaging, or even voice-delivered notifications. Don't be limited to simply sending emails or pages; be creative and use notifications to deliver the information required by the best possible means to ensure a response.

- External commands are both useful and powerful. They provide a very simple mechanism to integrate non-Nagios checks and data into your Nagios server. Rather than rewrite monitoring tools or applications, consider writing middleware that uses external commands to integrate these non-Nagios aware tools with Nagios.

Resources

There are a number of websites cited in this chapter, and they are listed in this section.

- Nagios Exchange Notification Scripts: `www.nagiosexchange.org/Notifications.35.0.html?&tx_netnagext_pi1[page]=0%3A10`

- Net-XMPP: `http://search.cpan.org/dist/Net-XMPP/lib/Net/XMPP.pm`

- Sendxmpp: `www.djcbsoftware.nl/code/sendxmpp/`

- NAN: `http://os.cyberheatinc.com/nan.php`

- NANS: `www.nachtwache.org/projects/netsaint/utilities/nans/`

- DBI: `http://search.cpan.org/~timb/DBI-1.48/DBI.pm`

- RRDtool: `http://people.ee.ethz.ch/~oetiker/webtools/rrdtool/pub/`

- RRDtool RPM: `http://dag.wieers.com/packages/rrdtool/`

- RRDtool Tutorial: `http://people.ee.ethz.ch/~oetiker/webtools/rrdtool/tut/rrdtutorial.en.html`

- Nagiosgraph: `http://sourceforge.net/projects/nagiosgraph/`

- Nagios Charting/Graphing Tools: `www.nagiosexchange.org/Charts.42.0.html`

■ ■ ■

## CHAPTER 7

Advanced Object Configuration

In Chapter 2 I explained how to configure the base objects you need to define your monitoring environment, including hosts, services, contacts, time periods, and commands. I also mentioned that other object types are available that allow you to define more advanced configurations for the monitoring of your environment. I'll examine these advanced object types in this chapter.

The two key functions provided by these objects are host and service dependency and host and service escalation. Host and service dependencies are a more advanced variation on the parent-child host relationships you can define with the `parents` directive. They allow you to make services and hosts dependent on each other and to influence the behavior of your service and host checks and notifications based on these dependent relationships.

The host and service escalation function allows you to develop escalation trees that enable you to escalate notifications to additional contacts on a defined schedule for your hosts and services. This is perfect for managing an environment that requires escalations to occur according to service levels, or that contains a hierarchical support or management structure where successive groups are notified of certain issues, or in which problems persist for long periods of time.

I'm also going to look at Host and Service Extended Information features. These features represent ways to enhance the display of your hosts and services in the web console by using images and adding the ability to add links and notes to the host and service displays. I'll only cover these briefly as they are fairly intuitive and easy to use, and are generally of limited value to most users.

The list of objects we'll look at in this chapter is shown in Table 7-1.

Table 7-1. *Advanced Object Types*

Object	Description
servicedependency	Allows a service or services to be dependent on other services.
hostdependency	Allows a host or hosts to be dependent on other hosts.
serviceescalation	Provides a notification escalation process for services.
hostescalation	Provides a notification escalation process for hosts.
hostextinfo	Host Extended Information changes and customizes the way hosts are displayed on the Nagios web console.
serviceextinfo	Service Extended Information changes and customizes the way services are displayed on the Nagios web console.

All of the objects in Table 7-1 are optional. You should use them in your monitoring configuration only if you require the functionality they provide.

Host and Service Dependencies

The first objects we'll look at are the servicedependency and hostdependency object types. They allow you to make services and hosts dependent on other services and hosts. You create these objects in your object configuration file or files, as described in Chapter 2. Like most Nagios configuration items, dependencies function slightly differently for hosts and services.

So what can we do with host and service dependencies? Dependencies allow us to structure relationships between one or more services or hosts. The uses for this can range from simple to highly complicated. On the simple end of the spectrum, a database may need to be running for a web application to function. Once you define services for both the database and the web application, you can make monitoring more effective by making the web application dependent on the database. You can do this by defining a service dependency using the servicedependency object. This means that if the database fails, you can configure Nagios not to execute service checks or send notifications for the web application because we already know it is not going to be working due to the dependency failure. This reduces the monitoring overhead and the number of notifications that your monitoring environment generates and simplifies the management of your environment.

In more complicated models, you can construct service dependencies that model your business processes with multiple services and hosts dependent on each other. For example, you can create chains of dependencies that mean multiple hosts and services that are used in a particular business process can be linked together.

Let's start by looking at service dependencies and then cover host dependencies.

Service Dependencies

Let's look at a simple example of service dependency. On the host kitten I have an httpd service. On the host puppy I also have two services, an ftpd and a smtpd service. I wish to make the httpd service on the kitten host dependent on the two services, ftpd and smtpd, on the puppy host. To do this I must configure two service dependency objects, one for each dependency. Example 7-1 contains the service dependency objects that achieve this objective.

Example 7-1. *A Service Dependency Example*

```
define servicedependency{
        host_name                          puppy
        service_description                ftpd
        dependent_host_name                kitten
        dependent_service_description      httpd
        execution_failure_criteria         w,c
        notification_failure_criteria      w,u,c
        }

define servicedependency{
        host_name                          puppy
        service_description                smtpd
        dependent_host_name                kitten
```

```
    dependent_service_description              httpd
    execution_failure_criteria                 n
    notification_failure_criteria              w,u,c
    }
```

Let's break down the service dependencies defined in Example 7-1. First I've defined two objects of type servicedependency. In each object, I've first defined the host_name and service_description directives. These are the hostname and service description of the services that are being depended on, in our case the ftpd and smtpd services both running on the puppy host. Nagios calls these master services.

Next are the dependent_host_name and dependent_service_name directives. These directives represent the hostname and service description of the dependent service, in this case the httpd service on the kitten host. The values of these directives in both objects defined in Example 7-1 are identical because I'm making one service dependent on two others.

■**Tip** Only these first four directives are mandatory for this object definition. The remaining directives are optional.

Next are the criteria under which Nagios should change the behavior of its active checks. The execution_failure_criteria directive tells Nagios not to execute active checks on the dependent services if the depended-on, or master, service is in a particular state. The potential states are listed in Table 7-2.

Table 7-2. *Execution Criteria States*

State	Description
o	Do not check the dependent service if the master service is in the OK state.
w	Do not check the dependent service if the master service is in the WARNING state.
c	Do not check the dependent service if the master service is in the CRITICAL state.
u	Do not check the dependent service if the master service is in the UNKNOWN state.
p	Do not check the dependent service if the master service is pending a check result.
n	Always check the dependent service, regardless of the state of the master service.

These states are fairly self-explanatory and are the standard service states that I discussed in Chapter 2. In Example 7-1 I've set the execution_failure_criteria directive for the first service dependency object to w,c (multiple states can be specified by separating them with commas). This indicates that if the ftpd service on the puppy host is in a WARNING or CRITICAL state, Nagios should stop executing service checks on the httpd service on the kitten host. The significant exception to the states discussed in Chapter 2 is the n state. The n state tells Nagios that it should always execute service checks on the dependent service no matter what the state of the depended-on, or master, service. Obviously, you must specify the n state on its own. It cannot be combined with any other states.

So how does this work? Well, when Nagios schedules an active check of a service it checks whether that service has any dependencies defined. If it finds one or more dependencies, it checks each master service in sequence to determine the status of each of the master services. If the state of one of those master services matches a state specified in the execution_failure_ criteria directive, Nagios stops checking and will not execute an active service check on the dependent service. This is not a permanent cessation of active checks of the dependent service; only the current active check is stopped. When the next check occurs, the cycle starts again. If, by this next check, the state of the master service has changed to one not specified in the execution_failure_criteria directive, the active check of the dependent service will proceed.

When doing this dependency checking, Nagios uses the hard service state of the master service. If the master service is in a soft state, this state will be ignored. You can override this default behavior by setting a directive in the nagios.cfg file called soft_state_dependencies. Setting this directive to 1, as you can see on the following line, will cause Nagios to use the soft state of the master service to determine whether to execute service checks on the dependent service:

soft_state_dependencies=1

■Note This directive may not be present in the sample Nagios configuration in nagios.cfg and you will have to add it to your file.

Setting the directive to 0 will turn off the use of soft states for dependency checks. 0 is the default setting for this directive.

■Note Dependency checking only applies to active checks. Only active checks of the dependent service will be stopped. Submitting a passive check will not be stopped by configuring a service dependency.

The last directive defined in both the service dependency objects in Example 7-1 is the notification_failure_criteria directive. This directive controls when notifications should not be sent out for a dependent service. Like execution criteria, this is controlled by the state of the master service and uses the same set of states described in Table 7-2. Hence in Example 7-1 the notification_failure_criteria directive for both the first and second service dependency object is set to w,u,c (again, multiple states can be specified if separated with commas). This indicates that if either the ftpd or the smtpd service on the puppy host is in the WARNING, UNKNOWN, or CRITICAL state, any notifications generated by the httpd service on the kitten host will be suppressed. The notification_failure_criteria directive can also be set to n to indicate that notifications should never be suppressed.

Notification execution dependencies operate in the same manner to service check execution dependencies. When a notification is generated on a service, Nagios checks whether that service has any dependencies. If it does, the Nagios checks the master service or services for their state; if that state matches a state defined in the notification_failure_criteria directive, the notification is suppressed.

This suppression is a temporary measure for that notification only. If another notification is generated on that service, Nagios performs the same checks again. If the state of the master service has changed to one not specified in the `notification_failure_criteria` directive, the notification is allowed to be sent.

Service Dependency Shortcuts

You can also use some shortcuts when defining your service dependency objects. For example, to define multiple hosts in the `host_name` or the `dependent_host_name` directive, you can separate each required host with a comma. This allows you to specify service dependencies for services of the same name running on multiple hosts. Many of the possible shortcuts can also be varied and combined. I recommend you experiment with a variety of combinations to achieve your objective.

Here's an example of defining multiple hosts in a service dependency:

```
define servicedependency{
          host_name                              kitten,puppy
          service_description                    vpnd
          dependent_host_name                    owlet,hatchling
          dependent_service_description    sshd
          ….
          }
```

In this service dependency definition, the `sshd` service running on the `owlet` and `hatchling` hosts would be dependent on the `vpnd` service running on the `kitten` and `puppy` hosts.

In addition to this, you can define service dependencies for services that run on all hosts in one or more host groups, as you can see on the following lines:

```
define servicedependency{
          hostgroup_name                         syd_servers,melb_servers
          service_description                    vpnd
          dependent_hostgroup_name               uk_servers,us_servers
          dependent_service_description    sshd
          …
          }
```

In this service dependency definition, the `sshd` service running on all hosts in the `uk_servers` and `us_servers` host groups would be dependent on the `vpnd` service running on all hosts in the `syd_servers` and `melb_servers` host groups.

Tip Remember, this in effect is defining multiple service dependencies and not a single service dependency. It is just a shorthand way of defining the multiple objects. Each service dependency would be checked individually as a service check or notification occurred. Thus, in all the examples in this section the service check and notification execution criteria would be identical for all service dependencies created with shortcuts.

Next you can create a shortcut definition of service dependencies for all services defined on a particular host. This is done using the * wildcard symbol, as you can see here:

```
define servicedependency{
            host_name                                   kitten
            service_description                         *
            dependent_host_name                         owlet
            dependent_service_description       *
            ….
            }
```

In this definition, all services on the owlet host would be dependent on all services on the kitten host.

You can also define service dependencies for multiple services on a single host:

```
define servicedependency{
            host_name                                   kitten
            service_description                         vpnd,routed,bgpd
            dependent_host_name                         owlet
            dependent_service_description       sshd,ftpd,smtpd
            ….
            }
```

Here the services sshd, ftpd, and smtpd on the owlet host would be all dependent on the vpnd, routed, and bgpd services on the kitten host.

Finally, you can define service dependencies for all services in one or more service groups:

```
define servicedependency{
            servicegroup_name                                   routing_services
            dependent_servicegroup_name         email_services
            ….
            }
```

In this shortcut, you only need to specify the master service group or groups and the dependent service group or groups because the membership of service groups already contains the service names of the services in it as well as the hostnames of the hosts that those services run on.[1] In the last service dependency definition, the service group email_services is dependent on the service group routing_services.

Inheritance

You can further complicate service dependencies by configuring inheritance. In this process, dependencies are chained together and a service can inherit the dependencies of services it is dependent on. For example, you define a service dependency and enable inheritance. If the master service in that dependency has any dependencies defined for it, then the depended-on

---

1. I described this in Chapter 2.

service will inherit these too. Inheritance is not enabled by default. So what does this mean? Well, it means you can chain together dependencies. Let's look at this in Example 7-2.

Example 7-2. *Service Dependency Inheritence*

```
define servicedependency{
                host_name                               puppy
                service_description                     ftpd
                dependent_host_name                     kitten
                dependent_service_description           httpd
                execution_failure_criteria              w,c
                notification_failure_criteria           w,u,c
                }

define servicedependency{
                host_name                               kitten
                service_description                     httpd
                dependent_host_name                     owlet
                dependent_service_description           smtpd
                inherits_parent                         1
                execution_failure_criteria              n
                notification_failure_criteria           w,u,c
                }
```

In Example 7-2 I've defined two objects. In the first service dependency object, I have specified that the httpd service on the kitten host is dependent on the ftpd service on the puppy host. If the ftpd service on the puppy host is in the WARNING or CRITICAL state, checks of the httpd service on the kitten host will be suppressed. Additionally, if the ftpd service on the puppy host is in the WARNING, CRITICAL, or UNKNOWN state, notifications from the httpd service on the kitten host will also be suppressed.

In the second object, I've defined that the smtpd service on the owlet host is dependent on the httpd service on the kitten host. I've also specified a new directive called inherits_parent and set it to 1. This turns on dependency inheritance. As a result, in addition to the service dependency of the smtpd service on the owlet host on the httpd service on the kitten host, this service has inherited any service dependencies that the master service has. This means that the smtpd service on the owlet host is now dependent on the httpd service on the kitten host and the ftpd service on the puppy host. Now this probably sounds complicated, but if you represent it visually as shown in Figure 7-1 (see the following page), then you can better make sense of it.

You can use multiple layers of inheritance to chain together numerous service dependencies so that a service inherits multiple levels of service dependencies. This can quickly get very complicated, and I recommend you carefully map out all your service dependencies using a flow charter or visual mapping tool so you fully understand the dependency model.

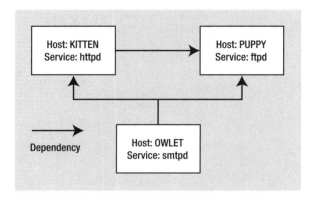

Figure 7-1. *Service dependency inheritance*

Host Dependencies

Along with service dependencies, you can define host dependencies. They are slightly different from service dependencies. The major difference is that unlike service dependencies they only suppress host notifications and not host checks. In addition, they do not perform the same function as the parents directive available in host object definitions. The parents directive structures your environment so that if a parent host is unavailable, all the child hosts of that parent are placed in an UNREACHABLE state. This allows you to design a monitoring environment that mirrors your network structure—for example, making all hosts in a site the child hosts of the gateway router to the site. In the vast majority of circumstances, you would use parent/child relationships rather than host dependency objects.

Host dependencies are only useful for controlling the behavior of your notifications. Let's look at Example 7-3, where I've defined a host dependency.

Example 7-3. *Host Dependency*

```
define hostdependency{
        host_name                               kitten
        dependent_host_name                     puppy
        notification_failure_criteria           d
        }
```

In Example 7-3 the host_name directive defines the name of the master host or the host being depended on. The dependent_host_name defines the dependent host. So in Example 7-3 the puppy host is dependent on the kitten host. The next directive, notification_failure_criteria, controls under what circumstances notifications are suppressed. In our example, if the master host is in the DOWN state, notifications will be suppressed. You can specify a number of different criteria, as shown in Table 7-3.

Table 7-3. *Notification Criteria States*

State	Description
o	Suppress notifications on the dependent host if the master host is in the OK state.
d	Suppress notifications on the dependent host if the master host is in the DOWN state.
u	Suppress notifications on the dependent host if the master host is in the UNREACHABLE state.
p	Suppress notifications on the dependent host if the master host is in the pending state.
n	Always check the dependent host, regardless of the state of the master host.

You can specify multiple criteria by separating them with commas. This excludes the n criterion, which must be specified on its own and indicates that Nagios should never suppress notifications.

Host dependency executions work exactly like service dependency executions. When a notification is generated on a host, Nagios checks if the host has any master hosts defined using host dependency objects. If the host is dependent, Nagios checks these master hosts to see if their status matches the status defined in the notification_failure_criteria directive. If the status does match, the notification generated by the dependent host is suppressed. This check occurs each time a new notification is generated; thus, if the status of the master host changes to one not listed in the notification_failure_criteria directive, the notification is allowed to be sent.

As with service dependencies, you can also set up host dependency inheritance using the inherits_parent directive. This functionality is not enabled by default, and you will need to add the inherits_parent directive, as you can see in Example 7-4.

Example 7-4. *Host Dependency Inheritance*

```
define hostdependency{
            host_name                               kitten
            dependent_host_name                     puppy
            notification_failure_criteria           d
            }

define hostdependency{
            host_name                               puppy
            dependent_host_name                     owlet
            inherits_parents                        1
notification_failure_criteria                 d
            }
```

In Example 7-4 I've added two host dependencies. In the first object, I've defined that the puppy host is dependent on the kitten host. In the event the kitten host is in the DOWN state, notifications on the puppy host will be suppressed. In the second object, the owlet host is dependent on the puppy host and also inherits the dependencies of the master host, puppy. The result of this is that the owlet host is actually dependent on both the kitten and puppy hosts; in the event that either of these hosts is in the DOWN state, notifications will be suppressed on the owlet host.

Additionally, as with service dependency definitions you can define objects using some shortcuts. The first shortcut is defining multiple hosts in a single host dependency, as you can see on the following lines:

```
define hostdependency{
            host_name                               puppy,kitten
            dependent_host_name                     owlet,hatchling
            ...
            }
```

In this object definition, the owlet and hatching hosts are both dependent on the puppy and kitten hosts.

You can also define host dependency objects using one or more host groups:

```
define hostdependency{
            hostgroup_name                          syd_servers
            dependent_hostgroup_name                uk_servers,us_servers
            ...
            }
```

In this object definition, all of the hosts in the uk_servers and us_servers host groups are dependent on all of the hosts in the syd_servers host group.

Notification Escalations

The next type of advanced objects I'm going to look at allows you to create notification escalation trees for hosts and services. These are optional and do not have to be used, but you might find them useful in complex or service level agreement (SLA)–driven environments where you need to notify multiple people at differing time periods. Host notification escalations are defined using hostescalation objects, and service notification escalations are defined using serviceescalation objects. They must be defined in your object configuration files, as I demonstrated in Chapter 2.

So what can we do with host and service notification escalations? Well, the key benefit is being able to tell other people about problems and issues in a staged manner. Most IT departments or organizations have a hierarchical structure, both in terms of support functions and management. For example, initial support queries may be answered by a help desk and then escalated to a second-level support group and then a third-level support group, and then potentially to a vendor or management if the issue cannot be resolved. This is usually done by a help desk or other ticketing system based on a series of predefined priorities and SLAs. Thus, an important help desk call that has not been resolved for four hours may be escalated automatically to a second-level support group and then, if still not resolved after a further four hours, to IT management.

Nagios host and service notification escalations allow you to perform a similar function. Using a service notification escalation, you can configure a service to send out a notification to a contact if it is a non-OK state. If the service remains in the non-OK state and has not been fixed after a period of time, then you can configure that future notifications be sent to the original contact and one or more additional contacts. You can also configure more than one escalation to allow sequential escalations, like the example I described in the previous paragraph.

Service Notification Escalations

Let's start by looking at service notification escalation objects. You can see one in Example 7-5.

Example 7-5. *Service Escalation Notifications*

```
define serviceescalation{
            host_name                      kitten
            service_description            httpd
            first_notification             3
            last_notification              5
            notification_interval          90
            contact_groups                 network_team,network_management
            }
```

So how do escalations work? Well, when a service generates a notification Nagios checks to see if an escalation has been defined and applies to this notification. The first two directives, host_name and service_description, in Example 7-5 define the name of the host and the service you wish to define an escalation for. Nagios also keeps count of how many notifications have been generated and uses this value to trigger the escalation.

The next two directives indicate which notifications will be the first and last notifications to be escalated. The first_notification directive indicates the first notification that should be processed by this service escalation object. In Example 7-5, this directive is set to 3. This indicates that on the third notification generated by the httpd service running on the kitten host that this escalation will be activated and that notification escalated. This means the httpd service on the kitten host has been in the state that generated the notification for long enough to generate two previous notifications.

The next directive, last_notification, indicates what will be the last notification that is escalated on. In Example 7-5, this is set to 5. This means that if more than five notifications have been generated, this escalation will cease to be in effect and the notifications will stop being escalated. You can make the escalation continual by setting this value to 0.

The interval between notifications is set by the next directive, notification_interval. This specifies the interval between escalation notifications in minutes. This overrides the notification interval specified in the service definition. In this case, I've defined 90 minutes between escalations. This means notifications would be sent every 90 minutes. If you specify an interval of 0, Nagios will send one notification and will then suppress all future notifications.

Finally in Example 7-5 there is the contact_groups directive, which specifies which contact groups will be escalated to by this service escalation object. In this case, on the third notification from the httpd service the network_team and network_management contact groups will be notified by this escalation definition.

There are two directives I've not used in Example 7-5 that are also available for service escalation objects: escalation_period and escalation_options. The escalation_period option tells Nagios in what time period to use the escalation. By default, the escalation is triggered whenever a notification is generated, which in turn is controlled by the notification_period directive in your host or service. You can further refine this by only escalating during a time period you specify. For example, if you had a service for which notifications were generated 24 hours a day, you could specify that escalations for that service only occurr during business hours. This would be done by specifying the name of a time period object that covers business hours in the escalation_period directive.[2] You can see this in the service escalation definition on the following lines:

```
define serviceescalation{
                host_name                       kitten
                service_description             httpd
                first_notification              3
                last_notification               5
                notification_interval           90
                escalation_period               bh
                contact_groups                  network_team,network_management
                }
```

The escalation_options directive allows you to control for which states you want the escalation to be active. This allows you to specify that only some types of notifications are escalated on. The valid options for a service escalation appear in Table 7-4.

Table 7-4. *Escalation Options*

State	Description
r	Sends an escalation if the service recovers to an OK state
w	Sends an escalation if the service is in the WARNING state
c	Sends an escalation if the service is in the CRITICAL state
u	Sends an escalation if the service is in the UNKNOWN state

You can specify multiple options by separating each with a comma.

A common way to define service escalations is to define multiple escalations for particular services, as shown in Example 7-6.

Example 7-6. *Multiple Service Escalations*

```
define serviceescalation{
                host_name                       kitten
                service_description             httpd
                first_notification              3
                last_notification               4
                notification_interval           90
                contact_groups                  network_team,network_management
                }
```

---

2. I discussed time period objects in Chapter 2.

```
define serviceescalation{
          host_name                    kitten
          service_description          httpd
          first_notification           5
          last_notification            0
          notification_interval        30
          contact_groups               network_team,network_management,it_manager
          }
```

In Example 7-6 I've defined two service notifications escalations. The first escalation for the httpd service on the kitten host will occur with the third notification from the httpd service. The fourth notification will also be escalated, and then the first service notification escalation definition will cease to be in effect. This is because the last_notification directive is set to 4.

But then the second service notification escalation object would take over. This second service notification escalation object would escalate the fifth notification and, because the last_notification directive is set to 0, it will never stop escalating the notifications. It also changes the notification interval to every 30 minutes and escalates to an additional contact group, it_manager.

■Note If you want a continuity of notification, remember that you should include all contact groups you specified in lower escalations in later escalation objects. This ensures that earlier contacts continue to be aware that a problem exists with a particular service. I do this in Example 7-6.

You can specify as many additional service escalations as you wish. You can also define service escalations that overlap in terms of their first and last notifications and their notification intervals. This means more than one service escalation notification can be sent for a service. In the case of overlapping notifications intervals for service escalations, Nagios will choose the smallest notification interval to send the notification escalation.

Finally, recovery notifications being escalated are a special case that you need to understand. In Example 7-7 I've defined two service escalation objects.

Example 7-7. *Recovery Notifications Escalations*

```
define serviceescalation{
          host_name                    kitten
          service_description          httpd
          first_notification           3
          last_notification            4
          notification_interval        90
          contact_groups               network_team,network_management
          }
```

```
define serviceescalation{
            host_name                        kitten
            service_description              httpd
            first_notification               4
            last_notification                0
            notification_interval            30
            contact_groups                   third_level_support
            }
```

In Example 7-7, using the first service dependency object, the first escalation will take place on the third notification for the service. The last escalation for this service dependency will be the fourth escalation. The fourth escalation will also trigger the second service dependency object. But what happens if the fourth notification is actually a recovery notification indicating that the service has now recovered? Who gets notified? Well, based on what I've discussed, you'd assume that both service escalations would be activated and that the network_team, network_management, and the third_level_support contact groups would be notified. In fact, this isn't what happens. The Nagios escalation engine has some intelligence built in and knows that a recovery notification escalated to the third_level_support contact group doesn't make a lot of sense. This is for two reasons. First, now there isn't a problem that needs to be escalated, and second, they weren't aware of the problem in the first place, and hence sending them the recovery notification makes no sense. Therefore, Nagios does not escalate the notification.

Note The same behavior is also applicable to host escalations.

Service Escalation Shortcuts

Like service dependencies, Nagios has some clever shortcuts for defining service escalation objects. Also, like service dependencies, using shortcuts actually generates multiple service escalations. Therefore, whatever you define as the other directives—for example, the notification interval and when the escalation is triggered—is identical for all the service escalations defined.

First, you can define service escalations for a service of the same name running on multiple hosts, as shown here:

```
define serviceescalation{
            host_name                        kitten,puppy,owlet
            service_description              httpd
            …
            }
```

Here I can define service escalations that will apply to the httpd service running on the kitten, puppy, and owlet hosts.

You also have the ability to define service escalations for multiple services running on one host:

```
define serviceescalation{
            host_name                          kitten
            service_description                httpd,ftpd,smtpd
            ...
            }
```

In this object definition I've defined service escalations for the httpd, ftpd, and smtpd services running on the kitten host.

You can also define a service escalation for a service that runs on all hosts in your environment using the regular expression symbol *, as you can see on the following lines:

```
define serviceescalation{
            host_name                          *
            service_description                httpd
            ...
            }
```

These service escalation definitions would escalate for the httpd service running on all hosts defined in your environment.

In a similar style, I can also define service escalations for all services running on a particular host. I've done this in the following object definition:

```
define serviceescalation{
            host_name                          kitten
            service_description                *
            ...
            }
```

This definition creates service escalations for all services running on the kitten host.

In addition, you can use a * wildcard symbol in both the host_name and service_description directives to define service escalations for all your services running on all your hosts:

```
define serviceescalation{
            host_name                          *
            service_description                *
            ...
            }
```

You can also define service escalations for services of the same name running on all hosts in a host group or groups:

```
define serviceescalation{
            hostgroup_name                     syd_servers,melb_servers
            service_description                httpd
            ...
            }
```

Here I've defined service escalations for the httpd service running on all the hosts in the syd_servers and melb_servers host groups.

Finally, you can also create service escalations that refer to all services contained in one or more service groups. To do this, exclude the host_name directive from the definition because service groups already contain references to both the hostname and service name.[3] Here's an example:

```
define serviceescalation{
                 servicegroup_description     email_services,web_services
         ...
         }
```

This object definition would provide service escalations for the service and host combinations contained in the email_services and web_services service groups.

Host Escalations

Host notification escalations are identical to service notification escalations except that they allow you to escalate host notifications. Let's look at an example of a host notification escalation in Example 7-8.

Example 7-8. *Host Notification Escalation Object*

```
define hostescalation{
              host_name                    kitten
              first_notification           3
              last_notification            10
              notification_interval        60
              contact_groups               field_support,support_management
              }
```

In Example 7-8 I've defined a host escalation for the kitten host. The third to tenth host notifications for this host will be escalated, once every 60 minutes, and sent to the field_support and support_management contact groups.

As with service escalations, you can also use a series of shortcuts for host escalations. I'll start with defining host escalations for multiple hosts, which you can see in the following object definition:

```
define hostescalation{
              host_name                                  kitten,puppy,owlet
              ...
              }
```

In this object definition I've defined host escalations for three hosts: kitten, puppy, and owlet. Host notifications for all these hosts will be escalated.

---

3. See Chapter 2 for a description of how service groups are created.

You can also specify a shortcut that defines host escalations for all hosts defined in your environment by using the * wildcard symbol:

```
define hostescalation{
            host_name                                              *
            ...
            }
```

Finally, you can define host escalations for all hosts in one or more host groups. You can see this shortcut on the following lines:

```
define hostescalation{
            hostgroup_name                      syd_servers,melb_servers
            ...
            }
```

In this object definition I've defined host escalations for all the hosts in the syd_servers and melb_servers host groups.

Extended Host and Service Information Definitions

The last of the advanced configuration objects we are going to examine are the Host and Service Extended Information objects. These objects are completely optional and allow you to extend the view and functionality of your hosts and services as they are displayed in the web console. They have no other effect on your monitoring environment. Thus, if you do not use the Nagios console, you will not need to use these object types.

Each object changes the view of your hosts and services in different CGIs. Changes caused by the directives defined in Extended Host Information objects are displayed in the status.cgi, statusmap.cgi, statuswrl.cgi, and extinfo.cgi CGI programs. Changes caused by the directives defined in Extended Service Information objects are displayed in the status.cgi and extinfo.cgi CGI programs.[4]

Let's look at hostextinfo objects first. In Example 7-9 I've shown a typical hostextinfo object.

Example 7-9. *Extended Host Information Object*

```
define hostextinfo{
            host_name                       kitten
            notes                           This is the primary web server
            action_url      http://intranet.yourdomain.com/hosts/kitten_actions.html
            notes_url       http:// intranet.yourdomain.com/hosts/kitten_notes.html
            icon_image                      apache.png
            icon_image_alt                  Web Server
            vrml_image                      apache.png
```

---

4. You can read about each CGI program at http://nagios.sourceforge.net/docs/2_0/cgis.html and I also discuss them in Chapter 4.

```
                    statusmap_image              apache.gd2
                    2d_coords                    100,250
                    3d_coords                    100.0,50.0,75.0
                    }
```

In Example 7-9 I've used all the possible directives in a hostextinfo object. The first directive, host_name, defines the host object that is referenced by this hostextinfo object. Its value is the short name of the host being referenced. It is also the only mandatory directive required for this object type; all others are optional. Of course, if you don't define any of the optional directives, the object will perform no function.

The next directive, notes, allows you to specify notes about the host that are displayed in the extended info CGI, extinfo.cgi.

The next two directives, action_url and notes_url, allow you to specify URLs that link to other websites. These sites can contain extra details, such as actions and information, about your hosts. These links appear in the extended info CGI, extinfo.cgi. The action_url appears as a link called Extra Host Actions and the notes_url as a link called Extra Host Notes. You can use these links to provide documents or links to other applications or tools that could interact with this host. For example, the notes_url link could connect to an operations manual or documentation for that host, and the action_url link could connect a page containing tools that could interact with the host or launch an SSH or Terminal Services session to the host.

■**Note** If you use a relative path for either the action_url or notes_url, that is, one not prefixed with a hostname, then Nagios will assume the root of the default path is the CGI path, usually /nagios/cgi-bin.

The next directive, icon_image, allows you to specify a GIF, JPEG, or PNG image that will be associated with this host. The icon image specified should ideally be around 40×40 pixels in size and is assumed by Nagios to be located in the logos directory, which is located by default at /usr/local/nagios/share/images/logos. Using the next directive, icon_image_alt, you can add an HTML ALT tag to the icon image you have defined.

The next two directives, vrml_image and statusmap_image, allow you to specify a texture map image in the statuswrl CGI program and an image that is associated with this host for the statusmap CGI program.[5] Nagios assumes both images are located in the logos directory, which is located by default at /usr/local/nagios/share/images/logos. For the status map image, it is recommended you use a GD2 image.[6]

The last two directives control the position of the host icons defined by the statusmap_image and vrml_image directives. The first directive, 2d_coords, defines coordinates for the host icon in the statusmap CGI program. The 2d_coords coordinates define the x (upper-left side of the image extending to the right) and y (upper-left side of the image extending downward) axes of the image. They need to be positive numbers.

---

5. See http://nagios.sourceforge.net/docs/2_0/cgis.html#statuswrl_cgi and http://nagios.sourceforge.net/docs/2_0/cgis.html#statusmap_cgi.

6. See a FAQ entry for details about GD2 images at www.nagios.org/faqs/viewfaq.php?faq_id=97.

The second directive, 3d_coords, defines coordinates for the host icon in the statuswrl CGI program. There are three dimensions representing the coordinates for the center of the cube to be defined. These can either be positive or negative numbers.

Extended Service Information objects are similar in nature to Extended Host Information objects. As we mentioned earlier, they allow you to alter the display output of the status and extinfo CGI programs. I've shown a typical Extended Service Information object in Example 7-10.

Example 7-10. *Extended Service Information Object*

```
define serviceextinfo{
            host_name           kitten
            service_description httpd
            notes               This is the primary web server instance
            action_url➡
http://intranet.yourdomain.com/hosts/kitten__httpd_actions.html
            notes_url ➡
http:// intranet.yourdomain.com/hosts/kitten_httpd_notes.html
            icon_image          httpd.png
            icon_image_alt      httpd server
            }
```

Example 7-10 shows a sample object definition that contains all the possible directives that can be used in the Service Extended Information object. The directives defined in the serviceextinfo object are similar to the hostextinfo object. The first directive, host_name, should contain the short name of the host the service runs on, and the service_description directive contains the short name of the service for which the extended information is being provided. As with the Host Extended Information objects, these are the only mandatory directives required for this object.

The serviceextinfo object can contain the notes, notes_url, and action_url directives. These perform the same function as they do when defined in the hostextinfo object. The notes and URLs defined by these directives will be displayed in the extended information or extinfo, CGI program.[7] The serviceextinfo object can also contain the icon_image and icon_image_alt directives, which perform an identical function as they do when defined in the hostextinfo object. The icon for the service will be displayed in the status and extinfo CGI programs.

Checkpoint

- Remember you don't need to use any of the objects described in this chapter. They are all optional and are only required if you need the specific functionality they provide. For example, unless you require service escalations, you do not need to define service escalation objects.

---

7. See http://nagios.sourceforge.net/docs/2_0/cgis.html#extinfo_cgi.

CHAPTER 8

■ ■ ■

Distributed Monitoring, Redundancy, and Failover

One of the important components of any enterprise monitoring application or tool is its ability to function in a disaster or high-availability situation. This is especially important for an enterprise management tool that is monitoring your hosts and services and warning you when issues arise or administrator intervention is required. If your enterprise-monitoring solution fails, you will have no warning or notifications of other problems in your environment. Often this includes being unable to provide you with warning or notification of the disaster or outage that has taken out both your enterprise-monitoring system and your production environment.

Also important for an enterprise-monitoring tool is the ability to function in a distributed model that allows the monitoring of assets in remote locations. This is especially true where monitoring of these assets is not possible from a central location due to issues with network visibility or network controls such as intervening firewalls. In this instance the ability to deploy distributed servers and send back the results of this monitoring to a centralized management server is important. Nagios has the ability to do this kind of distributed monitoring and to operate in redundant and failover modes. I'll address how to achieve both in this chapter.

Distributed Monitoring

Distributed monitoring allows you to offload the monitoring of your hosts and services onto multiple systems. This is designed to overcome two obstacles. First, it allows you to overcome performance limitations if you have numerous hosts and services and allows you to spread the monitoring load over multiple servers. Second, it allows you to monitor hosts and services in remote or segmented parts of your environment, such as in a remote geographical location or behind a firewall.

In a nondistributed environment, the Nagios server needs to be able to connect to all monitored hosts and services using the plug-in or mechanism you are using to monitor them and return the results of the check. For example, if you are monitoring a website the Nagios server needs to be able to make an HTTP connection to the website and receive the response. If there is a firewall between the Nagios server and the website that blocks this HTTP traffic, it is not possible to check this service.

To overcome this, Nagios uses another server, a distributed server, on the other side of the firewall to perform the check and then sends the results back to a central Nagios server. The distributed server uses service obsession and a special tool called NSCA (Nagios Service Check

Acceptor) to send these results to the central server.[1] Thus, you only need to open one hole in your firewall for the Nagios check results rather than all the possible protocol types required to monitor a collection of hosts and services. The central server receives these check results as passive checks and updates the status of the hosts and services based on this.[2]

As I mentioned, to facilitate the sending of these results there is a tool called NSCA, developed by the author of Nagios. This tool has two components: a plug-in that sends check results and a daemon that runs on your central Nagios server. The daemon accepts the transmitted results and submits them as passive check results using external commands to the Nagios server. This means you only need to have the NSCA traffic between your central and distributed servers. This limits both the bandwidth used and the number of ports you might need to open on your firewall or firewalls.

So how does this work in more detail? Well, you can see a distributed monitoring model in Figure 8-1.

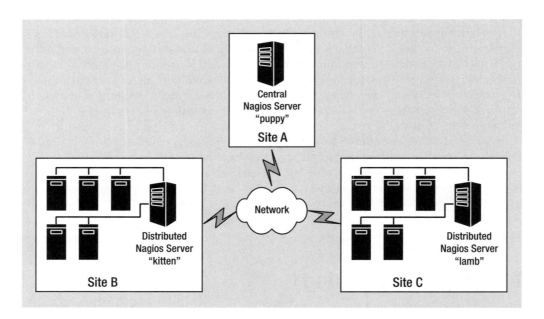

Figure 8-1. *Distributed monitoring model*

First, let's look at the architecture of our distributed environment. The major pieces of the solution are the central server and the distributed servers. In Figure 8-1 you can see our central server, puppy, located in Site A, and two distributed servers, kitten and lamb, located in Sites B and C. LAN or WAN connections would link these sites and potentially might have firewalls installed between them. If you had firewalls installed, traffic from the NSCA tool on the distributed servers containing the check results would need to be able to pass through these

---

1. I discussed service obsession in Chapter 2.

2. See Chapter 2 for a discussion of passive service checks.

firewalls. By default, the NSCA tool uses TCP port 5667 for this traffic. I'll cover installing and configuring NSCA to both send and receive check results later in this chapter.

■**Note** The sites in Figure 8-1 could also represent segmented sections of an internal network. The same design principles apply to both models.

The central server, puppy, located in Site A in Figure 8-1, is the collation point for all your check results. It generally would not perform any active checks itself. Or potentially it may perform checks for hosts and services local to it, for example, in the same site or network segment. As it is the collation point, the central server must contain object definitions for all hosts and services in your environment. This includes all hosts and services defined on your distributed servers, in this case, the kitten and lamb servers. If you do not add a host or service being monitored by one of your distributed servers to your central server, when the central server receives the check result it will discard the result since it has no knowledge of that host or service.

The distributed servers, kitten and lamb, perform the actual checks on your hosts and services. They then use the NSCA tool to send the results to the puppy server, where they are processed as passive check results and the status of the host or service updated. Thus, the distributed servers only need to have the object definitions for those hosts and services that you require them to monitor.

Your distributed servers are usually bare-bones installations of Nagios that only contains the Nagios server and any plug-ins required to perform checks. You should not need to install the web console. You also do not need to configure any notifications. The central server will perform all the notifications required based on the results it receives from the distributed servers.

Distributed Server Configuration

Let's start by configuring our distributed servers. As I have already mentioned, these can be a bare-bones installation of Nagios and you do not generally need to install the web console and hence a web server on these servers. So first install Nagios on the server. You can follow the instructions in Chapter 1 for this. Then define all the hosts and services that this server will be required to monitor.[3] Remember, you only need to define those hosts and services that this specific distributed server is going to monitor.

You also do not need to configure any notifications. Notifications will be performed by the central server. So you should set the enable_notifications directive in the nagios.cfg configuration file on the distributed server to 0 like so:

```
enable_notifications=0
```

---

3. See Chapters 1 and 2 for further information on how to do this.

■**Caution** If you have state retention enabled (using the `retain_state_information` and `use_retained_program_state` directives) as I discussed in Chapter 2, Nagios will ignore how this directive is set in the `nagios.cfg` configuration file in favor of what is contained in the state retention file. So if you have program state retention enabled on your distributed server and at some point enable notifications, remember that this setting will be kept through program restarts and the setting in the `nagios.cfg` file will be ignored. This can lead to confusion as to why your distributed server is sending notifications.

Installing NSCA

Next, we need to install the NSCA tool to allow the distributed server to send the check results to the central server. The NSCA package does have one prerequisite, the `libmcrypt` library. This library enables you to use encryption when sending results between your distributed and central servers. This is a very important security feature, and I recommend you install the library. You can find the `libmcrypt` library at `http://mcrypt.sourceforge.net/` or you can download it as an RPM from either `www.ottolander.nl/opensource/mcrypt/mcrypt.html` or `http://dag.wieers.com/packages/libmcrypt/`. The installation process for the `libmcrypt` library is very simple. Download the source package (I have chosen the Australian Sourceforge mirror but you should choose the mirror near you). Then configure, make, and install it like so:

```
kitten# wget http://optusnet.dl.sourceforge.net/sourceforge/mcrypt/➥
libmcrypt-2.5.7.tar.gz
kitten# tar -zxf libmcrypt-2.5.7.tar,gz
kitten# cd libmcrypt-2.5.7
kitten# ./configure
kitten# make
kitten# make install
```

Once you have `libmcrypt` installed, you can start the NSCA installation process. The NSCA tool is available from the Nagios Exchange website at `www.nagiosexchange.org/Communication.41.0.html?&tx_netnagext_pi1[p_view]=140` or via Sourceforge at `http://prdownloads.sourceforge.net/nagios/`. At the time of this writing the latest version of NSCA was 2.4.

Download and unpack the package on your distributed server like so:

```
kitten# wget http://optusnet.dl.sourceforge.net/sourceforge/nagios/nsca-2.4.tar.gz
kitten# tar -zxf nsca-2.4.tar.gz
```

Next change into the NSCA source package directory and configure the package using the `configure` script. There are some configuration options you can see if you run the `configure` script with the `--help` option (see Table 8-1), but generally you will not need these for compiling the send tool on the distributed server.

Table 8-1. *NSCA configure Options*

Option	Default	Description
`--with-nsca-user=`*user*	nagios	Specifies the username to run the NSCA daemon as
`--with-nsca-grp=`*group*	nagios	Specifies the group name to run the NSCA daemon as
`--with-nsca-port=`*port*	5667	Specifies the TCP port number that the NSCA tool uses

The first two options specify which user to run the NSCA daemon as; I recommend you use the same user and group that the Nagios server runs as. Both default to a setting of nagios. The third option controls which port NSCA will use to send and receive results. This defaults to TCP port 5667, and I recommend you leave this as the default unless your environment requires you define another port number. You cannot specify a privileged port number, that is, a port number below 1024.

You can then configure NSCA and run the make option to compile it:

```
kitten# ./configure
kitten# make all
```

■**Tip** You can also find an RPM of the NCSA tool at `http://dries.studentenweb.org/rpm/packages/nagios-nsca/info.html`.

When you want to install the NSCA tool, you need to manually install the required tool and configuration files. The compile process creates two binaries, nsca and send_nsca, located in the src directory beneath the NSCA package directory. The nsca binary is the NSCA daemon that runs on the central server and receives the check results. The send_nsca binary does the actual sending of the check results and is executed on the distributed server. There are also two configuration files, nsca.cfg and send_nsca.cfg, located in the root of the NSCA package directory. They are for the NSCA daemon and sending program, respectively. For the distributed server, you only need the send_nsca and send_nsca.cfg files. I recommend you install the send_nsca binary to the bin directory in your default Nagios directory structure, as I'm going to define it in a command shortly. This directory is /usr/local/nagios/bin by default. I suggest you place the send_nsca.cfg file into your Nagios etc directory, by default /usr/local/nagios/etc.

Configuring send_nsca

Once you have installed NSCA you need to configure it, both in terms of configuring it to the Nagios server and configuring the send_nsca program itself. Let's start with the send_nsca program. Its configuration is held in the send_nsca.cfg configuration file we placed in the /usr/local/nagios/etc/ directory earlier. Example 8-1 shows a sample configuration.

Example 8-1. *send_nsca.cfg configuration File*

```
password=password
encryption_method=3
```

■**Tip** You can add comments to the `send_nsca.cfg` configuration file by prefixing the line with a # symbol.

There are only two options in the `send_nsca.cfg` configuration file. Both of these options contain values that must be identical to their equivalent options in the `nsca.cfg` configuration file that will be located on the central server. The first option, `password`, specifies the password you will use to encrypt any data between the distributed and central servers. Therefore, it must be the same on both servers. You should replace the value *password* with a password of your choice. I recommend you chose a nondictionary word that includes special characters and is at least eight characters long.

■**Caution** I don't want people to read this option, so I'm going to secure this file to prevent casual users from seeing the password.

The next option, `encryption_method`, specifies what form of encryption you will use to encrypt the transmission of your check results. A variety of methods are available, ranging from no encryption, which I strongly recommend you don't use, to 3DES and Blowfish. Table 8-2 contains a list of the values you can use for this option and the type of encryption they represent.

Table 8-2. *NSCA Encryption Methods*

Value	Type of Encryption
0	None
1	Simple XOR (obfuscates but does not encrypt)
2	DES
3	Triple DES
4	CAST-128
5	CAST-256
6	xTEA
7	3WAY
8	Blowfish
9	Twofish
10	LOKI97
11	RC2
12	ARCFOUR
14	RIJNDAEL-128
15	RIJNDAEL-192
16	RIJNDAEL-256
19	WAKE

Value	Type of Encryption
20	SERPENT
22	Enigma (Crypt)
23	GOST
24	SAFER64
25	SAFER128
26	SAFER+

This is not a book about encryption, and I will not make any judgments about which encryption method is best. Obviously, the more complicated the encryption method, the greater overhead placed on your servers to encrypt and decrypt the transmissions. Generally speaking, though, the volume of data is quite small and most hosts will absorb the overhead required for more complex encryption. Additionally, it depends on the level of risk you perceive about the data being sent. I'll discuss this in more detail when I explain the security architecture and model of the NSCA daemon in the "Central Server Configuration" section.

Personally I use Triple DES (option 3). It is secure and is present on most distributions and systems. To be able to communicate with the distributed servers, the central server must use the same encryption method; I'll also show you how to do that when I look at configuring that server in the "Central Server Configuration" section.

Once you've configured the send_nsca.cfg file, you need to secure that file's ownership and permissions, as shown in Example 8-2.

Example 8-2. *Securing the send_nsca.cfg File*

```
kitten# chown nagios:nagios /usr/local/nagios/etc/send_nsca.cfg
kitten# chmod 0640 /usr/local/nagios/etc/send_nsca.cfg
```

In Example 8-2, I've changed the ownership of the configuration file to the nagios user and group (which I've used for the Nagios server on the distributed servers). I've also changed the permissions of the file to 0640 to only allow the nagios user to read the file.

Note I'll look at the exact functioning of the send_nsca binary later in this section when I define how to send the check results to the central server.

Now we've configured the NSCA sending program, we need to define this program to Nagios and configure the server to send its check results to the central server. To do this, let's use host and service obsession. Host and service obsession allow you to specify commands that will run after each host or service check. In this case, the commands will send the check results to the central server to allow the hosts and services status to be updated.

To do this you need to turn on two directives in the nagios.cfg file, specify a command to send service results and a command to send host results, and define those commands to some additional directives in the configuration file. The two directives you need to turn on are `obsess_over_services` and `obsess_over_hosts`, which turn on obsession for services and hosts, respectively:

```
obsess_over_services=1
obsess_over_hosts=1
```

Next, you need to define the commands that will be executed when a check is completed. These are defined in the `ocsp_command` and `ochp_command` directives; also in the `nagios.cfg` configuration file:

```
ocsp_command=send_service_check
ochp_command=send_host_check
```

■**Note** These directives may not be present in your `nagios.cfg` configuration file if you have used the sample configuration that comes with Nagios, and you may need to add them.

Sending Service Check Results

Now, the commands defined in these directives need to be defined to Nagios. We do this by adding them as command object definitions. You will need to create two commands: one for host check results and one for service check results. Let's first look at the service check results command, which is defined in the `ocsp_command` directive in Example 8-3.

Example 8-3. *ocsp_command directive Command Definition*

```
define command{
            command_name      send_service_check
            command_line      /usr/local/nagios/libexec/send_service_check ➡
$HOSTNAME$ '$SERVICEDESC$' $SERVICESTATEID$ '$SERVICEOUTPUT$'
            }
```

Let's break down the command defined in Example 8-3. I've defined a command called `send_service_check` (which is the same name I used in the `ocsp_command` directive in the `nagios.cfg` configuration file). The command executes a shell script (which I'll show you next) also called `send_service_check`. I'm passing a number of macro values to the shell script, which will in turn pass these to the `send_nsca` program. These are the hostname that the service is running on represented by the `$HOSTNAME$` macro. Next is the description of the service, which is defined in the `service_description` directive in the service definition object, and represented here by the `$SERVICEDESC$` macro. Next comes the `$SERVICESTATEID$` macro, which contains the state of the service as returned by the service check. In the case of services, these are `OK`, `WARNING`, `CRITICAL`, and `UNKNOWN`. But rather than being displayed by name, the service states in the `$SERVICESTATEID$` macro are represented by the return code values listed in Table 8-3.

Table 8-3. *Numeric Representation of Service States*

Value	State
0	OK
1	WARNNG
2	CRITICAL
3	UNKNOWN

You should use these numeric return codes because the send_nsca program requires the return code rather than the name of the status when submitting check results. I'll demonstrate this in the shell script I've created to submit the results that you can see in Example 8-5.

Finally, I've specified the $SERVICEOUTPUT$ macro. This macro contains the output of the service check result.

Note You will see I've placed two macros, $SERVICEDESC$ and $SERVICEOUTPUT$, in quotes. This is to ensure that if they contain multiword data that it is passed to the shell script cleanly.

Now that we have our command definition, we need to write the send_service_check shell script to use the send_nsca program to submit the results to the central server. To do this, you must understand how the send_nsca program works. The program looks very similar to a standard Nagios plug-in; Example 8-4 demonstrates a sample of how it might be run from the command line.

Example 8-4. *The send_nsca Program*

```
kitten# ./send_nsca -H 10.0.0.1 -c /usr/local/nagios/etc/send_nsca.cfg ➥
owlet local_disk 2 'Connection refused by host'
```

Example 8-4 executes the send_nsca program from the command line. It has a number of options. The first is the -H option, which specifies the IP address or hostname of the central server the check result is being sent to. In this case, it is 10.0.0.1. The next option, -c, specifies the location of the send_nsca.cfg configuration file. Finally, I've specified the actual check results: the hostname of the host the service is running on, the service description, the return code, and the output of the service check. By default each of these result values needs to be separated by a tab character.

There are also some additional options available for the send_nsca program, as shown in Table 8-4.

Table 8-4. *send_nsca Options*

Option	Description
-p *port*	The TCP port number on the central server where the NSCA daemon is running. Defaults to port 5667.
-to *seconds*	Connection timeout. Defaults to 10 seconds.
-d *delimiter*	The delimiter character for the check results. Defaults to the tab character.

The first option, -p, in Table 8-4 allows you to override the default port of 5667 on the central server. The second option, -to, lets you specify a different value for a connection timeout to the central server. The default is 10 seconds. The last option, -d, allows you to specify the delimiter that will be used between each item of the check results. By default, this is a tab character. You can override this with another character such as, or a ; symbol like so: -d "," or -d ";".

Now that you know how the send_nsca program works, let's use it in the shell script that will send the check results to the central server. Example 8-5 shows a sample shell script that will perform this function.

Example 8-5. *send_service_check Script*

```
#!/bin/sh

# Arguments:
# $1 = Hostname of the host (using the $HOSTNAME$ macro)
# $2 = Service Description of the service (using the $SERVICEDESC$ macro)
# $3 = Service Status ID of the service (using the $SERVICESTATUSID$ macro)
# $4 = Output of the service check (using the $SERVICEOUTPUT$ macro)

/bin/echo "$1","$2","$3","$4" | /usr/local/nagios/bin/send_nsca -H ip_address ➥
-c /usr/local/nagios/etc/send_nsca.cfg -d ","
```

In Example 8-5, you can see a very simple shell script that is designed to echo the check results, each separated by a , symbol (for which I've overridden the default delimiter symbol using the option -d ","), to the send_nsca program and from there to the central server. You would need to replace the *ip_address* value with the IP address or hostname of the central Nagios server that is running the NSCA daemon.

AN ALTERNATIVE TO THE SEND_NSCA SHELL SCRIPT

We don't precisely need the shell script. We could also just reference the send_nsca program in the command object definition and pass the macros directly to it, but I prefer using a shell script as it allows me to potentially add a data cleansing or manipulation stage to the sending process. An example of this alternative object definition might look like this:

```
define command{
            command_name                        send_service_check
            command_line /usr/local/nagios/bin/send_nsca -H ip_address ➥
-c /usr/local/nagios/etc/send_nsca.cfg -d "," $HOSTNAME$,'$SERVICEDESC$',➥
$SERVICESTATEID$,'$SERVICEOUTPUT$'
            }
```

You would need to replace the *ip_address* value with the IP address or hostname of your central Nagios server.

Sending Host Check Results

Now in order to send host check results to the central server, we'll need to create another command, in our case the send_host_check command, as defined in the ochp_command directive in the nagios.cfg configuration file. I've shown a sample of this command object definition in Example 8-6.

Example 8-6. *ochp_command Directive Command Definition*

```
define command{
            command_name      send_host_check
            command_line      /usr/local/nagios/libexec/send_host_check ➡
$HOSTNAME$ $HOSTSTATEID$ '$HOSTOUTPUT$'
            }
```

Note You will notice the send_host_check command is very similar to the send_service_check command except that I've used different macros, which I'll explain later.

Let's break down the command defined in Example 8-6. I've defined a command called send_host_check (which is the same name I used in the ochp_command directive in the nagios.cfg configuration file). The command executes a shell script also called send_host_check. I'm passing a number of macro values to the shell script, which will in turn pass these to the send_nsca program. These are the hostname of the host whose check results I'm sending; this is represented by the $HOSTNAME$ macro. Next comes the $HOSTSTATEID$ macro, which contains the state of the host as returned by the host check. In the case of services, these are UP, DOWN, and UNREACHABLE. But rather than being displayed by name, the status types in the $HOSTSTATEID$ macro are represented by the return code values, as you can see in Table 8-5.

Table 8-5. *Numeric Representation of Host States*

Value	State
0	UP
1	DOWN
2	UNREACHABLE

You need to use these numeric return codes because the send_nsca program requires the return code rather than the name of the status when submitting check results.

Finally, I've specified the $HOSTOUTPUT$ macro. This macro contains the output of the host check result.

Note You will see that I've placed the $HOSTOUTPUT$ macro in quotes. This is to ensure that if it contains multiword data it will be passed to the shell script cleanly.

Now that we have our command definition, we need to write the send_host_check shell script to use the send_nsca program to submit the results to the central server. It is again very similar to the send_service_check shell script, as you can see in Example 8-7.

Example 8-7. *send_host_check Script*

```
#!/bin/sh

# Arguments:
# $1 = Hostname of the host (using the $HOSTNAME$ macro)
# $2 = Host Status ID of the host (using the $HOSTSTATUSID$ macro)
# $3 = Output of the host check (using the $HOSTOUTPUT$ macro)

/bin/echo "$1","$2","$3" | /usr/local/nagios/bin/send_nsca -H ip_address ➥
-c /usr/local/nagios/etc/send_nsca.cfg -d ","
```

In Example 8-7 you can see a very simple shell script that is designed to echo the check results, each separated by a , symbol (for which I've overridden the default delimiter symbol using the option -d ","), to the send_nsca program and hence from there to the central server. You would need to replace the *ip_address* value with the IP address or hostname of the central Nagios server that is running the NSCA daemon.

Distributed Servers Final Steps

Once you've defined the required directives in the nagios.cfg file, configured NSCA, and created the required commands and shell scripts, you've completed the configuration of the distributed server to send the results of services and hosts to the central server. Let's quickly walk through the process of sending a service check to the central server to ensure we understand what is happening.

1. The distributed server executes a service check (or a host check).

2. After the check is completed, the command defined in either the ocsp_command or ochp_command directive executes (depending on whether it is a service or host check, respectively).

3. The command pipes the results of the check results to the send_nsca program.

4. The send_nsca command sends the check results to the central server.

Now that we have stepped through the events on the distributed Nagios server, let's see what happens on the central server and how it is configured.

Central Server Configuration

The central Nagios server should be configured much like a stand-alone Nagios server as it performs the majority of the same functions. Unlike with the distributed server, I recommend you install the web console. You will also have to ensure that all hosts and services defined on your distributed servers are also defined on your central server. The host and service definitions need to be essentially identical to those on the distributed server or servers.

Unlike with the distributed server, you will also need to enable notifications so that the central server can send any notifications generated. This is done by ensuring the enable_notifications directive in the nagios.cfg file is set to 1:

```
enable_notifications=1
```

There are also several other options you need to have enabled on your central server. First, your central server needs to be allowed to receive passive checks from both hosts and services. This means the accept_passive_service_checks and accept_passive_host_checks directives in the nagios.cfg file both need to be set to 1:

```
accept_passive_service_checks=1
accept_passive_host_checks=1
```

Second, the check_external_commands directive must be set to 1 to tell the Nagios server to check the external command file for commands to be processed:

```
check_external_commands=1
```

If this is not on, the submitted check results will not be processed.

Third, and last, you need to determine how your central server will handle active checks of hosts and services. There are a few scenarios here to consider. In the first instance, your central server may only be processing check results from distributed servers and not be performing any checks of hosts or services local to it. In this case, you should turn off all active host and service checking using the execute_service_checks and execute_host_checks directives in the nagios.cfg file. Setting these both to 0 will stop the central server from executing service checks:

```
execute_service_checks=0
execute_host_checks=0
```

In the second instance, your central servers may also be checking some local hosts and services. In this case, you should have the execute_service_checks and execute_host_checks directives set to 1 to enable active checks for these local hosts and services. To stop the central server from checking hosts and services that are being handled by the distributed server or servers, you need to set the active_checks_enabled directive in the object definition of each of the hosts or services being checked via distributed servers to 0. This will ensure that the central server will not perform active checks of them.[4] Instead, the central server will rely on the submitted passive check results to maintain the status of these hosts and services.

■**Caution** Using passive checks alone can be problematic, and I'll discuss this and some potential solutions in the upcoming section, "Distributed Monitoring and Freshness."

---

4. It will still schedule checks for them but will not execute those checks.

Installing the NSCA Daemon

You will also need to install the NSCA daemon. Follow the instructions in the "Installing NSCA" section, including adding the libmcrypt prerequisite, to do this. This same process will produce the required nsca binary and nsca.cfg configuration file. The nsca binary is the NSCA daemon that runs on the central server and receives the check results. The nsca.cfg configuration file controls the NSCA daemon. For the central server we need both files. I recommend you install the nsca binary to the bin directory in your default Nagios directory structure. This directory is /usr/local/nagios/bin by default. I suggest you place the nsca.cfg file in your Nagios etc directory, by default, /usr/local/nagios/etc.

Tip When you compile the NSCA package, I recommend you specify the same user and group name as your Nagios server for the daemon to run as. This is because the daemon is required to write to your external command file, and this is generally the easiest way to provide this access.

Configuring the NSCA Daemon

Once you have installed NSCA daemon, you need to configure it. The NSCA daemon works by listening for check results being sent via the send_nsca command on a remote server. It then submits these check results to the external command file to be processed by the Nagios server. Its configuration is held in the nsca.cfg configuration file you placed in the /usr/local/nagios/etc/ directory. I've shown a sample configuration in Example 8-8.

Example 8-8. *nsca.cfg Configuration File*

```
server_port=5667
server_address=10.0.0.1
allowed_hosts=127.0.0.1,10.0.0.10,10.0.0.20,10.0.0.30
nsca_user=nagios
nsca_group=nagios
debug=0
command_file=/usr/local/nagios/var/rw/nagios.cmd
alternate_dump_file=/usr/local/nagios/var/rw/nsca.dump
aggregate_writes=0
append_to_file=0
max_packet_age=30
password=password
decryption_method=3
```

There are a number of options in the nsca.cfg configuration file. I've listed them all in Table 8-6 and will explain their function in more detail next.

Table 8-6. *nsca.cfg Options*

Option	Description
server_port=port	Specifies the TCP port the nsca daemon should run on. Defaults to 5667.
server_address=ip_address	Contains the IP address the nsca daemon should bind to. Defaults to all addresses.
allowed_hosts=hosts	Contains IP addresses of the hosts that are allowed to connect to the central server.
nsca_user=user	Specifies the name of the user the nsca daemon should run as.
nsca_group=group	Specifies the name of the group the nsca daemon should run as.
debug=0 | 1	Turns on debug function.
command_file=file	Specifies the location of the external command file.
alternate_dump_file=file	Specifies the location of an alternative command file.
aggregate_writes=0 | 1	Turns on aggregate writes.
append_to_file=0 | 1	Specifies whether to open the command file for writing or appending.
max_packet_age=age	Specifies the maximum packet age in seconds.
password=password	Contains the password used between central and distributed servers.
decryption_method=method	Specifies the decryption method used.

Tip You can add comments to the nsca.cfg configuration file by prefixing the line with a # symbol.

The first two options in Table 8-6, server_port and server_address, specify the port number and IP address that the daemon will bind to. This defaults to all addresses on the host on TCP port 5667.

Tip For the server_port value, you cannot specify a privileged port (i.e., a port number lower than 1024).

The next option, allowed_hosts, requires that you specify the IP addresses of the distributed servers that are allowed to connect to this central server. The daemon only performs minor checking of these source addresses and thus these can be easily spoofed. The developer of Nagios recommends running the daemon under inetd or xinetd (and instructions on how to do this are provided in the README file in the NSCA source package). Personally I prefer not to use either and instead use a host-based firewall to lock down the daemon to the IP addresses of the distributed servers. Thus, I specify the allowed hosts in the allowed_hosts option and add `iptables` rules only allowing traffic from the required distributed servers to connect to the daemon on the central server via port 5667. A typical rule is shown here:

```
puppy# iptables -A INPUT -p tcp --dport 5667 -s 10.0.0.10 -j ACCEPT
```

The `iptables` rule on this line would only allow incoming connections to TCP port 5667 from IP address 10.0.0.10. You could specify additional rules for each distributed server.

The next two options, `nsca_user` and `nsca_group`, control the user and group that the daemon will run as. I recommend using the same user and group that the Nagios server runs as to ensure the daemon is able to write to the external command file.

The `debug` option allows you to turn on some debugging for the daemon. This results in debug information being outputted to `syslog`. I suggest when you're first testing the daemon you turn this on, but it is not required during general operation. Setting it to 1 enables debugging and 0 disables it.

The `command_file` and `alternative_dump_file` options specify the location of your external command file and an alternative destination for check results if the command file is unavailable. The `command_file` option would normally default to `/usr/local/nagios/var/rw/nagios.cmd`. As the command file is a named pipe, it only exists while the Nagios daemon is running. Therefore, if Nagios is down and check results are received, they are lost unless an alternate destination is specified. You can specify this alternate destination with the `alternative_dump_file` option. The results of the checks will be written into this file in the form of external commands. Many people check for this file as part of the Nagios `init` script or start-up process and dump the contents of the file into the external command file and then purge the file. This ensures any checks potentially received while Nagios was down are still processed. Alternatively, you could ignore checks received while the Nagios server is down by not specifying this option.

The `aggregate_writes` option specifies that if incoming connections contain multiple check results, such as a batch dump of results from a distributed server, you want to enable aggregate writing to the command file. Generally speaking, unless you are batching results you should leave this option as 0.

The `append_to_file` option specifies whether the daemon should open the command file for writing or appending. Unless you have a specific need (and I generally have never seen one), this should remain set to open for writing by specifying its value as 0.

Using the `max_packet_age` option is an additional method of ensuring the security of your incoming check results. This option should be set to the longest time period in seconds that your distributed servers are likely to take to send check results in. Any check results received in a longer time period will be discarded as a potential "replay" attack.[5] You cannot specify a value longer than 900 seconds, or 15 minutes. Ensure you set a high enough value for this age to accommodate any network latency issues you might have. This is especially important for check results being sent over the Internet where there might be delays.

Both of the `password` and `decryption_method` options contain values that must be identical to their equivalent options, the `password` and `encryption_method` options, in the `send_nsca.cfg` configuration file that is located on the distributed server.

The first option, `password`, specifies the password you will use to encrypt and decrypt any data between the distributed and central servers. Hence, it must be the same on both servers.

---

5. See `http://en.wikipedia.org/wiki/Replay_attack`.

I recommend you chose a nondictionary word that includes special characters and is at least eight characters long.

■Caution I don't want people to view the password contained in this option, so I'm going to secure this file to prevent casual users from seeing the password.

The next option, `decryption_method`, must match the value specified in the `encryption_method` option specified on the distributed servers, in our case, 3, which represents Triple DES encryption.

So why encrypt your check results? Well, in the case of the NSCA package, encryption provides both authentication and transmission security for the check results. The first function, authentication, enhances the daemon's ability to ensure that the source of the data is a trusted system. I've already recommended using `iptables` rules in conjunction with the `allowed_hosts` option (or you may prefer `inetd` or `xinetd`). If the password and encryption method on both the distributed and central servers are identical, the daemon assumes that the check result is valid and accepts it. This prevents an attacker from either maliciously submitting false check data or, worse, submitting malicious external commands via the daemon that could adversely impact your Nagios server or the host it is running on. The second function, transmission security, ensures that no one can sniff out your check results and use any data in them to provide some advantage when attacking your organization.

This is a very simplified explanation of how the NSCA package uses encryption and how it attempts to ensure the security and authenticity of connections. For a complete explanation, see the `SECURITY` file in the NSCA source package.

■Caution If you are transmitting check results via the Internet, this is especially important. Do not transmit your results over an untrusted network without a level of authentication and encryption that you feel comfortable with.

Lastly, once you've configured the `nsca.cfg` file you need to secure that file's ownership and permissions. Example 8-9 shows how.

Example 8-9. *Securing the nsca.cfg File*

```
kitten# chown nagios:nagios /usr/local/nagios/etc/nsca.cfg
kitten# chmod 0640 /usr/local/nagios/etc/nsca.cfg
```

Notice that I've changed the ownership of the configuration file to the `nagios` user and group (which I've used to run the Nagios server process on the central server). I've also changed the permissions of the file to 0640 to only allow the `nagios` user to read the file.

Starting the NSCA Daemon

Finally, once you've configured NSCA, you need to start the daemon. The daemon is controlled by the nsca binary. The binary has only two options: the -c option that specifies the location of the nsca.cfg configuration file and the mode you wish to run it in. The possible modes are --inetd, --daemon, and --single. The --inetd mode is used if you run the NSCA daemon from within inetd or xinted. The --daemon and --single modes run the NSCA daemon as a stand-alone daemon. The --daemon mode runs it as a multiprocess daemon, which I recommend for servers that have a heavy workload. The --single mode runs the daemon as a single process, which is better suited to a low-volume environment. If you do not specify a mode, the NSCA daemon defaults to the --single mode. Here's an example of how to start the daemon:

```
puppy# /usr/local/nagios/bin/nsca -c /usr/local/nagios/etc/nsca.cfg --single
```

■**Tip** Also in the NSCA package is an init script you can use to configure the NSCA daemon to start automatically when your host starts up. I recommend you modify this to suit your environment and use it to start and stop the NSCA daemon.

Distributed Monitoring and Freshness

There is one remaining major issue we need to consider with distributed monitoring. This issue concerns the veracity of the data being gathered from the distributed servers. The distributed monitoring solution relies on passive check results to perform its monitoring. I discussed passive check results in Chapter 2 and explained that this means Nagios simply has to assume that the source of these check results is accurate and up-to-date. It has no way of validating, as it normally would with active checks, that the incoming data represents the true state of the hosts and services being monitored.

There is, however, a way to enhance the value of these checks so you can be a bit more confident that they represent the true state of your assets. You do this using the concept of "freshness" checking.[6] Freshness checks monitor the age of the received check results, and if they exceed a set threshold, Nagios will trigger an active check of the device. This active check is conducted even if active checks are disabled for the host, service, or the entire server.

So how do you configure this? Well, let's have a quick refresher. In your nagios.cfg configuration file are four relevant directives that must be set. I've shown them in Example 8-10.

Example 8-10. *Freshness Directives in nagios.cfg*

```
check_service_freshness=1
service_freshness_check_interval=60
check_host_freshness=1
host_freshness_check_interval=60
```

---

6. I also discussed this concept in Chapter 2.

The check_service_freshness and check_host_freshness need to be set to 1 if you wish to enable service and host freshness checking for the server. The service_freshness_check_interval and host_freshness_check_interval specify how often in seconds the Nagios server will check the freshness of check results.

In our host and service definitions are three relevant directives: check_freshness, freshness_threshold, and check_command. The first directive, check_freshness, needs to be set to 1 for all hosts and services for which freshness checking is enabled. The freshness_threshold specifies the time period in seconds for which a check result is fresh. Any longer than this time period, and the check result will be declared stale. The freshness check will then be executed. This takes the form of the Nagios server executing the command contained in the check_command directive. On the following lines, I've specified an example service that uses freshness checking:

```
define service{
            host_name                owlet
            service_description      http
            active_checks_enabled    0
            passive_checks_enabled   1
            check_freshness          1
            freshness_threshold      300
            check_command            check_http
            ...
            }
```

In the previous service, the http service on the owlet host will not be actively checked. Instead, Nagios will rely on passive service check results to update the status of the service. Freshness checking is also enabled, and if the last passive check results are older than 300 seconds (5 minutes), Nagios will execute an active service check using the command check_http.

This model is fine if your central server is able to actually see the distributed hosts and services in your environment. But what if, as is common, one of the reasons you are using distributed monitoring is that you don't have network visibility of the host or service being checked? This means that, if you execute the check_http command and the Nagios server can't see the service, the check will time out. This response is of little value to us.

So what can you do to get a notification that there is potentially a problem with this service? Well, instead of using a check command that requires visibility of the host or service, configure a command that returns a status code and an error message just like a normal plug-in. Let's look at an example. In the following lines, I've defined a command called check_stale:

```
define command{
            command_name    check_stale
            command_line    $USER1$/check_dummy $ARG1$ $ARG2$
            }
```

The check_stale command uses a special plug-in called check_dummy, which comes with the Nagios plug-in package. The check_dummy plug-in returns a status and some optional text based on what is submitted to the $ARG1$ and $ARG2$ macros. On the next line, I've defined a potential check_command directive that would use this check_stale command:

```
define service{
        ….
        check_command          check_stale!2!'This service is stale'
        …
        }
```

The check_stale command has two arguments, 2 and the text 'This service is stale'. The 2 represents the return code for the status we wish the check_dummy plug-in to return (I discussed these numeric representations of service status in Table 8-3). The text 'This service is stale' represents the output we want from the plug-in. The check_dummy plug-in then returns the status of the service, based on us submitting the value 2, as CRITICAL and as the output of the plug-in as the text 'This service is stale'. As the check result is CRITICAL, the service would change into the CRITICAL status and generally, if configured, a notification would be generated. The service is then in a notification cycle until the problem is acknowledged or a more recent passive check result is received that changes the status of the service to an OK status.

Tip You could also write a script to produce the same results. You'll find an example of this way of handling this situation in the Nagios documentation at http://nagios.sourceforge.net/docs/2_0/freshness.html.

Central Servers Final Steps

Once we've defined the required directives in the nagios.cfg configuration file, configured the NSCA daemon, and duplicated the services and hosts defined on the distributed server (potentially editing them to configure how active checks and freshness are handled), we've completed the configuration of the central server. The central server should now be configured to receive the results of services and hosts from the distributed server or servers. Let's quickly walk through the process of sending and receiving a service check to ensure we understand what is happening:

1. The distributed server executes a service check (or a host check).

2. After the check is completed, the command defined in either the ocsp_command or ochp_command directive executes (depending on whether it is a service or host check, respectively).

3. The command pipes the results of the check results to the send_nsca program.

4. The send_nsca command sends the check results to the central server.

5. The NSCA daemon on the central server receives the check results and verifies the password and encryption method are valid. If they are not, the result is discarded.

6. The check result is submitted to the external command file.

7. The check result is processed and the status of the host or service is updated.

Your distributed monitoring configuration is now complete and you should be able to begin monitoring your hosts and services.

KEEPING YOUR CONFIGURATION SYNCRONIZED

In all the models I've described in this chapter, you generally need to keep your object definitions either exactly, or in the case of the distributed model, approximately synchronized between multiple Nagios servers. There are a number of ways to do this. I recommend you look at several potential tools. These range from standard Unix applications such as `rsync` to file replication tools such as Unison (`www.cis.upenn.edu/~bcpierce/unison/`) or cfengine (`www.cfengine.org/`).

I recommend that the two key attributes of any solution you chose be speed and security. This is especially true if you need to conduct file-synchronization activities over an Internet connection. Focus on a solution that will quickly and accurately replicate the required configuration files. A solution may potentially be required to only partially replicate a file or make more selective changes in the style of `diff` or `sdiff` where differences exist in the directives defined between central and distributed servers or master and slave servers. You should also consider a solution that allows you to tunnel or encrypt your file replication. This could consist of a scripted replication using a tool like `sftp` or another form of replication encapsulated in an SSL tunnel such as a Stunnel or HTTPS tunnel. Some of the available tools like Unison can be tunneled via `ssh`.

Redundancy and Failover

With Nagios there are two recommended methods for providing redundancy and failover. The first method is simple but, as a result of that simplicity, only protects against a limited type of failures. In this first method, you have two Nagios servers: one a master and one a slave. Both servers actively monitor the same hosts and services, but only the master server sends out notifications for any events on your hosts and services. In the event that master server is down or the Nagios process on the master server fails, the slave server takes over sending notifications. This is called redundant monitoring.

There are issues with this method, though. Principally, it doubles the bandwidth and performance requirements for your monitoring by duplicating your check processes across two servers. This is a rather inelegant way to provide this redundancy and resilience.

To address this issue, another method of implementation is possible. In this method, there is also a master and a slave server. The master server actively monitors all the hosts and services. The slave server contains an identical set of host and services definitions to the master server. But, unlike the redundant solution, the slave server does not actively monitor the hosts and services. Indeed, active checks and notifications are disabled on the slave server. Instead, using the NRPE tool, the slave server monitors the status of the Nagios process on the master server. If the slave server detects that the master server Nagios process has failed, it takes over the monitoring. Active checks and notifications are enabled using external commands, and the slave server takes over from the master server.

Of course, this means that the slave server does not have the current status of all the hosts and services being monitored. To overcome this, you must also configure host and service obsession on the master server and use the NSCA tool to send the check results to the slave server. This method of implementation is called failover monitoring.

You can see a high-level diagram of a failover monitoring model in Figure 8-2.

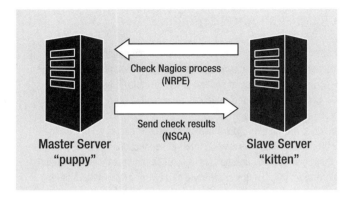

Figure 8-2. *Failover monitoring model*

This second method of implementation is far more elegant and allows considerably more flexible and less resource-intensive failover between Nagios servers. Therefore, I'll only cover this method of failover in this chapter.

■**Note** If you are interested in implementing the first method of redundancy, many of the same steps described in this section are also required. You can see more by reading the Nagios documentation at http://nagios.sourceforge.net/docs/2_0/redundancy.html.

Configuring the Master Server

So where do we start? Well, first we need to configure our master server. I set up a normal Nagios server, generally including the web console. I configured all the required hosts and services that I wish to monitor. I also enabled active checks of all these hosts and services and configured any required notifications.

This process involves turning on active host and service checking using the `execute_service_checks` and `execute_host_checks` directives in the `nagios.cfg` configuration file. Setting these both to 1 will ensure the master server executes service checks:

```
execute_service_checks=1
execute_host_checks=1
```

You should also enable notifications using the `enable_notifications` directive like so:

```
enable_notifications=1
```

Configuring the NRPE Daemon

Next you need to configure the nrpe daemon on the master server to allow the slave server to check the status of the Nagios process.[7] Let's quickly step through installing the nrpe daemon on the master server. Download the nrpe daemon and unpack it like so:

```
puppy# wget http://prdownloads.sourceforge.net/nagios/nrpe-2.0.tar.gz
puppy# tar -zxf nrpe-2.0.tar.gz
puppy# cd nrpe-2.0
```

To run the nrpe daemon on the master, you need a user and group. I recommend you use the same user and group that the Nagios process runs as, in our example the user and group nagios. Otherwise, you can create a user and group for the nrpe daemon.

We can run the configure script for the nrpe daemon like so:

```
puppy# ./configure --enable-ssl
```

Using the --enable-ssl configure option, we configured native SSL/TSL support. This will be used to encrypt and secure the connections between the master and slave servers. You will need to have OpenSSL installed for this functionality to be enabled.[8] I strongly recommend for security reasons you enable this functionality. If you do not enable it, an intruder could either eavesdrop or subvert the connections between your Nagios server and the remote host.

Next I recommend you use a host firewall and lock down the source and destination of all traffic on port 5666 (or the port you intend to use for NRPE). Let's look at a quick example using iptables:

```
puppy# iptables -A INPUT -p tcp -m tcp --dport 5666 -s 10.0.0.15 -j ACCEPT
puppy# iptables -A OUTPUT -p tcp -m tcp --sport 5666 -d 10.0.0.15 -j ACCEPT
```

On these lines I've locked down the NRPE traffic entering and leaving the remote host on port 5666 to only that traffic from and destined to host 10.0.0.15. This means that the slave server at 10.0.0.15 is the only host on our network that can send the puppy host NRPE traffic. You can obviously vary this to suit your environment.

Once you have configured the NRPE package, you need to make it:

```
puppy# make
```

The NRPE package does not have an automatic installation script. Once the make process is complete, you will need to manually install the required files. I normally copy the nrpe daemon binary into the /usr/local/nagios/bin directory. As you can see on the following line, the nrpe daemon is created in the src directory in the NRPE package:

```
puppy# cp src/nrpe /usr/local/nagios/bin
```

I also copy the nrpe.cfg configuration file. It is created in the root directory of the NRPE package. I usually place this in the /usr/local/nagios/etc directory:

```
puppy# cp nrpe.cfg /usr/local/nagios/etc
```

---

7. I discussed the nrpe daemon in Chapter 5.

8. You'll need at least version OpenSSL 0.9.7a or a more recent version.

In order for the nrpe daemon to work, you also need to change the ownership of the nrpe.cfg configuration file to the user and group that is running the nrpe daemon. This allows the daemon to read the file. I'll do this on the following line:

```
puppy# chown nagios:nagios /usr/local/nagios/etc/nrpe.cfg
```

You should change its ownership to the user and group you have specified that nrpe should run as, in our case nagios and nagios.

We also need one plug-in, the check_nagios plug-in, to allow the slave server to perform checks of the Nagios process on the master server to detect when it stops. This plug-in is installed as part of the standard Nagios plug-in package.

Next we need to configure the nrpe.cfg file. Example 8-11 shows a typical nrpe.cfg configuration file.

Example 8-11. *Master Server nrpe.cfg Configuration File*

```
server_port=5666
server_address=10.0.0.1
allowed_hosts=127.0.0.1,10.0.0.15
nrpe_user=nagios
nrpe_group=nagios
dont_blame_nrpe=0
debug=0
command_timeout=60
command[check_nagios]=/usr/local/nagios/libexec/check_nagios ➥
-e 1 -F /usr/local/nagios/var/nagios.log -C /usr/local/nagios/bin/nagios
```

Let's look at each of the options in Example 8-11. The first two options, server_port and server_address, allow you to specify the port and address the nrpe daemon will listen on. This defaults to all interfaces on port 5666.

The next option, allowed_hosts, specifies the IP addresses that are allowed to contact the nrpe daemon and transmit command requests. The loopback address, 127.0.0.1, is included by default, and you need to specify the IP addresses of the slave server that needs to be able to connect to the nrpe daemon. You should use commas to separate the IP addresses you're specifying.

The next two options specify the user and group that the nrpe daemon will run as. In this case I've used nagios and nagios.

The dont_blame_nrpe option is used to allow checks via NRPE to be submitted with arguments. For checks of the Nagios process, I don't require that arguments be allowed so I've set this option to 0.

The command_timeout is the period of time NRPE waits to see if a command completes before failing. The default of 60 seconds should be sufficient for most purposes.

The last option is the command option, which allows you to specify commands that the nrpe daemon will execute. For checks of the Nagios process from the slave server, I only require one command that executes the check_nagios plug-in. Let's quickly look at how that plug-in works. The check_nagios plug-in checks two variables: whether the Nagios process is active and running and the age of the status log file, nagios.log. You can see a command-line execution of the plug-in in Example 8-12.

Example 8-12. *Command-Line Execution of the check_nagios Plug-in*

```
puppy# /usr/local/nagios/libexec/check_nagios -e 1 -F ➥
/usr/local/nagios/var/nagios.log -C /usr/local/nagios/bin/nagios
Nagios ok: located 1 process, status log updated 3 seconds ago
```

The first option, -e, specifies after what period in minutes the age of the log file is considered stale. I've specified 1 minute. The second option, -F, tells the plug-in the location of the nagios.log log file. By default this is /usr/local/nagios/var/nagios.log. The last option, -C, specifies the location of the Nagios binary. By default this would be /usr/local/nagios/bin/nagios.

As you can see from the command-line execution in Example 8-12, it returns a status message saying Nagios is running and reports the age of the nagios.log status log file in terms of its last update. If the Nagios process was not running, it would return the following error message:

```
Could not locate a running Nagios process!
```

When I'll configure the slave server I'll use the results of this plug-in check to configure the slave server to take over from the master. I'll also discuss further how I might configure the check_nagios plug-in.

Finally, we need to decide how the nrpe daemon will run. Running the nrpe daemon locally is a simple process and you can see on the following line:

```
puppy# /ustr/local/nagios/bin/nrpe -c /usr/local/nagios/etc/nrpe.cfg -d
Aug 10 21:07:37 puppy nrpe[18728]: Starting up daemon
```

On the previous lines, you can see I've specified two options to the nrpe daemon: -c and -d. The -c option specifies the location of the nrpe.cfg configuration file. The -d option tells the nrpe daemon to run as a stand-alone daemon.

■**Tip** Also contained in the root directory of the NRPE source package are a series of init files for a number of different platforms. You can use these to automatically start, stop or restart the nrpe daemon. I recommend you use these init scripts for the nrpe daemon.

Configuring NSCA

Once the nrpe daemon is configured and running, we need to configure service obsession and NSCA to send passive check results to the slave server. To do this, follow the steps in the "Distributed Server Configuration" section earlier in this chapter. The master server performs the same function as a distributed server sending the check results, but instead of sending to a central server, it sends to the slave server. The slave server thus acts as the central server in the distributed monitoring model.

■**Tip** So what if you need to send results both as a distributed server and to a redundant or failover server? Well, there is nothing to stop you from configuring host and service obsession to run a shell script that sends the check results to two servers instead of just one.

Configuring the Slave Server

To configure the slave server, you need to install Nagios much like you installed it on the master server. I also recommend installing the web console as the slave server might have to take over monitoring of your environment. You configure all the required hosts and services that the master server is monitoring. You also disable active checks of all these hosts and services and notifications.

This means you should disable active host and service checking using the execute_service_checks and execute_host_checks directives in the nagios.cfg configuration file. Setting these both to 0 will ensure the slave server does not execute host and service checks.

```
execute_service_checks=0
execute_host_checks=0
```

You should also disenable notifications using the enable_notifications directive like so:

```
enable_notifications=0
```

You also need to ensure you have a few directives in the nagios.cfg configuration file turned on. The following list of directives should be set to 1:

```
accept_passive_service_checks=1
accept_passive_host_checks=1
check_external_commands=1
```

This ensures that the slave server will receive passive host and service checks using NSCA to check the status of the hosts and services being monitored. It also means that external commands will be checked, which will be important when I demonstrate how to monitor for and initiate the failover process.

Configuring NRPE

On the slave server let's use the check_nrpe plug-in to connect to the master server and check the status of the Nagios server process. This will allow the slave server to determine when it should take over monitoring of the environment. The first step in doing this is installing NRPE. Rather than the nrpe daemon that we required for the master server, let's only require the check_nrpe plug-in.

Let's quickly step through installing the check_nrpe plug-in on the slave server. Download the NRPE package and unpack it like so:

```
kitten# wget http://prdownloads.sourceforge.net/nagios/nrpe-2.0.tar.gz
kitten# tar -zxf nrpe-2.0.tar.gz
kitten# cd nrpe-2.0
```

Then run the `configure` script for the NRPE package like so:

```
kitten# ./configure --enable-ssl
```

As you can see, using the `--enable-ssl` `configure` option I've enabled native SSL/TSL support as I have on the master server. You must enable this option on both the master and slave servers if you wish to use SSL connections between them. As with the master server, you must also have OpenSSL installed on the slave server.[9]

After compilation you need to install the `check_nrpe` plug-in, located in the `src` directory of the NRPE package, into your plug-in directory. I've done this on the following line:

```
kitten# cp src/check_nrpe /usr/local/nagios/libexec
```

The `check_nrpe` plug-in executes commands defined in the `nrpe.cfg` configuration file on the master server. It does this by connecting to the `nrpe` daemon on TCP port 5666. In Example 8-11 I've defined a sample `nrpe.cfg` configuration file with the following command in it:

```
command[check_nagios]=/usr/local/nagios/libexec/check_nagios -e 1 -F ➡
 /usr/local/nagios/var/nagios.log -C /usr/local/nagios/bin/nagios
```

The `nrpe` daemon on the master server executes the `check_nagios` plug-in and returns the results of that check to the `check_nrpe` plug-in on the slave server. On the following lines, you can see this same check executed from the command line of the slave server:

```
kitten# ./check_nrpe -H 10.0.0.1 -c check_nagios
Nagios ok: located 1 process, status log updated 9 seconds ago
```

So how do we use this check to allow the slave server to determine when it should take over monitoring? I usually enclose this check into a shell script, monitor the exit status of the check, and initiate the failover process depending on the exit status. I then execute the script in a `cron` job. I've included the typical script I use in Example 8-13.

Example 8-13. *Nagios Process Monitor Script*

```
#!/bin/sh

cmd_file=/usr/local/nagios/var/rw/nagios.cmd

/usr/local/nagios/libexec/check_nrpe -H 10.0.0.1 -c check_nagios
return_code=$?

case "$return_code" in
        '0')
            TIME=`date +%s`
            echo "[$TIME] STOP_EXECUTING_SVC_CHECKS" >> $cmd_file
            echo "[$TIME] STOP_EXECUTING_HOST_CHECKS" >> $cmd_file
            echo "[$TIME] DISABLE_NOTIFICATIONS" >> $cmd_file
```

---

9. Again, you'll need at least version OpenSSL 0.9.7a or a more recent version.

```
        ;;
        '2')
        TIME=`date +%s`
        echo "[$TIME] START_EXECUTING_SVC_CHECKS" >> $cmd_file
        echo "[$TIME] START_EXECUTING_HOST_CHECKS" >> $cmd_file
        echo "[$TIME] ENABLE_NOTIFICATIONS" >> $cmd_file
        ;;
esac
exit 0
```

You can see in Example 8-13 that this is a very simple script. First, I define the location of the external command file, to which I am going to submit the commands that will trigger the failover process. In my default Nagios installation, this file is /usr/local/nagios/var/rw/ nagios.cmd. Next, I execute the check of the Nagios process using the check_nrpe plug-in. This plug-in will return a standard Unix exit status, and I assign that status to a variable called return_code. I then use a case statement to evaluate the exit status and perform actions based on its value.

If the script returns an exit status of 0, this indicates that the Nagios process is functioning and that the master server remains the active and primary server. This status triggers the submission of three external commands: STOP_EXECUTING_SVC_CHECKS, STOP_EXECUTING_HOST_ CHECKS, and DISABLE_NOTIFICATIONS.[10] These commands stop active service and host checks and disable notifications on the slave server.

The submission of these commands has two purposes. They are first a safety net to ensure that the slave server does not accidentally have active checks or notifications enabled. If this occurs when the master server is still available, these commands will disable those functions. Second, this creates an automated process of reversing the failover process. If the master server becomes available again, the slave server will stop active checks and notifications.

This is not a perfect model for reverting from the failed-over state. This is because if a failover has been initiated, the process of recovering the failover can be quite complicated. First, depending on how long the slave server took over from the master server, the check results on the master server may be out of date. The master server will also not know about any notifications generated, any performance or statistical data you are collecting, or the like. For example, there will be gaps in your availability reporting on the master server. Unfortunately, little can be done to alleviate these issues.

The next case statement is initiated when the exit status of the check is 2. This indicates that the Nagios process is not running, or that the check has failed or cannot be completed. In this case, three different external commands are submitted: START_EXECUTING_SVC_CHECKS, START_EXECUTING_HOST_CHECKS, and ENABLE_NOTIFICATIONS. These commands initiate the failover process and tell the slave server to take over active checks and notifications from the master server.

We then configure this shell script to be executed by the cron daemon on a regular basis. I recommend an interval of 1 to 5 minutes depending on how often you wish to check the status of your master server.

```
0-59/5 * * * * /usr/local/nagios/libexec/test_failover >/dev/null 2>&1
```

---

10. I discussed how to manually submit external commands in Chapter 7.

On the previous line you can see a `crontab` entry for a check at five-minute intervals (the `>/dev/null 2>&1` makes the `cron` job quiet and prevents the output from being generated).

Tip Remember, if you have a scheduled outage on your master server such as a reboot and it occurs during a check of the master service by the slave server, your slave server will take over monitoring. You may wish to disable checking of the master server during scheduled downtime.

Installing NSCA

Next we need to install the NSCA daemon to receive the passive check results from the master server. To do this follow the steps in the "Installing the NSCA Daemon" and "Configuring the NSCA Daemon" sections earlier in this chapter. You should also consider enabling freshness checking, as discussed in the "Distributed Monitoring and Freshness" section, to ensure the status information of your hosts and services is up to date.

Failover Process

Once you've set up both the master and slave servers, you should now have a functioning failover solution. Just to remind you how this will work, let's step through the process and interaction that occurs between the master and slave:

1. The master server monitors all the required hosts and services.

2. The master server uses host and service obsession and the `send_nsca` plug-in to send the results of checks to the slave server.

3. The slave server performs no checks itself but receives the results of the checks conducted on the master server using the NSCA daemon and applies these check results as passive host or service checks. This ensures the slave server has up-to-date status information for your hosts and services.

4. The slave server checks the status of the Nagios process using the `check_nrpe` plug-in. It connects to the `nrpe` daemon on the master server, executes the `check_nagios` plug-in, and returns the status of the Nagios process.

5. If the slave server receives an `OK` check result from the `check_nagios` plug-in on the master server, it submits external commands on the slave server disabling active checks and notifications. Checks of the Nagios process continue normally.

6. If the slave server receives a non-`OK` check result from the `check_nagios` plug-in on the master server, it assumes the server is unavailable. The process then submits external commands on the slave server enabling active checks and notifications. This indicates that the master server has failed over to the slave server.

7. If the master server becomes available again, the process will reverse the failover and the master server will become the active monitoring and notifying server. The slave server will return to the stand-by mode.

Checkpoint

- If you are using NSCA or NRPE, enable encryption to ensure that your communications are not compromised or intercepted, and that malicious commands are not submitted to your Nagios servers.

- If you are using distributed monitoring, consider adding freshness checking on your central server to ensure that your passive check results are up-to-date and accurate.

- You will need to keep your configurations objects synchronized between your Nagios servers. For both distributed monitoring and failover, the Nagios servers involved must have the appropriate object definitions defined on them.

- Be aware that if you fail over to your slave server any monitoring done by that server, notifications generated, or statistics gathered will not be replicated on the master server. Additionally, if there is a long period of failover, when your master server takes over again it might take some time for that server to check all the hosts and services and become up-to-date.

Resources

These are a list of sites that I have referred to in this chapter as well as other sites where you can seek further information.

Sites

- NSCA: www.nagiosexchange.org/Communication.41.0.html?&tx_netnagext_pi1[p_view]=140

- NSCA RPM: http://dries.studentenweb.org/rpm/packages/nagios-nsca/info.html

- MCrypt: http://mcrypt.sourceforge.net/

- MCrypt RPMs: www.ottolander.nl/opensource/mcrypt/mcrypt.html or http://dag.wieers.com/packages/libmcrypt/

CHAPTER 9

■■■

Integrating Nagios

Nagios is an excellent enterprise-monitoring tool, but it is not capable of doing everything you might require to monitor, report, and manage your environment. To enhance Nagios, you can easily integrate it with a number of other applications and tools that will assist in providing additional functionality or enhancing functionality areas in which Nagios is weak.

In this chapter, I look at integrating Nagios with a variety of tools. This includes sending syslog messages from syslog-NG to Nagios and how to configure Nagios to handle these incoming messages. I will also look at integrating Snort alerts into Nagios using similar methods to those used with syslog-NG.

I also look at retrieving data from MRTG, both from MRTG log files and RRD databases, and testing it against thresholds. The results of this testing can be submitted to Nagios as check results for services. The tool used to retrieve data from RRD databases will also allow you to query data from a number of other tools that use RRD as a backend, such as Cacti, Cricket, Munin, and Big Sister.[1]

Finally, this chapter contains a detailed explanation of how Nagios can interact with SNMP traps and notifications. I demonstrate how to receive SNMP traps from SNMP agents, including how to translate the traps into a more readable form using the SNMPTT tool. I also look at how to send SNMP traps from Nagios to an SNMP management station such as HP OpenView or similar products.

syslog-NG and Nagios

One of the more useful tools to integrate Nagios with are `syslog` daemons. This daemon allows you to send `syslog` messages from your hosts to your Nagios server. From your Nagios server, these messages can generate notifications or utilize other Nagios functions and capabilities. In this section, I'll look at how to integrate syslog-NG, a replacement for the default `syslog` daemon, with your Nagios server.

The syslog-NG daemon is an advanced replacement for the default `syslog` daemon that allows more control over where and how your `syslog` messages are processed. syslog-NG allows for more sophisticated message filtering, manipulation, and interaction. syslog-NG is freeware developed by Balazs Scheidler and is available from `www.balabit.com/products/syslog_ng/`.

By combining syslog-NG and Nagios, you can direct some or all of your `syslog` messages from syslog-NG to Nagios. This is achieved by sending `syslog` messages from syslog-NG into

---

1. You can see a list of tools that use RRD at `http://people.ee.ethz.ch/~oetiker/webtools/rrdtool/rrdworld/index.en.html`.

a named pipe and then processing this named pipe. Named pipes are a standard output destination for syslog-NG when sending `syslog` messages. The named pipe can then be processed
by a script on a regular basis to send the results to the Nagios server. In this integration example, I use a script that utilizes the `send_nsca` tool to send the check results to an NSCA daemon
running on your Nagios server and from there into the Nagios server to update the status of
hosts and services.[2]

In the process of sending the `syslog` messages, you can process each `syslog` message to
convert them all into Nagios check results. This will include assigning them to particular hosts
and services and setting a service status for each message, such as setting particular messages
to a service status of CRITICAL and others to WARNING or OK depending on how you wish the
message to be handled. The check result is then submitted for a host and service that you have
defined. The service can be configured to notify on messages according to your requirements
or utilize other Nagios capabilities such as escalation or event handlers.

■**Tip** Using this method, you can also forward `syslog` messages generated by a number of tools to
Nagios. Simply use syslog-NG's filtering capabilities to direct the particular `syslog` messages to Nagios
and a service or services defined for that tool.

Installing the Remote Host

In this section I'll quickly demonstrate how to install and start syslog-NG and NSCA on your
remote hosts. I'll then configure syslog-NG to process `syslog` messages and forward them to
a named pipe. I'll also show an example of a shell script to process this named pipe and use
the `send_nsca` tool to send the check results to Nagios.

Installing syslog-NG

First, let's quickly run through installing syslog-NG. You will need to install syslog-NG on all
of the hosts you wish to send `syslog` messages from. Start by downloading the current versions of syslog-NG and libol (an additional library required for installing syslog-NG) from
`www.balabit.com/products/syslog_ng/upgrades.bbq`. You'll need to build the libol package
first, so unpack the tar file you have downloaded and compile the libol package:

```
puppy# ./configure && make && make install
```

■**Tip** If you don't wish to install libol, you can omit the `make install` and when you configure syslog-NG
you need to tell it where to find libol using `./configure —with-libol=/path/to/libol`.

---

2. I introduced NSCA in Chapter 8 when I used it to send check results to a Nagios server.

Now unpack syslog-NG and enter the syslog-NG directory and configure the package:

```
kitten# ./configure
```

By default, syslog-NG is installed to /usr/local/sbin, but you can override this using

```
kitten# ./configure –prefix=/new/directory/here
```

Also by default, syslog-NG looks for its `conf` file in /usr/local/etc/syslog-ng.conf. You can override this also. We recommend using /etc/syslog-ng as the configuration directory, and you can set this using the `configure` option shown here:

```
kitten# ./configure –sysconfdir=/etc/
```

Then `make` and install syslog-NG:

```
kitten# make && make install
```

This will create a binary called `syslog-ng` and install it either to the /usr/local/sbin/ directory or to whatever directory you have specified if you have overridden it with the –prefix option.

Running syslog-NG

Once you have installed syslog-NG, you need to replace your existing `syslog` daemon and set syslog-NG to start automatically when your system starts. This involves stopping and removing the startup of your existing `syslog` daemon and replacing it with the syslog-NG daemon.

The syslog-NG package comes with a number of sample `init` scripts that you should be able to adapt for your system. Use one of these and set up syslog-NG to start when you boot up.

The Syslog-NG daemon has some command-line options, as you can see in Table 9-1.

Table 9-1. *Syslog-NG Command-Line Options*

Flag	Purpose
-d	Enable debug.
-v	Verbose mode—syslog-NG will not daemonize.
-s	Don't start; just parse the configuration file for incorrect syntax.
-f /path/to/conf/file	Tell syslog-NG where the `conf` file is located.

The first options, -d and –v, are useful to debug syslog-NG. In the case of -v, syslog-NG will start and output its logging messages to the screen and will not fork into the background. The -d adds some additional debugging messages. The next option, -s, or –syntax-only, does not start syslog-NG but merely parses through the syslog-ng.conf file and checks for errors. If it finds any errors, it'll dump them to the screen and exit. If it exits without an error, your syslog-ng.conf has perfect syntax!

Before you can start, you need to create or modify a configuration file. The syslog-ng.conf configuration file contains considerably more options than the traditional syslog.conf file. I recommend you make use of the sample syslog-ng.conf file.

■**Tip** I won't go in detail about how to configure syslog-NG. You can find further information on configuring it at www.balabit.com/products/syslog_ng/reference-2.0/syslog-ng.html/index.html and www.campin.net/syslog-ng/faq.html.

When it starts, syslog-NG looks for /usr/local/etc/syslog-ng.conf as the default configuration file unless you overrode that as part of the ./configure process. I recommend you create your configuration file in /etc/syslog-ng. You can also override the location of the syslog-ng.conf configuration file using the -f option.

Every time you change your syslog-ng.conf file, you need to restart the syslog-NG daemon. Use the provided init script to do this using the reload option. For example, on a Red Hat system you can reload the configuration like so:

```
kitten# /etc/rc.d/init.d/syslog-ng reload
```

Configuring syslog-NG for Nagios

Next you need to configure syslog-NG to forward syslog messages to a named pipe. To do this, you have to define four types of syslog-NG statements. The first is the source of the syslog messages. This can include the local host or messages received via a TCP or UDP connection. You can see a number of potential source statements in the sample syslog-ng.conf configuration file that comes with the package. The next statements are filters, which select the messages to be processed, and destinations, which specify where and how these messages are processed and written to. It is in our destination statements that the conversion from syslog message to Nagios check result will take place using a series of templates. Finally, you need to define log statements, which combine sources, filters, and destinations to log particular messages. For example, select all crit priority messages from the mail facility sourced from the local host using a filter and then send them to a specified named pipe defined in a destination.

■**Note** I don't explicitly define source statements in this section. These depend on your particular host. Refer to the syslog-NG documentation and the sample configuration files to see potential source statements.

One of the objectives of sending the messages is to send them to different services and with a different status depending on their criticality or how you wish Nagios to action them. To do this, you can construct a series of filters that allow you to classify certain messages. You can create filters in a number of ways. You can filter messages by host, priority, facility, the process or program that generated the message, the content of the message itself, or any combination of these variables. Example 9-1 shows three filters.

Example 9-1. *syslog-NG Filters*

```
filter f_mailcrit { level(crit) and facility(mail); };
filter f_namedcrit { level(crit) and program(named); };
filter f_warn { level(warn); };
```

The first filter selects all messages of crit priority from the mail facility. The second selects all crit priority messages from the named program. The last filter selects all messages of the warn priority. You can read about how to construct filters in more detail at www.balabit.com/products/syslog_ng/reference-2.0/syslog-ng.html/index.html#id2526069.

Tip Most syslog daemons generate a lot of messages; therefore, filters are very important. You risk being overloaded with messages unless you carefully use filters to see only those messages you require.

You also need to define a series of destinations for the messages you wish to select, all of which will point to a named pipe. As part of these destinations, a template for how the message will be written to the named pipe will be specified. This template allows you to process the message into the form of a check result that the NSCA daemon will be able to read and the Nagios server will be able to process. You can see these definitions in Example 9-2.

Example 9-2. *syslog-NG Destinations*

```
destination d_facility_crit {
pipe("/var/run/nagios.pipe"
template("$HOST,$FACILITY,2,'$MSG'\n") template_escape(no));
};

destination d_program_crit {
pipe("/var/run/nagios.pipe"
template("$HOST,'$PROGRAM',2,'$MSG'\n") template_escape(no));
};

destination d_nagios_warn {
pipe("/var/run/nagios.pipe"
template("$HOST,syslog-warnings,1,'$MSG'\n") template_escape(no));
};
```

I've defined three destinations. The first destination, d_facility_crit, writes to a named pipe called nagios.pipe in the /var/run/ directory. It writes messages to that pipe in the form of a template. This template converts the message into a form the NSCA daemon will accept as a submitted check result for a service. The NSCA daemon requires the following information: hostname, service, service status response code, and the actual output of the check. Normally for submission to the NSCA daemon each item should be separated by tab characters. But we're going to override this use of the tab character later when we configure the process of sending messages to the NSCA daemon and use commas to separate the items instead. This replacement makes handling the output easier.

Note The template string is enclosed in quotation marks. Some of the items inside these quotation marks are enclosed in single quotes for reasons that I'll discuss in a moment.

The first template in Example 9-2 starts by specifying the host, represented by the $HOST macro, and the facility using the $FACILTY macro. Both macros are available from the syslog-NG package that contains data from the syslog messages.

■**Tip** You can read about all the syslog-NG macros at www.balabit.com/products/syslog_ng/ reference-2.0/syslog-ng.html/index.html#macros.

In this case the $HOST and $FACILITY macros will be used as the value of the hostname and service description's of the Nagios objects that will receive the syslog messages. For the check result to be usable, you'll therefore need to create host and service objects for each host and facility combination you wish to process messages for. In this case we would need to create a host object for the host that generated the message and a service for each facility that we wish to process messages for. For example, if the host puppy was the source of the messages and we were using a filter to only select messages from the mail facility, we would need a host object for the puppy host and a service object called mail for the mail facility. I'll look at this in more detail when we configure the Nagios server to receive the messages.

The template then specifies the number 2, which represents the service status response code to be passed to the Nagios server. The 2 represents the CRITICAL status (0 represents OK, 1 represents WARNING, and 3 represents UNKNOWN). I've hard-coded this response code into the destination. Any message sent via NSCA to Nagios using this destination will be received as a service check result with a status of CRITICAL.

Lastly, the template contains another syslog-NG macro, $MSG, that represents the content of the syslog message being sent to Nagios and which will be passed as the output of the check result. I've enclosed the $MSG macro within single quotation marks as it generally will be a multiword data item and may include spaces and other characters that could be interpreted by the shell or the NSCA sending process. The enclosure in quotation marks allows the whole message to be passed without the risk of it being interpreted. You should generally enclose any items that might suffer this issue in single quotation marks.

■**Note** The last character in the template, \n, inserts a new line after the output. You should do this for all outputted data.

Finally, the template also has an option called template_escape that in all the destinations in Example 9-2 is set to no. This turns off syslog-NG's default escaping mechanism and protects the quotation marks we've used to enclose some items from being escaped.

The next two destinations, d_program_crit and d_nagios_warn, are similar to the first destination in that they both write to the same named pipe. They have different templates, though. The first destination, d_program_crit, is nearly identical to the d_facility_crit destination except that instead of using the $FACILITY macro it uses the $PROGRAM macro. The $PROGRAM macro represents the name of the program or process that generated the syslog message. For example, using this macro you could filter for all messages generated by a particular process,

such as sendmail or named. This would mean the Nagios server would need to have object definitions for the host generating the message and service objects for any program that you
wished to send messages for.

■**Note** I've enclosed the $PROGRAM macro in single quotes as it occasionally contains multiword data.

This template also hard-codes the service status of 2 for CRITICAL into it. Any message
passed through NSCA to the Nagios server using this destination will thus be received as
a CRITICAL status check result.

The last template, d_nagios_warn, is more generic. It passes the hostname of the host
generating the message with the $HOST macro and hard-codes a service name,
syslog-warnings, into the template. It also hard-codes a service status response code of 1,
representing the WARNING status, into the template. This will pass messages to the Nagios server
as check results in WARNING status for a service called syslog-warnings. You will need to define
a host object for each host generating these messages and a service object called
syslog-warnings for that host.

The syslog-NG daemon will not automatically create the required named pipe, so you will
need to use the mkfifo command to create the pipe like so:

```
puppy# mkfifo /var/run/nagios.pipe
```

Here I've chosen to locate the pipe in the /var/run directory. You can locate the pipe
wherever it suits your environment. You also need to change the ownership of the pipe so that
the user that will read the pipe can access it. I generally do this using the user and group running the Nagios process for this purpose. In my case, I am changing the user and group of the
pipe to nagios and nagios.

```
puppy# chown nagios:nagios /var/run/nagios.pipe
```

Finally, I need to specify log statements that combine the source, filter, and destination
statements to log the actual messages. In Example 9-3 I've specified three log statements.

Example 9-3. *syslog-NG Log Statements*

```
log { source(local); filter(f_mailcrit); destination(d_facility_crit); };
log { source(local); filter(f_namedcrit); destination(d_program_crit); };
log { source(local); filter(f_warn); destination(d_nagios_warn); };
```

The first log statement selects all messages from the local source (which I am assuming
here represents messages generated on your local host) that are of crit priority and generated
by the mail facility. It will then use the d_facility_crit destination to write them to the named
pipe. For example, if these messages were generated on the kitten host, it would write them
as a Nagios check result like so:

```
kitten,mail,2,'This is a syslog message'
```

where `kitten` is the host that generated the messages and `mail` is the service that Nagios will assign the check result to, 2 indicating that the check result is in the `CRITICAL` status and `This is a syslog message` being the output of the check result.

The second log statement will select all messages generated by the `named` program on the local host that are of `crit` priority and write them to the named pipe like so (again assuming the generating host is `kitten`):

```
kitten,'named',2,'This is a named message'
```

On this line the check result will be submitted for the `named` service running on the `kitten` host as a `CRITICAL` status check result with an output of `This is a named message`.

The last log statement is more general. It will log all messages of `warn` priority from the local host to the named pipe using a service called `syslog-warnings` as `WARNING` status check results. Messages written to the named pipe would look something like

```
kitten,syslog-warnings,1,'This is a warning message'
```

■**Caution** This is an extremely high-level introduction to syslog-NG configuration. I recommend reading the associated documentation and man pages for the package to gain a fuller understanding. I also discuss syslog-NG configuration in Chapter 5 of *Hardening Linux*.[3]

Installing and Configuring send_nsca

After installing and configuring syslog-NG, you must install the NSCA tool on the hosts that will send messages to the Nagios server. You will also need to install it on the Nagios server to receive the messages. I'll very quickly run through the installation of the `send_nsca` tool. You can refer to Chapter 8 for a more detailed explanation of how to do this.

The NSCA package has one prerequisite, the libmcrypt library. This is required to enable you to use encryption when sending data between the hosts sending `syslog` messages to the Nagios server. The libmcrypt library can be found at `http://mcrypt.sourceforge.net/` or you can download it as an RPM from either `www.ottolander.nl/opensource/mcrypt/mcrypt.html` or `http://dag.wieers.com/packages/libmcrypt/`.

The installation process for the libmcrypt library is very simple. Download the source package. Then configure it, `make`, and install it like so:

```
kitten# wget http://optusnet.dl.sourceforge.net/sourceforge/mcrypt/➥
libmcrypt-2.5.7.tar.gz
kitten# tar -zxf libmcrypt-2.5.7.tar.gz
kitten# cd libmcrypt-2.5.7
kitten# ./configure
kitten# make
kitten# make install
```

---

3. See `www.apress.com/book/bookDisplay.html?bID=395`.

Once you have libmcrypt installed, you can start the NSCA installation process. Download and unpack the package on your remote host like so:

```
kitten# wget http://optusnet.dl.sourceforge.net/sourceforge/nagios/nsca-2.4.tar.gz
kitten# tar -zxf nsca-2.4.tar.gz
```

Next change into the NSCA source package directory, and then configure the package using the configure script and make it:

```
kitten# ./configure
kitten# make all
```

Tip You can also find an RPM of the NCSA tool at http://dries.studentenweb.org/rpm/packages/ nagios-nsca/info.html.

When you want to install the NSCA tool, you need to manually install the required tool and configuration files. Install the send_nsca binary, which does the actual sending of the check results and is executed on the remote host. There is also a configuration file, send_nsca.cfg, located in the root of the NSCA package directory. I recommend you install the send_nsca binary to a directory such as /usr/local/bin. I suggest you place the send_nsca.cfg file in a directory such as /usr/local/etc.

Once you have installed NSCA, you need to configure it. Its configuration is held in the send_nsca.cfg configuration file; a sample configuration is shown in Example 9-4.

Example 9-4. *send_nsca.cfg Configuration File*

```
password=password
encryption_method=3
```

There are only two options in the send_nsca.cfg configuration file. The first option, password, specifies the password you will use to encrypt any data between the remote host and the Nagios server. You should replace the value *password* with a password of your choice. I recommend you chose a nondictionary word that includes special characters and is at least eight characters long. Remember this password as you will need to ensure it matches the password specified on your Nagios server in the NSCA daemon configuration.

The next option, encryption_method, specifies what form of encryption you will use to encrypt the transmission of your check results. I recommend using Triple DES (option 3). It is secure and is present on most distributions and systems. Remember this selection too, because the encryption chosen on the remote host needs to match the encryption method on the NSCA daemon on the Nagios server.

Once you've configured the send_nsca.cfg file, you need to secure that file's ownership and permissions. Example 9-5 shows you how.

Example 9-5. *Securing the send_nsca.cfg File*

```
kitten# chown nagios:nagios /usr/local/etc/send_nsca.cfg
kitten# chmod 0640 /usr/local/etc/send_nsca.cfg
```

You need to change the ownership of the configuration file to the user and group that will be sending the messages to the Nagios server. In our example, I've also changed the permissions of the file to 0640 to only allow the nagios user to read the file.

Sending the syslog-NG Messages

The syslog-NG tool will write the messages in the form of Nagios check results to a named pipe; for our example, I've specified a pipe called /var/run/nagios.pipe. From here we need to process the entries in the named pipe and send them using the send_nsca tool to the NSCA daemon on the Nagios server. We can do this using the simple shell script called syslog2nsca in Example 9-6.

Example 9-6. *syslog-NG to NSCA Script*

```
#!/bin/bash
while read line
  do
    /bin/echo "$line" | /usr/local/bin/send_nsca -H 10.0.0.31 ➥
    -c /usr/local/etc/send_nsca.cfg -d ","
  done < /var/run/nagios.pipe

exit 0
```

■**Tip** The shell script in Example 9.6 is very simple. You could greatly expand it to cater for a variety of different issues, such as checking for the existence of the named pipe or whether the syslog-NG daemon was running. But the core functionality to submit the check results is all that is required to actually get your syslog-NG and Nagios integration working.

The syslog2nsca shell script is very simple. It processes and reads the nagios.pipe named pipe in a do-while loop. The contents of the pipe are sent to the send_nsca command using the echo command. In the send_nsca command we've used the -d option to override the delimiter used to separate the check results being submitted. The normal delimiter is a tab character. But when designing the destination template in the syslog-NG configuration earlier in this chapter, we used a comma to separate the check results. The use of the -d "," option ensures that send_nsca will also use a comma.

Next you need to run this shell script to process the named pipe. You can execute the script from the command line like so:

```
kitten$ /usr/local/bin/syslog2nsca &
```

Or you can include the startup and shutdown of this script in your syslog-NG init script. I recommend this as the preferred method of execution.

Configuring the Nagios Server

On the Nagios server there are several configuration steps that need to take place. First, the NSCA daemon must be installed to receive the syslog messages in their check result form. You may already have the NSCA daemon installed but I'll quickly step through its configuration, and if required you can read about it in more detail in Chapter 8. Also needed are the Nagios host and service objects for the syslog messages being generated and received. The service objects to be defined will be configured to receive passive check results, perform no active checks themselves, and be set up as volatile services.

Installing and Configuring the NSCA Daemon

You will need to install the NSCA daemon. The NSCA daemon has the same prerequisite, the libmcrypt library, as the send_nsca program. This library is necessary to enable you to use encryption when sending data between the hosts sending syslog messages to the Nagios server. The libmcrypt library can be found at http://mcrypt.sourceforge.net/ or you can be download it as an RPM from either www.ottolander.nl/opensource/mcrypt/mcrypt.html or http://dag.wieers.com/packages/libmcrypt/.

The installation process for the libmcrypt library is very simple. Download the source package. Then configure it, make, and install it like so:

```
puppy# wget http://optusnet.dl.sourceforge.net/sourceforge/mcrypt/➥
libmcrypt-2.5.7.tar.gz
puppy# tar -zxf libmcrypt-2.5.7.tar.gz
puppy# cd libmcrypt-2.5.7
puppy# ./configure
puppy# make
puppy# make install
```

Once you have libmcrypt installed, you can start the NSCA installation process. Download and unpack the package on your remote host like so:

```
puppy# wget http://optusnet.dl.sourceforge.net/sourceforge/nagios/nsca-2.4.tar.gz
pippuy# tar -zxf nsca-2.4.tar.gz
```

Next change into the NSCA source package directory; then configure the package using the configure script and make it:

```
puppy# ./configure
puppy# make all
```

Tip You can also find an RPM of the NCSA tool at http://dries.studentenweb.org/rpm/packages/nagios-nsca/info.html.

This process will produce the nsca binary and nsca.cfg configuration file. The nsca binary is the NSCA daemon that runs on the central server and receives the check results. The nsca.cfg configuration file controls the NSCA daemon. For the NSCA server we need both files. I recommend you install the nsca binary to the bin directory in your default Nagios directory structure. This directory is /usr/local/nagios/bin by default. I suggest you place the nsca.cfg file in your Nagios etc directory, by default /usr/local/nagios/etc.

Now that you have installed the NSCA daemon, you need to configure it. The NSCA daemon works by listening for check results being sent via the send_nsca command on a remote server. It then submits these check results to the external command file to be processed by the Nagios server. Its configuration is held in the nsca.cfg configuration file we placed in the /usr/local/nagios/etc/ directory. I've shown a sample configuration in Example 9-7.

Example 9-7. *nsca.cfg Configuration File*

```
server_port=5667
server_address=10.0.0.1
allowed_hosts=127.0.0.1,10.0.0.10,10.0.0.20,10.0.0.30
nsca_user=nagios
nsca_group=nagios
debug=0
command_file=/usr/local/nagios/var/rw/nagios.cmd
alternate_dump_file=/usr/local/nagios/var/rw/nsca.dump
aggregate_writes=0
append_to_file=0
max_packet_age=30
password=password
decryption_method=3
```

There are only three major options you will need to change. First, you will need to list the IP addresses of any hosts that will be sending check results to NSCA in the allowed_ hosts option. If you are using other mechanisms, such as iptables, to further secure the sending hosts, you will also need to create rules for these hosts there. Additionally, both the password and decryption_method options contain values that must be identical to their equivalent options, the password and encryption_method options, in the send_nsca.cfg configuration file that is located on the sending hosts.

■**Tip** If you are having issues with sending and receiving check results, it may be worth turning on the debug option by setting it to 1. This will cause the NSCA daemon to output debug information and help you resolve any issues.

Finally, once we've configured the nsca.cfg file, we need to secure that file's ownership and permissions. I show how to do that in Example 9-8.

Example 9-8. *Securing the nsca.cfg File*

```
puppy# chown nagios:nagios /usr/local/nagios/etc/nsca.cfg
puppy# chmod 0640 /usr/local/nagios/etc/nsca.cfg
```

In our example, I've changed the ownership of the configuration file to the `nagios` user and group (which I've used to run the Nagios server process on the central server). I've also changed the permissions of the file to `0640` to only allow the `nagios` user to read the file.

Starting the NSCA Daemon

Once you've configured NSCA, you need to start the daemon. The daemon is controlled by the `nsca` binary. The binary has only two options: the `-c` option that specifies the location of the `nsca.cfg` configuration file and the mode you wish to run it in. The possible modes are –inetd, –daemon, and –single. The –inetd mode is used if you run the NSCA daemon from within inetd or xinted. The –daemon and –single modes run the NSCA daemon as a stand-alone daemon. The –daemon mode runs it as a multiprocess daemon, which I recommend for servers that have a heavy workload. The –single mode runs the daemon as a single process, which is better suited to a lower-volume environment. If you do not specify a mode, the NSCA daemon defaults to the –single mode. You can see an example of how to start the daemon here:

```
puppy# /usr/local/nagios/bin/nsca -c /usr/local/nagios/etc/nsca.cfg –single
```

■**Tip** Also in the NSCA package is an `init` script you can use to configure the NSCA daemon to start automatically when your host starts up. I recommend you modify this to suit your environment and use it to start and stop the NSCA daemon.

Configuring Nagios

Once the NSCA daemon is installed and running, you can receive `syslog` messages in the form of check results from your remote hosts. You then need to configure your Nagios server to receive these check results.

First, for each host that generates `syslog` messages you will need to create a host object definition. Additionally, for each facility, program, or defined service description, such as the `syslog-warnings` service description we created earlier in this chapter, you will need to define a service object definition.

A service object definition to process incoming `syslog` messages is a little different from a normal service object definition. This is because, unlike a normal service, each incoming message needs to be processed and reacted to no matter what state the service is currently in. In a traditional service object, only an incoming check result that changes the state of the service will be reacted to. For example, a service is in an `OK` state but receives a non-`OK` check result. The service goes into a soft non-`OK` state and checks the service the number of times specified in the `max_check_attempts` directive. If the service is still in that non-`OK` state after those checks, the state of the service moves from a soft non-`OK` state to a hard non-`OK` state. Any defined notifications, event handlers and logging will then occur. Then the service will stay in this hard non-`OK` state until an `OK` check result is received and processed. Any additional non-`OK` checks results received will not trigger additional notifications or event handlers or the like.

This model will not work for a service that receives `syslog` messages, where for each message we potentially want the service to react by generating notifications or executing event handlers. For example, I've defined a service called syslog-warnings. A non-OK status syslog message is received and sets the service to a non-OK status. For the service I've configured the max_check_attempts directive to 1 to ensure it immediately goes into a hard non-OK state and thus will execute any notifications or event handlers. The service then performs whatever notifications or event handlers I've configured. Another non-OK status syslog message arrives. But because the service is already in a hard non-OK state, nothing happens. No notification is generated and no event handlers are triggered, and so forth. This is because no state change has occurred.

So, unlike normal service object definitions, the definitions that should be created for processing syslog messages are slightly different and take advantage of a special feature of Nagios called volatile services. Volatile services are a special form of service that log, notify, and trigger an event handler every time a non-OK state is received even if the service is already in a hard non-OK state. In Example 9-9 I've specified a partial service object for the syslog-warnings service I described earlier in this chapter.

Example 9-9. *syslog-warnings Service Object*

```
define service{
            service_description      syslog-warnings
            is_volatile              1
            max_check_attempts       1
            active_checks_enabled    0
            passive_checks_enabled   1
            ...
}
```

In Example 9-9 you can see the service object is configured to only receive passive checks and has active checks disabled.[4] I've also set the max_check_attempts directive to 1. This will mean any non-OK result received by the service will set the service immediately to a hard non-OK state rather than attempting to retry the service. This will also immediately trigger any notifications or event handlers configured in the service.

Finally, I've added the is_volatile directive and set the directive to 1 to enable it. This will configure the service to be volatile. This means the service will react to all received non-OK results by logging, notifying, and/or executing any event handlers. Combined with setting the maximum check attempts to 1, this will cause any new incoming syslog message to trigger whatever logging, notification, or event handler that is configured for the service.

■**Note** In the Nagios console, only the last syslog message received will be displayed in the output of the service.

---

4. Active checks for the service will still be scheduled but not executed.

Wrapping Up

Once you have configured all the required components and set up the required host and service objects, you are able to receive `syslog` messages on your Nagios server. To confirm that you've completed all the required steps, let's review the whole process of how a `syslog` message gets from your remote host to your Nagios server:

1. The syslog-NG daemon has been installed and is running on the remote host and receiving `syslog` messages.

2. Selected or all `syslog` messages are configured in the `syslog-ng.conf` file using source, filter, destination, and log statements being sent to a named pipe. Using templates, the messages are manipulated into the form of Nagios check results, including specifying the status, such as `OK`, `WARNING`, or `CRITICAL`.

3. The `syslog` messages are added to the named pipe. A shell script running on the remote host processes the named pipe and sends the messages using the `send_nsca` command to an NSCA daemon running on the Nagios server.

4. The NSCA daemon submits the `syslog` messages as check results to the Nagios server through the external command file.

5. The check results require host and service objects configured to receive the results. Each host that generates `syslog` messages needs a host object. Each facility, program, or defined service also needs to have a service definition object created. The services defined must be created as volatile services to correctly process the `syslog` messages.

Remember the key factor with sending `syslog` messages to your Nagios is to be selective about what messages you do send. The `syslog` daemon can generate a large volume of messages, and most of them are either not relevant or not important enough to require logging or notification. Be sure to configure syslog-NG using filter statements to select only those messages that you wish to send to the Nagios server.

Snort

Snort is an open source intrusion-detection system (IDS) that runs on both Unix-like and Windows hosts. The Snort daemon runs on one of your hosts and samples the traffic on your network, compares it to a set of rules for bad or malicious traffic, and generates an alert if a particular packet matches a particular rule.

Next, I'll demonstrate how to integrate Snort alerts with Nagios. There are several methods that you could use to integrate Snort with Nagios. The first and easiest method utilizes Snort's ability to output alerts in the form of `syslog` messages. I'll use the syslog-NG daemon I've just examined to process and filter the appropriate messages and pass them to the NSCA daemon and from the Nagios server. A host and service (or potentially services) are then configured for the Snort alerts.

> **■Note** Another method to integrate with Nagios uses the Snort daemon's ability to output alerts to a Unix socket daemon. The alerts are sent to the Unix socket daemon and a script reads the alerts from the socket.[5] The alerts can then be processed in that script into Nagios check results and submitted to a Nagios server. Another method uses a modified version of Snort that outputs alerts as SNMP traps. The Nagios server is configured to receive and process these traps as check results for configured services.

I'll demonstrate how to integrate Nagios with the Snort daemon using the first method, processing alerts output as `syslog` messages using the method I described in the "syslog-NG and Nagios" section. If you don't wish to use syslog-NG to integrate Snort, I recommend you investigate the other options.

Configuring Snort for Integration

I'm not going to demonstrate how to install and configure Snort to act as an IDS. This is a complicated process that requires considerably more space than is available in this chapter. There are several excellent references for this process, including the books *Managing Security with Snort & IDS Tools* (O'Reilly, 2004) and *Snort 2.1 Intrusion Detection* (O'Reilly, 2004).[6] You'll also find a large collection of documentation on setting up and configuring Snort at the Snort homepage.[7]

I'll assume that you have already installed and configured your Snort daemon. To configure Snort to integrate with Nagios, you need to make some modifications to the `snort.conf` configuration file. This file is often located in the `/etc/snort` directory. The modifications include enabling, or confirming that it is already enabled, the `alert_syslog` output plug-in. Output plug-ins provide the mechanisms by which Snort can output IDS alerts or general log entries. The plug-ins can output to destinations such as databases, `syslog`, a Unix socket, and SMB messages. For the purpose of integrating with Nagios, we will look at the `alert_syslog` output plug-in, which provides `syslog` output for the Snort daemon. Output plug-ins are specified toward the end of the `snort.conf` configuration file, and can be identified as uncommented lines with the following syntax:

```
output plugin_name
```

Example 9-10 shows the `alert_syslog` output directive and syntax from the `snort.conf` file.

Example 9-10. *The alert_syslog Output Plug-in*

```
output alert_syslog: LOG_AUTH LOG_ALERT
```

---

5. I have included a sample script called `snort_unixsock.pl` that you can build on to perform this function in the Source Code section of the Apress website.

6. See www.oreilly.com/catalog/snortids/index.html and www.oreilly.com/catalog/1931836043/index.html.

7. See www.snort.org/docs/.

The options after the plug-in name allow you to specify the facility and priority of what is logged. In Example 9-10 we've specified the default facility, LOG_AUTH, which sends messages to the syslog server using the facility auth. You can change this to any facility that suits you. I prefer to use the facility authpriv to separate Snort messages from other auth facility messages. The LOG_ALERT option specifies what priority of messages will be sent to the syslog server. The LOG_ALERT setting sends syslog messages of alert and emerg to the syslog server. You can replace this with the required priority of messages to be sent. For the purposes of sending alerts to a Nagios server, the default is the best setting. In Example 9-11 you can see my preferred alert_syslog configuration.

Example 9-11. *Preferred alert_syslog Configuration*

```
output alert_syslog LOG_AUTHPRIV LOG_ALERT
```

■Note There are other settings, including the ability to log to a remote syslog server, that you can see in the Snort documentation at www.snort.org/docs/snort_htmanuals/htmanual_233/node15. html#SECTION00351000000000000000.

So either add the alert_syslog plug-in or change the configuration of your alert_syslog plug-in as I've specified here. You will need to restart your Snort daemon to activate the configuration change.

Configuring syslog-NG

Once you have configured Snort, you need to configure syslog-NG to send along your Snort alerts to the Nagios server. I won't detail the entire process of configuring syslog-NG, NSCA, and Nagios but I've assumed you have followed the instructions in the "syslog-NG and Nagios" section. Example 9-12 shows a filter, destination, and log statement for your Snort alerts.

Example 9-12. *syslog-NG Configuration for Sending Snort Alerts to Nagios*

```
filter f_snort { level(alert) and facility(authpriv) and program(snort); };

destination d_snort_nagios {
pipe("/var/run/nagios.pipe"
template("$HOST,'$PROGRAM',2,'$MSG'\n") template_escape(no));
};

log { source(local); filter(f_snort); destination(d_snort_nagios); };
```

In Example 9-12 the filter statement selects all messages generated by the Snort program of alert priority level and sent to the authpriv facility. I could also be more selective than this and only process certain types of Snort alerts using the filter option, match, which allows you to perform regular expression matching on the content of the syslog message. Here's an example:

```
filter f_snort { level(alert) and facility(authpriv) and program(snort) and ➡
match(" TCP Portsweep "); };
```

The filter statement on the previous line would select only those alerts whose descriptions contain the term TCP Portsweep. You can modify the match function to select alerts based on any regular expression you wish to use.

The destination statement then sends the Snort alerts to the nagios.pipe named pipe. The destination statement also uses the template option to modify the syslog message into the form of a Nagios check result. Prior to the modification, the syslog messages looks something like

```
Dec  4 23:59:54 puppy snort[3999]: [1:408:5] ICMP Echo Reply ➡
[Classification: Misc activity] [Priority: 3]: {ICMP} 10.0.0.5 -> 10.0.0.10
```

After the destination statement modifies the syslog message with the template, the message becomes a check result to be submitted to the NSCA daemon; it looks like this:

```
puppy,'snort',2,'[1:408:5] ICMP Echo Reply [Classification: Misc activity] ➡
[Priority: 3]: {ICMP} 10.0.0.5 -> 10.0.0.10'
```

You can see that the hostname, puppy, is passed as the value of the host the check result is to be submitted for. The name of the program that generates the messages, snort, is used as the value of the service. The status passed with the check result is 2 or CRITICAL. Then the syslog message itself is passed as the output of the check result.

Tip You could use another value for the service to be updated, especially if you are filtering individual alerts. An example is sending all alerts of a particular type, like TCP Portsweep, to a service called TCP_Portsweep.

Finally, the log statement combines the other statements and logs the selected messages to the destination.

Note You need to modify the source statement to use your local source or a network source if you are receiving syslog messages from a remote host.

Configuring Nagios

Much like the other syslog messages the Nagios server can receive from syslog-NG, the alerts that come from Snort should be sent to services that are configured to be volatile. Example 9-13 contains a partial service object called snort that is configured to receive the Snort alerts.

Example 9-13. *snort Service Object*

```
define service{
              service_description      snort
              is_volatile              1
              max_check_attempts       1
              active_checks_enabled    0
              passive_checks_enabled   1
              ...
}
```

You can see from Example 9-13 that I've configured the service to only receive passive check results, as submitted by the NSCA daemon. The service also has the max_check_attempts directive set to 1 to immediately react to HARD non-OK states. Finally, the service has the is_volatile directive set to 1 to mark this as a volatile service.

Wrapping Up

Let's quickly step through the process of sending Snort alerts to the Nagios server:

1. Alerts are sent using the alert_syslog output plug-in to your syslog daemon, in this case syslog-NG.

2. syslog-NG sends selected alerts to a named pipe after modifying them with a template.

3. A script processes the named pipe and sends the alerts in the form of check results to the NSCA daemon using the send_nsca command.

4. The NSCA submits the results to the Nagios server.

5. The check results are processed by the Nagios server and applied to the appropriate host and service objects. The notification, event handling, or escalation functionality that has been configured for the service is then initiated.

Integrating with MRTG, Cacti, and Related Tools

In Chapter 6, I described how to output Nagios performance data to RRDtool and have this data represented graphically. In that chapter, this was data being collected by Nagios. In addition, you may also have existing graphs and performance data from tools like MRTG and Cacti that you wish to query and report on in Nagios. This section will demonstrate how to query that data and use it in Nagios.

MRTG and Cacti are both network-monitoring tools that can produce graphs from data received from devices. This data can include elements like bandwidth, uptime or availability, and the status or components of the devices. These tools, however, do not have alerting or notifications functions embedded in them. They merely report, in graphical form, on the status of elements of your hosts and devices. But you can use plug-ins to retrieve the data contained in these tools and send it to Nagios in the form of a check result.

In this section I'll examine three plug-ins. The first two plug-ins, check_mrtgtraf and check_mrtg, are used to retrieve data from MRTG. The third plug-in, check_rrd.pl, is used to retrieve data from RRD databases that can include MRTG and other RRD-based tools. MRTG is a special case because it has two methods of storing data. The first method used by MRTG is a propriety logging format. The first two plug-ins, check_mrtgtraf and check_mrtg, can retrieve data in this format. The second method used by MRTG utilizes RRDTool to store and process the data. The third plug-in, check_rrd.pl, can retrieve data in this format.

Querying MRTG Log Files

As I mentioned earlier, MRTG can store data in both log files and RRD databases. Nagios has two plug-ins, check_mrtgtraf and check_mrtg, that can query MRTG data when stored in log files and submit the results of that query as check results. The results of these queries can be submitted to Nagios and monitoring, notification, and escalation functionality applied to the results. The two plug-ins are part of the Nagios plug-in package and are installed when it is.

Note I'll look at a Perl script called check_rrd later in this section that can interrogate RRD databases.

---

check_mrtgtraf

The check_mrtgtraf plug-in checks the average or maximum values from an MRTG log file but is specifically used for log files containing MRTG bandwidth and traffic data. The plug-in will check the maximum or average incoming and outgoing bandwidth and traffic volumes, measured in bytes per second, against WARNING and CRITICAL thresholds.

You can see an example of this plug-in on the following line:

```
puppy# ./check_mrtgtraf -F /var/log/mrtg/traffic.log -w 500,500 -c 10000,10000
Traffic WARNING - Avg. In = 2.0 KB/s, Avg. Out = 1.6 KB/s|in=1.976562KB/s;➡
500.000000;10000.000000;0.000000 in=1.615234KB/s;500.000000;10000.000000;0.000000
```

Let's look at each option of the check_mrtgtraf plug-in. The –F option specifies the location of the MRTG log file to be queried. The –w and –c options specify the WARNING and CRITICAL thresholds for incoming and outgoing bandwidth. The value for the incoming threshold is specified, followed by the value for the outgoing threshold, separated by a comma. The thresholds are specified in bytes per second. Thus to trigger the WARNING status in our example, the incoming or outgoing traffic (or both) would have to exceed 10,000 bytes per second, or 10Kbs. If the incoming or outgoing (or both) exceeded 50,000 bytes per second, or 50Kbs, the CRITICAL status would be triggered.

Note Like most thresholds in Nagios, the threshold must be rational, that is, the WARNING threshold must be less than the CRITICAL threshold.

If the bandwidth recorded is less than the WARNING threshold, the check_mrtgtraf plug-in defaults to an UNKNOWN status rather than an OK as you would expect. I usually change this to an OK status by editing the source code. To do so, change the following line in the check_mrtgtraf.c source file in the plugins directory of the plug-in source package

```
int result = STATE_UNKNOWN;
```

to

```
int result = STATE_OK;
```

I then recompile the plug-in using the make command and install the patched version. I don't recommend you make this change unless you understand what you are doing.

You can also have different values for the incoming and outgoing traffic like so:

```
puppy# ./check_mrtgtraf -F /var/log/mrtg/traffic.log -w 10000,20000 -c 50000,100000
```

On this line I've specified different values for the incoming and outgoing bandwidth levels for triggering both the WARNING and CRITICAL status. In this example the WARNING status would be triggered if the incoming bandwidth exceeded 10Kbs and/or the outgoing bandwidth exceeded 20Kbs. The CRITICAL status would be triggered if the incoming bandwidth exceeded 50Kbs and/or if the outgoing bandwidth exceeds 100Kbs.

There are also several additional options available for the check_mrtgtraf plug-in, as you can see in Table 9-2.

Table 9-2. *check_mrtgtraf Options*

Option	Description
-a AVG | MAX	Specifies whether to check the average or maximum values.
-e min	Specifies an expiry time in minutes for the MRTG data.
-t sec	Specifies the timeout for the command in seconds. Defaults to 10 seconds.
-h	Displays the help text for the command.
-v	Displays the version of the command.

The -a option determines whether the plug-in will select the average bandwidth or the maximum bandwidth from the MRTG log file. Average traffic is selected with the -a AVG option and maximum with the -a MAX option.

The -e option determines what age the data can be before Nagios will return a WARNING status. If the data contained in the MRTG log file is older than the time in minutes specified in the -e option, the plug-in will return a WARNING status. This option allows you to check whether MRTG is up to date and collecting data.

The -t option specifies the timeout in seconds of the plug-in, the -h option displays the help text, and the -v option displays the version of the plug-in.

Example 9-14 shows a Nagios command and partial service object that utilizes the check_mrtgtraf plug-in.

Example 9-14. *Command and Service Object Using check_mrtgtraf*

```
define command{
               command_name        check_mrtgtraf
               command_line        /usr/local/nagios/libexec/check_mrtgtraf ➥
                                   -F $ARG1$ -w $ARG2$ -c $ARG3$ -a $ARG4$

               }

define service{
               host_name           router
               service_description bandwidth_eth0
               check_command       check_mrtgtraf!/var/log/mrtg/router_eth0.log➥
                                   !5000,5000!10000,10000!MAX
...
               }
```

In Example 9-14 I've defined a command called check_mrtgtraf that is used in the bandwidth service of the router host. The command receives four arguments: the MRTG log filename, the WARNING and CRITICAL threshold, and whether the average or maximum value is being tested. You can see from the bandwidth service that all four arguments are passed from the check_command directive to the command.

check_mrtg

The check_mrtg plug-in will check the average or maximum value of one of the two variables contained in an MRTG log file. Example 9-15 shows the check_mrtg plug-in.

Example 9-15. *The check_mrtg Plug-in*

```
puppy# ./check_mrtg -F /var/www/html/mrtg/mem.log -w 5000 -c 15000 -v 2
CRITICAL - Avg. value = 17740|value=17740;14000;17000;
```

The check_mrtg plug-in works in a similar way to the check_mrtgtraf plug-in but allows you to query nonbandwidth data. Like the check_mrtgtraf plug-in, it uses the –F option to specify the location of an MRTG log file to be queried. It also requires the –w and –c options to specify the WARNING and CRITICAL status thresholds. Unlike the check_mrtgtraf plug-in, these thresholds are a single integer, not a pair.

Example 9-15 shows the –v option, which specifies which of the two possible variables to select from the MRTG log file. The two possible settings are –v 1 or –v 2.

■**Caution** Like the check_mrtgtraf plug-in, if the value recorded is less than the WARNING threshold, the check_mrtg plug-in defaults to an UNKNOWN status rather than an OK as you would expect. You can make a similar change to the code of this plug-in, as we made to the check_mrtgtraf plug-in in the previous section, to change this if you wish.

There are also some additional options available in the check_mrtg plug-in that you can see in Table 9-3.

Table 9-3. *check_mrtg Options*

Option	Description
-a *AVG* | *MAX*	Specifies whether to check the average or maximum values.
-e *min*	Specifies an expiry time in minutes for the MRTG data.
-l *label*	Specifies an optional label for the data.
-u *units*	Specifies an optional unit for the data.
-t *sec*	Specifies the timeout for the command in seconds. Defaults to 10 seconds.
-h	Displays the help text for the command.
-V	Prints version information.

The -a option specifies whether to test the average or maximum value from the MRTG log file. The -a AVG option tests the average values and -a MAX tests the maximum values.

The -e option specifies the expiry period of the MRTG data. When you specify this option, if the data returned from the MRTG log file is older than the time in minutes specified by the -e option, the WARNING status will be returned.

The -l and -u options allow you to specify a label and a unit value for the particular type of data being tested. You can see an example of this here:

```
puppy# ./check_mrtg -F /var/log/mrtg/mem.log -w 5000 -c 15000 -v 2 -a MAX ➥
-l Memory -u KBs
CRITICAL - Max. Memory = 17740 KBs|Memory=17740KBs;14000;17000;
```

Here I've specified a label of Memory and a unit of KBs. This label and unit have been reflected in the check results returned by the plug-in.

The last three options are standard for most plug-ins: the timeout for the plug-in, which defaults to 10 seconds, and options that return the help text and the version of the plug-in.

Finally, in Example 9-16, you can see a Nagios command and partial service object that utilizes the check_mrtg plug-in.

Example 9-16. *Command and Service Object Using check_mrtg*

```
define command{
            command_name              check_mrtg
            command_line              /usr/local/nagios/libexec/check_mrtgtraf ➥
                                      -F $ARG1$ -w $ARG2$ -c $ARG3$ -a $ARG4$
            }

define service{
            host_name                 router
            service_description       memory
            check_command             check_mrtg!/var/log/mrtg/router_mem.log➥
                                      !5000!10000!MAX
...
            }
```

In Example 9-16 you can see the check_mrtg command object takes four arguments, much like the check_mrtgtraf command object that I defined in the "check_mrtgtraf" section earlier in this chapter. The memory service object for the router host passes the required MRTG log filename, the WARNING and CRITICAL thresholds, and the value to check, either the average or maximum value.

■**Caution** At the time of this writing, the check_mrtg plug-in available in version 1.4.2 of the Nagios plug-ins package does not correctly function. You can find an updated version of the plug-in with the errors corrected in the Patches section of the Sourceforge site at http://sourceforge.net/tracker/ ?group_id=29880&atid=397599. If there is a more recent version of the plug-in package at the time of publication, this may have been corrected in that release.

Querying RRD Databases

MRTG, if it is using RRDtool to store data, and a number of other RRD-based tools such as Cacti and Cricket, can also be queried for data. There are two plug-ins available to perform this querying, neither of which is in the mainstream plug-in package. The check_rrd_data.pl plug-in is a Perl script that is provided in the contrib directory of the Nagios plug-in package. The check_rrd.pl plug-in is a Perl script written by Seva Gluschenko and is available from the following mailing list post: http://sourceforge.net/mailarchive/message.php?msg_ id=13455112. You'll also find it in the Source Code section of the Apress website.[8]

■**Tip** Both modules require that you install the RRDs Perl module that is contained in the RRDtool package. I provided instructions for installing RRDtool, including the RRDs Perl module, in Chapter 6.

For this section I am going to look at Seva Gluschenko's check_rrd.pl plug-in for the purposes of checking RRD databases. I've chosen this plug-in because I've found it is simpler to use than the check_rrd_data.pl script in the official Nagios plug-in package. Example 9-17 shows the check_rrd.pl plug-in being executed from the command line.

Example 9-17. *The Check_rrd.pl Plug-in*

```
puppy# ./check_rrd.pl -F /var/log/rrd/cpu.rrd -w 80 -c 90 -a AVERAGE -v 2
WARNING Average ds1=85
```

The first option in Example 9-17, -F, specifies the location of the RRD database to be queried. The next two options, -w and -c, specify the WARNING and CRITICAL thresholds to be checked by the plug-in. The -a option controls whether you are checking the average or maximum value from the database; the possible values are AVERAGE and MAX. The last option, -v, allows you to select the particular data source you wish to check from the RRD database.

---

8. Available for download from the Apress website at www.apress.com.

The data source is the particular metric you wish to test; for example, an RRD database measuring a dual CPU host might contain two data sources, one for the utilization of each CPU. You can select the data source by number; the first data source in an RRD database is numbered 1, the second data source is 2, and so forth. Thus in Example 9-17 I am selecting the second data source in the database. You can also select the data source by name:

```
puppy# ./check_rrd.pl -F /var/log/rrd/cpu.rrd -w 80 -c 90 -a AVERAGE -v ds1
```

Here I've selected the data source ds1 from the RRD database.

You can see the contents of an RRD database, including the data sources, by using the rrdtool binary. This will display each variable in the database and what it is:

```
puppy# /usr/local/rrdtool/bin/rrdtool info /var/www/html/mrtg/cpu.rrd
```

Here I've executed the rrdtool binary with the info option. This will display the structure of the cpu.rrd RRD database and assist you in determining which data source to select using the check_rrd.pl plug-in.

There are some additional options for the check_rrd.pl plug-in, and I've listed them in Table 9-4.

Table 9-4. *check_rrd.pl Options*

Option	Description
-e *min*	Specifies an expiry time in minutes for the MRTG data.
-l *label*	Specifies an optional label for the data.
-u *units*	Specifies an optional unit for the data.
-i	Lists only the integer of any result.
-t *sec*	Specifies the timeout for the command in seconds. Defaults to 10 seconds.
-x	Enables verbose mode.
-h	Displays the help text for the command.
-V	Prints version information.

The -e, -l, and -u options perform the same function for this plug-in as they do for the check_mrtg plug-in as I described in the previous section. The -i option tells the plug-in to only output the integer part of any result from the query.

The last four options are fairly self-explanatory. The -t option specifies the plug-in time-out, the -x option enables a verbose mode, -h displays the detailed help text for the plug-in, and -V lists the version information.

SNMP Traps and Nagios

SNMP traps are alerts and notifications generated by SNMP-enabled devices. The traps contain information about the status or an event on an SNMP-enabled device. For example, an authentication event or the change in status of an interface on a router may generate an SNMP trap that is sent to a management station of some sort, such as HP OpenView or CiscoWorks. There are two possible ways Nagios can interact with SNMP traps. The first is for Nagios to be the SNMP management station and receive traps as passive check results for a service. The second way is to send check results for hosts and services in the form of SNMP traps to a SNMP management station. I'll examine both ways of handling SNMP traps in this section.

■**Tip** I discussed briefly how SNMP works and how to check SNMP-enabled devices in Chapter 5.

For both ways of interacting with SNMP traps, the Net-SNMP package needs to be installed on your Nagios server. The Net-SNMP package is available from `http://net-snmp.sourceforge.net`.

■**Tip** The Net-SNMP site also contains quite a bit of useful information about SNMP and how to use it.

To install Net-SNMP, first download the current release from the Net-SNMP Sourceforge site located at `http://net-snmp.sourceforge.net/download.html`.

■**Tip** You need to have at least version 5.1.1 of the Net-SNMP package.

Then unpack it and run the `configure` script:

```
puppy# wget http://optusnet.dl.sourceforge.net/sourceforge/net-snmp/➥
net-snmp-5.3.pre4.tar.gz
puppy# tar -xzf net-snmp-5.3.pre4.tar.gz
puppy# cd net-snmp-5.3.pre4
puppy# ./configure —with-perl-modules
```

During the `configure` process, you will be prompted to answer a number of configuration questions. The default answers should be suitable for most installations, and the information provided about each option is extensive and clear if you wish to change the default answers. I've also provided the `—with-perl-modules` `configure` option that also configures and installs the Net-SNMP Perl module. This is useful for a number of tools, and I suggest you install it as well.

After configuring Net-SNMP, you need to compile and install it like so:

```
puppy# make
puppy# make install
```

▓**Tip** The Net-SNMP package is also available as a series of installable packages on many distributions. Indeed, it may already be installed on your system or you may be able to install it via your distribution's package management system, such as `yum`, `apt`, or the like. On Red Hat, SuSE, Debian, and Mandrake distributions, the required packages are called `net-snmp`, `net-snmp-libs`, and `net-snmp-utils`. You may also require some additional prerequisites for the Net-SNMP packages, but your package management system should identify them for you.

Receiving SNMP Traps

Much like Nagios can receive `syslog` messages, you can also configure it to receive SNMP traps from SNMP-enabled devices. The SNMP traps need to be converted into passive check results and then submitted to the Nagios server. To receive the traps from remote hosts, we will use the `snmptrapd` daemon that comes with the Net-SNMP package. This daemon listens for incoming traps and can send them on to `syslog`, a file, or some other form of output.

I could send the SNMP traps from the `snmptrapd` daemon to syslog-NG and from there to Nagios. But the textual and variable content of SNMP traps can be hard to decipher. They often require some translation and manipulation to provide meaningful information about the event that generated them. So in order to perform this translation and manipulation, I'll make use of a tool called SNMPTT, or the SNMP Trap Translator.

To do this, Management Information Base (MIB) files, which contain the definitions of all the objects being monitored on an SNMP-enabled device, are loaded into the SNMPTT tool and any traps or notifications contained in the MIB file translated into a more readable form. This is done using an automated tool that is provided with the SNMPTT package. You then select which traps you wish to monitor for and pass to Nagios. To do this, you add logic to selected trap definitions in SNMPTT so that if SNMPTT receives one of these traps, it should then submit it to Nagios as a passive check result.

▓**Note** MIB files may contain many traps and notifications, and you may not wish to pass all of them to Nagios. Thus, you may translate a lot of traps that you don't wish to do anything with. If you don't want to do anything with a particular trap, you simply don't add the sending logic to it.

When incoming traps are received from the `snmptrapd` daemon, they are passed to the SNMPTT tool. The SNMPTT tool will then try to match the incoming trap against the collection of trap definitions that it has translated. If the trap matches, SNMPTT will see if the translated trap definition contains logic to output it to Nagios and execute that logic. The trap is then output to Nagios as a passive check result.

I'll step through the steps required to configure all the components of this process in the following sections.

Configuring and Running the snmptrapd Daemon

The snmptrapd daemon comes with the Net-SNMP package. It is configured on the command line and uses a configuration file called snmptrapd.conf. It listens on UDP port 162 for incoming SNMP traps. The traps are then passed to the SNMPTT tool using a function called traphandle.

In Example 9-18 you can the snmptrapd daemon started via the command line.

Example 9-18. *Starting the snmptrapd Daemon*

```
puppy# /usr/local/sbin/snmptrapd -On -c /etc/snmp/snmptrad.conf ➥
-u /var/run/snmptrapd.pid
```

Example 9-18 shows the snmptrapd daemon being started with three options: -On, -c, and -u. The -On option tells the snmptrapd to output traps with numeric OIDs. This makes the translation process easier by preventing the SNMPTT tool from having to perform the conversion. The -c option specifies the location of the snmptrapd.conf configuration file. The last option, -u, specifies a location to store the process ID for the running daemon.

There are two other options that might be useful: -f and -D. The -f option stops the daemon from forking and leaves it running in the foreground. The -D option enables debugging. Both of these are useful for testing the daemon.

By default the snmptrapd daemon binds to all available IP interfaces on your host, but you can override this by specifying a particular IP address to bind to:

```
puppy# /usr/local/sbin/snmptrapd -On -c /etc/snmp/snmptrad.conf ➥
-u /var/run/snmptrapd.pid 10.0.0.10
```

The snmptrapd.conf file can contain a number of configuration items for controlling the daemon and how it handles traps. For the purposes of sending the traps to the SNMPTT tool, I only need to add one line to this file, as you can see in Example 9-19.

Example 9-19. *Sample snmptrapd.conf Configuration File*

```
traphandle                  default /usr/sbin/snmptthandler
```

The traphandle directive tells the snmptrapd daemon how to handle incoming traps and where to send them. Adding the default option tells the daemon that this is the default way to handle all incoming traps. All traps will be sent to the snmptthandler script located in the /usr/sbin directory. The use of this script assumes you are executing the SNMPTT tool in daemon mode. I'll demonstrate how to configure SNMPTT like this in the "Configuring SNMPTT" section.

■**Tip** You can see the full list of snmptrapd.conf configuration file options by displaying the snmptrapd.conf man page.

You can run the daemon from the command line or via an `init` script. The Net-SNMP source package and most of the packaged versions, such as the RPM, come with `init` scripts for starting and stopping the `snmptrapd` daemon.

Installing SNMPTT

Next we need to install the SNMPTT tool. The SNMPTT tool is written in Perl and uses a number of functions provided with the Net-SNMP package. The tool can either be called from the command line or run as a daemon. I recommend that you run it as a daemon for better performance, and I'll demonstrate that method here.

The SNMPTT tool has a number of prerequisites that must be installed for it to function:

- Perl version 5.6.1 or higher (the preferred version is 5.8.*x*)

- Net-SNMP version 5.1.1 or higher

- The `Text::Parse::Words`, `Getopt::Long`, `Posix`, `Config::IniFiles`, `Time::HiRes`, and `Sockets` CPAN modules

■Tip You can install the required CPAN modules via the `cpan` interface or from the command line. You can see instructions on using CPAN at `http://perl.about.com/od/perlmodule1/l/aa030500a.htm`.

You can get the SNMPTT tool from Sourceforge at `http://snmptt.sourceforge.net/`. This line shows how to download and unpack the SNMPTT tool:

```
puppy# wget http://prdownloads.sourceforge.net/snmptt/snmptt_1.0.tgz?➥
use_mirror=optusnet
puppy# tar -zxf snmptt_1.0.tgz
```

■Note I've used the Australian Sourceforge mirror. You should use the one closest to you.

The SNMPTT package has no installation script, so a number of manual installations steps need to take place. First, copy the SNMPTT binaries to a suitable directory and mark them as executable. I recommend using the `/usr/sbin` directory.

```
puppy# cp snmptt snmptthandler /usr/sbin/
puppy# chmod +x /usr/sbin/snmptt /usr/sbin/snmptthandler
```

These two commands copy the `snmptt` and `snmptthandler` binaries to the `/usr/sbin` directory and makes them executable. The `snmptt` binary provides the core functionality of the tool, and the `snmptthandler` binary allows you to interact with the tool in daemon mode. I specified the `snmptthandler` binary as the value of the `traphandle` option in the `snmptrapd.conf` configuration file in the previous section. When a trap is received, this binary is executed by default and the trap sent to the `snmptt` daemon.

Next, copy the SNMPTT configuration file, `snmptt.ini`, to the `/etc/snmp` directory like so:

```
puppy# cp snmptt.ini /etc/snmp/
```

■**Note** I'll come back to this file in the "Configuring SNMPTT" section.

Also needed are a user and group to run the SNMPTT daemon as. I typically use a user and group called `snmptt`, as you can see on the following lines:

```
puppy# groupadd snmptt
puppy# user –g snmptt snmptt
```

When executing the `snmptt` binary, the process will change to this user and group and drop privileges. This provides a greater level of security than running the daemon as the `root` user.

The `snmptt` user also needs to own the `snmptt.ini` configuration file, and you should change its ownership like so:

```
puppy# chown snmptt:snmptt /etc/snmp/snmptt.ini
```

The SNMPTT tool also needs a spool directory to hold the incoming traps. I usually use the default directory of `/var/spool/snmptt`. It needs to be owned by the user and group that will run SNMPTT. Create and change the ownership of the directory like so:

```
puppy# mkdir /var/spool/snmptt
puppy# chown snmptt:snmptt /var/spool/snmptt
```

Finally, in order to start the SNMPTT tool, you can either execute it from the command line or use the `init` script provided with the package. On the following line, you can see SNMPTT started in daemon mode:

```
puppy# /usr/sbin/snmptt –daemon
```

I recommend running the `snmptt` binary in daemon mode as it processes traps quickly and efficiently.

■**Tip** There are other command-line options for the `snmptt` binary you can see if you execute the binary with the `–help` option. The `snmptt` binary will automatically detect the `snmptt.ini` configuration file in the `/etc/snmp` directory and use its contents to determine the tool's other options.

The provided `init` script should work on Red Hat or Mandrake systems without modification and with minor changes on most other platforms. You can copy it to the standard location for your `init` scripts, for example, on Red Hat hosts the `/etc/rc.d/init.d` directory:

```
puppy# cp snmptt.init.d /etc/rc.d/init.d/snmptt
```

You can then add it to your startup process.

Configuring SNMPTT

You must take a number of steps when configuring SNMPTT. The first is configuring the `snmptt.ini` file. The file contains quite a large number of directives, but I'll only look at those relevant to the process of translating and transmitting the received traps to Nagios.

Example 9-20 contains a list of the directives from the `snmptt.ini` file that you should change in the sample `snmptt.ini` file to support the translation of traps to Nagios.

■**Tip** The sample `snmptt.ini` file contained in the SNMPTT package has detailed explanations of all the directives and options that you can specify. I recommend reading this file for further information and explanations about SNMPTT's configuration options.

Example 9-20. *snmptt.ini Configuration Directives to Be Changed*

```
mode = daemon
daemon_fork = 1
daemon_uid = snmptt
spool_directory = /var/spool/snmptt/
sleep = 5
dns_enable = 1
strip_domain = 1
log_enable = 0
syslog_enable = 0
exec_enable = 1
snmptt_conf_files = <<END
/etc/snmp/snmptt.conf
END
```

The first directives in Example 9-20 control how SNMPTT operates when running in daemon mode. The first directive, `mode`, controls whether SNMPTT will run in stand-alone or daemon mode. Specifying `daemon` will tell SNMPTT to run in daemon mode. The next directive, `daemon_fork`, when set to 1, will fork the SNMPTT daemon to the background and create a PID file called `snmptt.pid` in the `/var/run` directory. The next directive, `daemon_uid`, controls what user the daemon will run as. You can specify the username or the UID of the user. I've specified the user I created earlier, `snmptt`.

The `spool_directory` directive controls where the SNMPTT tool will store the incoming traps. I suggest leaving it at the default setting of `/var/spool/snmptt`. I created this directory in the previous section and changed its ownership to the `snmptt` user running the daemon.

The `sleep` directive tells the SNMPTT daemon how long to wait between checking the spool directory for new traps. It is measured in seconds. The default is 5. I'll discuss how the daemon processes traps in a moment.

The next two directives control how IP addresses, hostnames, and DNS are handled by the SNMPTT. By default, the `snmptrapd` daemon sends traps that contain the agent's IP address rather than the fully qualified domain name (FQDN). The `dns_enable` directive controls whether DNS resolution is performed on the agent's IP address. If this directive is set to 1,

DNS resolution is enabled and SNMPTT will use the host's default DNS servers, and the local host table, to resolve the agent IP addresses.

■Tip If you enable DNS resolution, I recommend you add all the hostnames that need to be resolved to the local /etc/hosts file on your host server. This prevents your DNS server from being a bottleneck or preventing SNMPTT from functioning if your DNS server is unavailable.

If set to 1, the strip_domain directive removes the domain name from the FQDN resolved by the SNMPTT tool. It leaves just the hostname, so that puppy.yourdomain.com becomes puppy. Setting it to 0 will leave the FQDN intact.

The next few options relate to how SNMPTT will log traps. The log_enable directive controls whether SNMPTT will log traps to a log file. As you are already sending these traps to Nagios, I recommend disabling this option by setting it to 0. The next directive syslog_enable controls whether SNMPTT logs to syslog. By default SNMPTT logs all incoming traps to syslog using the facility local0 and the priority warn. You can disable this also by setting the directive syslog_enable directive to 0.

The exec_enable directive controls whether EXEC statements are enabled in translated traps. I'll demonstrate the EXEC statement when I look at how you translate your traps. To send traps to Nagios, you will need to set this directive to 1 to enable EXEC statements.

The last directive in Example 9-20 defines the location of the trap definitions that have been translated by SNMPTT. This is done using the snmptt_conf_files directive. In the sample configuration file, the trap definitions are stored in a file called snmptt.conf in the /etc/snmp directory. You can specify this one file for all your translated traps, or you can specify multiple files by specifying them, one to a line, in between the <<END and END statements, as shown here:

```
snmptt_conf_files = <<END
/etc/snmp/snmptt.conf
/etc/snmp/snmptt-linksys.conf
/etc/snmp/snmptt-cisco.conf
/etc/snmp/snmptt-hp.conf
/etc/snmp/snmptt-as400.conf
END
```

In the next section, I'll demonstrate how to add trap definitions to these files and adjust the translated traps to send the trap as a Nagios check result.

Adding Trap Definitions and EXEC Statements

The second step in configuring SNMPTT is translating the trap definitions for all the traps you intend to monitor and modifying those trap definitions to send results to Nagios. This is done by adding the MIB[9] files for the devices or types of devices that are being monitored to the

---

9. See www.webopedia.com/TERM/M/MIB.html.

SNMPTT configuration file. An MIB file is a database of objects monitored by a device, including metrics, status information, and the like. For example, an object could consist of the metric of the amount of traffic transmitted through an interface or the amount of disk space consumed on a drive.

■**Tip** In Chapter 5, I discuss using the `snmpwalk` command to review the available objects on an SNMP-enabled device.

The translation process performs two functions. The first is to sort the traps and notifications from the other OIDs in the MIB file. This is because we only care about the traps and notifications, not the other types of OIDs. The second function is to translate or convert those traps and notifications into the more human-readable SNMPTT format. You can then add a special statement called an `EXEC` statement to these new, translated, definitions. This `EXEC` statement tells SNMPTT that when an incoming trap is matched against a translated trap definition, it should then execute a script, binary, or other function contained in that statement. In our case, the command in the `EXEC` statement will pass the trap to Nagios as a passive service check result.

The trap translation is done by a tool provided with the SNMPTT package called `snmpttconvertmib`. MIB files are loaded into the translation tool and output into files that are then referenced in the `snmtt.ini` configuration file using the `snmptt_conf_files` directive. These files are loaded when SNMPTT first starts and queried when SNMPTT tries to match incoming traps against translated traps.

■**Tip** To translate traps, you will need the MIB files for the devices you wish to monitor. In the Net-SNMP package is a directory called `mibs` that contains a number of MIB files. During installation, this directory is usually located in `/usr/share/snmp/mibs`. Additionally, most vendors provide MIB files for their products. You can see a list of sites in this chapter's "References" section that also contain MIB files.

The `snmpttconvermib` tool is provided with the SNMPTT package, and you can install it like so:

```
puppy# cp snmpttconvertmib /usr/sbin/
```

Example 9-21 shows the `snmpttconvertmib` tool translating an MIB file.

Example 9-21. *Translating an MIB File*

```
puppy# /usr/sbin/snmpttconvertmib —in=/usr/share/smnp/mibs/IF-MIB.txt ➥
—out=/etc/snmp/snmtt.conf
```

The `snmpttconvertmib` tool has two major options: `—in` and `—out`. The `—in` option specifies the location of the MIB file to be translated, and the `—out` option specifies the SNMPTT configuration file to receive the output. By default any translated traps are appended to the output file. In Example 9-21 I've translated the traps in the `IF-MIB.txt` file and appended them to the `snmptt.conf` file in the `/etc/snmp` directory. You can add all your traps to one file or to multiple files.

There are some options you can use with the `snmpttconvertmib` command, and you can list them using the `–help` option like so:

```
puppy# /usr/sbin/snmpttconvertmib –help
```

Example 9-22 shows a translated trap from the `IF-MIB.txt` MIB file (which contains traps dealing with the interface status of devices).

Example 9-22. *Translated Trap*

```
EVENT linkDown .1.3.6.1.6.3.1.1.5.3 "Status Events" Normal
FORMAT A linkDown trap signifies that the SNMP entity, acting in $*
SDESC
A linkDown trap signifies that the SNMP entity, acting in
an agent role, has detected that the ifOperStatus object for
one of its communication links is about to enter the down
state from some other state (but not from the notPresent
state).  This other state is indicated by the included value
of ifOperStatus.
Variables:
  1: ifIndex
  2: ifAdminStatus
  3: ifOperStatus
EDESC
```

In Example 9-22 you can see the translated trap is broken down into three sections: the `EVENT` and `FORMAT` lines and the information between the `SDESC` and `EDESC` directives that mark the start and end of a description of the trap. Later in this section I'll add another line, the `EXEC` statement, that will send the trap to Nagios.

The first directive, `EVENT`, is structured like so:

```
EVENT event_name event_OID "category" severity
```

The event line is broken down into the name of the trap and the OID number. These are followed by the category of the trap and the criticality of the trap. The category of the trap is the type of event, and there are also two special categories of trap: `LOGONLY` and `IGNORE`. If the category of the trap is set to either of these special categories, SNMPTT will not execute the `EXEC` statement. If you translate a trap and the category is set to either of these options, you will need to change it to allow the trap to be sent to Nagios.

The `FORMAT` line is used to create the text that is logged by SNMPTT to `syslog` or to a file. It is very similar to the `EXEC` line I'll add shortly. It can contain text and a number of possible variables, such as the hostname and IP address of the device generating the trap. You can see a full list of these variables in the SNMPTT documentation at `http://snmptt.sourceforge. net/docs/snmptt.shtml#Variable-substitutions`. I'll also look at some of these variables here.

You can see that the FORMAT line in Example 9-22 is not overly meaningful, even after translation, so I am going to rewrite it on the next line:

```
FORMAT Interface number $1 on $r is entering the $3 state
```

On this line I've rewritten the FORMAT line to output the message in more simple terms. I've also used several variables. The first variable, $1, captures the number of the interface (you can see a list of the available variables for this particular trap in the SDESC and EDESC sections). The $1 variable represents the ifIndex variable, $2 the ifAdminStatus variable and $3 the ifOperStatus variable. You can find details of particular variables in a trap in the MIB file, or they will be listed in the translated trap description. The $r is the hostname of the device that sent the SNMP trap. How this looks depends on how SNMPTT is configured; you should read the documentation about the dns_resolve and strip_domain directives in the snmptt.ini configuration file.

The text between the SDESC and EDESC directives is an optional description of the trap and its contents that generally comes from the MIB file. This text is ignored by SNMPTT.

Next we need to add the EXEC statement. As I mentioned, the EXEC statement is very similar to the FORMAT statement and can use the same variables that the FORMAT statement can. I generally add the EXEC statement after the FORMAT line, as you can see in Example 9-23. You will need to add EXEC statements to all of the traps you wish to send to Nagios.

Example 9-23. *The EXEC Statement*

```
FORMAT Interface number $1 on $r is entering the $3 state
EXEC /usr/local/nagios/libexec/eventhandlers/submit_check_result "$r" ➥
"snmp_trap" 2 "Interface number $1 is entering the $3 state"
```

To submit the check results to Nagios, you can use a script called submit_check_result (a copy of which is contained in the Nagios package in the eventhandlers subdirectory of the contrib directory).[10] You can see the script in Example 9-24. It submits service check results to the external command file using the PROCESS_SERVICE_CHECK_RESULT external command.

■Note I discussed external commands in Chapter 6.

Example 9-24. *submit_check_result Script*

```
# Arguments:
#  $1 = host_name
#  $2 = service_description (Description of the service)
#  $3 = return_code (An integer that determines the state
#       of the service check, 0=OK, 1=WARNING, 2=CRITICAL,
#       3=UNKNOWN).
```

---

10. I have also included a copy of the script in the resources file for this book.

```
#  $4 = plugin_output (A text string that should be used
#       as the plugin output for the service check)
#

echocmd="/bin/echo"

CommandFile="/usr/local/nagios/var/rw/nagios.cmd"

# get the current date/time in seconds since UNIX epoch
datetime=`date +%s`

# create the command line to add to the command file
cmdline="[$datetime] PROCESS_SERVICE_CHECK_RESULT;$1;$2;$3;$4"

# append the command to the end of the command file
`$echocmd $cmdline >> $CommandFile`
```

■**Tip** To be executed by Nagios, the `submit_check_result` shell script must be owned by the user running the Nagios server and have its permissions set so that it is executable.

As you can see, the script in Example 9-24 takes four arguments: the hostname, the service description, the return code for the service, and the plug-in output. These arguments are passed to the script in the EXEC statement in Example 9-23. First, the hostname of the device that generated the trap is passed using the $r variable. Next I've defined a service description called snmp_traps. In order for the check to be correctly received by the Nagios server, I would need to have a host object created for each SNMP device that will be sending traps. I'll also need a service description for each host called snmp_traps. Next, I pass the return code, for example OK, WARNING, CRITICAL, or UNKNOWN, in its numeric form. I've used the return code of 2 that would result in the service being placed in a CRITICAL status. You can pass whatever return code suits the particular trap you are sending.

I've included some text, enclosed in quotation marks to protect the text from being misinterpreted by the shell, to be sent as the output of the check. This text is what would be sent as a notification and/or displayed in the web console.

■**Tip** If the `snmptrapd` and SNMPTT daemons are not on the same host as the Nagios server, you could use the `send_nsca` command to send the passive check results to an NSCA daemon on a remote host running the Nagios server.

SNMPTT also has a regular expression–matching capability that allows you to use an EVENT line that matches multiple incoming traps, a catchall trap definition. This means you don't need to define individual translated trap definitions for each possible incoming trap. Example 9-25 shows a catchall trap definition with associated EXEC line.

Example 9-25. *Catchall Trap Definition*

```
EVENT CatchAll .1.* "SNMP Traps" Critical
FORMAT $D
EXEC /usr/local/nagios/libexec/eventhandlers/submit_check_result "$r" ➥
"snmp_traps" 2 "$O: $1 $2 $3 $4 $5"
```

As you can see, the EVENT line names the event CatchAll and then uses SNMPTT regular expression–matching capability to match all OIDs, by using the wildcard symbol, *. I could also be more selective and select OIDs from a particular vendor or class of trap either using a wildcard or regular expression pattern matching. I've added a category called SNMP Traps and severity of Critical. The FORMAT line only has the $D variable, which contains the description text from the MIB file.

The EXEC line is very similar to the EXEC line in Example 9-23. The line calls the submit_check_result shell script and passes in the hostname using the $r variable. It submits the trap to a service called snmp_traps as a CRITICAL status check result. Finally, as the output of the plug-in I am passing in the $O variable, which is the trap OID in symbolic format (i.e., the textual descriptive form rather than the numeric format). I also specify a range of variables $1 to $5 to cover all the possible defined variables from the trap and pass them to Nagios.

Tip To receive the traps in Nagios, you will need a service object called snmp_traps for each host that might be sending traps or use wildcards to create a service for all hosts.

Configuring Nagios

Lastly, much like receiving syslog messages and Snort alerts, the service objects defined to receive SNMP traps should be defined as volatile. Here's an example of a partial service object for the snmp_traps service I referenced in the previous section:

```
define service{
            host_name               puppy
            service_description     snmp_traps
            is_volatile              1
            max_check_attempts      1
            active_checks_enabled   0
            passive_checks_enabled  1
            ...
}
```

Tip You could also use a wildcard to create this service for all hosts or use the hostgroup_name directive to create the service for all members of a host group or groups.

I've defined the service as volatile and set the maximum check attempts to 1. This will cause Nagios to immediately set a HARD service state and trigger any configured notifications or event handlers. I've also configured it for passive checks only and disabled active checks.

Putting It All Together

Let's have a quick look at the process used to execute SNMPTT. The SNMPTT tool is called via the trap handler defined in the snmptrapd.conf configuration file I defined in the "Configuring and Running the snmptrapd Daemon" section. This trap handler calls the /usr/sbin/ snmptthandler script. The script reads the trap and then writes it to the spool directory defined in the spool_directory directive from the snmptt.ini configuration file. The script then exits.

From here the SNMPTT daemon takes over. It reads the trap from the spool file and searches for a match in its trap definitions. If it finds a match, it executes the EXEC statement in the matching trap definition. This EXEC statement sends the passive check result to the Nagios server using the submit_check_result script. The daemon then sleeps for the period specified in the sleep directive in the snmptt.ini file and checks the spool directory for additional traps; if it finds matches, it processes them and sends the check results to Nagios.

The Nagios server has to have host objects defined for every host that generates SNMP traps. Additionally, you need to define service objects for those hosts to receive the service check results. You should configure them to receive passive check results and as volatile services.

■Tip You can add considerable sophistication to this process by manipulating SNMPTT to select more than one trap or, for example, matching traps by severity or category and submitting them to particular service objects using this information. I recommend you experiment with SNMPTT's options and capabilities.

Sending SNMP Traps

As well as receiving SNMP traps, you can send them to a remote SNMP management station like HP OpenView or the like. The easiest way to do this is by using event handlers. When a change in status is detected in a host or service, you can trigger an event handler that generates an SNMP trap that is sent to your SNMP management station. You will remember from Chapters 2 and 6 that an event handler is executed when a service

- Changes into a SOFT error state

- Initially goes into a HARD error state

- Recovers from a SOFT or HARD error state

■Tip Another, equally viable, method to send SNMP traps from Nagios is to create a notification command that generates an SNMP trap. This way, you can use an SNMP management station as a notification destination. This will mean that the trap will be sent every time a notification is scheduled. The method described next can be easily modified to be used as a notification mechanism.

Unlike the other integrations in this chapter, I am going to start with the Nagios configuration and then add the additional components. In Example 9-26 you can see a service object configuration for a service that sends an SNMP trap.

Example 9-26. *Service with SNMP Generating Event Handler*

```
define service{
            host_name                   puppy
            service_description         disk
            event_handler               send_trap
            event_handler_enabled       1
            ...
}
```

In Example 9-26 a service object called disk on the host puppy is set to execute the event handler send_trap upon the conditions I listed. Example 9-27 shows the command object for the send_trap command.

Example 9-27. *The send_trap event Handler Command*

```
define command{
            command_name                send_trap
            command_line                /usr/local/nagios/libexec/send_trap manager ➥
                                        public $HOSTNAME$ $SERVICEDESC$ ➥
                                        $SERVICESTATEID$ $SERVICEOUTPUT$

            }
```

■**Tip** If you want to use notification logic to send traps, you can also just use this command as a notification command by specifying it in your contact objects.

In Example 9-27 you can see the send_trap event handler command that calls a shell script, also called send_trap, in the /usr/local/nagios/libexec directory. I pass the hostname or IP address of the destination management station and the target community string, manager and public, respectively.

■**Caution** If you are worried about exposing your community string, you could utilize a user macro to hold the community string. Your user macros are stored in resource configuration files and are generally harder for casual users to read. I discussed user macros in Chapter 2.

A number of macros are also passed to the shell script representing the hostname, the service description, the service state in numeric form, and the output of the service check.

Next let's look at the send_trap shell script. This script will execute the snmptrap tool that comes with the Net-SNMP package. The snmptrap tool generates SNMP traps and can send them to remote management stations. The traps are generated according to a Nagios MIB available from the same Sourceforge project as the Nagios plug-ins. You can download the MIB from http://prdownloads.sourceforge.net/nagiosplug/nagiosmib-1.0.0.tar.gz?download.

The package contains two MIB files: a root MIB file containing basic definitions for Nagios OIDs called NAGIOS-ROOT-MIB and an MIB containing events and traps called NAGIOS-NOTIFY-MIB. You will need to install both MIB files into your SNMP management device; for example, if your trap daemon is the snmptrapd daemon, you would generally copy these files to the /usr/share/snmp/mibs directory. When you start the snmptrapd daemon, you load the MIB files using the -m and -M options:

```
puppy# /usr/sbin/snmptrapd -m ALL -M /usr/share/snmp/mibs ➥
-Lf /var/log/smnptrapd.log
```

The -m option specifies which MIBs to load; I've used the special option ALL to load all MIB files. The -M option specifies the directory to check for MIB files to load. You can see more information on how to use these options in the snmpcmd man page.

```
puppy# man snmpcmd
```

■**Note** Your own SNMP management station, such as HP OpenView or the like, will have its own method of loading MIB files. You should refer to its documentation for that.

In Example 9-28, you can see the send_traps shell script.

Example 9-28. *send_trap Shell Script*

```
# Arguments:
#   $1 = Management Station
#   $2 = Community String
#   $3 = host_name
#   $4 = service_description (Description of the service)
#   $5 = return_code (An integer that determines the state
#        of the service check, 0=OK, 1=WARNING, 2=CRITICAL,
#        3=UNKNOWN).
#   $6 = plugin_output (A text string that should be used
#        as the plugin output for the service check)
#
#
/usr/bin/snmptrap -v 2c -c $2 $1 '' NAGIOS-NOTIFY-MIB::nSvcEvent nSvcHostname ➥
s "$3" nSvcDesc s "$4" nSvcStateID i $5 nSvcOutput s "$6"
```

The shell script receives all the incoming variables and passes them to the `snmptrap` command. Let's break this command down. The `-v` option specifies the version of SNMP you are using; in this case I am using `2c` for SNMPv2. You could also use `-v 1` for SNMPv1 and `-v 3` for SNMPv3.

Tip The `snmptrap` tool has a slightly different syntax for generating traps and notifications for each version of SNMP. You should review the `snmptrap` man page for details of each. This section focuses on the syntax for SNMPv2 notifications.

The `-c` option specifies the community string passed in the $2 command-line variable. The $1 variable contains the hostname or IP address of the SNMP management station you are sending the trap to. If you specify a hostname for this value and you are reliant on DNS resolution, the command will fail if that resolution is not available. This may mean that specifying the IP address is the preferred option.

The next two single quotes are special characters representing the uptime portion of a trap. They will be replaced with the current uptime of the system generating the trap when the `snmptrap` command is executed.

The enterprise OID is specified next; in this case it is `NAGIOS-NOTIFY-MIB::nSvcEvent`. The `NAGIOS-NOTIFY-MIB` is the name of the MIB module being referenced, and the `nSvcEvent` is the trap defined for sending service events. Together these form the enterprise OID.

Tip There are also traps for host events and notifications that you can use to send host notifications to remote management stations. You can modify the commands and scripts in this section to do this.

Next I've specified a list of individual OIDs and their variables that I'm passing as part of the trap. They are, in order, the hostname, the service description, the service status ID in numerical form, and the output of the service check. They are passed in the following form:

```
oid_name  type  value
```

For example:

```
nSvcHostname  s  "puppy"
```

The `nSvcHostname` OID holds the hostname of the host that generated the service event being sent. This has been passed into the script using the `$HOSTNAME$` Nagios macro. The `s` indicates the data type of the OID; in this case `s` represents a string.

The names of the OIDs available to be used are listed in the MIB file together with the data types of the OIDs. You can see how to represent these data types, such as `i` for integer and `s` for string, in the `snmptrap` command's man page.

Finally, as the values are being passed in from Nagios, I've enclosed the ones that might contain multiword data in quotation marks so that they are passed cleanly to the command.

■Tip You can find these and other OIDs that you can use with the traps and notifications defined in the NAGIOS-ROOT-MIB and NAGIOS-NOTIFY-MIB MIB files.

The script in Example 9-28 will generate a trap much like that contained in Example 9-29.

Example 9-29. *Sample Trap Generated by the send_trap Command*

```
2005-12-18 20:00:09 puppy.yourdomain.com [10.0.0.1]:
RFC1213-MIB::sysUpTime.0 = Timeticks: (119582652) 13 days, 20:10:26.52  ➡
SNMPv2-MIB::snmpTrapOID.0 = OID: NAGIOS-NOTIFY-MIB::nSvcEvent    ➡
NAGIOS-NOTIFY-MIB::nSvcHostname = STRING: "duckling"        ➡
NAGIOS-NOTIFY-MIB::nSvcDesc = STRING: "disk"      ➡
NAGIOS-NOTIFY-MIB::nSvcStateID = INTEGER: warning(1)    ➡
NAGIOS-NOTIFY-MIB::nSvcOutput = STRING: "WARNING: c:\\: Total: 9.77G - ➡
Used: 9.1G (93%) - Free: 685M (7%)  warning"
```

You can see the values passed from Nagios have been added as the OID variable values in the generated trap. This includes the service state ID that has been converted from the integer passed to the command to the name of the state as you can see here:

```
NAGIOS-NOTIFY-MIB::nSvcStateID = INTEGER: warning(1)
```

In our example, this trap is generated and sent to the manager host, which should be configured to receive and process incoming SNMP traps. You can obviously greatly extend and change this method to use different traps and notifications, such as sending host traps, and add additional OIDs, such as the time of the status change or the state type. You should review the MIB files to see what additional OIDs are available.

■Tip There is an excellent HOWTO on how to use snmptrap to send traps at http://net-snmp. sourceforge.net/tutorial/tutorial-5/commands/snmptrap.html. Also see Chapter 9 of the *Essential SNMP* book I mentioned earlier in this chapter.

Checkpoint

- If you are sending syslog messages to your Nagios server, remember to be selective. Most hosts generate thousands of syslog messages, and most of them are not worth alerting on. Selectively filter your messages to only send those messages that are critical or that you need to alert on or record in your Nagios server.

- There are problems with the check_mrtg plug-in provided in versions 1.4.1 and 1.4.2 of the Nagios plug-in package. You may need to check the Sourceforge patches site for a fix for this plug-in.

- Think about putting any community strings used to connect to SNMP agents or send traps to management station in user macros to protect them from casual snooping.

Resources

In the sections that follow you will find some of the resources cited in this chapter, as well as some additional sources of information that may assist you in further expanding and integrating Nagios with other tools.

Books

Mauro, D., and Schmidt, K., *Essential SNMP*, O'Reilly, September 2005.

Sites

- Syslog-NG: www.balabit.com/products/syslog_ng/

- Snort documentation: www.snort.org/docs/

- Net-SNMP: http://net-snmp.sourceforge.net

MIB Files

- Cisco MIB files: www.cisco.com/univercd/cc/td/doc/product/lan/cat5000/ent_mib/getmib.htm

- Miscellaneous MIBs: www.wtcs.org/snmp4tpc/FILES/Tools/SNMP/getif/GETIF-MIBS.ZIP and www.wtcs.org/snmp4tpc/mibs.htm

- Building your own MIB files from RFCs: http://net-snmp.sourceforge.net/docs/README.mibs.html

- Nagios MIB: http://prdownloads.sourceforge.net/nagiosplug/nagiosmib-1.0.0.tar.gz?download

■ ■ ■

Developing Plug-ins

The last thing I cover in this book is the development of Nagios plug-ins. This might sound like a difficult and complicated exercise, but Nagios plug-ins are actually very simple. A plug-in generally takes a few inputs, such as the IP address of a host, and then outputs a return code, output from the check, and optionally performance data. Due to this simplicity, unlike some other enterprise monitoring tools, plug-ins can be written in almost any programming language.

Note C, Perl, and shell script are all popular languages for plug-in development.

To maintain the simplicity and consistency of plug-ins, however, you must follow a few basic rules and guidelines. I cover these rules and guidelines in this chapter as I explore different types of plug-ins.

Additionally, I briefly discuss the Nagios Event Broker or NEB. The Nagios Event Broker is an integration interface and engine. The Event Broker can be compiled into Nagios. It is activated when events occur on the Nagios server such as check results being received or notifications generated. These events trigger callbacks that are written in modules called NEB modules. These modules can feed the data from events into other tools such as a database.

Note In this chapter I focus on plug-ins that can be used to check services. The same guidelines also apply to plug-ins that could be used to check host status. The need to develop any additional host checking plug-ins is limited.

Writing Your First Plug-in

In this section I look at writing a simple plug-in using shell script. In the process, I cover some of the guidelines and recommendations for developing plug-ins.

■**Note** There are broad developer guidelines for Nagios at http://nagiosplug.sourceforge.net/ developer-guidelines.html. I'll cover most of these using examples in this chapter.

The first of these guidelines is that the Nagios default plug-ins are developed to the GNU standard so that any operating system that is supported by the GNU standards can run them. I recommend that any new plug-ins you develop also be GNU-compliant.

■**Tip** You can see some broad GNU standards at www.delorie.com/gnu/docs/GNU/standards_toc. html.

To demonstrate the process of developing a plug-in, I'm going to show you a shell script template. This simple template can form the basis for plug-ins you develop using Bash shell script. All you need to do is add the check or test logic to the template—for example, whatever you wish the plug-in to check or test for. This template is not overly sophisticated, and you will probably find that you need to expand it to address all your requirements. The template is shown in Example 10-1.

Example 10-1. *Shell Script Plug-in Template*

```
#!/bin/sh
PROGNAME=`basename $0`
PROGPATH=`echo $0 | sed -e 's,[\\/][^\\/][^\\/]*$,,'`

. $PROGPATH/utils.sh

print_usage() {
        echo "Usage: $PROGNAME"
}

print_help() {
        print_revision $PROGNAME $REVISION
        echo ""
        print_usage
        echo ""
        echo "This plugin is a template written in shell script."
        echo ""
        support
        exit 0
}
```

```
case "$1" in
      --help)
            print_help
            exit 0
            ;;
      -h)
            print_help
            exit 0
            ;;
      --version)
            print_revision $PROGNAME $REVISION
            exit 0
            ;;
      -V)
            print_revision $PROGNAME $REVISION
            exit 0
            ;;
      *)
            testdata=`test -e t1`
            status=$?
            if test "$1" = "-v" -o "$1" = "--verbose"; then
                  echo ${testdata}
            fi

            if test ${status} -eq 1; then
                echo "UNKNOWN: The plug-in has failed to function"
                exit 3

              elif echo ${testdata} | egrep WARNING > /dev/null; then
                  echo "WARNING: The plug-in returned $status"
                  exit 1

              elif echo ${testdata} | egrep CRITICAL > /dev/null; then
                  echo "CRITICAL: The plug-in returned $status"
                  exit 2

              else test ${status} -eq 0 ;
                  echo "OK: The plug-in returned $status"
                  exit 0
            fi
            ;;
esac
```

Let's walk through the structure of the shell script template in Example 10-1. At the start
of the script I define two variables, PROGNAME and PROGPATH. The first variable, PROGNAME, uses
the basename command to retrieve the name of the plug-in being executed. The PROGPATH variable retrieves the directory where the script is located.

Next we look at another script, utils.sh. The utils.sh script is contained in the Nagios plug-in package and provides a series of standard variables; for example, it specifies the service state return codes and some default text to return when the version and help text for the plug-in is queried. This script is very useful, and I recommend that you include it with any plug-in you develop. By default, the utils.sh script is installed into the same directory as your plug-ins. The content of the utils.sh script from version 1.4.2 of the Nagios plug-in package appears in Example 10-2.

Example 10-2. *The utils.sh Script*

```
#! /bin/sh

STATE_OK=0
STATE_WARNING=1
STATE_CRITICAL=2
STATE_UNKNOWN=3
STATE_DEPENDENT=4

if test -x /usr/bin/printf; then
        ECHO=/usr/bin/printf
else
        ECHO=echo
fi

print_revision() {
        echo "$1 (nagios-plugins 1.4.2) $2"
        $ECHO "The nagios plugins come with ABSOLUTELY NO WARRANTY. ➡
        You may redistribute\ncopies of the plugins under the terms of the ➡
        GNU General Public License.\nFor more information about these matters,➡
        see the file named COPYING.\n" | /bin/sed -e 's/\n/ /g'
}

support() {
        $ECHO "Send email to nagios-users@lists.sourceforge.net if you have ➡
        questions\nregarding use of this software. To submit patches or suggest ➡
        improvements,\nsend email to nagiosplug-devel@lists.sourceforge.net.➡
        \nPlease include version information with all correspondence (when ➡
        possible,\nuse output from the --version option of the plugin ➡
        itself).\n" | /bin/sed -e 's/\n/ /g'
}
```

You can see that the script defines a series of variables for service state return codes: STATE_OK equals 0, STATE_WARNING equals 1, and so on. Next, two subroutines are defined: print_revision and support. The print_revision subroutine echoes the name of the plug-in that called the subroutine and outputs some default text about a warranty and license for the plug-in. The support subroutine returns some information about where to seek support for a Nagios plug-in. The text in both subroutines is for a plug-in that is part of the Nagios default plug-in package. You can create your own version of the `utils.sh` script for your own plug-ins if you require.

■**Tip** There is also a Perl module and C code that performs the same function as `utils.sh` for Perl and C plug-ins. For C plug-ins the program is called `utils.c` and is contained in the Nagios plug-in package. For Perl scripts the module is called `utils.pm` and is also provided in the Nagios plug-in package. I'll look at the `utils.pm` module briefly later in this chapter.

In our template in Example 10-1, I next define two more subroutines, `print_usage` and `print_help`. These subroutines complement the ones contained in the `utils.sh` shell script. They specify the output of the help and version options that I'll examine next.

Next in the template is a `case` statement that handles any command-line options specified when the plug-in is executed. Our template plug-in is very simple and uses a single positional command-line option. This is not an ideal model and is one of the reasons that plug-ins are often developed in more sophisticated languages such as C and Perl.

There are five possible `case` branches to follow. Four of them expect specific command-line options. These first four branches respond to the -V, --version, -h, and --help command-line options. The -V and --version options execute the `print_revision` subroutine, and the -h and --help options execute the `print_help` subroutine. The last branch is executed if no command-line options or any option other than the four I've previously cited is present on the command line. It is this branch that contains the test or check logic for the plug-in.

The test or check logic, in this case a dummy test, is shown in the following line:

```
testdata=`test -e filename`
```

Whatever test or check you want the plug-in to perform should be specified at this point. In Example 10-1 the result of the test will be stored in the `testdata` variable.

On the next line I've defined another variable called `status`, which contains the exit status for the test function I've executed. Most well-behaved Unix commands and programs should produce an exit status: 0 for successful completion and a nonzero value for unsuccessful completion, generally a value of 1.

I'll use the value of the `status` variable to partially determine what the overall exit status of the plug-in script will be. This overall status will determine what the status of the check result that is returned to Nagios will be OK, WARNING, CRITICAL, or UNKNOWN. I'll discuss this further in a moment.

■**Tip** In shell script, the exit status is controlled by the `exit` command in the script. You can read about the `exit` command by reading its man page.

Next, I test to see if a further command-line option was present. This option is -v or --verbose, which enables a verbose mode. All plug-ins should have an option for verbosity and preferably with escalating levels of verbosity. In this case I'm only specifying one level of verbosity, but if the test you are using has the ability to output varying levels of verbosity, you could configure further tests for different levels. The plug-in development guidelines recommend the use of multiple -v options for increasing levels of verbosity: -v, -vv, and -vvv, to a maximum of three iterations. You can see the general recommended level of verbosity in Table 10-1.

Table 10-1. *Verbose Output Levels*

Level	Description
None	Single line with minimal information
-v	Single line with additional information
-vv	Multiple lines with substantial output
-vvv	Multiple lines with debug level output

In the case of the template script in Example 10-1, the result of setting the -v option is to echo the full results of the test being performed by echoing the testdata variable. This data will be returned to the command line and the plug-in then moves on to checking the output of the test to determine what status to return.

Next in the template is an if…then…elif control structure that examines the results of the test that has been executed to determine what the final status of the plug-in will be and hence the status of the check result. There are four elements to the control structure. Each element checks the exit status or the data resulting from the test itself for one of the four possible return codes for the plug-in: OK, WARNING, CRITICAL, and UNKNOWN.

The first element checks the exit status of the test itself: if it returns a 1 or greater, it is assumed that the test has failed. This is designed to catch any failure in the execution of the test either due to bad input arguments, if there are any, or due to some inherent failure in the test application or command itself. This element assumes that the failure of the test will result in an error code of 1. Many plug-ins use an element like this as a catchall for all errors in the test or plug-in. You could modify this element to catch all potential error codes in the exit status from the test like so:

```
if test ${status} -gt 1; then
                    echo "UNKNOWN: The plug-in has failed to function"
                    exit 3
```

Instead of just matching on an exit code of 1 from the test, the element now matches any exit status of 1 or higher.

If matched, this element causes the plug-in to terminate with an exit status of 3. This is the return code of the plug-in that equates to the UNKNOWN status in Nagios.

The element also echoes the string:

```
UNKNOWN: The plug-in has failed to function
```

This string is passed to Nagios as the plug-in output. You could modify this to output whatever information, such as an error message generated by the failed check or test logic.

There are some rules and guidelines for the output of a plug-in that are worth discussing here. First, you should always output something to STDOUT to indicate whether the check has been successful or has failed. This output should be a single line and less than 80 characters long. This is because Nagios only grabs the first line of output to display it in the console. This output is often also sent as a notification via an email or pager or similar notification mechanism. Thus, the output must be short enough to accommodate this purpose. The guidelines also recommend that the output should also be in the form of

```
STATUS:     Plug-in output
```

■**Caution** The STATUS shown on the previous line is not the one Nagios uses to determine the check result. Nagios uses the return code of the plug-in to determine the status of the service.

There are four possible return codes that a plug-in should return, as shown in Table 10-2. They equate to the Nagios service status codes.

Table 10-2. *Plug-in Return Codes*

Code	Description
0	OK
1	WARNING
2	CRITICAL
3	UNKNOWN

The next three elements in the template in Example 10-1 are tests to determine whether the plug-in will return one of three remaining return codes: OK, WARNING, or CRITICAL. The second and third elements use the egrep command to parse the contents of the testdata variable for particular results. In the example, I've specified that the first element check whether the string WARNING is present in the testdata variable. If the string is present, the plug-in terminates with an exit status of 1 that equates to a return code of WARNING, and a check result with this status would be returned to Nagios. This obviously assumes that whatever command is executed as the test or check logic will potentially return the string WARNING. You would design your test to check for the appropriate output to trigger each status. Indeed, this check is very simple and you could add a great level of sophistication, including checking for thresholds or the like from the testdata variable.

The third element performs a similar check but looks for the string CRITICAL. If it matches this string, the plug-in terminates with an exit status of 2 that equates to a return code of CRITICAL, and a check result with this status would be returned to Nagios.

The fourth and final element checks if the exit status of the test or check is 0 and therefore if the check completed successfully. You could also check the contents of the testdata variable for some string or content that would indicate the same result, much the same way as the second and third elements, like so:

```
else echo ${testdata} | egrep OK > /dev/null;
                        echo "OK: The plug-in returned $status"
                        exit 0
```

If it matches this string or the correct exit status, the plug-in terminates with an exit status of 0 that equates to a return code of OK. A check result with this status would be returned to Nagios.

Tip Any output from a plug-in should respect the CRT screen size of 80×25 to allow plug-ins to be used on console devices.

This shell script template is a very simple example of how a plug-in could be written, and you could obviously add considerable sophistication and detail to it. For example, you can see that no performance data is output from the template. It may have become apparent from this section that it is sometimes simpler to develop more complicated plug-ins in other languages such as C or Perl. But if you are not a programmer, you should be aware that simple plug-ins, customized for your environment, can be developed quickly in shell script. An example I regularly use is a simple plug-in that checks the content of a temporary output file for particular data. Data is written to this temporary file when particular events occur. This plug-in reads that file and checks it for particular strings that will trigger respective statuses. This plug-in can obviously be developed in C or Perl, but if you use shell script, it is quick to develop and easy to maintain, and does not require that you have any advanced programming skills.

Writing Perl Plug-ins

The Perl programming language is a popular choice for writing plug-ins because of its speed, ease of use, and adaptability. Nagios also has an embedded Perl Interpreter built into it called Embedded Perl Nagios, or ePN. This interpreter can be enabled when compiling Nagios and can potentially speed up the execution of any plug-ins written in Perl.

Note I'll discuss ePN in a sidebar later in this chapter.

Like the shell script template in Example 10-1, most Perl plug-ins have a number of features in common. They should utilize the utils.pm modules, which is the Perl equivalent of the utils.sh script I demonstrated earlier. They should also be able to receive command-line options as inputs to the Perl script. The plug-in development guidelines recommend you use the Getopt::Long module to process these options. Perl-based plug-ins also need to exit with appropriate output and an exit status code.

There are also some Perl-specific guidelines you need to consider. First, any Perl plug-in should use the strict pragma. The strict pragma insists that bareword strings must be quoted, all variables must be declared and that you can't use symbolic references. Perl should also be called with the -w command-line option that turns on warnings.

In Example 10-3, you can see a partial Perl plug-in. It contains the framework for a basic plug-in, including demonstrating how to process command-line options, but does not contain any testing or check logic.

Example 10-3. *Example Perl Plug-in*

```perl
#!/usr/bin/perl -w

use strict;
use Getopt::Long;

use lib "/usr/local/nagios/libexec";
use utils qw($TIMEOUT %ERRORS &print_revision &support &usage);
use vars qw($PROGNAME);
use vars qw($opt_V $opt_h $verbose $opt_H $opt_w $opt_c);

$PROGNAME = "perl_plugin_template";

sub print_help ();
sub print_usage ();

$ENV{'PATH'}='';
$ENV{'BASH_ENV'}='';
$ENV{'ENV'}='';

Getopt::Long::Configure('bundling');
GetOptions
        ("V"   => \$opt_V, "version"   => \$opt_V,
         "h"   => \$opt_h, "help"      => \$opt_h,
         "v" => \$verbose, "verbose"  => \$verbose,
         "H=s" => \$opt_H, "hostname=s" => \$opt_H,
         "w=s" => \$opt_w, "warning=s" => \$opt_w,
         "c=s" => \$opt_c, "critical=s" => \$opt_c);

if ($opt_V) {
        print_revision($PROGNAME,'$Revision: 1.4 $'); #'
        exit $ERRORS{'OK'};
}

if ($opt_h) {
        print_help();
        exit $ERRORS{'OK'};
}

($opt_H) || ($opt_H = shift) || usage("Host name not specified\n");
my $host = $1 if ($opt_H =~ m/^([0-9]+\.[0-9]+\.[0-9]+\.[0-9]+|[a-zA-Z]➥
[-a-zA-ZO]+(\.[a-zA-Z][-a-zA-ZO]+)*)$/);

($opt_w) || ($opt_w = shift) || usage("You must specify a warning value.\n");
my $warning = $1 if ($opt_w =~ /([0-9]+)/);
```

```
($opt_c) || ($opt_c = shift) || usage("You must specify a critical value.\n");
my $critical = $1 if ($opt_c =~ /([0-9]+)/);

# Insert plug-in logic here

sub print_usage () {
        print "This section tells you what the plug-in does.\n";
}

sub print_help () {
        print_revision($PROGNAME,'$Revision: 1.4 $');
        print "Copyright (c) 2006 James Turnbull\n";
        print "\n";
        print_usage();
        print "\n";
        print "<warn> = The warning threshold should be...\n";
        print "<crit> = The critical threshold should be...\n\n";
        support();
}
```

In Example 10-3, you can see that the perl binary has been called with the -w command-line option. I've also set the strict pragma using the use strict; statement and included the Getopt::Long module with another use statement.

■**Note** You may need to download and install the Getopt::Long module from CPAN.

Next, using two more use statements, I've included the default plug-in directory and the utils.pm module. I've also included a number of subroutines and material from this module: $TIMEOUT, %ERRORS, &print_revision, &support, and &usage.

The $TIMEOUT variable contains a default timeout value that you can include in your plug-ins. The %ERRORS array contains default definitions for the Nagios service status codes that can also be included in the plug-in. The status definitions included in the %ERRORS array should be used to exit the plug-in rather than the exit statement. So if you wish to exit the plug-in with the OK status rather than using the statement

```
exit 0
```

you would instead use the statement

```
exit $ERRORS{'OK'}
```

■**Tip** The utils.pm module is installed with the Nagios plug-in package. You should review its contents and use it whenever possible in your Perl-based plug-ins to ensure consistency.

The three subroutines, &print_revision, &support, and &usage, all provide default information that can be included in the plug-in. The &print_revision subroutine contains copyright and warranty information for plug-ins. The &support subroutine contains support information including contacts. The last subroutine, &usage, provides a default response for usage checks—for example, for any errors that relate to the failure to provide a required option or the like. I'll look at this shortly.

The next two use statements define variables to be used in the plug-in. The first variable is the $PROGNAME variable that contains the name of the plug-in. The second set of variables contains the command-line options that can be passed into the plug-in.

Next I define two subroutines, print_help that I'll use when the plug-in is called with the -h or --help command-line options and the print_usage subroutine that contains information about what the plug-in does. I also set some environmental variables.

In the next section I configure the Getopt::Long module for the possible command-line options that I wish to pass to the plug-in. I've defined some default plug-in options for returning the version and help text for the plug-in and for setting verbose mode. I also provide examples of three other common command-line options for specifying a target hostname and a WARNING and CRITICAL threshold. I've specified a list of the generally reserved command-line options in Table 10-3.

■**Note** These reserved command-line options are used for all types of plug-ins, not just those written in Perl.

Table 10-3. *Reserved Command-Line Options*

Short Option	Long Option	Description
-V	--version	Prints the version of the plug-in.
-v	--verbose	Increases the verbosity. Used multiple times for increased verbosity.
-h	--help	Prints the help text for the plug-in.
-?	N/A	Prints a short usage statement.
-t	--timeout	Specifies the timeout for the plug-in.
-w	--warning	Specifies a WARNING threshold.
-c	--critical	Specifies a CRITICAL threshold.
-H	--hostname	Specifies the target hostname.
-C	--community	Specifies an SNMP community.
-a	--authentication	Specifies an authentication password.
-l	--logname	Specifies a login name.
-p	--port | --password	Specifies a port or password.

Note You can see full documentation for the `Getopt::Long` plug-in at `http://search.cpan.org/~jv/Getopt-Long-2.35/lib/Getopt/Long.pm`.

After defining the possible command-line options, I've specified how each option will be handled. In Example 10-3 the `-V` (`--version`) and `-h` (or `--help`) options execute the `print_revision` subroutine from the `utils.pm` module and the `print_help` subroutine defined later in the plug-in example, respectively.

EMBEDDED PERL INTERPRETER

The ePN interpreter is an embedded Perl interpreter that can potentially speed up your Perl-based plug-ins. It does this by loading them into the interpreter when the Nagios process is started. This model means that not all Perl-based plug-ins will work with ePN and you may need to modify them. This sidebar will discuss some of the guidelines for developing a plug-in that is to be used with ePN.

First, if you wish to use ePN or embedded Perl Nagios, you need to ensure it is activated when you compile Nagios. To activate ePN, add the following `configure` option to the `configure` command when you are compiling Nagios like so:

```
puppy# ./configure --enable-embedded-perl
```

Once you've compiled Nagios with ePN, it will be used it to interpret your Perl-based plug-ins. To ensure your plug-ins do function with ePN, follow these simple rules:

1. Plug-ins should operate in the `strict` pragma. As a result, you should also explicitly initialize all variables; otherwise ePN could execute your plug-in repeatedly with old variable values.

2. Perl should be executed with the `-w` command-line option.

3. Do not use global variables in named subroutines. Any variables used in subroutines should be passed in the argument list.

4. Do not use `BEGIN` and `END` blocks as these are only called once when Nagios is started. ePN will not reinitialize and rerun these blocks every time the plug-in is executed, and hence this may render your plug-in inoperable.

5. Do not use `<DATA>` handles as they will not compile under ePN.

6. Always ensure you control the runtime of the plug-in using a timeout, preferably using the `$TIMEOUT` variable imported from the `utils.pm` module.

7. Always explicitly use `close` statements to close any files that are open in a plug-in.

The ePN is a complicated framework and is most useful if you rely on a large number of plug-ins written in Perl. It can reduce the time spent running and the system impact of Perl-based plug-ins. But it can also be harder to code for and debug, and may have a slightly larger memory footprint than non-ePN Nagios. You can read about ePN in more detail at `http://nagios.sourceforge.net/docs/2_0/embeddedperl.html`.

The three example command-line options for hostname and the two thresholds are processed slightly differently. First, each option is checked to ensure it is present; if any of three options is not present, the plug-in will fail with an error message like so:

```
puppy# ./perl_plugin_template.pl -w 1 -c 2
Host name not specified
```

As I haven't specified the -H or --hostname option with a suitable value, the plug-in has ended with an error message indicating which command-line option is missing.

Next, if the command-line option is present, a regular expression is used to capture the value of the option and store it in a variable. This is not a very sophisticated method of grabbing the command-line option. For example, it does not perform any validation on the hostname or IP address to ensure it is in a valid format or that the WARNING or CRITICAL threshold is in a viable data type for whatever comparison is defined.

In the next section I've added a comment where the actual check or test logic for the plug-in would be located. This would use the command-line option data passed into the plug-in to perform some form of check and potentially compare the result of that check to input thresholds. You can see a number of examples of Perl-based plug-ins in the Nagios plug-in package that should provide insight into how a Perl-based plug-in should be constructed.

Last in the plug-in example, two subroutines are defined: one that provides a usage statement for the plug-in and another that provides help text for the plug-in.

Other Guidelines

There are also a number of other guidelines used for developing plug-ins. These guidelines become particularly relevant as your plug-ins become more complicated and require additional inputs and variables, such as specifying WARNING and CRITICAL thresholds; processing threshold ranges; outputting performance data; processing command-line options; and some general guidelines about how to handle files, system commands, and the like. I'm going to quickly cover the most important guidelines here, but you can refer to more complete documentation at http://nagiosplug.sourceforge.net/developer-guidelines.html.

Specifying Threshold Ranges

One of the common features of a plug-in is the ability to specify thresholds, including threshold ranges. These thresholds and threshold ranges can be configured to trigger different statuses if breached; for example, if disk space exceeds a certain threshold, the WARNING status is set and if it exceeds a further threshold, the CRITICAL status is set. Threshold ranges operate in the same manner, but the threshold that triggers each status is generally a range of integers or values. Threshold ranges are generally set in the format:

```
[@]start:end
```

There are a number of guidelines about how these threshold ranges should be set. First, and most important, they must be logical. The start threshold value needs to be less than the end threshold value. If you do not specify the start (including the :) value, it assumes that start is equal to 0 like so:

```
puppy# ./sample_plugin -w 50 -c 51:100
```

On this line the WARNING status would be triggered if the plug-in returned a value between 0 and 50, and the CRITICAL status would be returned if the plug-in returned a value between 51 and 100.

If you do not specify an end value but only specify start:, it is assumed that end is infinity:

```
puppy# ./sample_plugin -w 1:50 -c 51:
```

Here the WARNING status would be triggered if the plug-in returned a value between 1 and 50, and the CRITICAL status would be returned if the plug-in returned any value greater than 51.

If you wish to specify negative infinity, you should use the ~ symbol like so:

```
start:~
```

A status is normally generated if the value returned by the plug-in is outside the start and end values, including the endpoints. To reverse this behavior, you should prefix the range with the @ symbol like so:

```
@start:end
```

This will cause the alert to occur if the plug-in returns a value inside the range.

Specifying Performance Data

As I've discussed earlier in the book, performance data contains additional metrics and information returned from the plug-in. It is located after the plug-in output and should be separated from the output with the | symbol. It is structured like so:

```
|'label'=value[UOM];[warning];[critical];[minimum];[maximum]
```

After the | symbol, each metric returned by a plug-in is specified in a label and value pair. Each pair is separated by a space. The label portion of the metric can contain any character, and it is generally recommended that you enclose it in single quotes to preserve any spaces or other special characters it may contain, such as an = symbol, from being incorrectly interpreted. The value itself is followed by a unit of measure (UOM). This can be a number of different units of measure, as shown in Table 10-4.

Table 10-4. *Units of Measure*

Unit	Description
%	Percentage
s	Seconds
c	Continuous counter like the volume of traffic through an interface
B	Bytes
KB	Kilobytes
MB	Megabytes
GB	Gigabytes
TB	Terabytes
	None, for example an integer

The four items after the label and value pair are the values that would trigger the WARNING or CRITICAL status and the minimum and maximum possible values that could be returned. In Example 10-4, the check_disk plug-in is executed with the WARNING status triggered if there is less than 10 percent free disk space and the CRITICAL status if 5 percent or less disk space is free.

Example 10-4. *Performance Data*

```
puppy# /usr/local/nagios/libexec/check_disk -w 10% -c 5%
DISK OK - free space: / 9245 MB (51%); /boot 72 MB (73%); /dev/shm 124 MB (100%);➥
| /=8865MB;16299;17204;0;18110 /boot=26MB;88;93;0;98 /dev/shm=0MB;111;117;0;124
```

In Example 10-4 you can see three metrics in the performance data after the | symbol. These metrics represent the three partitions checked by the plug-in. The label of the metric is the name of the partition, and the value of the metric is the free space available on that partition. The value also has a unit of MB attached to it indicating megabytes.

The warning and critical values are the values that will trigger the respective status. In Example 10-4 for the / partition the WARNING threshold would be triggered if there was more than 16299Kb of disk space used and the CRITICAL status triggered if more than 17204Kb of disk space used. Lastly are the minimum and maximum values that represent the size of the partition. Again for the / partition in Example 10-4 the minimum value is 0 and the maximum value is the size of the partition, 18110Kb.

Any of these values can be null if they are not required, such as if there is no minimum or maximum, as is the case if the unit of measure is a percentage. Any leftover semicolons can be dropped. The warning and critical values are in range format (see the "Specifying Threshold Ranges" section earlier) and must have the same unit of measure. The minimum and maximum values must also both have the same unit of measure.

Commands and Files

Plug-ins should also exercise caution when using external commands and files, including temporary files. When executing external commands, such as a system command like grep, you should always specify the full path to the command being executed. This is simply good coding practice and prevents the substitution of Trojan programs higher in the path with the same name as the external command. These Trojan programs, being higher in the path, would be executed instead of the intended command.

If you are going to open any files, ensure you always check that you are opening a local file and that again you specify the full path to the file. Additionally, make sure you are not opening a symlinked file. Both these precautions mitigate any risk that your existing file could be replaced with malicious or incorrect data.

With temporary files, the best practice is simply not to use them. They open up a number of ways that a plug-in can fail—for example, if the file can't be found or written to, or the file system runs out of space. As with commands and other files, you should always specify the full path to your temporary files and preferably store them in an appropriate directory, such as /tmp.

If you must use temporary files, ensure that if one or more of these errors occurs the plug-in will exit cleanly and remove the temporary file. In the event of such a failure, it is recommended that your plug-in exit with an UNKNOWN status and an appropriate error message.

Plug-in Timeouts

All plug-ins should have a limited runtime. The usual default, which can be overridden using the reserved command-line option –t, is 10 seconds. The plug-ins should be coded to exit gracefully if this timeout is exceeded. I suggest that you code a plug-in to exit with the UNKNOWN status and an error message indicating that it has timed out. As with a normal exit from a plug-in, you should ensure that a timeout also cleans up after itself by removing any temporary files, sockets, locks, or the like. This is especially important for plug-ins that use some form of network connectivity.

Command-Line Options

Most plug-ins will have command-line options. Indeed, I've already discussed the use of reserved command-line options earlier in this chapter. But there are a few guidelines and rules around the use and processing of command-line options. The first guideline addresses how to process command-line options and arguments. Earlier in this chapter I also mentioned, while looking at a sample Perl plug-in, the CPAN module called Getopt::Long. The Getopt::Long module allows for the processing of command-line options. It performs a similar function to the standard C libraries getopt and Getopt_long. These modules and libraries allow the processing of command-line options without having to rely on positional arguments. Positional arguments are passed into a plug-in or program based on their order on the command line, for example:

```
puppy# ./sample_plugin $1 $2 $3 $4 $5
```

The guidelines for plug-ins strongly discourage from the use of positional arguments. Generally speaking, positional arguments are clumsy and can introduce errors into your plug-ins. I recommend you use the appropriate command-line option processing modules or libraries for your chosen language rather than positional arguments.

■**Note** If you are writing a plug-in in shell script, you will have to use positional arguments.

As I discussed earlier, most plug-ins should have a number of command-line options that should be specified in all plug-ins. These include the -V or --version option, which should return the revision of the plug-in. In the case of most plug-ins, it is recommended that you call a function or subroutine called print_revision from a module like utils.sh, utils.pm, or utils.c. This function or subroutine should return the current plug-in revision in a default format.

Additionally, the -? and the -h or --help options should always be present. When the -? option is specified, or in the event the plug-in receives a set of options that can't be parsed, a short usage statement should be printed. The usage statement is usually in a default format provided by a function or subroutine called print_usage that is specified in a module like utils.sh, utils.pm and utils.c.

The -h or --help command-line options should return a more complete help statement for the plug-in, including all possible command-line options and any examples of how to use the plug-ins. As with the -V option, the recommended approach is to execute a subroutine, this one called `print_help`. Generally this function or subroutine should execute a combination of functions or subroutines, usually the `print_revision` subroutine and the `print_usage` subroutine, and then display detailed help for the plug-in.

Finally, the `-v` or `--verbose` command-line option should be specified for all plug-ins. The option should increase the amount of information returned by the plug-in, and you should be able to specify it multiple times to increase the level of verbosity returned by the plug-in.

■Tip I discussed levels of verbosity earlier in this chapter.

Other Guidelines

Other guidelines deal with a variety of other facets of plug-in development. This includes developing test cases, coding guidelines (including commenting both in-line and in CVS), handling translations, and submitting new plug-ins or patches to plug-ins. You can see these guidelines at `http://nagiosplug.sourceforge.net/developer-guidelines.html`.

Nagios Event Broker

I discussed in Chapters 6 and 9 a number of ways to integrate Nagios with other tools, such as databases, SNMP-based tools, and `syslog` daemons. The Nagios Event Broker represents a far more advanced way to perform this integration. It uses callback routines that are executed when events occur in the Nagios server. Using NEB, you can convert these events, including data like check results, from Nagios into a variety of forms, such as a MySQL database, an SNMP trap, or a `syslog` message.

The Event Broker is essentially an integration interface. Shared code libraries, called NEB modules, are linked into the Nagios server process at runtime. Events occur in Nagios and the event broker sends the events to registered callback procedures in an NEB module. NEB modules can be written in C or C++.

To use the Event Broker, you need to enable it when Nagios is compiled, as discussed in Chapter 1. This is done using the `--enable-neb` configuration option. This option is enabled by default, and the Event Broker should be compiled into the Nagios daemon by default. In Example 10-5 you can see the `General Options` section of the output from the Nagios `configure` process that shows the Nagios Event Broker enabled.

Example 10-5. *Enabling the Nagios Event Broker Using configure*

```
General Options:
------------------------
        Nagios executable:  nagios
        Nagios user/group:  nagios,nagios
        Command user/group:  nagios,nagios
        Embedded Perl:  yes, without caching
        Event Broker:  yes
```

```
Install ${prefix}:  /usr/local/nagios
Lock file:  ${prefix}/var/nagios.lock
Init directory:  /etc/rc.d/init.d
Host OS:  linux-gnu
```

The Event Broker: yes line indicates that the Event Broker is enabled and will be compiled when Nagios is compiled.

An NEB module can monitor for and process a variety of events; here's a brief list:

- Events related to the Nagios daemon such as startup and shutdown

- Host and service checks

- Notifications

- Event handlers

- When external commands are initiated

- When retention data is loaded and saved

- When comments and downtime are added or deleted

- When flapping starts and stops for hosts and services

- When adaptive monitoring changes occur

- Log events including log rotation

Each of these events can have callbacks registered for them. You can register multiple callbacks for events, and thus multiple NEB modules can be loaded for different purposes. Then when an event occurs, the Event Broker checks to see if any callbacks are registered for that event. Each registered callback is then executed in order of registration.

Helloworld

The Nagios package comes with an extremely simple example of how to write an NEB module, and I'll look at that module, Helloworld, very briefly here to provide some further information. The module code is located in the module directory in the root of the Nagios package and consists of the helloworld.c source file and a Makefile. You can compile it like so:

```
puppy# gcc -shared -o helloworld.o helloworld.c
```

The resulting helloworld.o module can then be loaded into Nagios. To do this, the module needs must specified in the nagios.cfg configuration file, usually located in the /usr/local/nagios/etc, directory using a broker_module directive like so:

```
broker_module=/usr/local/nagios/bin/helloworld.o
```

The module is then loaded when Nagios is started and unloaded when it is stopped. Thus, if you add in a module you need to restart Nagios to have it take effect.

The Helloworld module is extremely simple and simply logs a message to the default Nagios log file, usually /usr/local/nagios/var/nagios.log, when Nagios is started and stopped, and when aggregated status updates start and finish. On the following lines, you can see the messages it logs when aggregated status updates start and finish:

```
[1137157196] helloworld: An aggregated status update just started.
[1137157196] helloworld: An aggregated status update just finished.
```

Let's quickly look at the code for this module. Example 10-6 shows the include statements for the module.

Example 10-6. *Module include Statements*

```
#include "../include/nebmodules.h"
#include "../include/nebcallbacks.h"
#include "../include/nebstructs.h"
#include "../include/broker.h"
#include "../include/config.h"
#include "../include/common.h"
#include "../include/nagios.h"
```

▪**Note** All the include files are located in the `include` directory of the Nagios source code package.

In Example 10-6, you can see the first two `include` statements, which contain the `nebmodules.h` and `nebcallbacks.h` include files. Every module needs to use these two includes as a minimum. Below them are two more `include` statements for the `nebstructs.h` and `broker.h` include files. The `nebstructs.h` file contains the data structures needed for the Event Broker. The `broker.h` include file contains all the Event Broker options, event types, event flags, event attributes, and functions.

Finally, the three default include files for most Nagios code, `config.h`, `common.h`, and `nagios.h`, are added. These provide the common functions and definitions for Nagios.

Next in the `helloworld.c` module code you can see the Event Broker API version specified like so:

```
NEB_API_VERSION(CURRENT_NEB_API_VERSION);
```

This version specification is required in all modules.

After this, the `helloworld.c` code includes the logic for the module. You can see further down in this logic the code that registers a callback so that the module is notified when status aggregation events occur:

```
neb_register_callback(NEBCALLBACK_AGGREGATED_STATUS_DATA,helloworld_module_handle,↵
0,helloworld_handle_data);
```

You can see a list of all the possible callbacks that can be registered in the `nebcallbacks.h` include file. This file also includes the registration and deregistration functions for callbacks. Here you can see the callback de-registered:

```
neb_deregister_callback(NEBCALLBACK_AGGREGATED_STATUS_DATA,helloworld_handle_data);
```

This module code should assist in the process of creating additional modules.

NDO Utilities

Also available as an example of an NEB module is the NDO utilities add-on. The NDO utilities add-on, written by Nagios developer Ethan Galstad, is designed to output events and data from Nagios to standard files or to a Unix socket. It also comes with a module called NDO2DB that allows Nagios data to be written to a MySQL or PostgreSQL database.

The add-on is made up of the NDOMOD Event Broker module, which is loaded by Nagios at runtime. It dumps all events and data from Nagios to a regular file or a Unix domain socket. It also contains the ndo2db daemon, which reads data that has been sent for the NDOMOD module to a Unix domain socket and dumps it into a MySQL or PostgreSQL database. You can dump into multiple databases and have multiple instances of the NDOMOD module writing to the same domain socket. There is also a utility called FILE2SOCK, which reads data from a standard file and dumps it into a Unix domain socket. Suggested uses are to dump data from NDOMOD that has been stored in a standard file into a Unix domain socket. Or if your Nagios server is remote from your database server, you can dump data into a standard file from NDO-MOD, send the file via SSH or SFTP to the database server, and then dump the data into a Unix domain socket and from there into a database. Finally, there is the LOG2NDO utility, which imports historical Nagios log files into the ndo2db daemon and sends them to a Unix domain socket or to standard output.

In this section, I set up this NEB module to output data from Nagios to a MySQL database. You can explore the other components of the add-on; if you are interested in developing your own NEB modules, the source code of this add-on will provide considerable information. Indeed, it should be possible to lift large chunks of the NDOMOD module code to perform a variety of possible functions, such as serving as the front-end of a module that outputs events as SNMP traps. Or you can simply use it to output data to a Unix domain socket or standard file and then use another tool to pick up and convert that data into another tool or application. I discussed similar applications without using an NEB module in Chapters 6 and 9.

To install the NDO add-on, you first need to download and unpack the module from the Nagios Sourceforge site at
`http://sourceforge.net/project/showfiles.php?group_id=26589&package_id=173832`, as you can see here:

```
puppy# wget http://optusnet.dl.sourceforge.net/sourceforge/nagios/➥
ndoutils-12272005.tar.gz
puppy# tar -zxf ndoutils-12272005.tar.gz
puppy# cd ndoutils-12272005
```

■Note The NDO utilities module is under considerable development, and you should download the latest version. You will also need to be using Nagios 2.0rc1 or later for the NDO utilities package to be functional.

Next you will need to compile and install the module. The module uses a `configure` script to create the `Makefile` and it can then be compiled.

```
puppy# ./configure --enable-mysql --disable-pgsql --with-mysql-lib=/usr/lib/mysql
```

On this line I've used the `configure` command with a number of options to compile the NDO utilities modules. At this point, the NDO utilities modules support MySQL and PostgreSQL databases. I've enabled MySQL support, disabled PostgreSQL support, and specified the location of the MySQL client libraries.

■**Note** You will need either the MySQL and PostgreSQL packages installed to use the NDO utilities module's database support.

I've listed the most important of the `configure` options in Table 10-5.

Table 10-5. *NDO Utilities* configure *Options*

Option	Description
`--enable-mysql`	Enables MySQL database support
`--enable-pgsql`	Enables PostgreSQL support
`--disable-mysql`	Disables MySQL support
`--disable-pgsql`	Disables PostgreSQL support
`--with-mysql-lib=`*dir*	Specifies the location of the MySQL client library files
`--with-mysql-inc=`*dir*	Specifies the location of the MySQL client include files
`--with-pgsql-lib=`*dir*	Specifies the location of the PostgreSQL client library files
`--with-pgsql-inc=`*dir*	Specifies the location of the PostgreSQL client include files

After you've configured the NDO utilities add-on, you need to `make` it:

```
puppy# make
```

The NDO utilities add-on does not have an automated installation script, so you will need to install it manually, which we'll look at in a moment. But first you need to set up a database to hold the outputted data. Create a database called `nagios` using the `mysql` interface:

```
puppy# mysql
mysql> CREATE DATABASE nagios;
Query OK, 1 row affected (0.08 sec)
```

The NDO add-on contains a script to populate this newly created database with the required tables. For MySQL, it is called `ndo-mysql.sql`, and it is located in the `db` directory in the root of the package:

```
puppy# mysql nagios < /ndoutils-12272005/db/ndo-mysql.sql
```

Next, you need to create a username and password for the database:

```
mysql> GRANT SELECT,INSERT,UPDATE,DELETE ON nagios.* TO nagios@localhost ➥
IDENTIFIED BY 'password';
```

You must grant the user you create, in this case nagios, the SELECT, INSERT, UPDATE, and DELETE privileges to the nagios database. Replace 'password' with an appropriate password for the database.

To install the NDO module itself, install the compiled ndomod.o module file located in the src directory. I recommend copying it into the Nagios bin directory, usually /usr/local/nagios/bin:

```
puppy# cp src/ndomod.o /usr/local/nagios/bin
```

You also need to copy the sample configuration file for the module, ndomod.cfg. It is located in the config directory in the NDO utilities package. I recommend installing it to the Nagios etc directory, usually /usr/local/nagios/etc:

```
puppy# cp config/ndomod.cfg /usr/local/nagios/etc
```

You also need to install the ndo2db daemon and its configuration file. They are also located in the src and config directories, respectively, and I suggest you copy them to the same locations in your Nagios installation:

```
puppy# cp src/ndo2db /usr/local/nagios/bin
puppy# cp config/ndo2db.cfg /usr/local/nagios/etc
```

Next, you need to modify your Nagios configuration file, nagios.cfg, to load the NDO module when Nagios starts. Add the following line to your nagios.cfg configuration file, usually located in /usr/local/nagios/etc:

```
broker_module=/usr/local/nagios/bin/ndomod.o ➥
config_file=/usr/local/nagios/etc/ndomod.cfg
```

This configuration directive will load the ndomod.o NEB module when Nagios is started. You will need to restart Nagios to make the module active. The config_file part of the directive must be modified to specify the location of the module configuration file.

You should ensure that the ownership and permissions of all these files is appropriate. They should generally all be owned by the user and group used by the Nagios server process and the configuration files only readable by that user:

```
puppy# chown nagios:nagios /usr/local/nagios/bin/ndo2db /usr/local/nagios/ ➥
bin/ndo2db.o /usr/local/nagios/etc/ndo2db.cfg /usr/local/nagios/bin/ndomod.cfg
puppy# chmod 0600 /usr/local/nagios/etc/ndo2db.cfg /usr/local/nagios/etc/ndo2db.cfg
```

You may also want to modify the two configuration files, ndo2db.cfg and ndomod.cfg. By default, the ndomod.o NEB module outputs data to a Unix domain socket, /usr/local/nagios/var/ndo.sock, which is created by the ndo2db daemon when it is started. You will also need to modify the ndo2db.cfg configuration file to update it with the correct database name, username, and password to allow the ndo2db daemon to write to the database.

■**Tip** Both sample configuration files are extensively documented internally if you wish to modify them.

Next you need to start the ndo2db daemon like so:

```
puppy$ su nagios
puppy$ /usr/local/nagios/bin/ndo2db /usr/local/nagios/etc/ndo2db.cfg
```

The daemon is launched with one command-line option, the location of the ndo2db daemon's configuration file ndo2db.cfg. The daemon will create the Unix domain socket, /usr/local/nagios/var/ndo.sock. As you can see, I used the su command to change to the user nagios before launching. You should run the ndo2db daemon as the nagios user to allow the Unix domain socket to be created with the correct ownership. This will allow the ndomod.o module, which is run with the ownership and permissions of the Nagios server process, to write to that domain socket.

■**Tip** You will need to write an init script, or other mechanism by which your host starts processes, for the ndo2db daemon; such a script is not contained in the current NDO utilities package.

With the ndo2db daemon running and the ndomod.o NEB module loaded into Nagios, events and data will now be logging to the specified database.

■**Tip** The module logs events and errors in the default Nagios log file, usually /usr/local/nagios/var/nagios.log. Check this file for errors and messages.

Other Sources of Information

This module and associated code should provide a good introduction to Nagios Event Broker modules and their functions. But where can you find out more about the Nagios Event Broker? Well, as I mentioned the NDO utilities package is an excellent example of a module, and the code contained in that package could easily form the basis for a number of variations.

■**Note** There is also a partially developed Nagios-to-database module, much like the NDO utilities add-on, at http://magoazul.com/proj/nagios/nag-db-0.0.1.tgz. This is also another useful source of information and code about NEB modules.

With regard to documentation, not a lot has been a lot produced about the NEB interface to date. Taylor Dondich of IT GroundWork has written two excellent articles (with more promised) about the NEB interface for the IT GroundWork weblog. You can read the first article at www.itgroundwork.com/blog/?p=13 and the second at www.itgroundwork.com/blog/?p=18. But other than these materials, there is a dearth of documentation regarding the NEB interface. Ethan Galstad has indicated that further documentation for the Nagios Event Broker will be forthcoming.

Checkpoints

- Always design and code your plug-ins using the established Nagios Plug-in Development Guidelines and in accordance with GNU standards.

- Avoid the use of positional arguments and rely on libraries and modules such as Getopt and Getopt::Long.

- Always specify the full path to any files, system commands, or objects referenced in your plug-in code to prevent insertion of malicious Trojans.

- Try to avoid the use of temporary files as they can create problems for the running of your plug-ins.

- Always ensure your plug-ins obey a timeout and that they are designed to exit cleanly and clean up any files, objects, or sockets that they have used.

Resources

- Nagios Plug-in Development Guidelines: http://nagiosplug.sourceforge.net/developer-guidelines.html

- Embedded Perl Nagios (ePN): http://nagios.sourceforge.net/docs/2_0/embeddedperl.html

- NDOutils: http://sourceforge.net/project/showfiles.php?group_id=26589&package_id=173832

- NEB HOW-TO Weblog Entries: www.itgroundwork.com/blog/?p=13 and www.itgroundwork.com/blog/?p=18

Index

▮Numbers and symbols

! character
    prefixed arguments with ! character, 201
? option
    plug-in reserved command-line options, 353
1 option
    check_by_ssh plug-in, 180
2 option
    check_by_ssh plug-in, 180
2d_coords directive, 266
3-D Status Map page
    Monitoring section, web console, 133
3d_coords directive, 267
4 option
    check_by_ssh plug-in, 180
    check_ssh plug-in, 155
    check_tcp plug-in, 157
6 option
    check_by_ssh plug-in, 180
    check_ssh plug-in, 155
    check_tcp plug-in, 157

▮A

a option
    check_http plug-in, 160
    check_mrtg plug-in, 321
    check_mrtgtraf plug-in, 319
    check_nrpe plug-in, 166, 198
    check_rrd.pl plug-in, 322
    plug-in reserved command-line options, 353
    service_perfdata_file_mode directive, 230
accept_passive_host_checks directive, 281
accept_passive_service_checks directive, 281
Acknowledge this service problem command
    Service Commands box, 121
ACKNOWLEDGEMENT notification type, 215
action_url directive, 266
active checks, 42
    author's tip, 44
    service dependencies, 252
active_checks_enabled directive, 40, 43, 57, 281
adaptive monitoring
    external commands for, 225–227
Add New Comments link
    Service Comments box, 124
address directive, 37, 38
addresses
    defining host address, 84
addressing directives, 74
addressx directive, 75
administration, 100–110
    external commands, 88–90
    init script, 106
    logging, 107–110
    Nagios init script, 107
    starting and stopping Nagios servers, 101–106
aggregate_writes option
    nsca.cfg file, 283, 284
aggregation
    notifications, 220–221
AIM
    sending notifications via, 220
Alert Histogram report, web console, 134
Alert History report, web console, 134
Alert Summary report, web console, 134
alerts
    integrating Snort alerts with Nagios, 313–317
    SNMP traps, 323
alert_syslog output plug-in
    configuring Snort for Nagios integration, 314, 315
    sending Snort alerts to Nagios server, 317
alias directive, 37, 73, 76, 78
    configuring web server for Nagios, 23
    defining, 38
    not specifying value for, 38
allow directive
    configuring web server for Nagios, 23, 24
allowed_hosts directive
    NSC.ini configuration file, 194, 195
allowed_hosts option
    nrpe.cfg configuration file, 169, 292
    nsca.cfg configuration file, 283, 310
AllowOverride directive
    configuring web server for Nagios, 23, 24
    web console authentication, 92
allow_arguments directive
    NSC.ini configuration file, 195, 196
allow_arguments option
    CheckDriveSize command, NSC.ini, 201
allow_nasty_meta_chars directive
    NSC.ini configuration file, 195, 196

alternate_dump_file option
    nsca.cfg file, 283, 284
Anon-DH function
    SSL/TLS functionality, 164
Apache Basic authentication, 93
Apache Digest authentication, 96
    checkpoint, 111
Apache directives
    see directives, Apache
Apache web server
    installing from RPM, 7–8
    installing from source, 6–7
    web console authentication with Apache,
        91–96
apachectl command
    restarting Apache, 26
APAN tool, 246
append_to_file option
    nsca.cfg file, 283, 284
archives
    Backtracked Archives option, 137, 138
    log_archive_path directive, 109, 135
arguments
    allow_arguments directive, 195, 196
$ARGx$ macros, 82
    check_local_disk command, 148
Assume Initial States option, 137
Assume State Retention option, 137, 138
Assume States During Program Downtime
        option, 137, 138
authentication, 97–100
    AllowOverride directive, 92
    Apache Basic authentication, 93
    Apache Digest authentication, 96
    authenticated contacts, 91, 92
    authenticated users, 91, 92
    authentication directives, 93
        in .htaccess file, 92
    authentication failure, 98
    checkpoint, 111
    check_by_ssh plug-in, 176
    default users, 99
    default_user_name directive, 99
    description, 91
    disabling, 97
    no users defined, 97
    NSCA package, 285
    use_authentication directive, 97
    web console authentication with Apache,
        91–96
authentication option
    plug-in reserved command-line options,
        353
AuthName directive
    web console authentication, 93

authorization, 97–100
    authorization directives, 98
        commented out by default, 99
    checkpoint, 111
    default authorization, 100
    description, 91
authorized_for_all_hosts directive, 99, 135
authorized_for_all_host_commands directive,
        99
authorized_for_all_services directive, 99, 135
authorized_for_all_service_commands
        directive, 99
authorized_for_configuration_information
        directive, 99, 141
authorized_for_system_commands directive,
        99
authorized_for_system_information directive,
        99
authorized_keys file, 177
    check_by_ssh plug-in, 179
    command option, 179
authpriv facility
    configuring Snort for Nagios integration,
        315
    configuring syslog-NG for Snort, 315
AuthType directive
    web console authentication, 93
AuthUserFile directive
    web console authentication, 93
availability
    deploying Nagios servers, 3
availability data interpretation, 137
Availability report page
    Reporting section, web console, 138
Availability report, web console, 134–139
    selecting host (step 2), 135
    selecting report options (step 3), 136
    selecting report type (step 1), 135
    undetermined state, 142

■B

Backtracked Archives option, 137, 138
backup of Nagios servers, 5
base installation directory
    directory structure, Nagios, 15
batch files
    check_batch command, 196, 197
BEGIN/END blocks
    ePN interpreter, 354
bigger.cfg configuration file
    starting configuration, 32
bin directory, 15
binaries
    location of, 15
    nagios binary, 101, 103
    using full paths for commands, 144

broker.h include file
  Helloworld module, NEB, 361
broker_module directive
  Helloworld module, NEB, 360

■C

C compiler
  installation prerequisites, 6
C option
  check_by_ssh plug-in, 175, 179-181
  check_nagios plug-in, 293
  check_rpc plug-in, 161
  check_smtp plug-in, 161
c option
  check_disk plug-in, 148, 150-151
  check_mrtg plug-in, 320
  check_mrtgtraf plug-in, 318
  check_nrpe plug-in, 166, 197
  check_nt plug-in, 193
  check_rrd.pl plug-in, 322
  check_tcp plug-in, 157
  htpasswd command, 94
  nrpe daemon, 170, 293
  nsca binary, 286
    starting NSCA daemon for syslog
      messages, 311
  plug-in reserved command-line options,
    353
  send_nsca program, 277
  send_trap script, 339
  snmptrapd daemon, 326
  snmpwalk command, 184
c service notification option, 64
c state, escalation, 251, 260
caching
  objects.cache file, 108
  object_cache_file directive, 108
Cacti, 317
capacity planning, 4
  Nagios hardware sizing figures, 4
case statement
  writing simple plug-in, 347
ceil function
  author's note, 59
central server
  introduction, 271
  receiving service checks, 288
central server configuration
  distributed monitoring, 280–288
    configuring NSCA daemon, 282–285
    freshness checks, 286–288
    installing NSCA daemon, 282
    starting NSCA daemon, 286
  passive checks, 281
cfengine
  Nagios server synchronization, 289

cfg_file directive
  in nagios.cfg, 33
  specifying configuration files, 32, 34
CGI alias
  configuring web server for Nagios, 22
CGI files
  information about CGI programs, 114
  location of, 15
  reading resource files, 81
  WAP-based CGI page, 115
CGI programs
  custom CGI headers and footers, 139
  incorporating into web console, 134
cgi.cfg file (web console configuration file), 30
  author's tip, 30
  comments, 97
  Nagios authentication and authorization,
    97
  syntax of directives, 97
cgiurl option
  Nagios critical configure options, 11, 12
  Nagios plug-in configure options, 19
  with-cgiurl option, 11
CGIWrap, 96
  checkpoint, 111
chaining object inheritances, 69
CHANGE_MAX_SVC_CHECK_ATTEMPTS
    command, 227
CHANGE_NORMAL_HOST_CHECK_
    INTERVAL command, 227
CHANGE_SVC_CHECK_COMMAND
    command, 226
characters
  escaping special characters, 80, 82
check commands, 79–82
  command_line directive, 80
  command_name directive, 80
CHECK PROCESSING INFORMATION
    heading, 105
check-host-alive command, 81
  monitoring hosts, 144
CheckAlwaysCRITICAL command, NSC.ini,
    199
CheckAlwaysOK command, NSC.ini, 199
CheckAlwaysWARNING command, NSC.ini,
    199
CheckCounter command, NSC.ini, 199, 202,
    204–205
CheckCPU command, NSC.ini, 198
CheckDisk.dll module
  NSC.ini configuration file, 192, 198
CheckDisk.dll, NSClient++, 199–202
CheckDriveSize command, NSC.ini, 198, 199
  allow_arguments option, 201
  thresholds, 199
  units of measurement, 200

CheckEventLog.dll module
  NSC.ini configuration file, 192, 198
CheckFileSize command, NSC.ini, 198, 199
CheckHelpers.dll module
  NSC.ini configuration file, 192, 193, 199
CheckMem command, NSC.ini, 199
CheckMultiple command, NSC.ini, 199
CheckProcState command, NSC.ini, 199, 203
checks
  active checks, 42
  active_checks_enabled directive, 43, 57
  command_check_interval directive, 89
  defining two checks intervals, 61
  freshness checks, 286–288
  host check directives, 40
  host_check_timeout directive, 40
  how Nagios works, 29
  log_passive_checks directive, 109, 110
  max_check_attempts directive, 41, 57
  max_concurrent_checks directive, 60
  max_service_check_spread directive, 60
  normal_check_interval directive, 57, 61
  obsess_over_host directive, 52, 53
  parallelize_check directive, 57, 61
  passive checks, 42
  passive_checks_enabled directive, 43, 57
  performance data, 227
  processing checks results with external
    commands, 224–225
  retry_check_interval directive, 57, 61
  service checking, 56–63
  service_check_timeout directive, 57
CheckServiceState command, NSC.ini, 199,
    202–203
  MaxCrit threshold, 204
  MaxWarn threshold, 204
CheckSystem.dll module
  NSC.ini configuration file, 192, 198
  NSClient++, 202–205
CheckUpTime command, NSC.ini, 199
check_batch command
  NSC.ini configuration file, 196, 197
check_by_ssh command/plug-in, 175–181
  indirect monitoring with NRPE, 173
  options, table of, 180
  passive mode, 178, 179
  protecting public and private keys, 205
check_command directive, 40, 57, 81, 82, 287
  indirect monitoring with NRPE, 172
  macro for, 40, 57
  monitoring using commands, 144
check_cpu command
  NSC.ini configuration file, 196
check_dhcp plug-in, 159
check_disk command/plug-in, 148–151
  help option, 149
  monitoring via NRPE, 163

  options, table of, 150
  remote monitoring using, 161
  setting thresholds, 148
  thresholds, 148
check_disk_fixed command
  FilterType argument, 201
check_dns plug-in, 159
check_dummy plug-in, 287
check_external_commands directive, 89, 281
  external commands, 222
check_file_age plug-in, 151, 152
check_fping plug-in, 159, 160
  plug-ins prerequisites, 18
check_freshness directive, 40, 43, 57, 287
check_game plug-in, 18
check_hpjd plug-in, 18
check_host_freshness directive, 45, 287
check_http plug-in, 159, 160
check_ifoperstatus plug-in, 187
  plug-ins prerequisites, 18
check_ifstatus plug-in, 187
  plug-ins prerequisites, 18
check_imap plug-in, 159, 161
check_interval directive, 40, 42
  author's tip, 42
check_ldap plug-in, 159, 160
  plug-ins prerequisites, 18
check_load plug-in, 151, 152
check_local_disk command, 148
check_local_user command, 82
check_log plug-in, 151, 152
check_log2 plug-in, 153
check_mailq plug-in, 151, 153
check_mrtg plug-in, 318, 320–322
  caution regarding, 322, 341
check_mrtgtraf plug-in, 318–320
check_mysql plug-in, 18
check_nagios plug-in, 292, 297
check_nntp plug-in, 159, 161
check_nrpe command/plug-in, 162, 166–167
  author's caution, 163
  check_batch command, NSC.ini, 197
  configuring NRPE, 294, 296
  failover process, 297
  indirect monitoring with NRPE, 171
  NSClient++, 188, 194
  prefixed arguments with ! character, 201
  testing, 170
check_nt plug-in, 188, 193
check_ntp plug-in, 159
check_period directive, 40, 57
check_ping plug-in, 160
  indirect monitoring with NRPE, 174
  monitoring hosts, 144
check_ping plug-in binary, 81
check_pop plug-in, 159, 161
check_pqsql plug-in, 18

check_procs plug-in, 151, 153
check_radius plug-in, 18
check_rpc plug-in, 159, 161
check_rrd.pl plug-in, 318, 322–323
check_rrd_data.pl plug-in, 322
check_service_freshness directive, 63, 287
check_smtp command, 80
check_smtp plug-in, 159, 161
check_snmp plug-in, 182, 185
    indirect monitoring with NRPE, 173
    modes of operation, 186
    plug-ins prerequisites, 18
check_ssh plug-in, 154–156
check_stale command, 287
check_swap plug-in, 151, 153
check_tcp plug-in, 156–158
    indirect monitoring with NRPE, 174
    monitoring services, 146
check_udp plug-in, 158
check_ups plug-in, 18
check_users plug-in, 151, 154
CLIENTVERSION check, NSClient++, 192
close statements
    ePN interpreter, 354
colorscheme directive, Nagiosgraph, 240
command-group option
    Nagios critical configure options, 11, 12
command groups
    with-command-user option, 13
command line
    escaping special characters, 80
command-line options
    developing plug-ins, 358–359
    plug-in reserved command-line options,
        353
command mode directory, 15
command object
    description, 31
    using check_mrtg plug-in, 321
    using check_mrtgtraf plug-in, 320
    using on-demand macros, 209
command option
    authorized_keys file, 179
    nrpe.cfg configuration file, 169
    nrpe.cfg file, 292
command types
    macros used in, 208
command-user option
    Nagios configure options, 13
commands
    authorized_for_all_host_commands
        directive, 99
    authorized_for_all_service_commands
        directive, 99
    check commands, 79–82
    check_command directive, 40, 57
    check_external_commands directive, 89

command_line directive, 214
    defining, 79–84
    event handler commands, 83
    external commands, 221–227
    host_notification_commands directive, 73,
        74, 214
    host_perfdata_command directive, 228
    how Nagios works, 29
    monitoring using, 144
    notification commands, 84, 214
    service_notification_commands directive,
        73, 74, 214
    service_perfdata_command directive, 228
command_check_interval directive, 89, 222
command_file directive, 89, 222
command_file option
    nsca.cfg file, 283, 284
command_line directive, 80, 214
    special characters, 214
    using full paths, 205
command_name directive, 80
command_name element
    external commands, 222
command_timeout directive
    NSC.ini configuration file, 195, 196
command_timeout option
    nrpe.cfg file, 292
comments
    author's tip, 32
    comment_file directive, 108
    NSC.ini configuration file, 190
Comments page
    Monitoring section, web console, 133
comments.dat file, 108
comment_file directive, 108
common.h include file, 361
community option, 353
community strings, 341
    exposing, 337
compilation
    compiling Nagios, 11–16
        Nagios compilation completion
            message, 14
    Nagios configure options, 13
    Nagios critical configure options, 11
    NRPE, 163–166
conf.d directory
    configuring web server with RPM
        installation, 26
config.h include file
    Helloworld module, NEB, 361
configuration
    authorized_for_configuration_information
        directive, 99, 141
    configuring for performance data, 241–242
    configuring for SNMP traps, 335
    configuring web server for Nagios, 21–26

basic configuration, 22–24
 restarting Apache, 26
 RPM installation, 25
 testing, 26
 virtual server configuration, 24–25
contact objects, 72–75
defining commands, 79–84
defining configuration objects, 35–36
defining first host, 36–54
defining services, 54–67
defining time periods, 78–79
enable-neb configuration option, 359
grouping objects, 75–78
how Nagios is configured, 30–35
Nagiosgraph, 239–241
NSClient++ client, 190–196
plug-ins configure options, 19
starting configuration, 32
syslog-NG daemon for Nagios, 302–306
using templates for object definition, 67–71
configuration files
 bigger.cfg, 32
 categorized configuration files, 35
 commenting out directives, 32
 comments, 32
 defining multiple configuration files, 33
 location of, 15
 minimal.cfg, 32
 Nagios server and web console
   configuration files, 30
 Nagios server software, 15
 nrpe.cfg file, 168
 object configuration files, 31
 ownership of, 35
 resource files, 30
 specifying configuration files, 32–35
 types, 30
configuration objects
 defining configuration objects, 35–36, 84
 Extended Host Information objects, 265
 Extended Service Information objects, 265
 synchronization, 298
Configuration section, web console, 140
 View Config page, 140
configure command
 compiling Nagios, 11, 13
configure script
 installing Apache web server, 7
 installing NSCA, 272
 installing RRDtool, 238
 Nagios plug-in configure statement, 18, 19
configure script, NRPE
 enable-ssl option, 164
 installing and compiling NRPE, 164
 installing Nagios plug-ins, 168
 nrpe daemon, 167
 options, table of, 164

connections
 security guidelines, 88
contact group objects, 77–78
 alias directive, 78
 contactgroup_name directive, 78
 members directive, 78
contact objects
 configuration, 72–75
 description, 31
$CONTACTADDRESSx$ macro, 75, 220
$CONTACTALIAS$ macro, 73
$CONTACTEMAIL$ macro, 75, 215
contactgroup object, 31
contactgroups directive, 73
contactgroup_name directive, 78
$CONTACTNAME$ macro, 73
$CONTACTPAGER$ macro, 75
contacts
 addressx directive, 75
 alias directive, 73
 authenticated contacts, 91
   access to hosts, 100
 basic contact directives, 73
 contact addressing directives, 75
 contact definitions, 72
 contact notification directives, 73
 contact objects, 72–75
 contactgroups directive, 73
 contact_name directive, 73
 email directive, 75
 host_notification_commands directive, 73,
   74
 host_notification_options directive, 73
 host_notification_period directive, 73
 how Nagios works - the basics, 29
 notifications, 85
   author's caution, 74
 pager directive, 75
 service_notification_commands directive,
   73, 74
 service_notification_options directive, 73
 service_notification_period directive, 73
contact_groups directive, 38, 55, 56, 259
 defining, 38, 39
contact_name directive, 73
context
 macro context, 208
COUNTER check, NSClient++, 192
counters
 CheckCounter command, NSC.ini, 204–205
CPU
 check_cpu command, 196
CPULOAD check, NSClient++, 192
CREATE DATABASE command, MySQL, 232
crit priority filter
 syslog-NG daemon, 303

critical option
    plug-in reserved command-line options,
        353
CRITICAL state, 63
    CheckAlwaysCRITICAL command, 199
    CheckDriveSize command thresholds, 200
    MaxXyz thresholds, CheckDriveSize
        command, 200
    MinXyz thresholds, CheckDriveSize
        command, 200
    monitoring hosts, 145
    setting thresholds, 148
    specifying plug-in performance data, 357
    specifying plug-in threshold ranges, 356
    writing simple plug-in, 349
Current Network Status box
    Service Detail page, 119

D

d command-line switch
    starting Nagios daemon, 101
d notification option, 46
D option
    check_tcp plug-in, 157, 158
    snmptrapd daemon, 326
d option
    log rotation, 108
    nrpe daemon, 170, 293
    sendxmpp, 219
    send_nsca program, 277, 278, 308
    syslog-NG daemon, 301
d service scheduling setting, 58
d state, notification criteria, 257
daemon mode, nsca binary, 286, 311
daemonchk.cgi program, 134
daemons
    integrating with syslog daemons, 299–313
    starting Nagios daemon, 101
    using appropriate privilege level, 12
daemon_fork directive, snmptt.ini file, 329
daemon_uid directive, snmptt.ini file, 329
DATA handles
    ePN interpreter, 354
databases
    inserting data into MySQL, 231–237
$DATE$ macro, 215
dates
    $LONGDATETIME$ macro, 215
date_format directive, 215
date_mask directive
    NSC.ini configuration file, 194
days of the week
    time period directives for, 78
db option, nagiosgraph, 244
DBI package
    inserting data into MySQL, 235, 237

DCHP server
    check_dhcp plug-in, 159
debug directive
    Nagiosgraph, 240
    NSC.ini configuration file, 194
debug option
    nrpe.cfg configuration file, 169
    nsca.cfg file, 283, 284
decryption_method option
    nsca.cfg configuration file, 283, 285, 310
default users, 99
    checkpoint, 111
default_user_name directive, 99
define directive
    closing, 36
    defining configuration objects, 35, 36
    opening, 36
Delete all comments link
    Service Comments box, 125
dependencies
    host dependencies, 250, 256–258
    service dependencies, 250–255
        inheritance, 254–255
        shortcuts, 253–254
dependent_host_name directive, 251, 256
dependent_service_name directive, 251
deploying Nagios servers, 1
DESCRIBE command, MySQL, 233, 234
destinations
    syslog-NG daemon, 303, 304
diff
    Nagios server synchronization, 289
Digest authentication
    see Apache Digest authentication
directive functionality
    checking host, 39–45
    defining configuration objects, 35
directives
    authentication directives, 93
    authorization directives, 98
    basic contact directives, 73
    contact addressing directives, 75
    contact notification directives, 73
    commenting out of nagios.cfg, 32
    host check directives, 40
    mandatory directives, 37
    nagios.cfg directives for obsession, 53
    regular expressions, 71
    service checking directives, 57
    service directives, 55
    state retention directives, 50
    syntax of, 97
directives (list of)
    2d_coords, 266
    3d_coords, 267
    accept_passive_host_checks, 281
    accept_passive_service_checks, 281

action_url, 266
active_checks_enabled, 40, 43, 57, 281
address, 37, 38
addressx, 75
alias, 37, 38, 73, 76, 78
authorized_for_all_hosts, 99, 135
authorized_for_all_host_commands, 99
authorized_for_all_services, 99, 135
authorized_for_all_service_commands, 99
authorized_for_configuration_information,
    99, 141
authorized_for_system_commands, 99
authorized_for_system_information, 99
broker_module, 360
check_command, 40, 57, 287
check_external_commands, 89, 281
check_freshness, 40, 43, 57, 287
check_host_freshness, 45, 287
check_interval, 40, 42
check_period, 40, 57
check_service_freshness, 63, 287
command_check_interval, 89
command_file, 89
command_line, 80, 214
command_name, 80
comment_file, 108
contactgroups, 73
contactgroup_name, 78
contact_groups, 38, 55, 56, 259
contact_name, 73
date_format, 215
default_user_name, 99
dependent_host_name, 251, 256
dependent_service_name, 251
downtime_file, 108
email, 75
enable_flap_detection, 48
enable_notifications, 281, 290, 294
escalation_options, 260
escalation_period, 259
event_handler, 49, 211
event_handler_enabled, 49, 211
event_handler_timeout, 83
execute_host_checks, 281, 290, 294
execute_service_checks, 281, 290, 294
execution_failure_criteria, 251, 252
first_notification, 259
freshness_threshold, 40, 43, 57, 287
global_host_event_handler, 50, 210
global_service_event_handler, 65, 210
high_host_flap_threshold, 48
hostgroups, 38
hostgroup_name, 55, 56, 76
host_check_timeout, 40
host_freshness_check_interval, 45, 287
host_inter_check_delay, 59
host_name, 37, 55, 56, 251, 256, 266, 267

host_notification_commands, 73, 74, 214
host_notification_options, 73
host_notification_period, 73
host_perfdata_command, 228, 234
host_perfdata_file, 230
host_perfdata_file_mode, 230
host_perfdata_file_processing_command,
    231
host_perfdata_file_processing_interval, 231
host_perfdata_file_template, 230
icon_image, 266
icon_image_alt, 266
illegal_macro_output_chars, 208
inherits_parent, 255, 257
is_volatile, 57, 62
last_notification, 259, 261
lock_file, 108
log_archive_path, 109, 135
log_event_handlers, 109, 110
log_external_commands, 109, 110
log_file, 107
log_host_retries, 109, 110
log_initial_states, 109, 110
log_notifications, 109, 110
log_passive_checks, 109, 110
log_rotation, 135
log_rotation_method, 108
log_service_retries, 109, 110
low_host_flap_threshold, 48
max_check_attempts, 40, 41, 57
max_concurrent_checks, 60
max_service_check_spread, 60
members, 76, 78
nagios_group, 88
nagios_user, 88
name, 67
normal_check_interval, 57, 61
notes, 266
notes_url, 266
notifications_enabled, 45, 63, 64
notifications_interval, 45, 63, 64
notifications_options, 45, 46, 63, 64
notifications_period, 45, 63, 64
notification_failure_criteria, 252, 256, 257
notification_interval, 259
notification_options, 213
notification_period, 259
object_cache_file, 108
obsess_over_host, 52
obsess_over_hosts, 53, 276
obsess_over_services, 66, 275
ochp_command, 53, 276, 279
ocsp_command, 66, 276
pager, 75
parallelize_check, 57, 61
parents, 38, 256
passive_checks_enabled, 40, 43, 57

perfdata_timeout, 229
process_performance_data, 241
process_perf_data, 52, 54, 67, 228
register, 68
resource_file, 81
retain_nonstatus_information, 51, 67
retain_state_information, 50, 108
retain_status_information, 51, 67
retention_update_interval, 50, 108
retry_check_interval, 57, 61
servicegroups, 55, 56
servicegroup_name, 77
service_check_timeout, 57
service_description, 55, 251, 276
service_freshness_check_interval, 63, 287
service_interleave_factor, 59, 60
service_notification_commands, 73, 74, 214
service_notification_options, 73
service_notification_period, 73
service_perfdata_command, 228, 234
service_perfdata_file, 230, 241
service_perfdata_file_mode, 230, 241
service_perfdata_file_processing_
    command, 241
service_perfdata_file_processing_interval,
    231, 241
service_perfdata_file_template, 230, 241
service_reaper_frequency, 61
soft_state_dependencies, 252
stalking_options, 52, 53, 66
state_retention_file, 50, 108
statusmap_image, 266
status_file, 108
timeperiod_name, 78
traphandle, 326
use, 68
use_authentication, 97
use_regexp_matching, 71
use_retained_program_state, 50, 51
use_retained_scheduling_info, 60
use_syslog, 109
use_true_regexp_matching, 71
vrml_image, 266
directives, Apache
    Alias, 23
    Allow, 23, 24
    AllowOverride, 23, 24
    AuthName, 93
    AuthType, 93
    AuthUserFile, 93
    Directory, 22, 24, 25, 93
    DocumentRoot, 25
    Include, 26
    Options, 23, 24
    Order, 23, 24
    Require, 94
    ScriptAlias, 22

ServerAdmin, 25
ServerName, 25
VirtualHost, 24, 25
directives, Nagiosgraph
    colorscheme, 240
    debug, 240
    heartbeat, 240
    icon_image, 243
    icon_image_alt, 243
    logfile, 240
    mapfile, 240
    notes_url, 243, 244
    perflog, 240
    rrddir, 240
directives, NSC.ini
    allowed_hosts, 194, 195
    allow_arguments, 195, 196
    allow_nasty_meta_chars, 195, 196
    command_timeout, 195, 196
    date_mask, 194
    debug, 194
    file, 194
    obfuscated_password, 194
    password, 194
    port, 195
    use_ssl, 195, 196
directives, snmptt.ini file
    daemon_fork, 329
    daemon_uid, 329
    dns_enable, 329
    exec_enable, 330
    log_enable, 330
    mode, 329
    sleep, 329
    snmptt_conf_files, 330
    spool_directory, 329
    strip_domain, 330
    syslog_enable, 330
Directory directive
    author's caution, 22
    configuring web server for Nagios, 22, 24
    virtual server configuration, 25
    web console authentication, 93
directory structure, 15
    author's tip, 17
    base installation directory, 15
    Nagios RPM, 17
disable-mysql options
    NDO utilities add-on, 363
disable-pgsql options
    NDO utilities add-on, 363
DISABLE_NOTIFICATIONS command
    configuring NRPE, 296
disk space
    capacity planning, 4
    check_disk plug-in, 148–151

disks
  CheckDisk.dll module, 192
Display Filters box
  Service Detail page, 119
distributed environment
  author's tip, 5
  distributed monitoring model, 270
distributed monitoring, 269–288
  central server configuration, 280–288
    configuring NSCA daemon, 282–285
    freshness checks, 286–288
    installing NSCA daemon, 282
    starting NSCA daemon, 286
  distributed server configuration, 271–280
    configuring send_nsca, 273–276
    installing NSCA, 272–273
    sending host check results, 279–280
    sending service check results, 276–278
  freshness, 298
distributed server configuration
  distributed monitoring, 271–280
    configuring send_nsca, 273–276
    installing NSCA, 272–273
    sending host check results, 279–280
    sending service check results, 276–278
  enable_notifications directive, 271
  retain_state_information directive, 272
  use_retained_program_state directive,
    272
distributed servers
  introduction, 269, 271
  sending service check to central server,
    280
DNS resolution
  checking host or services on host, 85
  enabled, 330
DNS server
  check_dns plug-in, 159
dns_enable directive, snmptt.ini file, 329
documentation
  web site references, 85
Documentation link
  General section, web console, 115
DocumentRoot directive
  virtual server configuration, 25
dont_blame_nrpe option
  nrpe.cfg configuration file, 169
  nrpe.cfg file, 292
DOWN state, 41
  d notification option, 46
downtime, 122
  Assume States During Program Downtime
    option, 137, 138
  scheduling downtime, 124
  scheduling service downtime, 123
  Service group pages scheduling, 129
  types of, 123

Downtime page
  Monitoring section, web console, 133
downtime.dat file, 108
downtime_file directive, 108
drives
  FilterType argument, 201
DSA keys, 176
dumb service scheduling method, 58

■E

e option
  check_disk plug-in, 150
  check_mrtg plug-in, 321
  check_mrtgtraf plug-in, 319
  check_nagios plug-in, 293
  check_rrd.pl plug-in, 323
  check_tcp plug-in, 157, 158
EDESC directive
  translated trap, 332, 333
email
  $CONTACTEMAIL$ macro, 215
  host-notify-by-email command, 216
  notify-by-email command, 214, 215
email directive, 75
embedded Perl interpreter, 354
empty files
  Nagios detecting, 34
  touch command, 34
enable-command-args option
  configure script, NRPE, 164, 165
enable-embedded-perl option, 13
enable-event-broker option, 13
enable-mysql options
  NDO utilities add-on, 363
enable-neb configuration option
  Nagios Event Broker, 359
enable-perl-site-install option, configure
    script
  installing RRDtool, 238
enable-pgsql options
  NDO utilities add-on, 363
enable-ssl option
  configure script, NRPE, 164
  configuring NRPE, 295
  configuring nrpe daemon, 291
enable_flap_detection directive, 48
  service flapping, 65
ENABLE_NOTIFICATIONS command
  configuring NRPE, 296
enable_notifications directive, 281, 290, 294
  distributed server configuration, 271
encryption
  NRPE, 164
  NSCA package, 274, 285
  public key encryption, 176
  using NSCA or NRPE, 298

encryption_method option
   nsca.cfg configuration file, 310
   send_nsca.cfg configuration file, 274, 284,
      307
end threshold value
   specifying plug-in threshold ranges, 355
environmental variables
   macro environmental variables, 209
   macros as environmental variables, 210
epager
   host-notify-by-epager command, 216
   notify-by-epager command, 216
ePN interpreter, 354
ERRORS array %ERRORS array
   writing Perl plug-ins, 352
escalation states, 260
escalations
   contact_groups directive, 259
   first_notification directive, 259
   host notification escalations, 258, 264–265
   introduction, 258
   last_notification directive, 259, 261
   notification_interval directive, 259
   service notification escalations, 258,
      259–264
      multiple service escalations, 260
      recovery notifications escalations, 261
      shortcuts, 262–264
escalation_options directive, 260
escalation_period directive, 259
escaping special characters, 82, 201
   command line, 80
etc directory, 15
etc/nagios directory, Nagios RPM, 17
Event Broker
   see NEB
event handler commands, 83
event handlers, 49–50, 210–213
   event_handler directive, 211
   event_handler_enabled directive, 211
   event_handler_timeout directive, 83
   execution of event handlers, 83
   global event handlers, 210
      precedence, 65
   global_host_event_handler directive, 50,
      210
   global_service_event_handler directive, 65,
      210
   host and service macros for event handlers,
      83
   local event handlers, 210
   log_event_handlers directive, 109, 110
   purpose, 211
   sending SNMP traps, 336
   service object definition, 211
   services, 65

EVENT lines
   translated trap, 332
Event Log report, web console, 134, 140
event logs
   CheckEventLog.dll module, 192
event_handler directive, 49, 211
event_handler_enabled directive, 49, 211
event_handler_timeout directive, 83
EXEC statements
   executing SNMPTT tool, 336
   SNMP traps, 330–335
execute_host_checks directive, 281, 290, 294
execute_service_checks directive, 281, 290,
   294
execution criteria states, 251
execution_failure_criteria directive, 251, 252
exec_enable directive, snmptt.ini file, 330
exit command, 347
Extended Host Information objects
   see also hostextinfo object
   CGI programs, 265
   example, 265
Extended Service Information objects
   see also serviceextinfo object
   CGI programs, 265
   example, 267
Extensible Messaging and Presence Protocol
   (XMPP)
   sending notifications via Jabber, 217
external command file
   author's caution, 15
   location of, 15
external command group
   creating, 10–11
External Command Interface page, 117
   disabling notifications via external
      command, 117
   Monitoring section, web console, 121, 122
   red fields, 142
external commands, 221–227
   adaptive monitoring, 225–227
   check_external_commands directive, 89,
      222
   command_check_interval directive, 89, 222
   command_file directive, 89, 222
   configuring Nagios to run, 14
   developing plug-ins, 357
   elements of, 222
   integrating non-Nagios aware tools, 247
   list of commands, 223
   log_external_commands directive, 109, 110
   permissions, 90
   processing checks results with, 224–225
   PROCESS_HOST_CHECK_RESULT
      command, 224, 225
   PROCESS_SERVICE_CHECK_RESULT
      command, 224

security and administration for, 88–90
START_EXECUTING_SVC_CHECKS
command, 223, 224
STOP_EXECUTING_SVC_CHECKS
command, 223
submitting, 225
submitting via shell script, 224
Windows checks, NSClient++, 197–198

∎**F**

f notification option, 46, 47
F option
check_log plug-in, 152
check_mrtg plug-in, 320
check_mrtgtraf plug-in, 318
check_nagios plug-in, 293
check_rrd.pl plug-in, 322
f option
check_by_ssh plug-in, 180
notifications_options directive, 215
sendxmpp, 219
snmptrapd daemon, 326
syslog-NG daemon, 301
f service notification option
description, 64
$FACILTY macro
configuring syslog-NG for Nagios, 304
failover monitoring, 289–297
configuring master server, 290–293
configuring NRPE, 294–297
configuring nrpe daemon, 291–293
configuring NSCA, 293
configuring slave server, 294–297
enable_notifications directive, 290
enable_notifications directives, 294
execute_host_checks directive, 290
execute_host_checks directives, 294
execute_service_checks directive, 290
execute_service_checks directives, 294
installing NSCA for, 297
interaction between master and slave, 297
model of, 290
file directive
NSC.ini configuration file, 194
FILE2SOCK utility
NDO utilities add-on, 362
FileLogger.dll module
NSC.ini configuration file, 192, 193
files
CheckDisk.dll module, 192
developing plug-ins, 357
filters
syslog messages, 302, 340
syslog-NG daemon, 302
FilterType argument
check_disk_fixed command, 201

firewalls
checkpoint, 110
distributed configuration, 2
security guidelines, 88
First Assumed Host State option, 137
First Assumed Service State option, 137
first_notification directive, 259
fixed downtime, 123
flapping, 47–49
enable_flap_detection directive, 48
f notification option, 47
flapping algorithm, 48
flapping status changes, 48
high_host_flap_threshold directive, 48
high_service_flap_threshold directive, 65
low_host_flap_threshold directive, 48
low_service_flap_threshold directive, 65
service flapping, 65
setting flap detection and thresholds, 48
FLAPPINGSTART notification type, 215
FLAPPINGSTOP notification type, 215
flexible downtime, 123
footers
adding content to Nagios web console, 142
custom CGI headers and footers, 139
FORMAT lines
translated trap, 332, 333
fping command
check_fping plug-in, 159, 160
fping package
installing Nagios plug-ins via RPM, 20
freshness
distributed monitoring, 298
freshness checks
check_command directive, 287
check_freshness directive, 287
check_host_freshness directive, 287
check_service_freshness directive, 287
distributed monitoring, 286–288
freshness_threshold directive, 287
host_freshness_check_interval directive,
287
service_freshness_check_interval directive,
287
freshness_threshold directive, 40, 43, 57, 287

∎**G**

GAUGE-based metrics, 246
gd includes
installing, 8–9
with-gd-inc option, 13
gd library
installing, 8–9
with-gd-lib option, 13
gd-inc option, 13
gd-lib option, 13

General section, web console, 115
geom option, nagiosgraph, 244
Getopt::Long module
    command-line options, 358
    full documentation for, 354
    writing Perl plug-ins, 350, 352, 353
global event handlers, 210
global_host_event_handler directive, 50, 210
global_service_event_handler directive, 65, 210
GRANT command, MySQL, 234
graphs
    Nagiosgraph creating additional graphs, 244–246
    Nagiosgraph displaying graphs, 242–244
Grid view
    Host and Service group pages, 129
        Host group grid view, 130
grouping objects
    configuration, 75–78
    contact group objects, 77–78
    host group objects, 76
    service group objects, 77
groups
    contact_groups directive, 259
    security guidelines, 87

■H

H option
    check_dns plug-in, 160
    check_http plug-in, 160
    check_nrpe plug-in, 166
    check_rpc plug-in, 161
    check_smtp command, 80
    check_smtp plug-in, 161
    check_snmp plug-in, 185
    check_ssh plug-in, 154, 155
    plug-in reserved command-line options, 353
    send_nsca program, 277
h option
    check_by_ssh plug-in, 180
    check_disk plug-in, 149, 150
    check_mrtg plug-in, 321
    check_mrtgtraf plug-in, 319
    check_nt plug-in, 193
    check_rrd.pl plug-in, 323
    check_tcp plug-in, 156
    log rotation, 108
    plug-ins, 156
    sendxmpp, 219
    writing Perl plug-ins, 354, 355
hard state, 41
hardware
    choosing, 3

Nagios hardware sizing figures, 4
    symmetric multiprocessing, 4
headers
    adding content to Nagios web console, 142
    custom CGI headers and footers, 139
heartbeat directive, Nagiosgraph, 240
Helloworld module
    NEB (Nagios Event Broker), 360–361
help flag, configure script
    installing RRDtool, 238
help option
    check_disk plug-in, 149
    plug-in reserved command-line options, 353
    writing Perl plug-ins, 354
helpers
    CheckHelpers.dll module, 192, 193
high_host_flap_threshold directive, 48
high_service_flap_threshold directive, 65
Home link
    General section, web console, 115
home partition
    check_disk plug-in, 151
$HOST macro
    configuring syslog-NG for Nagios, 304
Host and Service Extended Information objects, 249
host checks
    CHANGE_NORMAL_HOST_CHECK_INTERVAL, 227
    scheduling, 84
        author's tip, 59
    sending host check results, 279–280
Host Commands box
    Host Information page, 127
Host Comments box
    Host Information page, 127
host dependencies, 256–258
    description, 249
    inheritance, 257
    introduction, 250
    parents directive, 256
    shortcuts, 258
Host Detail page
    Monitoring section, web console, 125–127
host group objects, 76
    adding host to host group, 77
    alias directive, 76
    hostgroup_name directive, 76
    members directive, 76
Host group pages
    Monitoring section, web console, 127
        Host group grid view, 130
        Hostgroup Overview page, 127
Host Information page
    Monitoring section, web console, 126
        Host Commands box, 127

Find it faster at http://superindex.apress.com/

Host Comments box, 127
Host Status Information box, 126
host notification escalations, 264–265
    description, 249
    introduction, 258
    shortcuts, 264
host objects
    description, 31
    generic host object template, 70
    host object definition template, 67
    use directive, 68
host obsession, 53
Host Problems page
    Monitoring section, web console, 133
HOST SCHEDULING INFORMATION
        heading, 105
host states, 41
    DOWN, 41
    numeric representation of, 279
    OK, 41
    UNREACHABLE, 41
Host Status box
    Service Detail page, 119
Host Status Information box
    Host Information page, 126
host-notify-by-email command, 216
host-notify-by-epager command, 216
$HOSTADDRESS$ macro, 37, 80
    address directive, 38
    monitoring hosts, 144
    on-demand macros, 209
$HOSTALIAS$ macro, 37
$HOSTATTEMPT$ macro, 83
    event handling, 213
hostdependency object
    dependent_host_name directive, 256
    description, 31, 249, 250
    host_name directive, 256
    inherits_parent directive, 257
    notification_failure_criteria directive, 256,
        257
hostescalation object, 31, 249, 258
$HOSTEXECUTIONTIME$ macro, 227
hostextinfo object
    see also Extended Host Information objects
    2d_coords directive, 266
    3d_coords directive, 267
    action_url directive, 266
    description, 31, 249
    example, 265
    host_name directive, 266
    icon_image directive, 266
    icon_image_alt directive, 266
    notes directive, 266
    notes_url directive, 266
    statusmap_image directive, 266
    vrml_image directive, 266

hostgroup object, 31
hostgroups directive, 38, 39
hostgroup_name directive, 55, 56, 76
$HOSTLATENCY$ macro, 227
$HOSTNAME$ macro, 37
    macro context, 208
hostname option
    plug-in reserved command-line options,
        353
    writing Perl plug-ins, 355
$HOSTOUTPUT$ macro, 230, 279
    performance data, 228
$HOSTPERFDATA$ macro, 230
    performance data, 228
hosts
    allowed_hosts directive, 194, 195
    authorized_for_all_hosts directive, 99, 135
    authorized_for_all_host_commands
        directive, 99
    defining first host, 36–54
    description, 36
    directives checking hosts, 39–45
        author's tip, 42
    disabling host checking, 41
    First Assumed Host State option, 137
    First Assumed Service State option, 137
    flapping, 47
    global_host_event_handler directive, 210
    host check directives, 40
    host_notification_commands directive, 73,
        74
    host_notification_options directive, 73
    host_notification_period directive, 73
    how Nagios works, 29
    location of, 27
    log_host_retries directive, 109, 110
    managed devices, 181
    minimum number of directives, 36
    monitoring hosts, 144–145
    network elements, 181
    NRPE on remote host, 167–171
    obsess_over_host directive, 52
    obsess_over_hosts directive, 53, 276
    ochp_command directive, 53, 276, 279
    scheduling regular checks of, 42
Hosts box
    Tactical Monitoring Overview page, 116
$HOSTSTATE$ macro, 83
$HOSTSTATEID$ macro, 279
$HOSTSTATETYPE$ macro, 83
host_check_timeout directives, 40
host_freshness_check_interval directive, 45,
        287
host_inter_check_delay directive, 59
host_name directive, 37, 55, 56, 251, 256, 266,
        267

host_notification_commands directive, 73, 74, 214
host_notification_options directive, 73
host_notification_period directive, 73
host_perfdata_command directive, 228, 234
host_perfdata_file directive, 230
host_perfdata_file_mode directive, 230
host_perfdata_file_processing_command directive, 231
host_perfdata_file_processing_interval directive, 231
host_perfdata_file_template directive, 230
.htaccess file, 92
HTML Alias
    configuring web server for Nagios, 23
HTML files
    authentication, 111
    location of, 15
htmlurl option
    Nagios critical configure options, 11, 12
    with-htmlurl option, 11
.htpasswd command
    web console authentication with Apache, 94
HTTP
    check_http plug-in, 159, 160
httpd daemon
    installing Apache web server, 6, 7

■

i option
    check_by_ssh plug-in, 178
    check_rrd.pl plug-in, 323
    nrpe daemon, 170
ICMP (Internet Control Message Protocol) pings, 1
icon_image directive, 243, 266
icon_image_alt directive, 243, 266
ICQ
    sending notifications via, 220
if ... then ... elif control structure
    writing simple plug-in, 348
illegal_macro_output_chars directive, 208, 246
IMAP server
    check_imap plug-in, 159, 161
in option
    snmpttconvertmib tool, 331
Include directive
    configuring web server with RPM installation, 26
include option
    nrpe.cfg configuration file, 169
Include Soft States option, 137, 138
include statements
    Helloworld module, NEB, 361

include_dir option
    nrpe.cfg configuration file, 169
indirect monitoring with NRPE, 171–175
inetd
    running nrpe daemon, 170
    running NSCA daemon, 283
inetd mode
    nsca binary, 286, 311
inheritance
    host dependencies, 257
    service dependencies, 254–255
inherits_parent directive, 255, 257
init script, 106–107
    compiling Nagios, 14
    nrpe daemon, 293
    NSCA package, 286
    restarting Apache, 26
    running syslog-NG daemon, 301
    starting NSCA daemon for syslog messages, 311
    with-init-dir option, 13
init-dir option, 13
initial service scheduling, 58–60
inject function
    NSClient++ internal commands, 199
install command
    compiling Nagios, 14
installations
    Apache web server software
        from RPM, 7–8
        from source, 6–7
    gd library and gd includes, 8–9
    Nagios plug-ins, 5, 168
        from source, 17–20
        via RPM, 20–21
    Nagios server software, 5
        configuring web server for Nagios, 21–26
    Nagios server software from source, 9–16
        compiling Nagios, 11–16
        creating external command group, 10–11
    Nagios server software via RPM, 9, 16–17
        author's tip, 32
    Nagiosgraph, 239
    Net-SNMP package, 183
    NRPE, 163–166
    nrpe daemon, 167
    NSCA daemon, 282
    NSCA package, 272–273
    NSClient++ client, 189–190
    prerequisites, 5–9
    RRDtool, 237–238
    security guidelines, 87
    send_nsca program for syslog-NG, 306–308
    syslog-NG daemon, 300
instant messaging services, 217
Instant Messenger
    sending notifications via Jabber, 217–220

integration interface
  Nagios Event Broker, 359
Intel-based hardware
  author's note, 4
  choosing software and hardware, 3
interleaving
  scheduling, 59, 60
  service_interleave_factor directive, 59, 60
internal commands
  Windows checks, NSClient++, 198–205
intervals
  check_interval directive, 42
  normal_check_interval directive, 61
  notifications_interval directive, 45, 63, 64
  retention_update_interval directive, 108
  retry_check_interval directive, 57, 61
iptables rules
  configuring nrpe daemon, 291
  running NSCA daemon, 284
is_volatile directive, 57, 62
  configuring Nagios for Snort alerts, 317
  configuring Nagios for syslog messages, 312

■**J**
j option
  check_tcp plug-in, 157
  sendxmpp, 219
Jabber instant messaging service
  sending notifications via Instant Messenger, 217–220
  tutorial on setting up Jabber server, 217
  using sendxmpp command, 218–220

■**K**
k option
  check_disk plug-in, 150
kerberos
  with-kerberos-inc option, 164
keys
  DSA and RSA keys, 176
  protecting for check_by_ssh command, 205
known_hosts file
  ssh directory, 177

■**L**
l option
  check_disk plug-in, 150, 151
  check_mrtg plug-in, 321
  check_rrd.pl plug-in, 323
  plug-in reserved command-line options, 353
last_notification directive, 259, 261
LDAP server
  check_ldap plug-in, 159, 160

ldconfig command
  installing gd library, 8
libmcrypt library
  installing, 306
  installing NSCA, 272
  installing NSCA daemon for syslog messages, 309
libol package
  installing syslog-NG daemon, 300
Linux
  choosing software and hardware, 3
listeners
  NRPEListener.dll module, 192, 193
  NSClientListener.dll module, 192
listpdh option, NSClient++, 205
load
  check_load plug-in, 151, 152
local event handlers, 210
lockfile
  with-lockfile option, 13
lockfile option, 13
lock_file directive, 108
log block
  NSC.ini configuration file, 193
    sample file, 190
log files
  check_log plug-in, 151, 152
  location of, 15
  querying MRTG log files, 318–322
LOG2NDO utility
  NDO utilities add-on, 362
logfile directive, Nagiosgraph, 240
logging, 107–110
  authorization to access Nagios logs, 100
  downtime_file directive, 108
  FileLogger.dll module, 192, 193
  files containing log information, 108
  log rotation options, 108
  Nagios logging configuration, 107
  security guidelines, 88
  use_syslog directive, 109
logname option
  plug-in reserved command-line options, 353
LOG_ALERT option
  configuring Snort for Nagios integration, 315
log_archive_path directive, 109, 135
LOG_AUTH option
  configuring Snort for Nagios integration, 315
log_enable directive, snmptt.ini file, 330
log_event_handlers directive, 109, 110
log_external_commands directive, 109, 110
log_file directive, 107
  checkpoint, 111
log_host_retries directive, 109, 110

log_initial_states directive, 109, 110
log_notifications directive, 109, 110
log_passive_checks directive, 109, 110
log_rotation directive, 135
log_rotation_method directive, 108
log_service_retries directive, 109, 110
$LONGDATETIME$ macro, 215
losspct metric
    Nagiosgraph creating additional graphs,
        245
low_host_flap_threshold directive, 48
low_service_flap_threshold directive, 65

M

M option
    check_disk plug-in, 150, 151
    check_mailq plug-in, 153
    check_tcp plug-in, 157, 158
m option
    log rotation, 108
    snmptrapd daemon, 338
macro context, 208
macro environmental variables, 209
macros, 207–210
    as environmental variables, 210
    author's note, 19
    command types, used in, 208
    date and time macros, 215
    defining directives, 37
    handling multiword data, 277
    host and service macros for event handlers,
        83
    identifying, 38
    illegal_macro_output_chars directive, 208
    list of, 82
    meta-characters in macro values, 208
    on-demand macros, 208
    resource files, 81
    user-defined macros, 81
    using directives as, 37
mail binary
    with-mail option, 13
mail option, 13
Mail Transfer Agents (MTAs)
    check_mailq plug-in, 153
mailing lists
    web site references, 28
mailq
    check_mailq plug-in, 151, 153
make command, 13
make install command, 14
managed devices, 181
managed objects, 182
mandatory directives
    defining directives, 37

map file
    configuring Nagios for performance data,
        242
    configuring Nagiosgraph, 240
    installing Nagiosgraph, 239
    Nagiosgraph creating additional graphs,
        244
    regular expressions, 245
mapfile directive, Nagiosgraph, 240
master server
    configuring for failover monitoring,
        290–293
    failover process, 297
match function
    configuring syslog-NG for Snort, 316
MaxXyz thresholds
    CheckDriveSize command, NSC.ini, 200
    CheckServiceState command, NSC.ini, 204
max_check_attempts directive, 40, 41, 57
    configuring Nagios for Snort alerts, 317
    configuring Nagios for syslog messages,
        311, 312
    setting to 1, 61
max_concurrent_checks directive, 60
max_packet_age option
    nsca.cfg file, 283, 284
max_service_check_spread directive, 60
measurement
    units of measure, 356
members directive, 76, 78
MEMUSE check, NSClient++, 192
messages
    configuring Nagios server for syslog
        messages, 309–312
    configuring syslog-NG daemon, 302
    configuring syslog-NG for Nagios, 302, 303
    syslog-NG daemon destinations, 303
    syslog-NG filters, 302, 303
    syslog-NG sending, 308
meta characters
    allow_nasty_meta_chars directive, 195, 196
    escaping special characters, 201
    illegal_macro_output_chars directive, 208,
        246
    meta-characters in macro values, 208
metric option
    check_procs plug-in, 153
metrics
    performance data, 227
MIB (Management Information Base) files
    adding trap definitions and EXEC
        statements, 330
    receiving SNMP traps, 325
    web sites, 341
minimal.cfg configuration file
    specifying configuration files, 33
    starting configuration, 32

MinXyz thresholds
 CheckDriveSize command, NSC.ini, 200
mode directive, snmptt.ini file, 329
modes of operation
 check_snmp plug-in, 186
 host_perfdata_file_mode directive, 230
 service_perfdata_file_mode directive, 230,
  241
modules block
 NSC.ini configuration file, 191–193
  caution: enabling modules, 192
  sample file, 190
monitoring, 143–205
 distributed monitoring, 269–288
  central server configuration, 280–288
  distributed server configuration, 271–280
 during scheduled outages, 297
 external commands for adaptive
   monitoring, 225–227
 failover monitoring, 289–297
 hosts, 144–145
 indirect monitoring with NRPE, 171–175
 introduction, 144–147
 local Unix monitoring, 147–154
 network-based services, 154–161
 plug-in limitations, 161
 redundant monitoring, 289
 remote monitoring, 161–187
 services, 145–147
 via NRPE, 162–175
 via SNMP, 181–187
 via SSH, 175–181
 web site references, 206
 Windows-based hosts, 187–205
  clients available, 188
  NSClient++ client, 188–205
Monitoring Features box
 Tactical Monitoring Overview page, 117
Monitoring Performance box
 Tactical Monitoring Overview page, 115
Monitoring section, web console, 115–133
 3-D Status Map page, 133
 Comments page, 133
 Downtime page, 133
 External Command Interface page, 121, 122
 Host Detail page, 125–127
 Host group pages, 127
 Host Information page, 126
 Host Problems page, 133
 Network Outages page, 133
 Performance Info page, 133
 Process Information page, 130–131
 Scheduling Queue page, 132–133
 Service Detail page, 118–125
 Service group pages, 127
 Service Information page, 119
 Service Problems page, 133

 Status Map page, 133
 Tactical Monitoring Overview page,
  115–118
MRTG
 check_mrtg plug-in, 318, 320–322
 check_mrtgtraf plug-in, 318–320
 check_rrd.pl plug-in, 318, 322–323
 description, 317
 integrating Nagios with, 317–322
 querying MRTG log files, 318–322
 querying RRD databases, 322–323
$MSG macro
 configuring syslog-NG for Nagios, 304
multiple servers
 author's tip, 5
MySQL
 inserting data into MySQL, 231–237
mysql option
 Nagios plug-in configure options, 19

■**N**

\n character
 command_line directive, 214
n notification option, 46
n option
 check_by_ssh plug-in, 178, 179
 log rotation, 108
n service notification option, 64
n service scheduling setting, 58
n state, execution criteria, 251
n state, notification criteria, 257
Nagios
 how Nagios works, 29–30
 integrating with other tools, 359
nagios binary
 running in verification mode, 103
 starting Nagios daemon, 101
Nagios Event Broker
 see NEB
Nagios servers
 see servers
Nagios server software
 see server software
Nagios-DB package, 232
nagios-group option
 Nagios critical configure options, 11, 12
 Nagios plug-in configure options, 19
nagios-user option
 Nagios critical configure options, 11, 12
 Nagios plug-in configure options, 19
nagios.cfg
 NDO utilities add-on, 364
nagios.cfg file (server configuration file), 30
 author's tip, 30
 checkpoint, 111
 freshness directives, 286

logging, 107
    specifying configuration files, 32
nagios.conf file
    configuring web server with RPM
        installation, 25
nagios.h include file
    Helloworld module, NEB, 361
nagios.lock file, 108
nagios.log file, 107, 108
Nagiosgraph tool
    configuring, 239–241
    configuring Nagios for performance data,
        241–242
    creating additional graphs, 244–246
    displaying graphs, 242–244
    installing, 239
Nagiostat tool, 246
nagiostats program, 106
nagios_group directive, 88
nagios_user directive, 88
name directive, 67
named pipes
    configuring syslog-NG for Nagios, 305
    syslog-NG daemon, 300
naming conventions
    macro environmental variables, 209
NAN daemon (Nagios Notification Daemon)
    managing notifications with, 221
NANS (Netsaint Aggregate Notification
        System)
    managing notifications with, 221
ncmd group
    security considerations, 15
NC_Net client
    monitoring Windows-based hosts, 188
NDO utilities add-on
    configuration options, 363
    development of, 362
    installing, 362, 363
    NEB (Nagios Event Broker), 362–365
ndo2db daemon
    installing, 364
    NDO utilities add-on, 362, 365
NDOMOD module
    NDO utilities add-on, 362
NEB (Nagios Event Broker), 359–366
    broker_module directive, 360
    documentation, 365
    enable-event-broker option, 13
    further information, 365
    Helloworld module, 360–361
    NDO utilities add-on, 362–365
nebcallbacks.h include file, 361
nebmodules.h include file, 361
nebstructs.h include file, 361
Net-SNMP package, 182
    commands, 183

distributions, 183
    installing, 183, 324, 325
    SNMP traps, 324
    snmpget commands, 183
    snmpwalk command, 183–185
network elements, 181
Network Health box
    Tactical Monitoring Overview page, 116
Network Outage box
    Tactical Monitoring Overview page, 116
Network Outages page
    Monitoring section, web console, 133
network visibility
    deploying Nagios servers, 1
    locating Nagios servers, 27
network-based services
    author's tip, 154
    check_tcp plug-in, 156
    monitoring network-based services,
        154–161
Net::XMPP
    installing via CPAN, 217
    sending notifications via Jabber, 217
NNTP server
    check_nntp plug-in, 159, 161
no service scheduling method, 58
normal_check_interval directive, 57, 61
notes directive, 266
notes_url directive, 243, 244, 266
notification commands, 84
    DISABLE_NOTIFICATIONS command, 296
    ENABLE_NOTIFICATIONS command, 296
    sending SNMP traps, 336
notification criteria states, 257
notifications, 45–47, 213–221
    ACKNOWLEDGEMENT notification type,
        215
    aggregating notifications, 220–221
    cmd.cgi page for disabling notifications,
        130
    command_line directive, 214
    commands, 214
    contact notification directives, 73
    contacts, 85
        author's caution, 74
    detecting flapping, 47
    disabling notifications via external
        command, 117
    enable_notifications directive, 281
    FLAPPINGSTART notification type, 215
    FLAPPINGSTOP notification type, 215
    host notification escalations, 264–265
    host_notification_commands directive, 73,
        74, 214
    host_notification_options directive, 73
    host_notification_period directive, 73
    how Nagios works - the basics, 30

lifecycle of, 214
log_notifications directive, 109, 110
managing with NAN daemon, 221
managing with NANS, 221
mechanisms for sending, 216, 246
multiple notification option, 47
options, 46
PROBLEM notification type, 215
RECOVERY notification type, 215
sending notifications via Instant
    Messenger, 217–220
sending via AIM, 220
sending via ICQ, 220
service notification escalations, 259–264
    shortcuts, 262–264
service notifications, 63–64
service_notification_commands directive,
    73, 74, 214
service_notification_options directive, 73
service_notification_period directive, 73
SNMP traps, 323
state change, 46
state changes, 213
suppressing notifications, 220–221
throttling_notifications.pl script, 221
Notifications report, web console, 134
notifications_enabled directive, 45, 63, 64
notifications_interval directive, 45, 63, 64
notifications_options directive, 45, 46, 63, 64,
    85
    f option, 215
notifications_period directive, 45, 63, 64
$NOTIFICATIONTYPE$ macro, 215
notification_failure_criteria directive, 252, 256,
    257
notification_interval directive, 259
notification_options directive, 213
notification_period directive, 259
notify-by-email command, 214, 215
notify-by-epager command, 216
notify-by-im command, 220
notify_outage command, 44
NRPE
    check_nrpe plug-in, 162, 166–167
    configure script, table of options, 164
    configuring for failover monitoring,
        294–297
    encryption, 164
    indirect monitoring with NRPE, 171–175
    installing and compiling NRPE, 163–166
    monitoring via NRPE, 162–175
    on Nagios server, 166–167
    on remote host, 167–171
nrpe binary, 167
NRPE block
    NSC.ini configuration file, 194
        sample file, 191

nrpe daemon
    allowed_hosts directive, 195
    allow_arguments directive, 195, 196
    allow_nasty_meta_chars directive, 195, 196
    author's caution, 163
    command_timeout directive, 195, 196
    configuration options, 164, 165
    configuring for failover monitoring,
        291–293
    configuring NRPE, 295
    indirect monitoring with NRPE, 171
    installing, 167
    monitoring via NRPE, 162, 167–171
    monitoring Windows-based hosts, 187
    nrpe.cfg file ownership, 168
    options, 293
    port directive, 195
    special characters and, 165
    use_ssl directive, 195, 196
NRPE Handlers block
    NSC.ini configuration file, 195, 196
        sample file, 191
NRPE traffic
    Stunnel-generated tunnel, 165
nrpe.cfg file, 168
    configuration file, 168
    configuring NRPE, 295
    configuring nrpe daemon, 292
NRPEListener.dll module
    NSC.ini configuration file, 192, 193
nrpe_group option
    nrpe.cfg configuration file, 169
NRPE_NT client
    monitoring Windows-based hosts, 188
nrpe_user option
    nrpe.cfg configuration file, 169
NSC.ini configuration file, 190–196
    allowed_hosts directive, 194, 195
    allow_arguments directive, 195, 196
    allow_nasty_meta_chars directive, 195, 196
    CheckAlwaysCRITICAL command, 199
    CheckAlwaysOK command, 199
    CheckAlwaysWARNING command, 199
    CheckCounter command, 199, 202,
        204–205
    CheckCPU command, 198
    CheckDisk.dll module, 192, 198
    CheckDriveSize command, 198, 199
    CheckEventLog.dll module, 192, 198
    CheckFileSize command, 198, 199
    CheckHelpers.dll module, 192, 193, 199
    CheckMem command, 199
    CheckMultiple command, 199
    CheckProcState command, 199, 203
    CheckServiceState command, 199, 202–203
    CheckSystem.dll module, 192, 198
    CheckUpTime command, 199

check_batch command, 196, 197
check_cpu command, 196
command_timeout directive, 195, 196
comments, 190
date_mask directive, 194
debug directive, 194
file directive, 194
FileLogger.dll module, 192, 193
log block, 193
    sample file, 190
modules block, 191–193
    sample file, 190
NRPE block, 194
    sample file, 191
NRPE Handlers block, 195, 196
    sample file, 191
NRPEListener.dll module, 192, 193
NSClient++
    argument numbering, 202
    installing NSClient++, 189
NSClientListener.dll module, 192
obfuscated_password directive, 194
password directive, 194
port directive, 195
sample file, 190
Settings block, 194
    sample file, 190
SysTray.dll module, 192, 193
use_ssl directive, 195, 196
nsca binary
    configuring NSCA daemon for syslog
        messages, 309
    description, 282
    options, 286
    starting NSCA daemon for syslog messages,
        311
NSCA daemon
    configuring, 282–285
    configuring for failover monitoring, 293
    configuring for syslog messages, 309
    installing, 282
    installing for syslog messages, 309
    receiving syslog messages on Nagios server,
        313
    running under inetd or xinetd, 283
    sending Snort alerts to Nagios server, 317
    starting, 286
    starting for syslog messages, 311
NSCA package
    compilation, 282
    configuration options, 272
    configuring send_nsca program, 273–276
    encryption, 285
    encryption methods, 274
    init script, 286
    installing, 272–273

installing for failover monitoring, 297
installing send_nsca program for syslog-
    NG, 306–308
send_nsca.cfg configuration file, 307
nsca.cfg configuration file
    configuring NSCA daemon, 282
        for syslog messages, 310
    description, 282
    options, 282
nsca_group option, 283, 284
nsca_user option, 283, 284
NSClient client
    monitoring Windows-based hosts, 188
NSClient++ client, 188–205
    check features, 192
    check_nt plug-in, 193
    configuring
        see NSC.ini configuration file
    external commands, 197–198
    inject function, 199
    installing, 189–190
    internal commands, 198–205
    listpdh option, 205
    modes, 188
    monitoring Windows-based hosts, 188
        using NRPE-like daemon mode, 205
    starting, 189
    stopping, 190
    uninstalling, 189
    Windows checks, 196–205
        CheckDisk.dll, 199–202
        CheckSystem.dll, 202–205
NSClientListener.dll module
    NSC.ini configuration file, 192
NTP server
    check_ntp plug-in, 159

■O
O option
    check_by_ssh plug-in, 179
    check_log plug-in, 152
o option
    check_snmp plug-in, 185
o state, execution criteria, 251
o state, notification criteria, 257
obfuscated_password directive
    NSC.ini configuration file, 194
object configuration files, 31
    checking syntax of, 103
object definition
    using templates for object definition,
        67–71, 85
object identifiers
    see OIDs
object inheritance, 68
    author's tip, 70

chaining object inheritances, 69
recursion and, 68
object types, 31
objects
contact objects, 72–75
grouping objects, 75–78
regular expressions, 71
objects.cache file, 108
object_cache_file directive, 108
obsession
configuring for failover monitoring, 294
host obsession, 53
nagios.cfg directives for, 53
ocsp_command directive, 66
service obsession, 66
obsess_over_host directive, 52
obsess_over_hosts directive, 53
configuring send_nsca program, 276
obsess_over_services directive, 66
configuring send_nsca program, 276
ochp_command directive, 53, 276, 279
central server receiving service checks, 288
distributed server executing service checks, 280
ocsp_command directive, 66, 276
central server receiving service checks, 288
distributed server executing service checks, 280
OIDs (object identifiers), 182
SNMP OID, 182
snmpwalk command, 184
variables available for specific devices, 185
OK state, 41
CheckAlwaysOK command, 199
r notification option, 46
writing simple plug-in, 349
on-demand macros, 208, 209
On options
snmptrapd daemon, 326
ongoing service scheduling, 61
OpenSSH
check_by_ssh plug-in, 175, 176
ssh-keygen command, 176, 177
openssl option
Nagios plug-in configure options, 19
OpenSSL versions
SSL/TLS functionality, 164
options
check_by_ssh plug-in, 178, 180
check_dhcp plug-in, 159
check_disk plug-in, 148–151
check_dns plug-in, 160
check_file_age plug-in, 152
check_http plug-in, 160
check_load plug-in, 152
check_log plug-in, 152
check_mailq plug-in, 153

check_nrpe plug-in, 166
check_nt plug-in, 193
check_procs plug-in, 153
check_rpc plug-in, 161
check_smtp plug-in, 161
check_snmp plug-in, 185
check_ssh plug-in, 154–156
check_swap plug-in, 154
check_tcp plug-in, 156–158
check_users plug-in, 154
configure script, NRPE, 164–165
nrpe daemon, 170
nrpe.cfg configuration file, 168–169
snmpwalk command, 184
Options directive
configuring web server for Nagios, 23, 24
Order directive
configuring web server for Nagios, 23, 24
out option
snmpttconvertmib tool, 331
output data
inserting performance and output data into RRDtool, 237–246
Output in CSV Format option, 138
output plug-ins
alert_syslog output plug-in, 314
Overview view
Host and Service group pages, 127
Hostgroup Overview page, 127

■P
p option
check_by_ssh plug-in, 180
check_disk plug-in, 148, 150, 151
check_http plug-in, 160
check_nrpe plug-in, 166
check_nt plug-in, 193
check_rpc plug-in, 161
check_smtp plug-in, 161
check_ssh plug-in, 155
plug-in reserved command-line options, 353
sendxmpp, 219
send_nsca program, 277, 278
p state, execution criteria, 251
p state, notification criteria, 257
packages
author's tip, 6
pager directive, 75
parallelize_check directive, 57, 61
parents
inherits_parent directive, 255, 257
parents directive, 38, 256
defining, 38, 39
passive checks, 42
central server configuration, 281

description, 286
service dependencies, 252
passive mode
check_by_ssh plug-in, 178, 179
passive_checks_enabled directive, 40, 43, 57
passphrase key
check_by_ssh plug-in, 177
password directive
NSC.ini configuration file, 194
password option
nsca.cfg configuration file, 283, 284
configuring NSCA daemon for syslog
messages, 310
plug-in reserved command-line options,
353
send_nsca.cfg configuration file, 274, 284,
307
passwords
obfuscated_password directive, 194
paths
log_archive_path directive, 135
using full paths for commands, 144, 205
perfdata_timeout directive, 229
perflog directive, Nagiosgraph, 240
performance
deploying Nagios servers, 3
distributed monitoring, 269
process_perf_data directive, 52, 54, 67
performance data, 227–246
configuring Nagios for, 241–242
host_perfdata_command directive, 228, 234
host_perfdata_file directive, 230
host_perfdata_file_mode directive, 230
host_perfdata_file_processing_command
directive, 231
host_perfdata_file_processing_interval
directive, 231
host_perfdata_file_template directive, 230
inserting data into MySQL, 231–237
inserting performance and output data into
RRDtool, 237–246
metrics, 227
Nagiosgraph creating additional graphs,
244–246
Nagiosgraph displaying graphs, 242–244
perfdata_timeout directive, 229
processing performance data, 228–231
to file or pipe, 229–231
using commands, 228–229
process_performance_data directive, 241
process_perf_data directive, 228
service_perfdata_command directive, 228,
234
service_perfdata_file directive, 230, 241
service_perfdata_file_mode directive, 230,
241
service_perfdata_file_processing_
command directive, 241
service_perfdata_file_processing_interval
directive, 231, 241
service_perfdata_file_template directive,
230, 241
specifying plug-in performance data,
356–357
units of measure, 356
uses, 231
Performance Info page
Monitoring section, web console, 133
PERFORMANCE SUGGESTIONS heading, 105,
106
Perfparse tool, 246
Perl
embedded Perl interpreter, 354
enable-embedded-perl option, 13
with-perlcache option, 13
writing Perl plug-ins, 350–354
perl-Net-SNMP package
installing Nagios plug-ins via RPM, 20
prerequisites for, 20
Perl regular expressions, 245
perlcache option
Nagios configure options, 13
permissions
external commands, 90
pgsql option
Nagios plug-in configure options, 19
ping
check_fping plug-in, 159, 160
check_ping plug-in, 144
with-ping-command option, 19, 20
ping-command option
Nagios plug-in configure options, 19
ping6-command option
Nagios plug-in configure options, 19
pipes
see named pipes
plug-ins
alert_syslog output, 314
author's tip, 18, 149
common options, 156
configure options, 19
default plug-ins package, 154
installing Nagios plug-ins, 5, 168
installing Nagios plug-ins from source,
17–20
installing Nagios plug-ins via RPM, 20–21
local service monitoring, 151
monitoring limitations, 161
Nagios plug-in configure statement, 18
performance data, 228
prerequisites, 18
return codes, 349

send_nsca, 297
setting thresholds, 148
using full paths for commands, 144
plug-ins (list of)
check_by_ssh, 175–181
check_dhcp, 159
check_disk, 148–151
check_dns, 159
check_dummy, 287
check_file_age, 151, 152
check_fping, 159, 160
check_http, 159, 160
check_ifoperstatus, 187
check_ifstatus, 187
check_imap, 159, 161
check_ldap, 159, 160
check_load, 151, 152
check_log, 151, 152
check_log2, 153
check_mailq, 151, 153
check_mrtg, 318, 320–322
check_mrtgtraf, 318–320
check_nagios, 292
check_nntp, 159, 161
check_nrpe, 162, 166–167
check_nt, 193
check_ntp, 159
check_ping, 144
check_pop, 159, 161
check_procs, 151, 153
check_rpc, 159, 161
check_rrd.pl, 318, 322–323
check_rrd_data.pl, 322
check_smtp, 159, 161
check_snmp, 182, 185
check_ssh, 154–156
check_swap, 151, 153
check_tcp, 146, 156–158
check_udp, 158
check_users, 151, 154
plug-ins, developing, 343–366
coding guidelines, 359, 366
command-line options, 358–359
developing test cases, 359
external commands, 357
files, 357
handling translations, 359
patches, 359
reserved command-line options, 353
return codes, 349
shell script templates, 344
specifying performance data, 356–357
specifying threshold ranges, 355–356
timeouts, 358
utils.sh script, 346
writing Perl plug-ins, 350–354
writing simple plug-in, 343–350

POP server
check_pop plug-in, 159, 161
port directive
NSC.ini configuration file, 195
port option
plug-in reserved command-line options, 353
prefix flag, configure script
installing RRDtool, 238
prefix option
configure script, NRPE, 164, 165
installing syslog-NG daemon, 301
Nagios critical configure options, 11, 12
Nagios plug-in configure options, 19, 20
print_help subroutine
writing Perl plug-ins, 353
writing simple plug-in, 347
print_revision subroutine
utils.sh script, 346
writing simple plug-in, 347
&print_revision subroutine
writing Perl plug-ins, 353
print_usage subroutine
writing Perl plug-ins, 353
writing simple plug-in, 347
privilege levels
using appropriate privilege level, 12
PROBLEM notification type, 215
process information
authorization to access, 100
Process Information page
Monitoring section, web console, 130–131
process-host-perfdata command, 228, 235
process-host-perfdata-file command, 231, 235
process-service-perfdata command, 228, 229, 235
process-service-perfdata-file command, 241
processes
check_procs plug-in, 151, 153
PROCESS_HOST_CHECK_RESULT command, 224, 225
process_performance_data directive, 241
process_perf_data directive, 52, 54, 67, 228
PROCESS_SERVICE_CHECK_RESULT command, 224
submitting service check results, 333
PROCSTATE check, NSClient++, 192
PROGNAME variable
writing simple plug-in, 345
$PROGNAME variable
writing Perl plug-ins, 353
PROGPATH variable
writing simple plug-in, 345
$PROGRAM macro
configuring syslog-NG for Nagios, 304

public key
    check_by_ssh plug-in, 177
public key encryption, 176

■Q

q option
    check_log plug-in, 152
    check_tcp plug-in, 157

■R

\r character
    command_line directive, 214
r notification option, 46
R option
    check_http plug-in, 160
    check_smtp plug-in, 161
r option
    check_dhcp plug-in, 159
    check_snmp plug-in, 186
    check_ssh plug-in, 155, 156
    check_tcp plug-in, 157, 158
r service notification option, 64
r state, escalation, 260
Re-schedule the next check of this service
        command
    Service Commands box, 121
RECOVERY notification type, 215
red fields
    web console, 142
Red Hat
    author's note, 4
    checking RPMs are installed, 8
    installing Nagios plug-ins via RPM, 20
    installing Nagios via RPM, 16–17
redundancy of Nagios servers, 5, 27
    author's tip, 5
redundant monitoring, 289
    implementing, 290
register directive, 68
regular expressions
    directives, 71
    map file, 245
    Perl, 245
    SNMPTT tool matching, 334
    use_regexp_matching directive, 71
    use_true_regexp_matching directive, 71
reload option, init script
    running syslog-NG daemon, 302
remote hosts
    configuring syslog-NG daemon for Nagios,
        302–306
    installing syslog-NG daemon on, 300
    NRPE on remote host, 167–171
    running syslog-NG daemon on, 301
remote monitoring, 161–187
    monitoring via NRPE, 162–175

monitoring via SMNP, 181–187
    monitoring via SSH, 175–181
Reporting section, web console, 134–140
    Availability report page, 138
reports, web console
    Availability report, 134–139
    Event Log report, 140
    table of, 134
Require directive
    web console authentication, 94
resource configuration files, 30
resource files, 81
    CGI files reading, 81
    resource_file directive, 81
    user-defined macros, 81
resources
    see web site references
resource_file directive, 81
restarts
    retention of status, 50–51
retain_nonstatus_information directive, 51,
        67, 85
retain_state_information directive, 50, 108,
        272
retain_status_information directive, 51, 67
retention of status, 50–51
retention.dat file, 108
retention_update_interval directive, 50, 108
retry_check_interval directive, 57, 61
return codes
    plug-ins, 349
root partition
    check_disk plug-in, 151
root user
    author's caution, 12
    author's note, 9
    checkpoint, 110
    security guidelines, 88
RPC services
    check_rpc plug-in, 159, 161
RPM
    configuring web server for Nagios, 25
    installing Apache web server from, 7–8
rpm command, 8
RRD databases, 242
    check_rrd.pl plug-in, 318, 322–323
    querying, 322–323
rrd directory, 242
rrddir directive, Nagiosgraph, 240
rrdgraph tool, 246
rrdopts option, nagiosgraph, 244
RRDtool
    inserting performance and output data
        into, 237–246
    installing, 237–238
    tutorial, 237

rrdtool binary
  querying RRD databases, 323
RSA keys, 176
rsync
  Nagios server synchronization, 289
rta metric
  Nagiosgraph creating additional graphs,
    246

■S

s command-line switch, 104, 105
S option
  check_smtp plug-in, 161
s option
  check_by_ssh plug-in, 178, 180
  check_dhcp plug-in, 159
  check_dns plug-in, 160
  check_http plug-in, 160
  check_nt plug-in, 193
  check_snmp plug-in, 186
  check_tcp plug-in, 157, 158
  syslog-NG daemon, 301
s service scheduling setting, 58, 59
sbin directory, 15
Schedule downtime for this service command
  Service Commands box, 122
scheduling
  checking using -s switch, 104
  displaying for hosts and services, 104
  host checks, 85
  initial service scheduling, 58–60
  interleaving, 59, 60
  ongoing service scheduling, 61
  retention_update_interval directive, 108
  service checks, 85
  services, 57
  use_retained_scheduling_info directive, 60
scheduling engine, 122
Scheduling Queue page
  Monitoring section, web console, 132–133
ScriptAlias directive
  configuring web server for Nagios, 22
  Nagiosgraph displaying graphs, 242
scripts
  using full paths for commands, 144
SDESC directive
  translated trap, 332, 333
sdiff
  Nagios server synchronization, 289
security, 87–100
  deploying Nagios servers, 3
  external commands, 88–90
  guidelines for running Nagios server, 87–90
  nagios_group directive, 88
  nagios_user directive, 88
  ncmd group, 15

root user, incorrect use of, 88
  securing web console, 90–100
  send_nsca.cfg file, 275
  transmission security, NSCA package, 285
sendxmpp
  caution using d option, 219
  downloading and installing, 218
  options, 219
  sending notifications via Jabber, 217
  using sendxmpp command, 218–220
send_host_check command, 279, 280
send_nsca binary
  installing, 307
send_nsca plug-in
  failover process, 297
send_nsca program
  alternative to shell script, 278
  central server receiving service checks, 288
  configuring, 273–276
  distributed server executing service checks,
    280
  host check results, 279, 280
  installing for syslog-NG, 306–308
  obsess_over_hosts directive, 276
  obsess_over_services directive, 276
  options, 277
  sending syslog-NG messages, 308
  service check results, 276
  service check results to, 277
send_nsca.cfg configuration file
  options, 274, 307
  securing, 275
send_service_check script, 276, 278
send_trap event handler command, 337
send_trap script, 338
  options, 339
  sample trap generated by, 340
server configuration files, 30
server software
  compiling, 11
    configuring Nagios to run external
      commands, 14
    Nagios configure options, 13
    Nagios critical configure options, 11
  configuration files, 15
  configuring web server for Nagios, 21–26
  installation prerequisites, 5–9
  installing from RPM, 9, 16–17
    installing from source recommended, 27
  installing from source, 9–16
    compiling Nagios, 11–16
    creating external command group, 10–11
ServerAdmin directive
  virtual server configuration, 25
ServerName directive
  virtual server configuration, 25

servers
  capacity planning, 4
  configuring Nagios server for syslog
      messages, 309–312
    configuring Nagios server, 311–312
    configuring NSCA daemon, 309
    installing NSCA daemon, 309
    starting NSCA daemon, 311
  deploying servers, 1
  distributed configuration, 2
  independent Nagios servers, 2
  locating, 27
  monitoring requirements, 27
  Nagios server startup failure, 102
  Nagios server validation, 102
  NRPE on Nagios server, 166–167
  placing on the Web, 91
  redundancy and backup, 5, 27
  security guidelines for running, 87–90
  specifying configuration files, 32–35
  starting and stopping, 101–106
  synchronization, 289
  virtual server configuration, 24–25
server_address option
  nrpe.cfg configuration file, 168
  nrpe.cfg file, 292
  nsca.cfg file, 283
server_port option
  nrpe.cfg configuration file, 168
  nrpe.cfg file, 292
  nsca.cfg file, 283
service checking, 56–63
  accept_passive_host_checks directive, 281
  accept_passive_service_checks directive,
      281
  active_checks_enabled directive, 281
  central server receiving service checks, 288
  CHANGE_MAX_SVC_CHECK_ATTEMPTS
      command, 227
  CHANGE_SVC_CHECK_COMMAND
      command, 226
  check_external_commands directive, 281
  distributed server executing service checks,
      280
  enable_notifications directive, 281
  execute_host_checks directive, 281
  execute_service_checks directive, 281
  ocsp_command directive, 276
  parallelize_check directive, 61
  scheduling, 85
  sending service check results, 276–278
  service_description directive, 276
Service Commands box
  Service Information page, 121
Service Comments box
  Service Information page, 124

service dependencies, 250–255
  active checks, 252
  description, 249
  inheritance, 254–255
  introduction, 250
  multiple service dependencies, 253
  passive checks, 252
  shortcuts, 253–254
Service Detail page
  Monitoring section, web console, 118–125
    Current Network Status box, 119
    Display Filters box, 119
    Host Status box, 119
    list of services section, 119
    Service Status box, 119
service directives, 55
service flapping, 65
service freshness, 62
  check_service_freshness directive, 63
  service_freshness_check_interval directive,
      63
service group objects, 77
Service group pages
  Monitoring section, web console, 127
    commands, 128
    scheduling downtime, 129
    Servicegroup Summary page, 128
Service Information page
  Monitoring section, web console, 119
    Service Commands box, 121
    Service Comments box, 124
    Service State Information box, 121
    syslog_upd service, 119
    View Xyz links, 119
service notification escalations, 259–264
  description, 249
  introduction, 258
  multiple service escalations, 260
  recovery notifications escalations, 261
  shortcuts, 262–264
service notifications, 63–64
service object
  description, 31
  event handler definition, 211
  on-demand macros, 209
  service object definition, 54
  using check_mrtg plug-in, 321
  using check_mrtgtraf plug-in, 320
service obsession, 66
Service Problems page
  Monitoring section, web console, 133
service reaping, 61
  service_reaper_frequency directive, 61
service-restart event handler, 211, 212
service scheduling, 57–61
  initial service scheduling, 58–60
  ongoing service scheduling, 61

SERVICE SCHEDULING INFORMATION
heading, 105
service stalking, 66
Service State Information box
Service Information page, 121
service states, 41, 63
CheckServiceState command, NSC.ini,
202–203
numeric representation of, 277
Service Status box
Service Detail page, 119
$SERVICEATTEMPT$ macro, 83
event handling, 213
servicedependency object
dependent_host_name directive, 251
dependent_service_name directive, 251
description, 31, 249, 250
example, 250, 251
execution_failure_criteria directive, 251,
252
host_name directive, 251
inherits_parent directive, 255
notification_failure_criteria directive, 252
service_description directive, 251
soft_state_dependencies directive, 252
$SERVICEDESC$ macro, 276
macro context, 208
serviceescalation object
contact_groups directive, 259
description, 31, 249, 258
escalation_options directive, 260
escalation_period directive, 259
first_notification directive, 259
last_notification directive, 259, 261
notification_interval directive, 259
notification_period directive, 259
$SERVICEEXECUTIONTIME$ macro, 227
serviceextinfo object
see also Extended Service Information
objects
description, 31, 249
example, 267
host_name directive, 267
Nagiosgraph displaying graphs, 243
servicegroup object, 31
servicegroups directive, 55, 56
servicegroup_name directive, 77
$SERVICELATENCY$ macro, 227
$SERVICEOUTPUT$ macro, 229, 277
performance data, 228
$SERVICEPERFDATA$ macro, 229
performance data, 228
serviceperf_mysql.pl script, 235, 237
services
authorized_for_all_services directive, 99,
135

authorized_for_all_service_commands
directive, 99
contact_groups directive, 55, 56
defining services, 54–67
event handling, 65
flapping, 47
global_service_event_handler directive, 65,
210
high_service_flap_threshold directive, 65
hostgroup_name directive, 55, 56
host_name directive, 55, 56
how Nagios works, 29
log_service_retries directive, 109, 110
low_service_flap_threshold directive, 65
max_service_check_spread directive, 60
monitoring network-based services,
154–161
monitoring services, 145–147
obsess_over_services directive, 66, 275
ocsp_command directive, 66, 276
other service checking directives, 63
process_perf_data directive, 67
retain_nonstatus_information directive, 67
retain_status_information directive, 67
security guidelines, 87
servicegroups directive, 55, 56
stalking_options directive, 66
volatile services, 62
Services box
Tactical Monitoring Overview page, 117
$SERVICESTATE$ macro, 83
SERVICESTATE check, NSClient++, 192
$SERVICESTATEID$ macro, 276
$SERVICESTATETYPE$ macro, 83
service_check_timeout directive, 57
service_description directive, 55, 251, 276
service_freshness_check_interval directive, 63,
287
service_interleave_factor directive, 59, 60
service_inter_check_delay_period directive,
58
service_notification_commands directive, 73,
74, 214
service_notification_options directive, 73
service_notification_period directive, 73
service_perfdata_command directive, 228, 234
service_perfdata_file directive, 230, 241
service_perfdata_file_mode directive, 230, 241
service_perfdata_file_processing_command
directive, 241
service_perfdata_file_processing_interval
directive, 231, 241
service_perfdata_file_template directive, 230,
241
service_reaper_frequency directive, 61

Settings block
    NSC.ini configuration file, 194
        sample file, 190
sftp tool
    Nagios server synchronization, 289
share directory, 15
shell script templates
    writing simple plug-in, 344
shortcuts
    host dependencies, 258
    host notification escalations, 264
    service dependencies, 253–254
    service notification escalations, 262–264
$SHORTDATETIME$ macro, 215
SHOW DATABASES command, MySQL, 232
SHOW TABLES command, MySQL, 233
single mode
    nsca binary, 286, 311
slave server
    configuring for failover monitoring,
        294–297
    failover process, 297
    replication of monitoring on master server,
        298
sleep directive, snmptt.ini file, 329
smart service scheduling method, 58, 59, 85
SMP (symmetric multiprocessing)
    author's note, 4
SMTP server
    check_smtp plug-in, 159, 161
SNMP
    check_snmp plug-in, 182, 185
    monitoring via SNMP, 181–187
    monitoring Windows-based hosts, 188
    Net-SNMP package, 182
    versions and security, 205
    writable SNMP variables, 184
SNMP OID, 182
SNMP traps, 323–340
    adding trap definitions and EXEC
        statements, 330–335
    configuring Nagios for, 335
    configuring snmptrapd daemon, 326
    configuring SNMPTT tool, 329–330
    description, 323
    installing SNMPTT tool, 327–328
    Net-SNMP package, 324
    receiving, 325–336
    running snmptrapd daemon, 326, 327
    sending, 336–340
snmpd daemon, 181
snmpget commands
    Net-SNMP package, 183
snmptrapd daemon
    configuring, 326
    options, 326, 338
    receiving SNMP traps, 325

        running, 326, 327
        sending SNMP traps, 338
        traphandle directive, 326
    snmptrapd.conf file, 326
    SNMPTT (SNMP Trap Translator) tool
        configuring, 329–330
        executing, 336
        installing, 327–328
        regular expression matching, 334
    snmptt binary, 327, 328
    snmptt.ini file, 328, 329
        configuration directives, 329
    snmpttconvertmib tool
        installing, 331
        options, 331
        trap translation, 331
    snmptthandler binary, 327
    snmptt_conf_files directive, snmptt.ini file,
        330
    snmpwalk command
        Net-SNMP package, 183–185
    Snort alerts
        configure syslog-NG for, 315–316
        configuring for Nagios integration, 314–315
        configuring Nagios for, 316
        integrating with Nagios, 313–317
    snort.conf configuration file
        configuring Snort for Nagios integration,
            314
    soft recovery
        state types, 41
    soft state, 41
        Include Soft States option, 137, 138
        soft_state_dependencies directive, 252
    software
        see also server software
        choosing, 3
        installing Nagios software, 5–21
            see also installations
    soft_state_dependencies directive, 252
    source
        installing Apache web server from, 6–7
    special characters
        command_line directive, 214
    spool_directory directive, snmptt.ini file, 329
        executing SNMPTT tool, 336
    SSH
        check_by_ssh plug-in, 175–181
        check_ssh plug-in, 154–156
        monitoring via SSH, 175–181
    ssh directory, 178
        known_hosts file, 177
    ssh-keygen command, OpenSSH, 176, 177
    sshd daemon, 178
        check_by_ssh plug-in, 175
    sshd daemons
        check_ssh plug-in, 154

ssi directory, 139
SSL
  checkpoint, 111
  check_http plug-in, 159, 160
  configuring web server for Nagios, 21
  enable-ssl option, 164
  use_ssl directive, 195, 196
  with-ssl-inc option, 164
  with-ssl-lib option, 164
ssl option
  check_http plug-in, 160
SSL/TLS functionality, 164
stalking_options directive, 52, 53, 66
start option
  NSClient++ client, 189
start threshold value
  specifying plug-in threshold ranges, 355
START_EXECUTING_HOST_CHECKS
        command
  configuring NRPE, 296
START_EXECUTING_SVC_CHECKS
        command, 223, 224
  configuring NRPE, 296
state
  Assume Initial States option, 137
  Assume State Retention option, 137, 138
  Assume States During Program Downtime
        option, 137, 138
  check_ifoperstatus plug-in, 187
  check_ifstatus plug-in, 187
  CRITICAL, 63
  DOWN, 41
  escalation states, 260
  execution criteria states, 251
  files containing status information, 108
  First Assumed Host State option, 137
  First Assumed Service State option, 137
  flapping, 47–49
  host states, 41
    numeric representation of, 279
  log_initial_states directive, 109, 110
  not retaining nonstatus information
        author's caution, 51
  notification criteria states, 257
  notifications, 45–47
  OK state, 41, 63
  retain_nonstatus_information directive, 51,
        67
  retain_state_information directive, 50, 108
  retain_status_information directive, 51, 67
  retention of status, 50–51, 85
  retention_update_interval directive, 50
  service state stalking, 66
  service states, 63
    numeric representation of, 277
  state retention directives, 50
  state_retention_file directive, 50, 108

status_file directive, 108
  undetermined state, 139, 142
  UNKNOWN state, 63
  UNREACHABLE state, 41
  use_retained_program directive, 50, 51
  WARNING state, 63
state change, 46
  event handlers, 210
  event handling, 49–50
  execution of event handlers, 83
  flapping status changes, 48
  notifications, 213
state stalking, 52
  author's tip, 52
  directive for hosts, 53
  recommendation, 53
  stalking_options directive, 52, 53
state types, 41
  hard state, 41
  soft recovery, 41
  soft state, 41
statements
  syslog-NG daemon, 305
state_retention_file directive, 50, 108
Status Information column
  Service Detail page, 119
Status Map page
  Monitoring section, web console, 133
status.dat file, 108
statusmap_image directive, 266
status_file directive, 108
stop option
  NSClient++ client, 190
STOP_EXECUTING_HOST_CHECKS
        command
  configuring NRPE, 296
STOP_EXECUTING_SVC_CHECKS command,
        223
  configuring NRPE, 296
strict pragma
  ePN interpreter, 354
  writing Perl plug-ins, 350, 352
strip_domain directive, snmptt.ini file, 330
Stunnel-generated tunnel, 165
Submit passive check result for this service
        command
  Service Commands box, 121
submit_check_result script, 333
sudo command
  event handling, 213
suEXEC
  checkpoint, 111
Summary view
  Host and Service group pages, 128
&support subroutine
  utils.sh script, 346
  writing Perl plug-ins, 353

suppression
  notifications, 220–221
swap space
  check_swap plug-in, 151, 153
synchronization
  configuration objects, 298
  Nagios servers, 289
syslog
  use_syslog directive, 109
syslog daemons
  check_tcp plug-in, 156
  integrating Nagios with, 299–313
syslog messages
  configuring Nagios server for, 311–312
  configuring NSCA daemon for, 309
  configuring Snort for Nagios integration,
    315
  configuring syslog-NG for Snort, 315
  filtering, 302, 340
  installing NSCA daemon for, 309
  receiving on Nagios server, 313
  starting NSCA daemon for, 311
syslog service
  indirect monitoring with NRPE, 174
syslog-NG daemon
  command line options, 301
  configuring for Nagios, 302–306
  configuring for Snort alerts, 315–316
  configuring Nagios server for syslog
    messages, 309–312
  configuring on remote hosts, 306
  description, 299
  destinations, 303
  filters, 302
  installing on remote host, 300
  integrating Nagios with syslog daemons,
    299–313
  receiving syslog messages on Nagios server,
    313
  running on remote host, 301
  sending messages, 308
  sending Snort alerts to Nagios server, 317
  statements, 305
syslog-ng.conf file
  configuring syslog-NG for Nagios, 302
  running syslog-NG daemon, 301, 302
syslog-warnings service
  configuring Nagios for syslog messages, 312
syslog_enable directive, snmptt.ini file, 330
syslog_upd service
  Service Information page, 119
system commands/information
  authorized_for_system_commands
    directive, 99
system updates
  security guidelines, 87

systems
  CheckSystem.dll module, 192
SysTray.dll module
  NSC.ini configuration file, 192, 193

■T
\t character
  command_line directive, 214
t option
  check_by_ssh plug-in, 180
  check_disk plug-in, 150, 151
  check_mrtg plug-in, 321
  check_mrtgtraf plug-in, 319
  check_nrpe plug-in, 166
  check_rpc plug-in, 161
  check_rrd.pl plug-in, 323
  check_ssh plug-in, 155
  check_tcp plug-in, 156
  plug-in reserved command-line options,
    353
  plug-ins, 156
  sendxmpp, 219
Tactical Monitoring Overview page
  Monitoring section, web console, 115–118
    Hosts box, 116
    Monitoring Features box, 117
    Monitoring Performance box, 115
    Network Health box, 116
    Network Outage box, 116
    Services box, 117
TCP/IP (Transmission Control
    Protocol/Internet Protocol)
  check_tcp plug-in, 156–158
  deploying servers, 1
template option
  configuring syslog-NG for Snort, 316
templates
  author's tip, 72
  chaining object inheritances, 69
  configuring syslog-NG for Nagios, 304, 305
  defining template before object, 68
  defining template or real object, 68
  generic host object template, 70
  host object definition template, 67
  host_perfdata_file_template directive, 230
  name directive, 67
  name of template definition, 67
  object inheritance, 68
  overriding template directives, 69
  register directive, 68
  service_perfdata_file_template directive,
    230, 241
  use directive, 68
  using template with object definition, 68
  using templates for object definition, 67–71
  writing simple plug-in, 344

template_escape option
    configuring syslog-NG for Nagios, 304
temporary files
    developing plug-ins, 357
tftp server
    check_tcp plug-in, 156
thresholds
    CheckDriveSize command, NSC.ini, 199
    freshness_threshold directive, 57
    high_service_flap_threshold directive, 65
    local Unix monitoring, 148
    low_service_flap_threshold directive, 65
    setting CRITICAL and WARNING, 148
    specifying plug-in threshold ranges,
        355–356
throttling_notifications.pl script, 221
time
    $LONGDATETIME$ macro, 215
    $TIME$ macro, 215
time periods
    alias directive, 78
    defining, 78–79
    directives for days of the week, 78
    timeperiod_name directive, 78
timeout option
    plug-in reserved command-line options,
        353
$TIMEOUT variable
    ePN interpreter, 354
    writing Perl plug-ins, 352
timeouts
    command_timeout directive, 195, 196
    developing plug-ins, 358
    host_check_timeout directive, 40
    perfdata_timeout directive, 229
    service_check_timeout directive, 57
timeperiod object
    check_period directive, 40
    description, 31
timeperiod_name directive, 41, 78
timestamps
    converting to more readable format, 107
$TIMET$ macro, 215
timetick, 185
tmp partition
    check_disk plug-in, 151
to option
    send_nsca program, 277, 278
touch command, 34
traceroute.cgi program, 134
trailing / at the end of URL
    author's caution, 12
transmission security
    NSCA package, 285
traphandle directive, 326

traps
    SNMP traps, 323–340
    trap translation, 331
Trends report, web console, 134
Triggered By option
    External Command Interface page, 122
trusted-path option
    Nagios plug-in configure options, 19

■U

u notification option, 46
u option
    check_disk plug-in, 150
    check_mrtg plug-in, 321
    check_rpc plug-in, 161
    check_rrd.pl plug-in, 323
    sendxmpp, 219
    snmptrapd daemon, 326
u service notification option, 64
u state, execution criteria, 251, 260
u state, notification criteria, 257
udp
    check_udp plug-in, 158
undetermined state, 142
    author's tip, 139
Unison
    Nagios server synchronization, 289
units of measure, 356
Unix
    local Unix monitoring, 147–154
Unix epoch timestamp
    converting to more readable format, 107
UNKNOWN state, 63
UNREACHABLE state, 41
    u notification option, 46
UPTIME check, NSClient++, 192
URLs
    action_url directive, 266
    notes_url directive, 266
&usage subroutine
    writing Perl plug-ins, 353
use directive, 68
use statements
    writing Perl plug-ins, 352, 353
USEDDISKSPACE check, NSClient++, 192
user-defined macros, 81
    restricting access to, 85
users
    authenticated users, 91
    check_users plug-in, 151, 154
    default users, 99
    security guidelines, 87
    user_name directive, 99
$USERx$ macros, 81
    macros as environmental variables, 209
use_authentication directive, 97

use_regexp_matching directive, 71
use_retained_program_state directive, 50, 51, 272
use_retained_scheduling_info directive, 60
use_ssl directive, 195, 196
use_syslog directive, 109
use_true_regexp_matching directive, 71
usr/bin/nagios directory, 17
usr/lib/nagios/cgi directory, 17
usr/lib/nagios/plugins directory, 17
usr/share/nagios directory, 17
utils.c script
    writing C plug-ins, 347
utils.pm module
    writing Perl plug-ins, 350, 352
utils.sh script
    writing simple plug-in, 346

V

v command-line switch, 102, 103
V option
    check_by_ssh plug-in, 180
    check_disk plug-in, 150
    check_tcp plug-in, 156
    plug-in reserved command-line options, 353
    plug-ins, 156
v option
    check_mrtg plug-in, 320, 321
    check_mrtgtraf plug-in, 319
    check_nt plug-in, 193
    check_rrd.pl plug-in, 322, 323
    check_ssh plug-in, 155
    sendxmpp, 219
    send_trap script, 339
    snmpwalk command, 184
    syslog-NG daemon, 301
    verbose output levels, 348
    writing Perl plug-ins, 354
validation
    Nagios server validation, 102
var directory, 15
var partition
    check_disk plug-in, 151
var/archives directory, 15
var/log/nagios directory, 17
var/log/nagios/rw directory, 17
var/rw directory, 15
verbose option
    plug-in reserved command-line options, 353
    writing Perl plug-ins, 354
verbose output levels, 348
verification mode
    running nagios binary in verification mode, 103

version option
    plug-in reserved command-line options, 353
versions
    author's tip, 16, 31
    object configuration syntax changed, 31
View Config page, 140
View Xyz links
    Service Information page, 119
virtual hosting
    author's tip, 25
virtual server configuration
    configuring web server for Nagios, 24–25
VirtualHost directive
    configuring web server for Nagios, 24, 25
volatile services, 62
    is_volatile directive, 57, 62
vrml_image directive, 266
vv option
    check_disk plug-in, 150
    verbose output levels, 348
vvv option
    verbose output levels, 348

W

w command-line option
    ePN interpreter, 354
    writing Perl plug-ins, 350
w option
    check_by_ssh plug-in, 180, 181
    check_disk plug-in, 148, 150
    check_mrtg plug-in, 320
    check_mrtgtraf plug-in, 318
    check_nt plug-in, 193
    check_rrd.pl plug-in, 322
    check_tcp plug-in, 157
    log rotation, 108
    plug-in reserved command-line options, 353
    service_perfdata_file_mode directive, 230
w service notification option, 64
w state, execution criteria, 251, 260
WAP-based CGI page, 115
warn priority filter
    syslog-NG daemon, 303
warning option
    plug-in reserved command-line options, 353
WARNING state, 63
    CheckAlwaysWARNING command, 199
    CheckDriveSize command thresholds, 200
    MaxXyz threshold, 200
    MinXyz threshold, 200
    monitoring hosts, 145
    setting thresholds, 148

specifying plug-in performance data,
    357
specifying plug-in threshold ranges,
    356
writing simple plug-in, 349
Web
    placing Nagios server on the Web, 91
web console
    authenticated contacts, 92
    authenticated users, 92
    configuration alternatives, 27
    configuration files, 30
    Configuration section, 140
    considerations, 113
    General section, 115
    illustration of, 114
    introduction, 113
    Monitoring section, 115–133
        3-D Status Map page, 133
        Comments page, 133
        Downtime page, 133
        External Command Interface page, 121,
            122
        Host Detail page, 125–127
        Host group pages, 127
        Host Information page, 126
        Host Problems page, 133
        Network Outages page, 133
        Performance Info page, 133
        Process Information page, 130–131
        Scheduling Queue page, 132–133
        Service Detail page, 118–125
        Service group pages, 127
        Service Information page, 119
        Service Problems page, 133
        Status Map page, 133
        Tactical Monitoring Overview page,
            115–118
    Nagios authentication and authorization,
        97–100
    red fields, 142
    Reporting section, 134–140
        Availability report page, 138
    reports
        Availability, 134–139
        Event Log, 140
        table of, 134
    securing, 90–100
    version 3.0 replacing, 113
    web console authentication with Apache,
        91–96
        AllowOverride directive, 92

AuthName directive, 93
AuthType directive, 93
AuthUserFile directive, 93
Directory directive, 93
Require directive, 94
website references, 28, 111
    authentication and authorization, 111
    documentation, 85
    mailing lists, 28
    monitoring, 206
webpages
    check_http plug-in, 159, 160
Wieers, Dag
    installing Nagios plug-ins via RPM, 20
    installing Nagios via RPM, 16
Windows
    monitoring Windows-based hosts, 187–205
        NSClient++ client, 188–205
Windows checks, NSClient++, 196–205
    CheckDisk.dll, 199–202
    CheckSystem.dll, 202–205
    external commands, 197–198
    internal commands, 198–205
with options
    Nagios configure options, 13
    Nagios critical configure options, 11
    Nagios plug-in configure options, 19
with-mysql-inc option
    NDO utilities add-on, 363
with-mysql-lib option
    NDO utilities add-on, 363
with-nsca-xyz options
    NSCA configuration options, 273
with-pgsql-inc option
    NDO utilities add-on, 363
with-pgsql-lib option
    NDO utilities add-on, 363
with-xyz options
    configure script, NRPE, 164
without-openssl option
    Nagios plug-in configure options, 19

■X
x option
    check_disk plug-in, 150, 151
    check_rrd.pl plug-in, 323
xinetd
    running nrpe daemon, 170
    running NSCA daemon, 283
XMPP (Extensible Messaging and Presence
        Protocol)
    sending notifications via Jabber, 217

You Need the Companion eBook

Your purchase of this book entitles you to its companion eBook for only $10.

We believe this Apress title will prove so indispensable that you'll want to carry it with you everywhere, which is why we are offering the companion eBook for $10 to customers who purchase this book now. Convenient and fully searchable, the eBook version of any content-rich, page-heavy Apress book makes a valuable addition to your programming library. You can easily find, copy, and apply code—and then perform examples by quickly toggling between instructions and the application. Even simultaneously tackling a donut, diet soda, and complex code becomes simplified with hands-free eBooks!

Once you purchase this book, getting the $10 companion eBook is simple:

❶ Visit **www.apress.com/promo/tendollars/**.

❷ Complete a basic registration form to receive a randomly generated question about this title.

❸ Answer the question correctly in 60 seconds and you will receive a promotional code to redeem for the $10 eBook.

2560 Ninth Street • Suite 219 • Berkeley, CA 94710